Gardeners
vs.
Designers

MORE PRAISE FOR
GARDENERS VS. DESIGNERS

Brian Lee Crowley's "Gardeners Versus Designers" is a refreshingly provocative analysis of the increasingly "progressive" trend in Canadian politics, which he sees as anything but progressive. Crowley juxtaposes the machine-like doctrines of experts (the "Designers"), who see themselves as all-knowing custodians of truth and are adamant about what is best for society, with those (the "Gardeners") who claim no monopoly on truth but are inspired by the spirit of individual dynamism and a never-ending quest for knowledge. The book is a rallying cry "in support of a society that prefers to act by accommodation and negotiation not by authority and command." Crowley explodes policy distortions prevailing on health care, the environment, mass transit and urban planning and explains convincingly why sensible resource development makes sense both for most indigenous communities and for Canada. A compelling delightful read that should command the attention of anyone concerned about the quality of our governance.

    – Derek H. Burney, OC, former Canadian ambassador to Washington

For all those despairing that choice, liberty, individual responsibility and free trade are in full retreat, Brian Crowley invites us to think more deeply about how and why we can make better decisions for ourselves, our neighbours and our nation in this important new book. Three cheers for the gardener's loving gratitude and respectful humility!

    – Tom Long, Mike Harris Campaign Chair, 1995 and 1999.

Gardeners versus Designers is at once provocative and hopeful. Brian Lee Crowley challenges Canadians to expect more from their politicians and civil servants, and to fight hard for a better future, and to rekindle their belief in the great Canadian experiment. This is uncommonly wise counsel. This book shows that effective and sustainable public policy is really hard work. But it must begin with a comprehensive understanding of the global landscape, a deep passion for Canada, and a belief that the people of Canada deserve better than they're getting from politicians of all stripes and the institutions that have been hijacked by the designers' agenda.

    – Ken Coates, Canada Research Chair, University of Saskatchewan

I am an entrepreneur, not a scholar, and I don't buy big books. But this one is different. Crowley helps me understand how the world works today with wit and useful examples.

    – Brendan Calder, Entrepreneur and Professor
of Management, Rotman School of Management.

Crowley has done it again! He refuses to kneel for nonsense and bullying while working hard to rescue Canadian politics from progressives' woke revolution. *Gardeners Versus Designers* revives the Canadian dream for those willing to work for it: innovation, diversity, and prosperity, all within a "protected sphere" of individual freedom. The chapter on Canadian health care alone is worth the price of admission. This book is not light but wraps challenging concepts in easy and engaging reading.

— Shawn Whatley, former President, Ontario Medical Association, author *No More Lethal Waits: 10 Steps to Transform Canada's Emergency Departments*

Crowley's two previous books, *Fearful Symmetry* and *The Canadian Century* were so good I thought he would never be able to top them. Yet this remarkable book, *Gardeners versus Designers,* not only does so but draws the reader into a wonderfully complex, subtle and fun account of why Canada is "a rare jewel in human experience." It then goes even further and shows how ill-informed politicians, often with the best of intentions, are endangering Canada's continued success. Astute and brilliant in its insights into politics, business and the conditions in which human beings flourish best, this book will restore your faith in this country, its institutions, its history and its future, provided we don't let the politicians mess it up!

— Conrad Winn, founder and former CEO, Compas Research

This book provides a powerful, thoughtful, and intelligent discussion of competing political philosophies in Canada today. It holds a mirror that reflects two very different approaches to public policy, and provides a warning to us that our prosperity, our ability to innovate, and our ability to choose will be restricted by politicians and officials who think they know best. It is a call for citizens to be both active and vigilant. For thoughtful readers, this book advances an unvarnished critique of what is not working in current Canadian public policy and offers an explanation of why that is. I recommend leaders in all fields, as well as students everywhere.

— Doug Black, elected senator from Alberta

Brian Lee Crowley has written a beautiful book which brilliantly asks us to think of governing as gardening. The gardener has a sense of what he needs to do and what he can't do, with the goal of growing a pleasing and beautiful garden. What he's not is a designer who tries to impose an abstract plan that inevitably results in something unpleasant and ugly. So too for public policy.

— F.H. Buckley, Foundation Professor, Scalia Law School, author of *The Once and Future King*

Brian Lee Crowley helps us to think about old ideas and contemporary problems within a new and creative paradigm. Reshaping a conversation and long-held beliefs takes an unconventional thinker and a creative genius. Crowley hits that mark with clarity and accessibility. It is not left versus right or Liberals versus Conservatives but gardeners versus designers. On the surface, both labels have attraction and proponents. But Crowley shows us something new on every page as he majestically weaves together theory, practice, failure, and success. Storytelling is an art and Crowley is a master. But perhaps he is an even better gardener.

– Bob Plamondon, author, *The Shawinigan Fox:*
How Jean Chrétien Defied the Elites and Reshaped Canada

Brian Lee Crowley's metaphor of designers versus gardeners brings alive the wisdom of his intellectual mentors, Michael Oakeshott and Friedrich Hayek. They saw that society is, in Hayek's term, a spontaneous order that emerges from human interaction but cannot be consciously planned without catastrophic loss of information. Government should be the gardener—the custodian—of that order, not the architect. 'Progressives' never understand this. They want to forcibly impose their own abstract and limited conceptions of order upon institutions such as social customs and the economic market, which amalgamate the choices of individuals without coercion. This book explains why the good intentions of reformers produce so much havoc. Everyone who cares about the future of Canada needs to read this book.

– Tom Flanagan, author, *Harper's Team:*
Behind the Scenes in the Conservative Rise to Power

Brian Lee Crowley has been a strong defender of the right of Indigenous peoples not to be an afterthought but to be incorporated as true economic, social and political partners in Canada's development. In this fascinating and important book, he incorporates Indigenous governments, people, and issues as central elements in his analysis of the forces shaping Canada. At last, a prominent Canadian thinker who recognizes that Indigenous people are no longer on the periphery but at the centre of Canada's future.

– Stephen Buffalo, President, Indian Resource Council of Canada

Inspired by the deeply grounded wisdom of gardeners, Crowley invites his readers to recover their ambitions for Canada. He rolls up his sleeves and vividly demonstrates how ill-conceived policies have hindered our prosperity and our access to services that can actually make a difference in making our country a happier place. This book is not for unimaginative public servants or for politicians and their worn-out orthodoxies. It is for Canadians who demand better governance

and better decisions. Reach for the policy tools and instruments that free the mind and the energies of this country, and discover a new approach to policy making!
— Patrice Dutil, author and Professor of Politics and Public Administration, Ryerson University

Brian Lee Crowley has written a truly outstanding book, one that should be read by anyone interested in Canada and its future as a democratic country and a healthy and prosperous nation. He demonstrates how Canada can find its path to an even better future. More particularly, he shows how that better future lies not in a system of coercion led by the state through infinite regulations, but in a system which allows each and every one of us to pursue their lives to the outmost of their talent and abilities. He explains that Canada has not achieved its admired world status by chance and that our greatness as a country can be traced to our past, although not perfect, of which all Canadians, present and future, should be proud.
— Hon. Mr. Justice Marc Nadon

Do "Black Lives Matter," "Me Too," and all the other "progressive" ideologies of the modern world have the exclusive roadmap for the future in this time of turmoil? Brian Lee Crowley says no. To him, "progressives" are "designers" at heart. Motivated by a belief that they alone possess the moral imperative required to redefine society, they have a design for everything, a plan to mold an infinitely malleable society into a grand vision that only produces benefits and never suffers costs. A much more realistic approach in his view is that of the "gardener" who recognizes that change is in no-one's hands, but instead results from co-operative and incremental efforts based on the accumulated wisdom of previous generations and the institutions and behaviours that have defined us, from rule of law and property rights to civic freedoms and mutual respect. This is not a defense of the status quo. Far from it. It is a thoughtful, detailed argument about today's great political divide between "progressives" and "conservatives."
— Hon. Janet Ecker, former Ontario Minister of Education and Community and Social Services

This book is a must-read for Canadians of all ilks, especially Immigrants for whom the Canadian political system sometimes seems hard to comprehend. Brian Crowley has gently and kindly explained the differences between the designer (or progressive) and gardener mindsets. The book goes into details about the problems of individualism and collectivism, knowledge and ignorance, social co-operation arising from authority and social co-operation arising from incentives, the limits of designed institutions versus the possibilities of grown social institutions, the key differences between individual and group identity and the nature of justice in a society of free people. Reading the book certainly gave me clarity.

— Raheel Raza, President, Muslims Facing Tomorrow

In the eighteenth-century, Scottish economist Adam Smith took issue with the "man of system" who imagines he can arrange different members of society as though they were pieces on a chess board, forgetting that in human society "every single piece has a principle of motion of its own." Crowley brings this idea up to date in a Canadian context, using the provocative analogy of "gardeners" and "designers." Canadian society is a garden, he argues, the key characteristic of which is that "no-one is in charge." Rather, it is a co-operative effort. Designers believe that every part of society is infinitely malleable, that every problem can be fixed with the correct application of money and expertise. Crowley demonstrates that while this view is in the ascendancy, "it is demonstrably false and misleading." The book is very lucid in its structure and the prose flowed beautifully, as always.

— John Ivison, national political columnist, *National Post*

This book is an ingenious interpretive key to success and failure in policy-making. Crowley's effort belongs in the pantheon with Thomas Sowell's *A Conflict of Visions*. The gardener from experience works within lived reality; the designer believes he can re-engineer creation, banishing the gardener for good measure. I hope many liberal-progressives read it: they need it most.

C.P. Champion, editor, *The Dorchester Review*

This book, from a leading voice on our most important public questions, including trade and health care and foreign relations, reads like a magnum opus. If the author could teach us nothing else, it's the error of an engineer's mindset in politics. Society is not a machine and our country does not need to be "fixed." Instead, we should build on our inheritance, identify our faults in good faith, and continue to make Canada more like its best self. As Crowley recognizes, he's not the first to point out the beauty and practicality of evolved institutions. But his approach to cultivating a better country forms a solid and original work. Liberals and Tories alike should read and enjoy it.

— Jackson Doughart, Editor-in-Chief, *Brunswick News Inc.*

Brian Lee Crowley's new book clarifies why debates over the most critical issues in Canadian politics—particularly, environmental policy, the public health care system, and Indigenous relations—so often seem futile. He is decidedly open-minded and empathetic to both sides in our culture wars. Nevertheless, he makes a clear case for the gardener paradigm as both faithful to the spirit of Canada's founding, as well as

fitting to the current and future reality of Canada as a pluralistic and technologically sophisticated country. This marvellous book is a paean to diversity, epistemic humility, equality, the rule of law, and tolerance – the quiet greatness of this fine country.
   – Joanna Baron, Executive Director, Canadian Constitution Foundation

Brian Crowley is a rare public intellectual who doesn't resort to political schism to explain his philosophy. In 'Gardeners versus Designers' he takes a panoramic view of Canada's glorious achievements and charts a course for a future that will ensure Canada's continued glory as a free society.
   – Anil Shah, chair, Canada-India Foundation

Many of us have been brought up to believe in the mechanics of politics, as if our societies were machines, clean, functional, deprived of life. They are not. As Dr. Crowley so accurately writes, societies are more like gardens, to be nurtured and cultivated. Gardens can be full of dirt and weeds, but they are also full of life in all its splendour and complex majesty. As politicians, we should nurture more than engineer, cultivate more than speculate, and not be afraid of that which does not fit into the narrow mould of contemporary times. I highly recommend this very *humane* book to everyone who wishes to expand their understanding of our societies and what drives them forward.
   – Sven Otto Littorin, former Swedish Minister for Employment

Canada has its share of problems. But as Crowley reminds us, unlike most other countries we also have admirable institutions and freedoms which have evolved over hundreds of years to provide us with a free and prosperous society almost without peer and without parallel in history. At a time of temptation for governments to increasingly engage in large scale economic and social intervention, Crowley shows why this can be counterproductive and indeed destructive. He makes the case that our best path forward starts with acknowledging the power of our institutions, extending them to people who do not yet fully benefit from them, and unleashing the knowledge and power of our people, respecting society as a garden to be nurtured and shaped from the bottom, not as a machine to be directed from the top.
   – Vaughn MacLellan, Partner, DLA Piper

In this terrific new book, Brian Lee Crowley diagnoses the main political divide in Canada today: not between Conservatives and Liberals, but between those who see society as a garden to be tended with a gentle respectful hand, and those who see it as a machine to be directed with a hard fist. Creative, comprehensive, and eminently readable, Gardeners versus Designers profiles the visions battling for the future of our country.
   – Bruce Pardy, Professor of Law, Queen's University

GARDENERS VS. DESIGNERS

Understanding the Great Fault Line In Canadian Politics

BRIAN LEE CROWLEY

Foreword by Theodore Dalrymple

SUTHERLAND
HOUSE
TORONTO, 2020

Sutherland House
416 Moore Ave., Suite 205
Toronto, ON M4G 1C9

First edition, September 2020

If you are interested in inviting one of our authors to a live event or
media appearance, please contact publicity@sutherlandhousebooks.com
and visit our website at sutherlandhousebooks.com for more
information about our authors and their schedules.

Manufactured in Canada
Cover designed by Lena Yang
Book composed by Karl Hunt

Library and Archives Canada Cataloguing in Publication
Title: Gardeners vs. designers : understanding the great fault
line in Canadian politics / Brian Lee Crowley.
Other titles: Gardeners versus designers
Names: Crowley, Brian Lee, author.
Description: Includes bibliographical references.
Identifiers: Canadiana 20200293842 | ISBN 9781989555354 (softcover)
Subjects: LCSH: Conservatism—Canada. | LCSH: Political leadership—Canada.
Classification: LCC JC573.2.C3 C76 2020 | DDC 320.520971—dc23

ISBN 978-1-989555-35-4

Table of Contents

Foreword

A S I WRITE THIS INTRODUCTION to Brian Lee Crowley's book, the full effects on the western world, both economic and social, of the COVID-19 epidemic have yet to be revealed, but there is already no shortage of calls for a thorough change in economic and social models.

The word "model" in this context is very revealing, for it implies two things: first that our societies are possessed of and are built upon a pre-conceived model, and second that societies can and ought to be redesigned and rebuilt according to such a preconceived model, this time a better one. This is rationalism gone mad, and is rightly the object of the author's criticisms. One might have hoped that by now the disastrous practical results of politics conceived of as the fulfilment of a blueprint of perfection would have been clear to everyone, but in politics no defeat of bad ideas is final and illusion springs eternal in the human mind. The temptation, especially for intellectuals, to criticize what exists by reference to a perfection that has never existed and never will exist is more or less permanent, and must at all times be resisted.

Mr. Crowley's book is about Canada, a country that has been exceptionally fortunate (and wise) by comparison with the standards of most societies throughout human history. He readily admits that there have been failures and failings, but one would expect no less from a society of fallen creatures such as Man. Nor is it true that Canada, though by no means an ideological state, was founded on no principles whatever. On the contrary, its founders understood what many people seem unable to understand at the present conjuncture, namely, that to have no principles at all is to be a scoundrel, but to have only principles is to be a fanatic. The founding principles of Canada, then, were those to limit the power of the state such that the population that lived within its jurisdiction was free (within limits, of course) to pursue its own ends and to allow it as wide a margin of freedom as possible as was consistent with civilized living.

The maintenance of such a dispensation requires restraint, modesty and tolerance – the kind of tolerance that is a habit of the heart rather than only a justiciable demand. The author is particularly persuasive on the kind of modesty that is required: an awareness of the inevitable limitations of human knowledge and foresight, both individual and collective. Having divided thinkers about society into two large categories, the designers and the gardeners, he tells us that the designers believe that they have sufficient knowledge or data to bring about precisely the end that they desire (or at least that they say that they desire, though their drive to power should never be underestimated) without any deleterious unintended consequences, whereas the gardeners are more modest and are content to work with what already exists, especially where whatever already exists has virtues or beauties. This is not a call to inaction or passivity: gardeners have a profound influence on the gardens that they cultivate, but they do not fall prey to the delusion that they can create anything they like irrespective of the climate, soil, nature of the plants available, etc.

Canadians are more than usually fortunate in what they have inherited, says the author, and judging by the people who vote with their feet to move to Canada, he is not alone in his judgment. Canada has managed to combine individual freedom with social decency as few countries have managed.

But there is no room for complacency. As he rightly warns, there are those in Canada, as everywhere else, who would make the best conceivable (best, that is, as decreed by them) the enemy of the good. They find in Canadian history instances of the country failing to live up to its promises and then conclude, like political Savonarolas, that the promises were nothing but hypocrisy and smokescreen for private interests. They are evangelical preachers denouncing sin and calling on everyone to repent. They want to destroy to perfect.

These are the people who would destroy the delicate balance necessary to combine individual freedom with social decency. They are the kind of people who see in differences in outcome between different social groups nothing but injustice and the workings of illicit prejudice, and never differences in tastes or propensities. To take an absurd example, they would demand that until people of Vietnamese origin become heavyweight champion boxers, the boxing authorities be denounced as anti-Vietnamese. In other words, they do not accept that a free and just society is bound to result in group differences.

Mr Crowley's book is an invaluable study in how a still-fortunate society may reconcile freedom with fairness and decency without resort to supposedly all-knowing, all-powerful and totalitarian-leaning experts who would enslave millions to bring about their reign of virtue. But its balance is not immutable.

Theodore Dalrymple

Preface

WE FATALLY MISUNDERSTAND OUR politics in Canada if we think that the main divide is that between the principal political parties, Grits versus Tories, say, or progressives versus reactionaries, as the left would like to frame it. Having misconceived the nature of what divides us politically, we then profess to find ourselves disappointed by the shallow nature of the political debate that results.

This book calls on Canadians to reimagine this nation's politics by sharply redefining the main fault line at the heart of our politics. As you will see, my starting point for this redefinition is to point out that there are two main ways of thinking about any society from a political point of view. On the one hand there are people who conceive of society as a machine. A machine is invented by human beings following a carefully engineered plan. Every part has a purpose and a function that can only be understood and made to work by the folks who designed it in accordance with highly specialized expert knowledge. And like almost any machine, it can be made to do pretty much what you want. If you want it to speed up, you pull this lever; if you want it to use less fuel, you twiddle that dial. And if the machine gets old and clapped out you can replace it with a "new and improved" model.

In this view of politics, the key players are the engineers, the designers, the experts, who understand machines. When our social machine disappoints, they can always come up with something better, and in the meantime they can fiddle endlessly with the current model to get it to do what they think is best.

The progressive mindset which is in the ascendant in Canada today leans heavily toward this mechanistic model. Every social problem can be solved by expertise, every part of society is infinitely malleable and every reform proposed by well-meaning politicians guided by disinterested and selfless experts (medicare, pharmacare, urban transit, the transition to the green economy and so forth) will only produce benefits and never costs in an ever-upward spiral of benevolent social progress. Harvard and Queen's Ph.Ds, McKinseyites and international organizations like the UN and the World Economic Forum marshal the world's knowledge and chivvy us along to social progress by making us act in accordance with their superior knowledge. I call this the designer approach to society and politics.

The only real flaw in the designer worldview is that it is demonstrably false and misleading. Yet it has become so fashionable and ubiquitous that many Canadians are literally in danger of forgetting that there is an alternative vision of how society works which is, on every point, more in keeping with what we know of human experience, desires and knowledge than the society-as-machine approach.

I draw the contrast with a competing analogy to the mechanistic one. Canadian society is no machine, but rather a garden. The key characteristic of a garden, as any real gardener will tell you, is that no one is in charge. A garden is a co-operative effort among many different factors, like climate, predators, soil, nutrients and, of course, the efforts of gardeners. But unlike a machine, whose purpose was imagined by its designers and which is a servant of their will, gardens are made up of many disparate plants, each of which has its own energy, intelligence and will. Gardeners can help to create the conditions in which a garden flourishes but they cannot overmaster natural processes and they succeed best when they accept that each plant knows what conditions help to elicit its best self and no amount of gardening "expertise" can shove nature aside. Gardeners can and do profoundly influence their garden, but they are the servants, not the boss, of what goes on there. A true gardener who sits and admires her garden at the height of its beauty does not think, "Behold what I have created." She thinks, "There is nothing more beautiful than that which emerges when humanity and nature find a harmonious balance and each respects what the other has to contribute."

This book walks the reader through the differences between the designer (or progressive) and gardener mindsets and shows all the reasons why the pretensions of designers have little basis in human experience, while the gardener philosophy has been the secret of the success of many of the greatest societies known to history.

As befits a book that teases out universal ideas and then applies them to Canada, this work is divided into two parts.

The first is called "The Gardener's Creed." In the first chapter I lay out why I think the designer/gardener distinction is the key one for any modern politics and how it illuminates our understanding of Canadian history. It lays out the case for why the Canadian garden, as it has been forged from centuries of experience, is worthy of our love, respect and deference and needs to be cultivated and cherished if it is to continue helping Canadians flourish as few peoples in the world are able to do. The Canadian garden comprises a number of institutions such as the common law, independent courts, markets, private property, contract, money, language and others that no one invented but which grew rather than were engineered and which embody more knowledge than designers can ever hope to acquire, let alone act on. Replacing them with "designed" institutions is a regressive, not a progressive step. Despising the garden that Canadians' lived experience has created for us and replacing it with expert-designed machinery will make us less successful than we have been and the cost will be measured in the frustrated plans individual Canadians have for how to live their best lives.

The other four chapters in this first part walk the reader through how the gardener thinks about the problems of individualism and collectivism, knowledge and ignorance, social co-operation arising from authority and social co-operation arising from incentives, the limits of designed institutions versus the possibilities of grown social institutions, the key differences between individual and group identity and the nature of justice in a society of free people.

The chief division between designers and gardeners is what they think human beings can and do know. If designers are right that political authorities can and do know more than everyone else then there is a strong case for the rest of us to defer to those authorities in the design of our institutions and society. By contrast, gardeners think that grown institutions embody more knowledge than anyone, including our political leaders, can ever hope to gather, let alone understand. If gardeners are right then acquiescing in the designing ambitions of ignorant political leaders will make us a less successful society. Chapter II, therefore, focuses entirely on what rulers and the rest of us can and do know and the different kinds of knowledge that are available, how we can make use of them and the limits they impose on us. It basically lays out the case for deference to grown institutions because there are rational reasons for thinking they embody more knowledge than any alternative, including bureaucracy guided by expertise.

Gardeners believe that the most successful societies are the ones where each individual member's chances of defining and then living a successful life are maximized. Chapter III asks, if gardeners are right in their understanding of the nature of the knowledge humanity possesses, what does that teach us about how to organize society so that people are as successful as they possibly can be in pursuing the life plans they have chosen for themselves.

Chapter IV contrasts gardener and designer versions of democracy. It makes the case that people get more of what they want from grown social institutions more of the time and at less cost than they do from political institutions (parties and elections and parliaments) as they are conventionally understood.

The chapter that follows enquires into the nature of identity and justice. One of the key arguments of designers is that grown social institutions produce unhappy outcomes for identifiable groups and that these differential outcomes are unjust and license all kinds of "correction" by political authorities. The gardener rejects both how designers understand identity and the idea that justice is defined by social outcomes for favoured groups.

The second part of the book, "Gardening in a Cold Climate," applies these gardener insights to a representative sample of political issues that preoccupy Canadians today. This selection is meant to be illustrative, not definitive. There are many other issues I could have chosen that would also make the dry discussion of the difference between the worldview of designers and gardeners come alive. The ones that commended themselves to me were to show how gardeners would: help Canadians live together successfully in our cities; manage the natural environment; work toward reconciliation with Indigenous people; develop our natural resources; and care for the sick. These themes provide the central thread for the discussions in Chapters VI through IX. Chapter X wraps up the discussion and includes a coda on the COVID-19 pandemic and how it fits into the designer versus gardener debate.

Happy reading.

Before you move on to the meat of the book, though, please allow me to thank a few people who made a huge contribution to this book. My good friend Tony Daniels wrote the brilliant Foreword. In countless books and articles under his pen name, Theodore Dalrymple, Tony has been one of the world's most insightful and trenchant critics of how bureaucracy guided by expertise has consistently failed the most vulnerable in Britain and elsewhere. As always when I undertake a major project like this one I felt at my shoulder the benevolent shade of my tutor and friend at the LSE, the late Alan Beattie. People who read and provided feedback on chapters or early drafts bore a huge burden for little recompense and the least I can do is to say thank you. The list includes Tom Adams, Ken Coates, Wendell Cox, Philip Cross, Janet Ecker, Norbert Eschborn, Brian Ferguson, Tom Flanagan, Laura Jones, Jonathan Kay, Patrick Luciani, Jack Mintz, Marc Nadon, Sam Staley, David Watson and Shawn Whatley. My research assistant was Lucas Donovan and Dave McDonough helped with the index. My absolutely invaluable and disciplined editor was Kristin McCahon. Ken Whyte, my publisher, has been extremely supportive throughout the whole process of getting this book done. As always my greatest thanks go to my sternest critic, most assiduous reader and staunchest moral support, my wife Shelley. I wish I could blame all these people for anything that isn't up to standard in this work and take all the credit for everything therein that is true and compelling. Alas, it is the other way around.

The book is dedicated to my colleagues at the Macdonald-Laurier Institute. A finer, more collegial, smarter and harder working team it would be hard to imagine and they are deserving of my grateful thanks and highest esteem.

PART ONE

The Gardener's Creed

CHAPTER I

Introduction

Tradition is a matter of much wider significance. It cannot be inherited, and if you want it you must obtain it by great labour.

T.S. Eliot

CANADA SEEMS TO MANY to be firmly embarked now on the "progressive" path, exemplified by Justin Trudeau and the Liberal Party of 2020. The NDP, the Greens, and the Bloc are all merely variants on this central theme; each could be aptly characterized by Jack Pickersgill's famous phrase as "Liberals in a hurry." The Conservatives give in to the progressive temptation far more often than they resist it.

The adoption of "progressive" to describe this policy direction is relatively new and is imported from the United States, where the terms "left-wing" and "liberal" were successfully turned by the left's opponents into terms of abuse. But the ideas that preoccupy today's progressives are essentially the same as those the left was pursuing before the fall of the Berlin Wall: inequality between groups (the One Percent and the rest, men and women, whites and racial minorities), redistribution, and alleviation of sickness, poverty and suffering through direct state action.

To this has been added more recent moral anxieties over inequalities between heterosexuals and sexual minorities, relations between Indigenous and non-Indigenous Canadians, guilt over the past and climate change, plus a dwindling belief in the loyalty owed to the nation-state, exemplified by a reluctance to police the borders (particularly against illegal immigration and aggressive refugee claimants) and an increasing enthusiasm for following the lead of international organizations like the United Nations in policy-making.

Progressivism, as least in its Canadian incarnation, promises that nothing will be allowed to stand in the way of people in quiet possession of the compelling moral truth that no grievance is too small, no inequality too slight, and no environmental sin too minor to be allowed to escape correction, or at least notice, as the topic of a finger-wagging lecture on the moral inadequacies of Canadians. The purpose of progressive politics is to identify these failings, talk endlessly about them and, perhaps, to take action to correct them. The more quickly and determinedly a government roots these shortcomings out, deaf to the pleas of traditionalists, the more worthy it is of the "progressive" adjective.

So comprehensively has this program been bought by some that any opposition to the march of this "progress" is seen as itself a moral failing, making the objections of those who do not share this ideology nothing but the rantings of racists, homophobes, and apologists for a rapacious capitalism, none of them deserving of a platform. The objectors should not be accorded the status of legitimate intervenors in the political debate, representing a current of thought worthy of respect and consideration. It is this moral certainty, the intellectual blinkers that it brings in its train, and the accompanying belief that the purpose of government is to root out all of which progressivism disapproves that poses the greatest challenge to the continued existence in Canada of a remarkable civil society that is the envy of the world.

But what is the alternative to progressivism? Names are a powerful tool of communication, as evidenced by the left's continuing struggle to find a term for their ideas that doesn't repel mainstream voters. The evolution of the name for their ideas is, however, not the result of their adversaries' propaganda victories, but rather of the painful truth that almost everywhere their ideas have been put into action the results have been vigorously repudiated by voters. Progressivism both needs and feeds on the magnification of conflict between identifiable groups and the destruction of institutions, behaviours and practices that, while handed down to us by tradition, have evolved to suit the character of our society and ensure its harmonious operation and future success.

Because of this connection to the past, the alternative to "progressivism" is often termed "conservatism" but I think both names are historically and lexicographically wrong. Using them leads to confusion in and about political debates and what is at stake. I am going to lay out here the case for reimagining our way of conceiving of the main political forces contending for power in Canada today even if neither of the forces corresponds exactly to any major political party. While one of the approaches to politics I will describe is in the ascendant in the Liberal Party and the other is somewhere (barely) within hailing distance of the mainstream of the Conservative Party, there is division and confusion *within* the parties over exactly these issues. This book is intended to make a contribution to redrawing our mental categories in politics differently and therefore to illuminate our political choices in a way that may make them easier to see and to weigh.

To understand the real differences between the forces now contending for our loyalty in the political sphere it is less necessary to know about progressives and conservatives, constitutions and legislatures, and policies and regulations, than it is to understand what distinguishes two different casts of mind.

No one has better drawn the distinction between these two types of mind than Michael Oakeshott, the late English political thinker. Read Oakeshott's description of the rationalist mind and see if it brings to mind a certain type of political practitioner. He says:

At bottom the Rationalist stands (he always *stands* for something) for independence of mind on all occasions, for thought free from obligation to any authority save the authority of 'reason' . . . He is the *enemy* of authority, of prejudice, of the merely traditional, customary or habitual. His mental attitude is at once sceptical and optimistic: sceptical because there is no opinion, no habit, no belief, nothing so firmly rooted or so widely held that he hesitates to question it and to judge it by what he calls his 'reason'; optimistic, because the rationalist never doubts the power of his 'reason', when properly applied, to determine the worth of a thing, the truth of an opinion or the propriety of an action. . . .[H]e is something also of an individualist, finding it difficult to believe that anyone who can think honestly and clearly will think differently from himself.

Of the alternative, traditionalist or small-c conservative cast of mind, by contrast, Oakeshott has this to say:

> To be conservative is to prefer the familiar to the unfamiliar . . ., the tried to the untried, fact to mystery, the actual to the possible, the limited to the unbounded, the near to the distant, the sufficient to the superabundant, the convenient to the perfect, present laughter to utopian bliss.
>
> . . . the inclination to enjoy what is present and available is the opposite of ignorance and apathy and it breeds attachment and affection. Consequently, it is averse from change, which first appears always as deprivation. A storm which sweeps away a copse and transforms a favourite view, the death of friends, the sleep of friendship, the desuetude of customs of behaviour, the retirement of a favourite clown, involuntary exile, reversals of fortune, the loss of abilities enjoyed and their replacement by others – these are changes, none perhaps without its compensations, which the man of conservative temperament unavoidably regrets.

What can this have to do with a discussion of the merits of progressivism vs conservatism? Why everything, of course. Each of these casts of mind will, in the modern world, offer a different answer to the question of "how ought people to be governed in a liberal-capitalist democracy like Canada?"

In understanding the different answers, it is important to clarify that Oakeshott is *not* saying that the traditionalist is irrational. It would not be accurate to say that he or she does not believe in the power of the human mind to understand and to solve humanity's problems. On the contrary, he is saying that when we engage in the project of "inventing" institutions from so-called "first principles," when individuals, committees, constitutional conventions and even entire generations consult only their own experience and knowledge in seeking to solve their problems, the answers they come up with are bound to be less effective and less suited to the character and dispositions of the people called to live under them than the answers that have grown up over generations of careful and controlled experimentation that values the affection in which the tried and true and familiar is held by the population. This contrast between the "grown" and the "invented" or "designed" is the key one we need to understand.

If this seems impossibly abstract, let me bring it down to earth with a chicken-and-egg analogy. Which came first: the ordinary speaker of English (or indeed any other natural language) or the grammarian? The rationalist cast of mind is always on the lookout for first or definitional principles by which to judge specific performances or utterances or institutions, so the rationalist answer to which came first must be "the grammarian." Grammarians define the rules of proper speech based on logic and reason, and the things we say and write are judged against that standard.

But language was not invented by grammarians. It grew. It grew out of the blooming buzzing confusion of attempts by generations of people to communicate with each other. To do so successfully they needed to develop certain regularities in the way they talked to one another. Language simply *is* the existence of these established and shared regularities in the creation of which all speakers of the language participated. *After the fact*, the grammarians came along and teased out those regularities, described them and gave them names which we rather inaccurately refer to as the "rules" of grammar. But they did not invent language nor did the rules guide its emergence. Grammarians and rules are *the product of language* and not the other way around.

Take something as simple as the order in which adjectives appear before the noun they modify.[1] In *The Elements of Eloquence: How to Turn the Perfect English Phrase,* the author, Mark Forsyth, points out that adjectives, "absolutely have to be in this order: opinion-size-age-shape-colour-origin-material-purpose Noun. So you can have a lovely little old rectangular green French silver whittling knife. But if you mess with that order in the slightest you'll sound like a maniac."

When the BBC's Matthew Anderson tweeted this quotation (under the observation "Things native English speakers know, but don't know we know"), it was retweeted over 47,000 times, prompting one observer to comment, ". . . this came as a complete surprise to many people who thought they knew all about English." And indeed grammarians only twigged to this regularity of the English language relatively recently. They did not *cause* the regularity; they only drew it to our attention *while native speakers had all been using it effortlessly for centuries* before the grammarians (or we) noticed that it existed.

This is a classic example of the kind of complex but undesigned rule that is grown by social institutions all the time. We all use it, but even the grammarians didn't notice it. No one needed to know it for it to be a useful guide for us in communicating with each other.

Moreover, all attempts to extirpate from language all the irregularities and contradictions, to abandon "grown" language and replace it with "invented" and wholly "rational" languages based on first principles, such as Esperanto, have been abject failures, certainly when measured by the number of people who speak them. The traditionalist understands that language *grows* in the tension between the search for rules on the one hand and the constantly evolving circumstances and experiences of native speakers that the rules can never fully capture or fix for all time on the other. Natural grown language will always be richer, subtler and more elusive than is dreamt of in the philosophy of rationalist grammarians and the inventors of rational languages no one speaks.

If that example doesn't help, try this one. The late Norman Barry, a British professor of political thought, told me that in the US Midwest he knew of two universities built near one another at roughly the same time. In the first, the rationalist planners designed a campus that looked spectacular from the air, with lovely landscaping and curving symmetrical pathways that gave the whole a pleasing aspect – at least from 30,000 feet. To do so, however, those pathways had to follow routes that were inconvenient and awkward for those on the ground who were using them to get to where they needed to go, *which is actually the purpose of pathways*. The result was that people abandoned the paths and tramped across the lawns, spontaneously creating pathways that were less pleasing to look at but actually got you where you wanted to go quickly and conveniently. The campus became a battleground between authorities trying to get people to respect their utopian but impractical "first principles" or "invented" design and the students who were late and needed to get to class.

The other campus, under the authority of traditionalists, took a different tack. They built their buildings but held off landscaping for a year or two so that they could observe where students actually wanted to go and the paths that they trod to get there. Once established, the university simply paved over the paths and landscaped around them. The result was not so nice to look at from the air, but resulted in a harmonious relationship between the authorities and those who were trying to get from their dorm to the lecture hall and then the cafeteria. Put another way, the pathways on the campus "grew" out of the needs and experiences of those who had to use them. Unlike the rationalist designer approach, the students participated, through their choices and actions, in the creation of a framework that supported rather than tried to supplant their vision of how to succeed.

So rationalist designers try to impose their will on the world, which they feel must give up its stubborn attachment to the old and the conventional and acquiesce in the dictates of what they think of as "reason." To their mind, human society is a machine, and its operation can always be tweaked by twiddling the right dial, improving the information technology, or installing a better valve. And the whole machine can be costlessly replaced with a new "high performance" model when necessary; the fact that people loved the look or feel or sound of the old machine is mere sentimentality that must be ignored in the name of a higher social good.

Gardeners is the name I give to those who think of society more as a garden than a machine, and who see humans as autonomous beings whose choices and actions allow the unfurling of their character over time, not as dials to be twiddled. For gardeners, therefore, grown institutions are, on the whole, more effective and held in higher esteem than invented ones. Gardeners in nature are mindful of the fact that while they certainly wish to put their stamp on their garden, they are very far indeed from being in total control. They are participants among many, not masters of all the others. They must make their peace with the effects of predators, of climate, of weather, of soil, of nutrients and of the life cycle and characteristics of the plants they seek to cultivate. Gardeners know that they can create the conditions in which a garden will flourish, but they cannot overmaster the natural processes on which they depend; you cannot make flowers grow faster by pulling on them.

Gardeners of human institutions, too, apply reason to their work, but they must reason knowing the nature of their raw material and its behaviour under different conditions and, more importantly, the limits of their power to shape the world closer to their heart's desire, since *everyone in the garden has their own heart and their own desires.*

The two casts of mind I have described, what I will call *the gardeners* and *the designers* (even though I accept that, like all analogies these are imperfect and not to be taken literally), differ on the wellsprings of authority in political institutions.

The designers believe that institutions derive their legitimacy from their conformity to some set of abstract first principles, such as, say, that all authority derives from "the people" or that "democracy" must always trump established interests, or that perfect equality of outcome is the ideal social arrangement.

They further believe that the worth of institutions can be determined by how their results conform to an abstract pattern that they find aesthetically pleasing. Thus an economy that does not produce identical outcomes for men and women, or whose income distribution is too "skewed" or whose distribution of jobs among ethnic groups is not as these "designing minds" think it ought to be, or a city that is "too" dispersed or "too" reliant on cars instead of transit, or a voting system that "underrepresents" certain groups relative to their weight in the population, is an arrangement that is morally suspect and subject to correction or preferably wholesale replacement by something "better."

The worth of institutions will be judged by designers by how closely they hew to such foundational principles and abstract patterns that are allegedly the measure of justice and efficiency.

The traditionalist gardener, by contrast, will be of the view that human action does not proceed from abstract first principles, but from messy and very untheoretical practical experience of what works and has passed the test of time and is acquiesced in by the population regardless of how it appears to those who value only abstractions and not practical success.

Mention of "first principles" makes me think a brief digression on this idea is warranted.

Marxism or radical feminism or Chavismo or progressivism or any of the other fashionable critiques of liberal capitalism start from theoretical premises: society is corrupt because of inequality or sexism or colonialism and because it does not measure up in theory, it must be discarded and replaced with one "designed" to eliminate the evil *du jour*.

But what our society's critics do not realize is that those who think the liberal-capitalist order worth defending *are not engaged in the same enterprise* as they are. They do not proceed from anything like the same theoretical premises. Instead they are preoccupied with practice. They do not measure vast complex societies such as Canada against our puny understanding or passing aesthetic preferences. They measure them against how well they work in allowing people to pursue the goals they have chosen for themselves.

Liberal capitalism was not "designed" by anyone. There is no presiding designing genius, no Karl Marx, no Betty Friedan, no Malcolm X, no Franz Fanon, no Mao Zedong. The society we have inherited grew up out of the lived experience of uncounted generations of those who went before us. The job of gardeners is therefore not to theorize, but to untangle and interpret, to understand not to design, to respect the seasons and the nature of the garden's residents, to create the conditions in which the garden can flourish. We gardeners seek to understand why society works, because a society that works as well as ours is indeed a rare jewel in human experience, and certainly one not to be tossed aside because some academic scribbler who can't even remember to keep his university office hours or pick up his dry cleaning thinks he can redesign society from the ground up based on his superior insights and understandings.

The people who liberal-capitalism's opponents therefore think of as its founders or designers, the Edmund Burkes, the Adam Smiths, the David Humes, the F.A. Hayeks, are nothing of the sort. They are the ones who realized that the practical workings of our social order, designed by *no one*, nonetheless required defenders against the onslaught of the theoreticians. There is no "return to first principles" *because this approach isn't based on first principles*. Society isn't an "enterprise" seeking to dragoon people into pursuing the goals of a few or so-called "majorities" under the authority of the state. It is not a journey nor an enterprise but a conversation among people of differing temperaments, inclinations and values, which has no "destination" and which for its success requires the respect of all those who participate and their acceptance on their own terms. There is no "discussion leader."

This idea that institutions and behaviours might not have been designed by *anyone*, that they are not the result of theorising, that they have not been imposed by the will of those in authority but have grown incrementally out of experience is completely foreign to the progressive mindset, but is the central understanding of gardeners.

The gardeners' mindset is guided, not by a central idea or policy, but by two emotional dispositions. They are first and foremost *grateful* for what we as a society have; one might even say that we *love* the peculiar and unique institutions, history, experiences and behaviours that constitute Canada because all of these have *made us who we are*. Second, gardeners are *humble* about the ability of present-day men and women to substitute their own necessarily limited knowledge and experience for that embodied in the institutions, traditions and culture of which we are the inheritors.

The kind of loving gratitude in the gardener's breast arises from an awareness of where we have come from. Poverty, disease, ignorance and intolerance are humanity's default condition. Only a handful of societies have, slowly and painfully, evolved the institutions and behaviours that allow people to escape these ills on a broad front.

Canada is one of those nations. Our greatest endowment is thus neither our natural resources nor our people but a set of institutions and behaviours that includes the rule of law and equality before the law, judicial independence, meritocracy, robust property rights, respect of contracts, non-corrupt police and bureaucracy, a relatively stable regulatory and tax burden, abjuring violence as a way of settling disputes, civility and respect toward one another, a strong work ethic and the certainty that elections actually choose governments with the vanquished relinquishing power. Add to that the civil freedoms of speech, religion, conscience and assembly and this makes an inheritance of order and freedom almost without peer in the world. It is of this edifice of grown institutions and behaviours that Canadian gardeners think when they read Oakeshott's moving words about the conservative inclination to enjoy what is present and available [that] is the opposite of ignorance and apathy and . . . breeds attachment and affection. We have been made by Canada and we think it is not to be tossed lightly aside.

As for the respectful humility that is the constant companion of loving gratitude, gardeners do not think society is perfect; they think rather that the imperfections signal a permanent need for incremental adjustments that promise genuine improvements without endangering the gains of the past. That bit about endangering what we have, what the past has bequeathed us, is crucial. So many schemes for social reform assume that the preoccupations and insights of the people who happen to be alive today are all that need concern us, that we can recast institutions and values that have stood the test of time in any way we wish in accordance with our transitory heart's desire, that we can change anything we want about how our society operates serene in the certain knowledge that we have foreseen all the consequences that will flow from such decisions. Everything is known, plastic, malleable, changeable; nothing is beyond our powers of analysis and understanding. We can keep everything we value, discard what annoys us and only indisputable progress will result.

Gardeners, on the contrary, are mindful that what we have has emerged from a generations-long tempering in the furnace of human experience. Our humility causes us to believe, not that nothing can be changed, but rather that change is always and inevitably accompanied by unintended consequences and that we are often largely or wholly ignorant of all the advantages bestowed upon us by institutions that work in practice, however quaint or Byzantine they may appear to ignorant but plausible-sounding theorists. *Theory is not the yardstick by which our past and our institutions should be measured; rather they should be measured by the practical success they confer on those who use them.*

This loving gratitude for and respectful humility about our inheritance is in contrast to progressivism's obsession with our mistakes, our moral, environmental and racial failings, for example. The past is no source of inspiration for progressives, but is composed of endless sins whose stain can only be removed by limitless self-flagellation, the abandonment of tradition and the reconstruction of our institutions and behaviours in accordance with fashionable opinion.

A corollary of the gardener's loving gratitude and respectful humility is a deep scepticism of grand schemes of social reconstruction. Too often have such great upheavals not only failed to improve conditions for the many, but they have destroyed the progress that had already been made in growing the institutions which confer success.

Gardeners thus look with favour, to choose a modern but relatively minor political controversy that perfectly illustrates the principle, on the vast network of programs and private insurance that have grown up over the years to give the vast majority of Canadians affordable access to pre-scription drugs. Gardeners equally agree, however, that this should be supplemented by a scheme that extends coverage to the small minority not served by the current system.[2] A universal "pharmacare" system that arrogantly and heedlessly sweeps away approaches that work well for an untried government monopoly unnecessarily risks compromising benefits enjoyed by the majority in order to worship at the left's altar of uniformity and bureaucratic control.

Moreover, gardeners understand that some of our greatest social challenges do not come from the *failure of our institutions and practices* but rather our *failure to extend them to people who do not yet fully benefit from them.* In the case of Indigenous people, for example, their challenge is not that they have had too much local autonomy and personal freedom and access to basic social and educational services. On the contrary, many of their ills arise from their longstanding exclusion from opportunity, education, infrastructure, self-government and many other things the rest of us take for granted. Indigenous leaders are reading from the gardeners' manual when they call for the yoke of Ottawa's bureaucracy to be lifted, for their communities to be granted self-government and for them to be able to build their economies to generate enough wealth for Indigenous people to make their own choices.

Loving gratitude and respectful humility for what we have inherited from our forebears entails an obligation to resist those who, from ignorance or self-interest, would damage this patrimony. It was thus a gardener's impulse that saw Canadians rise up in disgust against the corruption and the abuse of the rule of law and equality under the law that underpinned the SNC-Lavalin scandal. We are united in not wishing to import such behaviour and in rooting it out wherever it is to be found. That same impulse animated outrage at the attack on a rules-based society represented by asylum-seekers letting themselves into Canada by simply walking across the border at Roxham Road in defiance of the spirit of a fair and orderly immigration and refugee system.

What progressives usually try to characterize as racism vis-à-vis immigrants is almost always the perfectly reasonable fear that immigrants not committed to Canada's way of life will import into Canada behaviours or traditions that are destructive of what we have built and value, such as equal treatment of men and women, religious neutrality by the state, respect for the rule of law and absence of corruption in our public institutions.

On the vexed question of identity, gardeners hold that in a society of free people it is neither possible nor necessary for us all to agree with each other's choices of how to worship, conduct our sex lives, or interpret our history.

In the gardeners' worldview, people are not first and foremost black or transgender or Chinese or Muslim or Irish or Indigenous. They are Canadians who enjoy the freedom to choose the identities that matter to them. And the identities that they *choose* will almost certainly be different from the identities that progressive designers think matter.

This can be true because identity is best thought of as *an internal self-understanding*, the way I as an individual decide to define and weigh the parts of my character and personality and experience, what I put to the fore and what I consider to be secondary; what I invest time and effort in and what I leave in the dusty attic of memory. But identity can also be seen from the outside, without the benefit of the self-understandings that give identity meaning. Thus we can say that some percentage of the population "are" or "identify as," say, black or indigenous or bisexual or Sikhs or university graduates or parents or homeowners or suburbanites or soccer mums. These are objective, countable things. Either you live in the suburbs or you don't. Either you have children or you don't.

Where progressives get into trouble is in assuming that objectively observable characteristics actually define individual identity and, there-fore, interests. "Visible minorities" have interests that distinguish them from "whites." "Women" have interests that distinguish them from "men." "Muslims" have interests that distinguish them from "Jews and Christians." The "working class" has interests that distinguish it from "owners of capi-tal." The "middle class's" aspirations are crushed by the greed of the "One Percent."

The larger the objective countable group, the more political power ought to be exercised to promote their "interests." Similarly, the more vulnerable a group is thought to be, the greater the moral claim for political power to promote "their" interests. But the gardener believes that attributing interests to complex individuals based on their observable "objective" characteristics leaves out of the account the single most important thing about any particu-lar individual: what that person wants for him or herself. In fact, gardeners deny that you can know much of anything important about people by totting up their externally observable characteristics.

Progressives, who sees these disparate objective identities as founda-tional, are outraged by the resistance shown by ordinary Canadians when they are told by law they must use someone else's choice of pronoun or refrain from saying anything that might be construed as critical of Islam or must renounce their religious convictions to get government grants.

Gardeners say that generations of bloody and painful experience have taught us that in practical terms it must not be the business of the state to have preferences among the many and varied ways of life people can and do choose for themselves. All identities are private, and therefore not the domain of government, which must limit itself to the public domain. As private matters that fall within the protected sphere of individual auton-omy that our history, laws and tradition grant to individuals, identities are just self-chosen facts that must be accepted by everyone (including governments), not inconvenient behaviours to be rooted out by our wise rulers. Similarly, because ways of life and identities are private matters that do not and must not require the endorsement of others, no one must be forced to endorse such choices.

When Justin Trudeau says he has spent his time in office bringing Canadians together, what he really means is he has demanded that ordinary Canadians be forced to embrace ever smaller and more militant minorities who demand not acceptance but enthusiastic endorsement by the state, private organizations and private individuals. It is not enough to say that sexual minorities, for example, are entitled to the same protections and respect as all other Canadians. You must march in the pride parade or be labelled a bigot. Gardeners believe in a single public Canadians-of-All-Identities Pride Parade, followed by private side parties for those who want to celebrate particular identities.

I want to be clear that I personally have no problem marching in pride parades, but in keeping with the idea of the complexity of identities and the many ways they can be highlighted and show themselves, I note that there are specific pride parades in which I will not march. This is not for reasons of anti-gay bigotry, but for reasons of the choices that have been made by specific organizers in specific circumstances that raise important questions that must not be ignored.

For example, I wouldn't march in the Toronto Pride Parade for two principal reasons. One is that I abhor the organizers' decision to cave in to pressure from Black Lives Matter (not itself a gay rights organization) to ban the Toronto police from official participation in the parade. This exclusionary attitude is not acceptable especially when it concerns the people who put their lives on the line every day to maintain the public order that makes events like pride parades possible. The second reason is the similar threat of exclusion of the Toronto Public Library from participation in the parade on the grounds that that institution gave a platform to a feminist speaker giving a talk about the nature of sexuality and identity of which many trans activists disapproved.[3] One can approve wholeheartedly of gay rights but not wish to endorse or enable hijacking of that approval to justify an attack on free speech.

Beyond the Toronto Pride Parade, there are some parades in different locations that involve aggressive, vulgar and prurient displays of naked and near-naked male bodies that have nothing to do with celebrating great advances in gay rights and everything to do with thumbing one's nose at ordinary standards of common decency. Such parades are not a display most parents would want their children to see and supporters of gay rights and indeed gay individuals are not obliged to find such displays tasteful or acceptable.

These are not arguments against pride parades, but they constitute legitimate reasons why someone might not want to attend one without attracting the homophobia epithet.

Is Canada something to celebrate?

Unsurprisingly, designers want us to celebrate Canada because of programs they have designed (like social welfare and medicare) and concepts they endorse (like multiculturalism and diversity), but they are wrong to see these recent relatively minor side benefits as what makes Canada a society to be treated with love and gratitude, respect and humility. As befits a gardener, my view is that the best way to explain what makes Canada great and worthy of our love and respect is with stories, not abstract programs and statistics.

When my paternal ancestors, Laurence and Honora Crowley, set sail from Ireland in the 1820s for what was to become Canada, they didn't come for free visits to the doctor. They didn't wrestle a prosperous farm from a hostile wilderness for the quality of our public services. There weren't any. And yet Laurence and Honora and millions of others flocked to Canada. Why?

Plenty of people move to Canada from countries with more generous social programs, but not many Canadians move the other way. What, then, (with apologies to Donald Trump) makes Canada great?

My maternal great-grandparents, Henry and Edith Bierschied, came from the United States in search of the free homestead land that had been largely exhausted south of the border but was still relatively easily available in the great Dominion. When they crossed the border from North Dakota at North Portal, Saskatchewan, in August 1911, they brought with them seven-year-old Grace, my grandmother. Henry was of German immigrant stock, and it was not unusual for the many ethnic immigrants – the Poles, the Russians, the Germans, the Ukrainians, the Galicians, the Swedes and others – who ended up in the Canadian west to have tried their luck in the US first.

The Bierschieds were one of the tiny trickles that together added up to a mighty torrent of humanity sweeping into Canada at that time. And just like the Crowleys, who arrived nearly a century earlier, they did not come for medicare or subsidized university tuition. Again, these things did not exist. And yet they came. Why?

Because there is something about Canada that doesn't just make it a pleasant place to live with good public services and people from many countries; there is something about Canada that makes it one of a handful of societies on which the rest of the world looks in envy. If we opened the doors to this country tomorrow, the torrent of humanity that would sweep in would be beyond imagining. As a politician I heard once said, "this place would look like Walmart on a Saturday morning."

Let me suggest that there are three things that gardeners believe make Canada a great nation and a nation worth celebrating.

The first is that, like America and Australia, we are a creature of the New World. We are not an ancient civilization like Europe or the Middle East or China. We have escaped much of the prejudice and many of the social and cultural barriers that disfigure the Old World. Our life prospects are not determined by our religion, our ethnicity, our accent, our caste, our party membership, or our social class. That does not mean that people don't fail in Canada – they do – or that poverty does not exist – it does. It means that the barriers I've described are not impermeable here as they are in many other societies.

Of course, there has been prejudice. My forebears suffered from the prejudice against the Catholic Irish common in the nineteenth century, and it cannot have been easy to be native Irish speakers who were, in my great-great-grandmother's case, illiterate, according to the Canada West census taken a few years after they arrived. But that prejudice has been overcome, and we have worked successfully to defeat many other such prejudices over this country's history, including for example the decision to extend to gays and lesbians of the right to marry, an innovation of which Canadians are justly proud. Some prejudices remain; the disgraceful plight of many Indigenous people in Canada, for instance, tells us that there is still work to be done and I believe that it falls to this generation of Canadians to heal the wounds that have been created by generations of neglect, abuse and prejudice toward Aboriginal people.

But such blemishes in no way negate what we have accomplished. People come to Canada so that the sum of their life choices is not determined at their birth. Many people born here literally cannot imagine what that's like, and so don't appreciate how rare an achievement it is. But those who come here from elsewhere know, and often make great sacrifices to come here so that their children will never know a society where your fate is sealed before you take your first breath.

What makes Canada great is not, say, multiculturalism, although there is nothing wrong with multiculturalism per se. But as Sir Wilfrid Laurier said in his great speech on the admission of Alberta into the Dominion, it is fine to celebrate where your parents came from and the traditions they brought with them, but surely what matters most of all is how we work together here and now, not looking backward at what we were, at our different origins or our diverse points of departure, but looking forward *to what we are becoming together* and working toward creating a better country here for our children, all of whom are Canadians, every one of them.[4]

What makes Canada great, then, is in part that we do not care where you came from. What we care about is where we can go together.

The second thing that makes Canada great is freedom. Canada is free and freedom is her nationality, proclaimed Sir Wilfrid Laurier. In so saying, he encapsulated the great tradition of freedom which has been bequeathed to us, a tradition that finds its roots in the British liberal tradition, but whose benefits have been conferred on every Canadian, regardless of their ethnic origin, their religion, or their language.

Too many people seem to believe that freedom was somehow introduced to Canada by the Charter of Rights and Freedoms. That is not so. The

Charter is such an important document because it codifies (imperfectly) part of a tradition that reaches back deep into our colonial past and beyond that to the common law, Sir Edward Coke, the Glorious Revolution and the Magna Carta, a tradition of freedom that drew Laurence and Honora across the Atlantic and Henry and Edith across the border with barely the clothes on their backs, knowing almost nothing of how they would make their living here but knowing that energy and commitment and hard work would find their reward and they would be entitled to keep the fruits of their labour.

That freedom includes those very institutions I referred to earlier as our greatest endowment, institutions, beliefs, and behaviours that most of the rest of the world still have not mastered, an inheritance of freedom almost without peer in the world. And those, including our prime minister, who look in vain for the Canadian mainstream,[5] for the Canadian values that unite us, have not looked here or they would understand their error. The Canadian mainstream doesn't merely exist; it is the foundation on which repose the diverse identities of Canadians which so preoccupy progressives.

That mainstream is deeply imbued with gardener's values. The fact that no political party has been able to articulate and defend it is the greatest reason for our divisive and fractured politics. And we must never lose sight of this Canadian mainstream because without it we are forced to fall back on superficialities such as diversity and multiculturalism and so forth as the explanation for what makes Canada great.

If there is no *here* here, then all that is left of Canada is the angry intersection of our differences; this is the place where we all happen to be different together. But the unexamined corollary of such a viewpoint is that there is nothing beyond our differences that unites us, that we welcome newcomers *because they are different* rather than because they are enriched by Canada just as we are enriched by them, that people add themselves to Canada but Canada adds nothing to them.

Gardeners believe it is exactly the other way around – people flock here *to be changed by the well-tended garden that is the Canada we love;* not to live as they would have in the societies from which they came, but to live as

Canadians do, heedless of points of origin, and focused on a shared destination of self-respect, dignity and freedom *as Canada has come to understand these things.*

Multiculturalism in Canada isn't the cause of our success, but a result. Diversity isn't our strength; our strengths attract diversity. People from all nations come here because of the freedom, stability and opportunity Canada offers, not because people from all nations come here.

Freedom plus the New World together make a society in which each of us has been given more latitude to shape our lives according to our individual beliefs and desires than anywhere else on the face of the earth. That deserves loving gratitude and respectful humility.

Finally, what makes Canada great is our willingness to sacrifice to protect this precious and rare inheritance. Indeed, as Thucydides, the classical Greek who was the father of the study of history, once so wisely observed, "The secret of happiness is freedom, and the secret of freedom is courage." So if we celebrate our freedom here in Canada, we must ask ourselves what evidence there is that we have discovered that secret.

When Laurence and Honora Crowley arrived in the 1820s, they could not have known that their grandson, my grandfather, Lee, would fight in the Great War or that his son, my father, Lawrence, named for that first Laurence to arrive on our shores, would serve in both the Second World War and Korea. Whether facing down Nazism or Communism or Salafi Jihadism, whether in Korea, in Kosovo, in Afghanistan, in Iraq and Syria or in Latvia, Canadians have always been willing to put everything on the line so that the things we most value will be protected at home and abroad because, as Tommy Douglas so sagely observed, what we want for ourselves we desire for all.

Gardeners believe in a robust defence against predators, in standing up to bullies like China, Russia and North Korea, who see our freedom and prosperity as a threat to their power and who seek to undermine the international order to which Canada has contributed so mightily. If American leadership of the Western alliance flags (as I believe it is flagging), Canada must, in partnership with other like-minded middle-powers, pick up the mantle of leadership, even if it means forgoing some economic opportunity in places like China. Forgoing some export earnings from such places is a small price to pay to protect our freedom and of our ability to defend the weak and vulnerable, whether Hongkongers, Uighurs, or Ukrainians. It is of more of this Canada that the world is in desperate need, not the finger-wagging moralizer who, to quote a former deputy prime minister, talks a good game on the international stage but quietly heads for the bathroom when the waiter brings the bill.

The willingness to make sacrifices in order to protect the freedoms uniquely available to us in the New World: now that is a country worth loving, respecting and celebrating. One of the premises of this book, however, is that these foundation stones on which Canada's greatness are built are under threat. We are in danger of creating new privileged classes whose success depends not on their ability to contribute, but on their dependence on an ever-expanding state. Our freedoms are at risk of being lost through a failure to understand how and why they work and a cavalier belief that they can survive unscathed the unrelenting expansion of overweening government. Our willingness to sacrifice is being transmogrified from a willingness to put everything on the line to face down the world's bullies into a willingness to watch as our neighbours don balaclavas and thuggishly seek to prevent the perfectly legal exercise of our legitimate freedoms (whether to build pipelines and other critical infrastructure or to express unpopular opinions on university campuses and in public libraries).

These dangers to our established order call for a response that challenges the half-truths, falsehoods, distortions and falsifications that seek to turn our past and our achievements into sources of shame and derision rather than celebration.

But perhaps this is an old-fashioned and historically ignorant patriotism of a now unfashionable kind. According to Samuel Johnson, patriotism is the last refuge of a scoundrel. If the views of Canada's young people (as revealed in an Angus Reid/CBC poll[6]) are anything to go by, they largely agree with Johnson.

As the poll notes, "Massive generational differences affect Canadians' sense of pride and attachment to their country: nearly three-quarters (73%) of those sixty-five years or older profess a 'deep attachment' to Canada, this shrinks to less than half (45%) among those aged 18-24."

The Angus Reid/CBC poll further points out that in the recent past, ambivalent or negative sentiment about Canada was concentrated in Quebec; differences among Canadians on this question were therefore chiefly regional. Today the young right across the land are far more conditional in their enthusiasm for Canada than their elders.

If this is just a new manifestation of the old phenomenon of idealistic youth versus worldly-wise experience, it is perhaps nothing to worry about. If, by contrast, it portends a long-term shift in Canadians' commitment to and love for Canada, I think that would not just be a pity, but a loss to the world as well as to Canada.

In a way, I am not surprised that young Canadians view Canada with some suspicion. Talk to many of them and you may be dismayed by how little they know about our country, how it came to be and what it represents. Equally, much of what they have been taught is that our past is nothing but a repository for all that is retrograde and shameful. They believe it is filled with racism, sexism, homophobia, colonialism, militarism, genocide and environmental destruction.

It is easy to criticize the past and the decisions made there. But it is a conceit of each and every generation that they alone are free from poor judgements and intellectual shortcomings and historical myopia.

Looking solely at our past errors – and we have made our share – is not the right standard by which to measure Canada and its great achievements. Again, only a handful of societies have figured out, slowly and painfully, the institutions and behaviours that allow us to corral the horsemen of the apocalypse: pestilence, war, famine and death.

Canada is at the forefront of those nations and it is thanks to our history of struggle against the worst human afflictions that we now enjoy the conditions where our young people can look back in horror at how things used to be. It is the progress made possible by the economic, social and, yes, moral advances of our forebears that have allowed us to enjoy peace, order and good government in generous measure.

As the head of an institution that bears the name of our two greatest founding prime ministers I cannot help but observe that Confederation itself was no exercise in crude majoritarian triumphalism, but was an exquisitely wrought compromise between contending cultures, languages and religions that has made us one of the longest-enduring political orders on the planet. We have constantly expanded our notion of rights in response to genuine wrongs and real grievances. Canadian blood and treasure were expended in righteous struggles like World War Two and Korea because when the world called we were not found wanting. As we have become wealthier we have worked hard and with great success to improve our environment, our education and our social supports. As I have already remarked, it appears that this generation is the one called upon to right the many wrongs done to Aboriginal peoples in our history.

We cannot change the past, but our determination to ensure that past mistakes will not recur does not require us to despise our past. I have always believed that the true measure of a man or a woman or a country is not mistakes – for who among us has never made a mistake? – but how those mistakes are answered, by taking responsibility, making amends, and making every effort to ensure they don't happen again. On this measure, Canada has little of which to be ashamed and much of which to be proud.

The progressives and designers among us reject this account. Their argument is roughly this: you say that Canadian society is inextricably bound up with values of freedom and equality before and equal treatment under the law and yet look at how we over time have so signally and consistently failed to live up to those ideals, which are far more rhetorical than real. Look at the treatment Canadian society has dealt out over the years to women, Indigenous people, racial and sexual minorities, immigrants and would-be immigrants and others. Only a vicious society of which we should be ashamed could have acted in this way.

But I look at our history, recognize those undoubted abuses and failures, and draw exactly the opposite conclusion. The institutions we so value, which are at the heart of Canadian society, and whose operation reveals to us the ideas on which our success as a society depends, those institutions themselves are the result of an evolutionary process by which the dross of self-interest and prejudice is slowly purged and their reach is progressively extended to embrace more and more of society's members, as in the example of the extension of the traditional right to marry to those previously excluded, such as gays and lesbians.

Progressives' hostility to the traditional, and particularly traditional institutions, arises from a misunderstanding both of the origins of institutions and practices on the one hand and of the relationship between history and liberal-democratic ideals on the other.

It may be that many of our common institutions find their origins in the interests of particular groups. Private property, for example, may have its origins in the need of those who had wealth to protect themselves from those who did not (I do not think that this is the case, but let's accept it for the sake of the argument). But once in place, such institutions can be and are turned to the benefit of those who had no hand in their creation. Indeed, one might argue, for example, that what Indigenous groups in Canada are now claiming is a particularly robust form of property right to Indigenous lands that is intended to protect them from interference from the non-Indigenous.

Similar things could be said about the right to political representation, which sprang from a clash of interests between revenue-hungry sovereigns and wealthy aristocrats. As people began to understand better the ramifications of what had been created, the many arbitrary exclusions from the basic principle of representation were slowly stripped away. Indeed, a marked tendency of our ever more individualistic society is to strip privileges (literally "private laws") from particular groups by opening up those rights to all, thus turning them into public institutions.

Something similar was at work in the taming of political power. Following the Norman invasion of Anglo-Saxon England the monarch ruled with largely untrammeled power, although that power was somewhat diluted by the need to conciliate the nobles on whose land, soldiers, and wealth the king depended in the pursuit of his aims. When the king became too overbearing, demanding and dismissive of the role and authority of the barons, they allied against him and at Runnymede forced him to commit himself in writing to respect their traditional power and rights. The result was the Magna Carta. But why do we hark back to the Great Charter when in fact it was merely a deal worked out between a handful of the most powerful in society and conferred few benefits on the many?

The answer is because it began an evolutionary process by which political power had to extend the range of those whose interests were to be considered in the exercise of that power and whose rights had to be protected in consequence. Magna Carta unleashed a process by which more and more members of the population were included in the circle of those who enjoyed rights. That process moved through stages that included the toleration of religious dissent and recognition of rights of conscience and belief, enjoyment of private property and of freedom from arbitrary arrest and detention, the Reform Acts of the nineteenth century, the enfranchisement of women and various minorities, the abolition of slavery, the elimination of property-ownership requirements and many other reforms. Each of these changes was made to eliminate defined abuses and in no case did the authors' intentions include universal suffrage or universal enjoyment of rights, however much that might have been in the minds of those who agitated for reform.

Universalizing these rights was an incremental process whose full outcome few foresaw. Indeed, at each stage those who legislated often explicitly said that this outcome was not their intention. The point, however, was that those who enjoyed power had over time to share what had hitherto been their privileges with ever greater swathes of the population, turning "private laws" into public benefits. As the protected sphere belonging by right to individuals was gradually extended it became clear to those who thought about these things that the unintended benefit was institutions that protected and buttressed human freedom, flourishing and prosperity. But it was a long and slow process to purge these institutions from the dross of partiality and privilege.

When the British political order, culture and institutions crossed the Atlantic they eventually inspired both the American Founding and Canada's Confederation. In both instances our founders were moved by the same vision of human freedom and flourishing implicit in the British political heritage, but being imperfect human beings their prejudices prevented them from understanding the potential of every human being to benefit from the rights and freedoms they so rightly extolled. The subsequent history of both countries has been shaped in part by the struggle to enlarge the circle of those rights and freedoms to all: women, oppressed minorities, Indigenous people and others. Americans fought a civil war, not to repudiate their founding, but to extend its benefits to those wrongly excluded.

Every time we expanded the franchise, enlarged the circle of immigration, enhanced minority rights and, most recently, sought reconciliation between Indigenous and non-Indigenous Canadians, we have done so using language, concepts and aspirations that informed Confederation and the British political heritage from which Canada drew inspiration.

That is why the argument of those previously excluded had such moral force: They appealed to concepts such as rights and equality that have long been part of our heritage but were imperfectly understood and applied. A balanced view of our past acknowledges the imperfections of what was done, but also the soundness of the vision that inspired it and the effort made to fix our errors and overcome the partiality of our vision. We cannot change the past, but it does not require us to despise our past to say that our job is to ensure past mistakes shall not be tolerated on our watch.

To draw it all together, what makes Canada a society worthy of our grateful love and respectful humility is not the values of progressive designers embodied in invented things like social programs and diversity and multiculturalism, although these are all quite reasonable (if imperfect) extensions of the core of what makes us Canadians. They are nice add-ons, not the essence of Canadianism.

Three attributes form the core of what makes us Canadians: our inheritance of the institutions of opportunity and freedom that in practice have conferred great success on us collectively and individually; our status as a New World society that has escaped many of the ills and prejudices that disfigure the Old World; and finally the willingness to make sacrifices to protect and nurture these values at home and abroad.

Our past, while helping to highlight areas where we can and must do better, is no reason to hang our head in shame. On the contrary, it is reason for us to thank our lucky stars that those who went before us built as solidly as they did and gave us the tools necessary to extend over time the benefits of Canada's strengths to all who live here and those yet to come. Canadian gardeners are thus patriots who believe that our little patch of the world's garden is one that has been rather well tended and one of which we have every reason to be extraordinarily proud.

As Aristotle taught us, true patriotism, like all real virtues, is a mid-point between two extremes. On the one hand is narrow, bellicose, xenophobic nationalism – of which we have perhaps seen all too much in recent times; on the other hand is a bloodless, rootless cosmopolitanism that loves an abstract humanity but not any actual flawed community of real people.

True patriots love Canada because it has made us (and "us" most emphatically includes those who have come to join us from other countries) who we are; and who we are, for all our flaws, is a standard to which much of the rest of the world aspires, and with very good reason. The rest of this book tells us how gardeners see Canada's achievements and how to protect those achievements from the predators, foreign and domestic, who want to feed on and even crush its success, heedless of the fact that in so doing they endanger its bounteous harvest in the future.

CHAPTER II

The problem
of ignorance

G ARDENERS AND DESIGNERS AGREE that knowledge *is* power. We just disagree about what knowledge is, how it works, who has it and, most importantly, the corresponding role of ignorance in human affairs.

Humankind has never possessed more knowledge than it does today. True knowledge is the most potent instrument of human power, for acting on it allows us to be successful in realizing our intentions, which is at the heart of human freedom. Ignorance, by contrast, is a pitfall waiting to trap us, even in the pursuit of our best laid plans.

But while humanity has every reason to worship at the altar of Sophia, goddess of knowledge and wisdom, gardeners and designers have a very different view of what knowledge is, how it operates, and crucially, of its limitations.

Designers believe that once knowledge is acquired, it is a permanent feature of life, as indeed some knowledge is. The truths of mathematics, for example. They further believe that all knowledge is at least in principle available to everyone. Finally, because knowledge is in principle available to all, they believe that it is possible to achieve a comprehensive overview of human knowledge and that that overview can best be achieved by governments that use a vast, professional, knowledge-gathering and processing bureaucracy to acquire and analyse everything that is known. And since knowledge is the prerequisite for success in human affairs, a wise humanity hands over to government, at the apex of the knowledge hierarchy, the design, organization and execution of the most important and complex of human affairs.

A choice between letting ordinary people, communities and groups organize their affairs in accordance with their own understandings of what matters and what is important (usually referred to dismissively by designers as a "patchwork"), and a government able to marshal vast resources to find the "best" solution, is really no choice at all. Who would choose to be guided by ignorance and partial knowledge and prejudice when disinterested and comprehensive "expert" knowledge is available, especially when backed by a "democratic" mandate? And for the designer there are only two alternatives: either individuals and groups stumble around in the dark of human ignorance as they try to achieve their goals and ambitions, or the designing power of all-wise, all-seeing, beneficent government bestows the gift of clever and generous programs tailored precisely to the needs of a struggling citizenry.

The gardener, by contrast, is keenly aware that knowledge is variegated and subtle. Far from being easily assembled in a god-like overview of the operation of society, much knowledge is irremediably locked in both nature and the minds and hearts of billions of people. Moreover, new knowledge about ourselves, about nature, and about society is constantly being discovered. Furthermore, new knowledge, as Galileo taught us, is often seen by those in power as deeply subversive, for it undermines not only faith (in God or government) but the authority that safeguards and propagates that faith.

Gardeners thus believe that it is an enduring and pernicious prejudice of our age that governments are somehow endowed with more, and more certain, and more expert knowledge than anyone else. In fact, for gardeners, the designer's knowledge hierarchy is upside down. Governments, far from being at the apex of knowledge, know the least, because humanity's greatest store of knowledge resides in individual hearts and minds, in local communities and in specialized organizations that can know a very great deal about a few things, like how to generate electricity or make a car or design software or deliver packages or organize retirement savings.

In a later chapter I will talk about how human diversity is best fostered by knowledge-rich grown social institutions, not by governments whose knowledge is necessarily incomplete. In fact, many government programs can only survive their own ignorance by relying on the law to shield them from the vigorous challenge offered by the new knowledge which time and human imagination will inevitably throw in their path.

For now, let me talk a bit more about this scepticism, central to the gardener's vision, that governments can and do possess a comprehensive overview of the state of human knowledge and that they are therefore not merely entitled but morally obliged to act on this knowledge for the betterment of humanity, and that the knowledge designers possess should trump the knowledge on which people decide things for themselves and create the "patchwork" that so offends designers.

There are few prejudices more firmly anchored in the designing mind than the one that holds that we can always take the merely traditional grown institution and, by taking thought, replace it with a modern, well-designed replacement with none of the defects and many positive new features. Can this prejudice be sustained? Here are just a few reasons why I think it cannot.

We don't know nature

Once upon a time, in ancient Greece, sailors were transporting a cargo of natron, a washing powder, somewhere in the Mediterranean. They stopped to prepare a meal on a fine white sandy beach. Lacking stones on which to support their kettle, they used lumps of natron to hold the kettle over the fire. The heat from the fire fused the natron and the sand creating something of which humanity had been ignorant since the dawn of time. For all we know, similar accidents may well have occurred earlier without anyone seeing and appreciating what had happened. In this case, however, the accident and an intelligent observer worked together to bring a highly valuable creation to humanity, increasing, not by design but by happy circumstance, our power to achieve our purposes.

The nameless sailor who saw the shiny crust that had formed under the fire had discovered, by accident, a single bit of useful information, one of nature's slumbering secrets: that heat, sand, and natron, when brought together, create glass. By seizing it, experimenting with it, and then exploiting it, he and those who came after him unknowingly unleashed a series of powerful transformations and innovations. It became possible to have both warmth *and* natural light in buildings. Pots could be glazed. The seeds of mason jars, petri dishes, and the great stained glass masterpieces of Chartres were planted by the sailors and that fire.

Now a more modern example: originally founded on coal mining, Springhill, Nova Scotia, had been in decline for decades following the closure of the mines. One snowy winter's day, a man was out walking his dog in the town and noticed a patch of ground where the snow had melted and steam was rising. His curiosity was piqued and on investigation he discovered that the mine shafts underneath the town had filled with water that was geothermally heated. A chance surface leak, together with a man who was not content merely to see, but able to observe, changed the town. New businesses have sprung up, built on the exploitation of this cheap, plentiful, but strictly local and accidental source of energy.

What can we conclude from these examples? That in spite of our vast knowledge, we do not know more than a tiny fraction of the world around us. Most of what we know about the world has been discovered by accident and curiosity. The chief way to increase our knowledge, therefore, is to accept our ignorance of the world and give people freedom to try new things, because we cannot know what they will discover.

One of the main justifications for *freedom* is precisely our *ignorance*. If we give people freedom to try new things, to experiment in trying to achieve their own goals, we will inevitably discover knowledge that serves not only our own purposes but those of others. Remember that our Greek sailor friends were not looking to discover glass. They were looking for lunch. The man in Springhill wasn't looking for a source of energy. He was walking his dog.

Lest you think that this relationship between chance and human curiosity and nature's secrets has been overcome by the modern scientific method, you are bound to be disappointed. Several years ago, when one of that year's three Nobel laureates in physics, Duncan Haldane, was notified of the prize, he said he was "very surprised and very gratified." He made the additional remarkable observation that the laureates stumbled onto the discoveries that earned them the prize.

"Most of the big discoveries are really that way," he said. "At least in theoretical things, you never set out to discover something new. You stumble on it and you have the luck to recognize what you've found is something very interesting." One of his colleagues went on to say he was in his twenties at the time of their discovery (about superconductivity) and that his "complete ignorance" was an advantage in challenging the established science.

"I didn't have any preconceived ideas," he said. "I was young and stupid enough to take it on."

Genuine scientists, then, are humble about what they know, individually and collectively, just as they are aware that orthodoxy can gain control of any field of human activity, including science, and that ignorance is a powerful tool out of which human knowledge grows.

We as a culture pride ourselves on an impressive body of knowledge, and so an emphasis on our ignorance does not sit well with many of us. Yet this may just be precisely the overweening arrogance of the ignorant at work. While we pride ourselves on our knowledge of the physical world, for example, in fact much of it is brought to us by people who happened by chance to witness some accident and understood at least part of the practical significance of what they saw.

The Greek sailor who discovered glass is merely the earliest recorded example that I know of this principle at work. Many other discoveries that were the fruit of fortuity have changed the course of human life for the better. Aniline dyes, photography, x-rays, the discovery of the relationship between electricity and magnetism, the curing of rubber, the telephone, the phonograph, welding, steelmaking, the telescope, and penicillin are only a few choice examples. We knew nothing about the potential of the physical world to supply us with such wonders until someone stumbled upon them and *really* saw what they meant. We could not have sought them directly without knowing what they were, and had we known what they were, we would already have discovered them!

Some of these discoveries were the so-called "black swans" that options trader Nassim Taleb did so much to popularize, and more black-swan-type examples will follow. The point is that the future is going to be populated with many more such discoveries, some about the natural world, some about the human-made world, and some about ourselves as individuals. Some of these will change everything and yet, by definition, we know nothing about them today.

The designer thinks that we are knowledgeable about the physical world. The gardener thinks, on the contrary, that we are ignorant of the world we inhabit and this must make us humble in our assumptions about human knowledge.

We don't know who we are or what we are becoming

The ignorance of the physical world is by no means the only kind of ignorance to which we are subject. We are also ignorant about ourselves.

Consider a man I once met who makes Scottish Highland paraphernalia, things like sporrans, daggers, and bagpipe fittings. One day he was reading the newspaper and his eye happened to fall on a call for tenders from an aircraft manufacturer looking for subcontractors to make aircraft parts. He ran his eye idly over the advertisement. Suddenly, he realized that with the equipment he had for making Highland paraphernalia, he had the capacity to make the aircraft parts that were described there. In that brief moment, this man's understanding of himself and his capabilities was transformed; he now saw himself not only as a maker of daggers and sporrans, but as an aircraft manufacturing subcontractor. He went on to employ a number of people in the aircraft parts business, as well as carrying on his traditional activities.

Let's stop for a moment to ponder what this example tells us about the ability of government authorities to achieve the overview of all of society's productive resources. After all, such knowledge, the ability to identify and then rationally employ all of society's resources is the designer's promise; he promises to do it better than the unplanned and grown processes of social co-operation. But remember that my maker of Highland paraphernalia *did not himself know* that he possessed the capacity to make aircraft parts, and he only learned it about himself by the purest happenstance.

Note that no government official or statistician who wanted to get a comprehensive overview of the aircraft making capacity of the national economy would therefore be capable of doing so, because if he did a survey and asked this fellow, "Are you an aircraft parts maker?" the answer would have been "no." Why? Because the man lacked the self-knowledge needed to answer in the affirmative. He did not know all of which he was capable. If we do not know these things about ourselves, how can distant bureaucrats in national or provincial capitals know them on behalf of all of us? How can such knowledge be programmed into computers or be captured by Big Data or be part of the National Economic Recovery Plan?

So, just as we established that we don't know the world we inhabit, we don't know who we are. Who we are is subject to constant transformation as we learn new things, and what we will learn about ourselves and how we will be changed by this new knowledge is one of the inscrutable mysteries of human life.

Indeed, I suggest that most of the really important things that have happened to you in life have been the result not of planning but of accident. Where you were born, the abilities, talents, and interests you were born with, the community you grew up in and where you went to school, the teachers you had, the friendships you made, and the romantic attachments that you form are all good examples. My wife and I, for instance, are together because we had the great good fortune to have had three accidents befall us: to grow up in the same community in Vancouver, to be in Grade Eight together and then after thirty years of adult life, to be brought back together through the merest chance. And yet meeting her is literally the single most important thing that has happened to me in my life.

The knowledge that makes humanity so powerful and successful is by its nature dispersed and locked in many minds. Its central characteristics are exponential growth, constant creative destruction and revision, adaptability, decentralization and resistance to central gathering and analysis. It can be used but it cannot be controlled because it is a dynamic force constantly evolving in response to unforeseen and unforeseeable changes in circumstances. Ironically, one consequence is that as we become more developed, more evolved, and more technologically sophisticated, we become less and less able to control and direct society, or even the complex systems of which it is composed. In other words, as humans, taken together, become more knowledgeable, the justification for allowing those in authority to tell us what to do declines.

Yet we increasingly live in a society in which no one has a complete overview of everything that is going on and therefore we are ever more interdependent. I can't do what I do if oil refiners and miners and farmers and administrators and bankers and money managers and restaurant cooks and servers and airline pilots and everybody else don't do what they're supposed to do.

The miracle of modernity is that I can rely on the entire body of knowledge of society without having to possess that knowledge myself and without government officials telling people what to do in accordance with some "rationally-designed" plan. Through a set of institutions and behaviours like personal accountability and responsibility, markets, property, contract, the rule of law, and a whole series of others, people are rewarded for putting their specialist knowledge at your disposal without them having to know you, what you are trying to do, or whether they agree with what you're doing.

This is the trade-off we have made: *greater knowledge at our disposal and therefore more power to achieve our purposes, but in return less and less power to control the activities of each other and of institutions and complex systems.*

We don't know what we're doing

Here's another thing we don't know: we don't know what we're doing. Technology, like all human actions, has both intended and unintended consequences. One example of unintended consequences is how the emergence of collateralized debt obligations and various forms of derivatives contributed to a transformation of the American housing market in ways that no one foresaw, and with devastating consequences in the recession of 2007-08.

Some argue that climate change is an unintended consequence of technological shifts in energy generation to carbon-based fuels. The list of unintended consequences of technological innovations is long: loss or theft of intellectual property, proprietary data and customer information, EM pulses, cyber-attacks, identity theft, privacy invasion, nuclear proliferation, high-tech terrorism, and the destruction of national borders are just a few that come to mind.

Here is an example from the finance industry. In the span of just two minutes in Asia in early trading a few years ago, the British pound plunged more than 6 percent, sending the fourth most-traded currency on the planet to its lowest level in thirty-one years. Possible explanations offered by experts included France's president pushing for a hard-line approach on Britain's exit from the European Union, and recycled rumors of a "fat finger" trade, but nothing that would justify a drop of this magnitude. It was, however, widely thought that the sell-off was probably exacerbated by computer-driven automated traders reacting at speeds faster than any human could manage. So-called algorithmic transactions in the foreign-exchange market have more than tripled in recent years, accounting for hundreds of billions of dollars of daily turnover. This move in the pound followed a flash crash in the South African rand and a similarly unexplained move in New Zealand's dollar. This is a classic example of the unintended consequences of our actions and creations. We simply don't know what we have created.

We don't know how to explain ourselves

As for the touching claim that all of this inventory of the types of ignorance suffered by fallible humanity is irrelevant because we can program all this information into computers and achieve the kind of comprehensive and analytical overview of our situation that I am saying is not possible – well, anyone who believes this has not been paying attention.

For computers to know something, a human being must both possess the knowledge as a fully articulated idea and also must realize that it is important enough to tell the computer. Yet much of human knowledge is not consciously known by anyone and can never be comprehensively stated.

This may be a startling thing to say and yet a moment's thought reveals that every one of us has had this experience. We may know how to make excellent spaghetti sauce or how to speak well or how to influence people or how to raise money for charity. If asked to give a comprehensive statement of how we achieve what we do, however, we are often reduced to saying, "I can't put it into words. I just know when it is right." Try putting that into your planning process. In fact, the best statement of this kind I have read comes from Michael Oakeshott. He quotes a parable from Chuang Tzu, as follows:

> A wheelwright asks a duke what book he is reading. On being told that it is the collected wisdom of the sages, he dismisses the book as "the lees and scum of bygone men." Outraged, the duke challenges him to justify his statement or face death. The wheelwright responds:
>
> "As a wheelwright I look at the matter in this way. When I am making a wheel, if my stroke is too slow, then it bites deep but is not steady; if my stroke is too fast then it is steady, but it does not go deep. The right pace, neither slow nor fast, cannot get into the hand unless it comes from the heart. It is a thing that cannot be put into words [rules]; there is an art in it that I cannot explain to my son. That is why it is impossible for me to let him take over my work, and here I am at the age of seventy still making wheels. In my opinion it must have been the same with the men of old. All that was worth handing on dies with them; the rest they put in their books."

There is a famous (and possibly apocryphal) anecdote about the virtuoso violinist Isaac Stern. Whether it is true or not is irrelevant. It captures a profound truth. A fan, collaring Stern backstage after a magisterial concert exclaimed, "I'd give my life to play like you!" to which Stern replied, "Lady, that I did."

My gloss on that is that Stern went to many teachers, some of them the best in the world. If they could simply have communicated to him what was needed to play brilliantly, they would have done so. But all they could do was to put into inadequate words and exercises and demonstrations examples of what they wanted him to learn. But there was no substitute for actually putting his hands on the violin and going through the hard slog of mastering the skill for himself. And like those who taught him, he surely said to the students who followed him: "this is what I do. Now go away and figure out for yourself how it is done and how you will build on it to create your own style. Keep coming back to me from time to time and I will tell you if you are getting close."

"You can't describe it – it's a feel," said Scott Podsednik, an outfielder for the White Sox when asked to describe the magic in a perfect bat. It is not easy to define. "When you pick it up and take a couple of swings with it, you just know."

In his eulogy on the death of Sir John A. Macdonald, Canada's founding prime minister, the Opposition leader, Sir Wilfrid Laurier, opined that Sir John ". . . was also endowed with those inner, subtle, undefinable graces of soul which win and keep the hearts of men."[7] Undefinable because they are an art that can be known in the soul but never fully stated by those who enjoy their mastery or by those who study them.

This is a wonderful way of getting at the important truth that many of the most important things we do we cannot express in words. We know *how* to do them, but we cannot *put into words* what we do. We often express this truth in the phrase "those who can, do; those who can't, teach." The examples are legion of, say, hockey players who are brilliant on the ice but utter failures as coaches. Why? Because they know how to do what needs to be done, but they are incapable of expressing in words how it is done. And if those who study different topics could analyse and then master them easily, they would be able to pass them on in their university classes. But like the wheelwright, we all know that those who come out of formal education are far from achieving the mastery they will acquire over a career spanning decades, a mastery that they themselves will then find impossible to communicate fully to the succeeding generation.

We don't know how complicated most things are

Let us think for a moment about the complexity of the world that the designers seek to understand comprehensively, to master, to control. Nobel laureate and economist Paul Romer tells us that if you take something as simple as a chair which can be constructed out of ten parts that can be assembled in any order, the number of possible alternative moves in constructing the chair gives us a number that as I recall is ten to the 42nd power (that is to say ten followed by forty-two zeros), or more seconds than have elapsed since the Big Bang that created the universe. All those alternative courses of action in something as simple as assembling a basic chair.

But does that matter? Who cares what order you do things in? Well, of course, the order in which you do things is only one of many choices that are available to us in deciding what is to be done in public policy or any other field. And it can be of overriding importance. There is a documented case of one batch of a certain aircraft engine that was involved in several crashes, while another batch of identical engines was not involved in crashes. After an exhaustive investigation it was determined that the difference was that the second batch of engines was dismantled for maintenance in a particular order. The first batch of engines was dismantled in a different order. That was the only distinction, and it caused the planes to go down.

There was a similar case of a manufacturer who used a number of extremely expensive heavy stamping machines. All the costly machines had to be replaced after a relatively few years, except for one, which the same man had operated over many years. That machine outlasted all the others by a wide margin. After some investigation, it was discovered that the reason for this difference was that this man came in in the morning and turned on his machine and then went for coffee, while his colleagues went and got their coffee first, then came to their machines, turned them on, and went immediately to work. It was the act of allowing his machine to warm up for fifteen to twenty minutes each day that made an operating difference worth millions of dollars to the company. When you think of all the things that could be done differently than they are, and the time and effort required to try all out all the permutations, you realize the absurdity of the designers' pretensions.

Deceptively simple looking things are actually the result of incredibly long and complex chains of highly specialized activities executed by a series of people each of whom possesses part of the puzzle but none of whom knows it all.

An American named A.J. Jacobs decided a few years ago to thank personally every person who made a contribution to delivering his morning cup of coffee (yes, I know, those Americans really are inexplicable aren't they? But that's my point). He started with the obvious ones, the baristas and the cashiers and the cleaners. But that wasn't enough. As one reviewer wrote, he talked to

> . . . the shop's head of purchasing, the inventor of the lid for his paper cup, the guy who designed the shop's logo, and the city employees charged with food safety and water quality. He talked to truck drivers, warehouse employees, coffee importers, and farmers. And, he acknowledges, he only scratched the surface of the immense web of industries and workers who contributed to the physical and intellectual infrastructure required to bring him one perfect cup of coffee.

Jacobs spent an entire year on this project and recognizes that he didn't get to everyone. He did, however, find the time to write a book and a TED talk about his experience. Please don't try to do what he did for everyone who worked to make his book or his TED talk possible, because the list would be different but just as long and convoluted and hard to pin down.

Member of the European Parliament Daniel Hannan, in an after dinner speech I once heard, told the story of another American who decided to make himself a chicken sandwich. He didn't decide to make it by going to the store and buying bread and chicken and mayonnaise and lettuce, however. He decided to do every process required from scratch. He grew the grain, which he then ground to make flour for his bread. He raised, slaughtered, and prepared the chicken; he grew the lettuce, pickled the cucumber, went to the seaside and evaporated seawater to make salt, and so on. It took him months and the process cost him thousands of dollars. All for a sandwich inferior in quality to the crispy chicken sandwich he could have purchased at Wendy's for $3 and five minutes' effort.

The point is not about chair assemblers or coffee suppliers or sandwich makers. The point is the incredible complexity of even the "simplest" human service or product. Every one of them involves thousands of bits of sophisticated knowledge seamlessly coordinated in the absence of a Ministry of Chicken Sandwiches or a Department of Chair Assembly.

What is more, every sandwich seller who competes with Wendy's and every coffee maker who competes with Timmy's does so using their own unique process, based on their unique knowledge and skill sets. There is therefore no one *right* answer about how to do any of these things. There are many, many ways of doing each one of them, each with their characteristic strengths and weaknesses, and each better suited to one kind of customer or set of circumstances than another. It is not wasteful having more than one supplier; it is the condition of there being a wide variety of products that allows each person to get just what they want within the limits of what they can pay. And what they can pay is itself not a fixed amount but will vary according to circumstances and, for example, what other things cost that they also want.

And as for the notion that government officials can always arrive at the "right" solution based on a comprehensive study of the problem, I offer you this gem of a parable from the airport in Halifax. In order to avoid the problem of fog, an official did a comprehensive survey of the region around the city to identify the place that was least foggy. They found it, cut down the forest, and built the airport. What they did not realize was that in cutting down the trees they effectively created a "fog sink," and the airport is now one of the foggier places in the region.

I don't talk about the Halifax airport because it somehow proves that the private sector always gets it right and the public sector always gets it wrong. That's nonsense. Everybody gets it wrong sometimes. The issue is how do you maximize your chances of getting it right and how can you fix it when it is wrong?

Remember, there is no one right answer about how to do things, and an enormous number of variables (remember how many ways there are to assemble something as simple as a chair, and how devastating the consequences can be of the wrong choice of the order in which to do things). In grown social institutions premised on human ignorance and the likelihood of failure, you maximize the chances of getting things right by having lots of people using their own unique knowledge to do tasks as well as they can and then competing against one another. You handle failure by allowing poorly performing or incompetent companies or people to go bankrupt and letting others who have a better idea fill the gap left by the failure. When Eaton's closed it was a tragedy for the people who worked there, but the people who bought Eaton's goods simply moved their custom to Sears or the Bay, just as today they move to Amazon or Walmart or specialized retailers. Customers would barely have noticed Eaton's failure beyond the momentary inconvenience of having to find another supplier for the things they were used to buying there. And as for the affected employees, many will have gone on to work at other retailers or in different careers altogether.

If you are the public sector and you get one shot at what you're aiming to achieve based on "the best available knowledge" and there is no back-up in the case of failure, you get fogged in when you need to fly and there are no alternatives.

So far we have established that we:

- don't know what we're doing,
- don't know who we are,
- don't know how complicated the world is,
- don't know what we are capable of,
- don't know how to explain ourselves,
- don't know what we are becoming, and
- don't know what the future will bring.

We don't know what we want

But there is more ignorance to catalogue.

If, for example, the social question that should most preoccupy us is, how do we go about satisfying human wants and needs, the logically precedent question must be: How do we know what these wants and needs *are?*

What people want depends on what they know – about themselves, their resources, and the real choices open to them. To discover what people really want, we must be constantly striving to offer them ever-changing choices, letting them know that these choices exist. Since by its very nature this information can never be complete, we are embarked, in a society of free people working within grown social institutions, on a permanent quest for knowledge. This quest is for knowledge about our fellow humans: about their expectations, their wishes, their desires, and their thoughts.

What we want is driven by what we know. If we change what we know, we change what we want. Change what we want and our grown social institutions change in response.

A brief example: some years ago, the price of oat bran shot through the roof. Why? A published study purported to show that eating oat bran lowered your chances of developing cancer. Overnight, oat bran went from being a commodity of marginal interest and economic value to selling like hot cakes. All because an idea was introduced into the human mind, an idea that changed our wants and desires. When it was later established that this idea about oat bran was wrong, our behaviour changed yet again.

Coca Cola is probably the most successful consumer product in the history of the world. It was originally marketed in syrup form as a mouthwash and tonic, not as a soft drink. And it was quite unsuccessful. People didn't want this tonic. In fact, Coke was invented as a soft drink by somebody who had a supply of the useless syrup. He mixed it with carbonated water and sold it at his pharmacy's soda counter to get rid of the unwanted stock. He and Coke never looked back. Yet all he did was to change the idea people had about Coke. It was no longer a health product, but a leisure product: a drink, not a tonic.

Joseph Schumpeter wrote about the "creative destruction" inherent in capitalism, the ceaseless questing for change that seethes within a liberal-capitalist society.[8] That change is driven by the intertwined forces of constantly changing human needs and the constant discovery of new knowledge. The destructiveness of this process of change can, of course, be deeply disquieting, so political authorities often resist this transformative force in the name of the preservation of a comfortable status quo.

Yet change which at first looks destructive often brings great and quite unexpected benefits later. No one, and particularly not those who spark these changes, can foresee all the consequences of what they have unleashed.

Consider in this regard something as simple as the invention of the motorcar.[9] No one foresaw the myriad social transformations that would be wrought by this invention as people began to see and exploit its potential. Certainly its inventors were no better at crystal-ball gazing than anyone else; they believed that the total number of cars in the world would be forever limited by one insurmountable obstacle: the number of members of the working class intelligent enough to be trained as chauffeurs.

Yet the car was nearly to destroy, for example, the horse industry. Almost twenty million horses lived and worked in North America at the turn of the last century, creating work for blacksmiths, livery boys, and makers of nails, harnesses, and saddles. Hay and oats were major cash crops. Of all this, almost nothing remains today. Local institutions like the rural school and church fell victim to the school bus and the Sunday drive. City centres shrank, suburbs blossomed, hemlines, drive-ins, and highways went up – barns, travel time, and (arguably) sexual mores came down. Millions of individual ideas, adjustments, desires, and innovations all conspired to work a transformation on the face of society which even the most prescient could not have envisioned.

Once they could see what was happening, many lawmakers early in the last century resisted the automobile's rise, fearing the economic and social transformations they dimly sensed would come in its train.

Now we may find Zimbabwean chrome and Malaysian tin, French tires and Dutch chemicals, Taiwanese steel and German robots running on American software being used by Canadian workers under Japanese management to make cars for export to the Far East. Most of the jobs performed in the manufacture of a car didn't even exist at the turn of the last century, yet now the industry directly or indirectly employs millions of people in literally every corner of the globe.

A similar transformation occurred as thousands of feudal peasants moved from the countryside to the city during the Industrial Revolution. If authorities had had the power to stop such social transformations, to prevent the kind of experimentation I am describing, some immediate suffering might have been prevented and some established interests protected. But we would still be working the land, and few of us would have horses, let alone automobiles.

When the Wright brothers flew their plane at Kitty Hawk they could not have envisioned that Airbuses and Boeing 777s would be the result or that within three or four generations or so commercial space travel would be within our grasp, just as they could not have imagined that their invention would destroy the trans-Atlantic ocean liner industry or most long-distance passenger rail travel.

Limited brain vs. unlimited complexity

Consider that by most estimates the stock of knowledge is exploding at an unprecedented rate. In his 1981 book *Critical Path*, visionary R. Buckminster Fuller estimated that by 1900, the body of human knowledge doubled every century. By 1945 the doubling period was down to 25 years and in the year of his book's publication it was down, he estimated, to perhaps a year. IBM not so long ago predicted that by this year, 2020, it would be down to every 12 *hours*.[10] Of course not all fields of knowledge advance at the same rate; in cutting-edge technical fields such as computer science or nanotechnology it doubtless doubles more quickly than in, says, classics or the study of Jane Austen novels. Taken as a whole, however, these numbers mean that *one half of everything that is known today by somebody somewhere was not yet known yesterday, and humanity collectively will know twice as much tomorrow as we do today.* Whether the doubling period is in fact a day or a week or a month or even a year is largely irrelevant to the nature of the challenge represented by this accelerating knowledge tsunami.[11]

Importantly, new knowledge discovery *displaces* old knowledge, so not only are we constantly learning new things, but we must constantly *unlearn* things that we were convinced only yesterday were true. This is sometimes referred to as the "half-life of facts (or knowledge)."[12] A measure of the practical significance of this is found in Shane Parrish's estimate of the half-life of an engineering degree (i.e., how long it takes for one half of what an engineering graduate has learned to become obsolete): "A century ago, it would take 35 years for half of what an engineer learned when earning their degree to be disproved or replaced. By the 1960s, that time span shrank to a mere decade . . . Modern estimates place the half-life of an engineering degree at between 2.5 and 5 years."[13]

Set this explosion of knowledge against the capacity of the human mind to process information. This is what is known as its channel capacity, and that capacity is finite because "the number of signals and information that can be processed in attention, short term memory and working memory etc. are limited,"[14] and is essentially unchanged since homo sapiens emerged many millennia ago. That channel capacity has been estimated to be roughly five to nine ideas (or as expressed by Harvard's George Miller, the originator of this concept, seven plus or minus two[15]); that is, the number of ideas we can hold in our minds and consider, that we can juxtapose one against the other to see how they connect. And that's on a good day. God knows what the channel capacity of the mind is on a Monday morning after Spring Break.

What does this mean? Among other things, it means that we as individuals are *condemned* to ignorance. Our brain's channel capacity is relatively fixed, while the knowledge known by all human beings collectively is expanding exponentially.

With minds so limited, and knowledge so vast and varied, you and I are condemned to see a narrowing slice of what is known at the same time as humanity has never had access to more knowledge. As Karl Popper, the philosopher of science, once remarked, "Our knowledge can only be finite, while our ignorance must necessarily be infinite."

This is a bitter pill for "experts" to swallow, especially ones that make a living pontificating (yes, I am guilty, but demand calls forth supply) and prognosticating about the future. But you will perhaps not be surprised to learn that careful studies have been made about the ability of "experts" with fancy PhDs and impressive organizations behind them to make successful predictions. You will further fail to be surprised if I reveal to you that their track record is pitiful, as documented, for example, by Philip Tetlock in his classic work, *Expert Political Judgment*.[16]

Tetlock doesn't just find that expert predictions in field after field are frequently dead wrong, but compare badly to well-informed non-expert opinion and simple extrapolation from current trends. He then asks the $64,000 question: Is there an approach that works better than kowtowing to "expert" opinion? His answer gladdens the heart of gardeners everywhere. As one summary of the book has it:

> Classifying thinking styles using Isaiah Berlin's prototypes of the fox and the hedgehog, Tetlock contends that the fox – the thinker who knows many little things, draws from an eclectic array of traditions, and is better able to improvise in response to changing events – is more successful in predicting the future than the hedgehog, who knows one big thing, toils devotedly within one tradition, and imposes formulaic solutions on ill-defined problems. He notes a perversely inverse relationship between the best scientific indicators of good judgement and the qualities that the media most prizes in pundits – the single-minded determination required to prevail in ideological combat.[17]

And British political (and self-admittedly "expert") commentator Helen Dale uses this as a leaping off point for a discussion of human characteristics that often lead expert opinion to be not only wrong but spectacularly wrong:

> I learnt that those with higher education levels[18] and academic aptitude[19] tend to be less attuned than most to ambiguity, complexity, and limitations in their own knowledge – and less likely to [engage in]

innovative or creative thinking. Even worse, people tend to grow more politically doctrinaire as their scientific literacy and numeracy increases, while deploying scientific studies[20] or statistics[21] in the context of political arguments seems to polarise debate even further.[22]

Sounds like Tetlock's criticism of experts for thinking like Berlin's hedgehogs rather than like his foxes. Let's be clear: I am not asking you to accept my expert opinion on how to organize society in preference to some other expert's. I am inviting you to engage in the gardener's justified scepticism *about all forms of "expertise" that purport to tell you how to garden* in the absence of real knowledge of your concrete and particular circumstances and that persists in that advice in the teeth of the evidence. Grown social institutions don't care about your theory and don't respond to what experts think would be good for the rest of us. But as I demonstrated earlier, they are unapologetically and constructively brutal in ending experiments that do not work and moving on to try something new.

The gardener's solution to this problem of expert ignorance isn't to get you to prefer one expert to another, but to look instead for a social order that doesn't rely on expert opinion to "fix" what's "wrong" with it as seen from the top. Instead grown social institutions are themselves self-correcting because they stop doing what isn't working and seek solutions to problems we know we have and ones we don't even know about yet. And all that knowledge is put to use without any designing expert in charge. *As long, that is, as you are willing to accept that these institutions will produce what people want, not what you think they should want.*

Grown social orders are like the rules of the road. They don't specify where you should go. They simply assume you want to go *someplace,* a place you have chosen for your own reasons. The rules of such an order simply tell you that if you want the co-operation of others along the way, if you don't want other people to crash into you, then you have to obey the rules of the road. They specify *how* to get where you want to go, but don't concern themselves with *why* you want to get there, or how people and incomes and other things are distributed once you get there.

The map is not the territory

Designers are usually dismissive of this kind of argument because they think it ignores other sources of knowledge that do give designers special insight, particularly that made available by social science. Designers believe that policy-makers at the top can, by judicious use of the scientific method, obtain all the knowledge they need about people and society. Indeed it is this delusion that largely motivated their outrage at the Harper government's cancellation of the long form census in 2010. Without the statistics such censuses generate, they warned, policy-makers wander in the dark, knowing nothing of the people that they serve.

I hold no brief one way or the other on the census issue. What I do hold a brief on, however, is the delusion that statistics and computer modelling and all the other apparatus of modern social science can somehow improve upon and replace the knowledge that grown social institutions, not designed or controlled by anyone, effortlessly make use of every day. And as I have already said repeatedly, the best way to promote the success of each of us is to maximize the knowledge on which each of us acts. So let's compare the knowledge made available by the grown social institutions that are the gardener's delight with those instruments of social science that so gladden the heart of designers.

Human action is essentially a coordination problem. What I mean by that is that everything we do rests on the bedrock of human knowledge, but that knowledge is – and by its nature has to be – widely dispersed and locked in the minds of millions of individuals. If our minds are as limited as I have just described and our collective knowledge is vast and "uncatalogueable," then we must become ever more specialized in a few fields, and we must allow ourselves to be ever more dependent on the knowledge of others similarly specialized in their fields.

This social truth, however, is also one of the chief obstacles to designers' ambitions. If the knowledge on which individuals, corporations, governments, and societies depend is, in fact, so widely dispersed, so subject to change and revision, so locked in experience and therefore not articulated anywhere, how do we call forth this knowledge? How do we get it to the people who need it? No one can possibly possess all the knowledge necessary to decide who should do what, and when. Even at the level of corporations, which operate on a much smaller scale than governments, we have discovered the limitations of top-heavy, highly centralized control. It doesn't work because *orders from the top are based solely on what the people at the top know and what people at the top want* – and that will always be a tiny fraction of what is known by the people who are being ordered about.

The answer to this problem – how do we coordinate all the things that have to be done by different people possessing different bits of knowledge? – is that, most of the time, we use grown social institutions like the market and its mechanisms of supply and demand, guided by prices.

Most of us, when we travel by plane, do not devote a moment's thought to all the knowledge on which we depend to get us safely to our destination. When we buy our airline ticket, we buy knowledge about piloting, computing, air traffic control, airport administration, (bad) catering, safety measures and regulation, metallurgy, navigation, fuel, maintenance, propulsion, and so on. But we don't need to know anything about any of these things, for as soon as we lay our credit card on the counter (and think about the complex knot of knowledge a credit card represents!), the people who possess all the necessary bits of knowledge come running to put them at our service. You can use them without knowing anything about them and yet they will work together to achieve the result of you flying safely from Winnipeg to St. John's. That is quite miraculous.

Yes, government regulation oversees part of that, but government regulators don't build the planes, or conceive new alloys for their construction or new software for their navigation or run the credit cards that allow you to buy your ticket and call an Uber when you arrive. Governments used to do far *more* to regulate air travel than they do today, and air travel was more expensive, less convenient and less accessible. No serious person thinks we should go back to the days when governments decided how many flights would connect which cities and what a ticket should cost.

Grown social institutions like these enable us all to make use of more knowledge than we possess as individuals or organizations because such institutions are highly sensitive interactive communication networks. In these networks, people are rewarded for supplying others with what they need, just as those who supply things that no one wants are driven out. The marvel is that this is true even though no human mind possesses an overview of the whole and directs the various parts to play their roles. All these activities are coordinated by this communication network based on the signals offered by prices.

Let me give you a bucolic example of how grown institutions signal things to us. You may have heard of America's northern spotted owl. A proposal some years ago to protect this owl's habitat by restricting lumbering in the northwestern United States caused lumber prices in Chicago to rise considerably, despite a slump in housing starts.

This is a clear example of the ultra-sensitive nature of the knowledge embodied in the grown social institution of prices. What was being signalled here to consumers? That they should seek alternative building supplies: because they became cheaper, perhaps it would be more sensible for the consumer to buy aluminium studs rather than wooden studs. The price change was also a signal to foreign suppliers that they may possess a cost advantage relative to their American competitors. The price changes may have led to an increase in timber production in New Brunswick, or even in Australia or Malaysia, not because people in those places knew about the northern spotted owl's ecological troubles, but because the price mechanism signalled to them the practical effects of that knowledge: Higher prices indicate an increased demand for their product.

Prices, very simply, are the grown social institution par excellence; they bring together and summarize very quickly vast quantities of information about supply and demand, and do so in a way that is infinitely flexible and sensitive to technological innovation, supply fluctuations, and changes in what people want.

Prices can be a guide for both gardeners and designers. They can, in fact, be the best guide because they represent the sum of all knowledge existing in society about not only the current state of supply and demand, but also the sum of informed guesses about what supply and demand are likely to do in the future.

Prices, however, have a drawback, at least from the designer's point of view. We do not and cannot know all the particular facts that are known to individual people and firms that, together, are moving prices. The knowledge is global, but mute. It reacts immediately to changes in supply and demand, but is silent on the reasons for those changes. We can make well-informed guesses, but those guesses will frequently be wrong, for reasons that we will see in a moment.

This makes designers feel that they are flying blind when they depend on prices as the guide for their designs. They want more precision, more dependability, and more specific information. They want the details that prices summarize.

Because prices are volatile – and what seemed a good investment or a good labour contract last year looks like it will ruin you this year – there is also a desire on everyone's part to find something more stable, something firmer upon which to base our actions. Surely all these ups and downs in prices and in supply and demand could be eliminated if we could discover the forces driving the economy directly. We could turn them to our own purposes, design the economy directly and scientifically, manage trade, set labour costs, invent industrial strategies, and pick today the technologies that will win people's hearts tomorrow.

From these desires is born a faith in science, in economics, in statistics, in that whole scientific edifice which humanity wants to believe gives us verifiable scientific knowledge about the state of society and the forces driving it. By collecting vast quantities of specific information, designers think they can grasp directly what is affecting the cost of labour and the supply of raw materials, and they can identify the new technologies that we should be developing and keep abreast of the changing consumer preferences that make or break corporations. They could know more than prices tell us, and know it in advance, rather than reacting as we so often do to price movements.

The problem, however, is that the information or knowledge contained in all our impressive scientific studies of our corporation, our industry, or our economy *is not the information that is missing from prices.* Still less does this information allow us to dispense with the signals prices flash at us every hour of every day. The knowledge contained in statistics is not more complete. In fact, it is considerably less complete than prices. Those statistics on which designers place such reliance in designing for the future are, in fact, strikingly limited.

I am not just talking here about the notorious lag between the collection of data and its appearance as statistics (although that lag is serious and may have cost George H.W. Bush the 1992 U.S. election). It is true, of course, that by the time we get statistics that paint as good a picture of the real economy as statistics can, it is far too late to use them for designing purposes. The lag makes them primarily of historical interest and not useful for designing.

That is not the fundamental problem, however. The fundamental problem with the whole social scientific approach is that it assumes that the people collecting the information know what information to collect. It also assumes that all the relevant information is available to be collected. Neither of these assumptions is justified.

Think back to what I said earlier about the limited capacities of the human mind. It has rightly been observed that the mind cannot fully understand something more complex than itself. If we want to make the complexity of the whole of human society graspable to our limited intelligence, we have to simplify it. We have to strip it down to what we can manage – and that is precisely the function of statistics, including economic statistics. Statisticians begin with a vast and complex reality of relations – millions of actors engaging in billions of transactions for trillions of reasons every day. They then take arbitrary aspects of those activities on arbitrary bits of territory and reduce what the statisticians think is important about those activities to abstract numbers. In this sense, economic statistics are a bit like a map or any other symbolic representation of a concrete reality. They extract a few useful facts from a larger whole, so that people with our limited capacity to understand are given the illusion of powerful insight.

Like any such simplification, maps and statistics are undeniably useful, but we must be clear about what exactly that use is, or we risk using them improperly, or to do jobs for which they were not intended. A map takes a three-dimensional reality and renders it in two dimensions. By its very nature, then, a map must distort reality. It is notoriously the case with the standard map of the world, the Mercator projection. On such a map Greenland appears to have the same surface area as South America. In reality, however,

South America is about 11 times larger. This is a feature, not a bug: without it the two landmasses wouldn't be able to appear on the map in the correct relationship to one another under the rules of the Mercator projection.

More important than the distortion, however, is the simplification of reality that is the fundamental feature of maps. If you've ever made a road trip you will be drearily familiar with the fact that each stretch of road (to pick just one example) can present features of capital importance that no map, paper or digital, can represent in their entirety, especially during construction season. The reason is quite straightforward: no mapmaker (including a computerized one reliant on human beings to update its data) possesses more than a two-dimensional snapshot of a complex and ever-evolving three-dimensional reality. Every map, in pursuit of its ambition to be simple and easily usable, distorts reality.

As with maps, so it is with statistics representing a society, an economy, or an industry. There are thousands of examples of things that no planner could know, or would be unlikely to know on the basis of the statistical representations of the activities of people, which are the maps that are used to simplify complex social reality. I have already given many examples of why this is the case, but let me just remind you here of the single most important one: the limited knowledge that we have about the most basic fact that drives the shape of society and the economy, i.e., what individual people like you and me actually want. If the success of human institutions is best judged by their ability to satisfy human wants and needs, how can we know what these are? What human beings desire depends on what they know about themselves and their resources, and about the different goods and services available to them.

We could not have measured the demand for smartphones before they were invented because it was only after people saw what they were and what they made possible that people wanted them. IBM got into trouble because it did not keep abreast of how the new personal computing products from small competitors were making their own mainframe products progressively less attractive. People's opinion of what IBM was supplying them was changing not because of anything that IBM did, but because of what its competitors were doing. IBM planned to go on doing what it had always done in the attractive but dangerous belief that the world is a stable place and that tomorrow will be like today.

This means, of course, that planners and their plans are always at the mercy of new and unexpected bits of information which change desires and expectations, and, hence, the behaviour of people.

Now, before an actuary objects, I must hasten to add a caveat about what I am saying regarding the usefulness of statistics and the predictability of human life. After all, the actuarial profession is grounded on the justified assumption that there are identifiable statistical regularities in human life. We know that we all tend to catch more colds in winter, that multiplying the number of scientists at work on a well-defined problem will increase the probability that it will be solved sooner rather than later, that your husband or wife is more likely to murder you than a criminal stranger, that the suicide rate rises in late spring and early summer (*not* around Christmastime), and that everything tends to be bigger in Texas, including the homicide rate.

Remember, however, that successful institutions, in the long run, require more than simply identifiable regularities such as this. On the one hand, there is nothing eternal about the regularities that we can identify at any one moment. For instance, we used to think that human body temperature was a constant 37C; now we learn it is falling over time.[23] At the beginning of the twentieth century, men lived longer than women, and now the reverse is the case. On the other hand, these regularities can be identified without our understanding their causes; we simply do not have reliable information about the reasons for many of these regularities, and many of our beliefs about their causes have proven false. Before Galileo, no one would have had any difficulty predicting that the sun would rise each day and cross the sky. But these same people who were able to predict with such confidence and success were utterly mistaken about *why* this was the case; they were convinced that it was because the sun orbited the earth. And it is surely right to think that without a proper understanding of the causes of such regularities, they are of limited value as guides to indulging the designing impulse successfully.

So we must simplify if we are not to be overwhelmed by the complexity of the world and often we will know facts about the world but be mistaken or ignorant about the "why" behind those facts. But this in turn means that designers who rely on statistics, which are merely simplified symbolic representations of society's complexity, are always necessarily acting on a partial and limited view of the facts. Our principal sources of information, prices and statistical and other scientific studies, each have characteristic and insurmountable limitations.

Underlying all the other limitations is the brutal fact that the needs and desires of individual people – the fundamental forces that have created grown social institutions like markets and the common law, and human behaviour, which is the raw material of statistics – are evolving and elastic. This is, in part, because we are always discovering new facets of ourselves and, therefore, changing our behaviour and needs.

For these reasons, the plans of mice and men, no matter how well laid, can, at best, be a partial and fallible guide to action, including especially public policy that seeks to displace the decisions that individuals and groups make for themselves about what is important to them. Indeed, the key difference between plans made on our behalf by governments and the plans that we make for ourselves is that while those who make public policy must rely on simplified and generalized abstractions as their guiding information, *this is the least useful form of human knowledge.* The most useful knowledge is specific, practical and time-bound. But this is exactly what statisticians must leave out because by their nature statistics count what is common between one set of circumstances and another, while what is often most important about them is what distinguishes them. It can never be repeated too often: *statistics are abstract and general; the knowledge most useful to people is concrete and particular.*

Aside from the general argument I have been making, there is another very particular reason for why specific knowledge, knowledge of oneself, of one's specific place and circumstances is the knowledge that really matters. When scientists study the physical world, they study something immutable, which follows laws that we can, with effort, discover and harness, although even here the philosophers of science are careful to remind us that such knowledge is never final but always provisional and subject to correction as new discoveries are made and new insights gained.

The human world, however, is a quite different matter because it is composed of people with unique minds, wills, knowledge and experiences. Unlike, say, atoms, we are not an eternally fixed, changeless subject mindlessly following natural laws. We *learn*. In fact as Michael Oakeshott tells us, this is the central fact of human nature: we are condemned to learn. Even when we don't want them, new ideas that emerge from the minds of others and then become part of life around us force themselves on our notice and we must come to terms with them. And when new ideas enter our heads, we change who we are, what we want, what our priorities are, what we are trying to achieve in life.

Thus scientists may fairly make the claim that all atoms that present a specific set of characteristics (so many electrons, protons, neutrons, etc.) will behave the same, but they cannot make the same claims about people. Our external and observable characteristics actually tell you relatively little about the person who is at the core of those characteristics. We will talk more about this in the chapter on identity.

For now, it is enough to say that planning is necessary if we are to carry out the grand projects we each have for our lives, and if our greatest intentions as individuals are to be realized. *Who* does the planning will affect enormously the success of the enterprise, however. Contrary to the superstitions of an age dazzled by the achievements of science, the people who know the least about the complexity of our lives and our communities and our society are the faraway people who claim the mandate of science for their decisions: those who govern us.

Our grand projects always turn out differently than we imagined them, and our intentions must be brought to fruitful compromises with an inconstant world. That is the gardener's creed.

The designing mind meets uncontrollable complexity and the unpredictable future

None of the foregoing is an argument for complacency or inaction in human affairs. But it does set the stage for discussion of what policy-makers can reasonably expect to do and what *kinds* of policies are likely to succeed. Political authorities, when deciding how to pursue their policy goals, basically have two options open to them. Not surprisingly, one of them is the gardener's strategy, while the other commends itself to designers.

Option One is to make use of all the widely-dispersed knowledge available, and to be open to the discovery of new knowledge, thus harnessing the forces of innovation and disruption. Option Two is to rely on the limited knowledge that policy-makers inevitably possess when designing their programs and then resist the forces of disruption and innovation. No prizes for guessing which one works best.

Unfortunately, people led by fear of unintended and poorly understood consequences of innovation and technology often try to curtail the freedom and the openness that progress depends on. When Matt Ridley, author of the brilliant book *The Rational Optimist*, is asked what he worries about, he usually responds, "superstition and bureaucracy," because superstition can obstruct the accumulation of knowledge, and bureaucracy can stop us from applying that knowledge in new technologies and businesses.[24]

When you try to solve problems by harnessing the forces of technology and widely dispersed knowledge responding to thoughtful incentives, you increase your chances of success by essentially rewarding people for coming up with a workable solution to your problem, but not dictating what that solution should be. You specify the direction of travel, but not the means of transport, travelling companions, or the final destination. By contrast, when you decide you know enough to come up with THE best solution and impose it on everyone regardless of how well it fits their circumstances, circumstances about which you must inescapably be largely ignorant, you resist the forces of innovation and technology. When you harness human ingenuity you get effective answers but cannot predict exactly what they will be. When you oppose human ingenuity, your solution becomes an obstacle to be defeated and bypassed by that same ingenuity.

Let me illustrate with a current example. Because of climate change concerns, governments around the world are seeking to reduce humanity's carbon footprint. There are basically two ways to do this. One is to put a price on carbon (either through a tax or tradeable permits), which then becomes a useful piece of data for people engaged in activities that produce carbon. A carbon price doesn't tell them *how* to reduce carbon; it merely offers a useful and objective measure of the problem and, incidentally, rewards people for successfully reducing carbon emissions by whatever means works *and* achieves those reductions at the lowest overall economic cost. That is a knowledge-harnessing strategy. It is not without its flaws in that it misrepresents what the market, with its amazing ability to synthesize instantaneously the consequences of all that is known, thinks about the value of carbon. People will be guided in their decisions about how to use carbon, not by an objective price that incorporates all knowledge, but by government propaganda about what the price of carbon *should* be, but let's set that objection aside for the moment.

The alternative strategy says that bureaucrats know enough about the economy, transport, natural resource supply, the environment, energy generation and more, to be able to dictate the precise means by which carbon emissions should be reduced. Rather than leaving all options open but changing the incentive structure, as harnessing does, it attempts to decide what avenues are most fruitful, regardless of cost, for carbon reduction. This attempts to force people trying to solve the carbon reduction problem to use means they would not choose themselves based on their intimate awareness of their unique knowledge and circumstances. This means that not all the knowledge available will be brought to bear on the problem and that the solutions that are chosen will, on the whole, be more costly to society and less effective overall than those they might have chosen if left alone to act on their own knowledge in response to the proper incentives. Or, as George Gilder so felicitously put it, "regulation is an attempt to replace knowledge with power."[25]

In the next chapter I'll talk in more detail about exactly how the gardener's vision of who knows what and why in society and how that shapes the role and potential of government as opposed to the role of grown social institutions and voluntary action by people and organizations.

CHAPTER III

What gardeners know about what works and what doesn't

THE TASK OF THE DEFENDERS of a liberal-capitalist democracy like Canada's is not to engage in theoretical exercises allegedly showing the inferiority of our practice to some idealized alternative. We do not rely on "returning to first principles." Our society was not founded on first principles. In fact, neither Canada nor America were ever "founded" as societies. The political framework surrounding that social order, yes. But even the American Revolution left essentially undisturbed the grown social institutions like the common law, private property, law of contract, the rule of law, and a thousand other institutions and behaviours that grew from a thousand years and more of history reaching back to William the Conqueror and beyond. Ditto for Confederation in 1867. Edmund Burke deplored the French Revolution because it was premised on the designer's belief that society could be constructed from first principles, from "reason," overwriting what history and experience had bequeathed the French. By contrast, Burke celebrated the American Revolution as a modernization and extension of what generations of experimentation and incremental adjustment had created.

The gardener's job is akin to Burke's: to defend properly the existing social order against the onslaughts of clever but ultimately ignorant theoreticians and people who believe that only the consciously designed has any real value. It is no criticism of such a defence that it is messy or not theoretically sound or internally inconsistent. Gardeners are trying to understand *why our society works*, why it exhibits the features that it does, how its various pieces are connected and why it appears, of all the alternatives, best suited to human nature as it is revealed in the day-to-day choices of real people.

The way our society works has an internal logic I find compelling (while theoreticians often do not), but there is an asymmetry in our society that means that the designing theoreticians, being clever and articulate people, seem to have the microphone a lot and are able to offer what seems a profound (although deeply mistaken) critique of our institutions.

The asymmetry arises from the fact that, since our institutions are based in practice not in theory, since no one invented them and the people who find them congenial are mostly engaged in enjoying their benefits without devoting too much thought to how they work, these institutions' defenders are often ill-organized and lack the theoreticians' shared script, which often sounds good, however impractical it may be. Since the grown institutions on which our social order depends are constantly under attack, with ill-informed politicians of all parties constantly grinding away at them, we are in danger of losing the vast benefits they confer. If these institutions are to be destroyed, let us at least be clear-eyed about what we are doing.

So in what follows I am not laying out a "theory" of liberal-capitalist democracy in Canada, holding up our practice to see how it conforms to the theory. I am trying to distill from the practice its underlying logic. Like the grammarian trying to understand a complex grown or evolved language not invented or designed by anyone, I am not inventing that logic, but describing it and doing what I can to explain how it works to achieve a better result for people compared to all the theoretical alternatives that could be invented. And I concede that if a theoretical alternative were put into practice that actually achieved better results for people, a powerful defence of our way of life would be undermined, perhaps fatally. Just don't hold your breath.

Canadian society has largely grown up in the care of gardeners. It has not yet been overly damaged by designers. Gardeners are engaged in a co-operative exercise in which they understand that the ideal garden that exists in their mind must make real world compromises with the raw materials to hand. Those raw materials are human beings, complex individuals who grow and evolve and have plans for themselves and those they care about. It is therefore impossible for any top-down designer to impose their vision of an ideal world without frustrating the plans that people have laid for themselves.

The gardener's central insight is that knowledge is the scarcest and most precious resource of all and that knowledge is *by its nature* scattered in the arms and hearts and minds of billions of individuals and cannot be comprehensively gathered, sifted, understood and applied successfully by any central authority. On the other hand, grown maximally participatory social institutions like tradition, language, the family, civil society, the market and the common law can co-ordinate the use of all the knowledge in society, bypassing the limitations of the intelligence of individuals and organizations (including governments). If you like to think of it this way, grown social institutions are *knowledge economizing devices*. By following the rules that have emerged from centuries of trial and error by those who came before us, we can benefit from the knowledge they acquired without having to know it ourselves.

Wise gardeners, then, are humble and limit their ambitions to tending these grown social institutions and understanding what they reveal about human nature and the conditions in which the vast dispersed array of human knowledge is made as widely available as it can be. The result of such careful and thoughtful tending is that each of us can make use of the knowledge of the generations who preceded us in pursuing the life we are trying to make for ourselves. And since *all* knowledge makes its way into society through individual people and never more than a tiny fraction of it can be known by society's rulers or designers, wise gardeners know that the vast co-operative enterprise that is society can only function at its best when institutions give everyone in society reasons to *want* to share their knowledge with others. But how?

A good starting point is the most basic question of all: what are we all doing? Gardeners would be of the view that what we are all doing is *learning*, and what we are learning *about* is chiefly ourselves. Life is the process of the unfolding of our individual character, of learning what it means to be the person we are in a unique set of complex relationships of family, of affection, of place, of community, of profession or trade and a lot more. The more institutions accommodate that blossoming of identity, the more people will co-operate with those institutions and other people by putting their knowledge at the service of others.

This is the best account I can offer of the reason why gardeners do not think in abstract terms like groups or classes or races, for none of these things have minds. None of them learn. None of them make choices. None of them have experiences or characters or life plans. Only individuals do or have these things. And because it is in the hearts and minds of individuals that characters unfold and judgments are made about the success or failure of the choices each of us make, individuals and not groups are the focus of grown social institutions and the gardeners who tend to them. The groups that exist only matter because they were chosen by individuals. According to Aristotle, there are only two exceptions to this rule: family and the state. We chose neither of those; they are handed to us by fate and circumstance, although we can choose to leave them.

So individuals, not our governors, possess all knowledge and no one possesses it in its totality; this is an inescapable fact of human life. The inescapable corollary is that all of us depend for our success on others sharing what they know. But using authority or political power to force people to share what they know against their will is costly and inefficient because no one wants to be used as a mere instrument of the will of another and because authorities don't know all that you know. You don't even know yourself.

What gardeners have learned from patient observation of generations of trial and error embodied in grown social institutions is that the best way to get people to share their knowledge comes in two parts. The first is to give them *freedom to make their own choices*, so they are motivated in life by what matters to them. The second is to reward them for sharing voluntarily with others the knowledge they possess, so that *they earn their way in life by being of service to others*, not because they are forced to do so, but because in so doing they earn the means to pursue what matters to them. This is no "theory of liberal individualism"; this is the distillation of a thousand years and more of practical experience in our tradition.

Nor is this a materialist philosophy, one preoccupied with money and material goods. Even non-materialists must cater to their material needs (unless you are a hermit in a cave and even then you need a loincloth, firewood and food).

The gardener makes no judgments about whether it is better to use your money and time in Buddhist contemplation or NASCAR racing, symphony orchestras or grunge bands, disaster relief or fine wine, helping the developing world or vacationing there. The value of what you choose lies not in the thing or activity chosen but in the dignity that your choices confer on the things chosen.

And the justification of wealth isn't the outsized consumption it makes possible but the outsized service to humanity, as we will see in a moment.

The gardener's philosophy *is* quite concerned with how wealth is created and who gets it, but only because the way those things happen has a powerful impact on everyone's ability to live the best life they can according to their lights. Wealth isn't the end pursued by gardeners, but it most emphatically is an indispensable *means* to the end of making human life as comfortable and satisfying as it can be for as many people as possible.

Gardening permits something quite subtle in the way wealth is created and parcelled out. Wealth isn't "distributed," on this view, according to whether we agree with each other's choices or way of life. There is too much disagreement in a free society over such values. Instead, what you get is in direct proportion to what you give. What you give is your knowledge, what you know how to do. What you get in return isn't decided by people in authority. In fact it is not *anyone's* decision. What you get is the going rate for what you do, as determined by quite impersonal social forces. It is thus a system that makes humanity freer and smarter than the alternatives. But how does it work?

Part One: Freedom to choose; freedom to fail

Gardeners eventually came to understand that societies based on a shared vision of the good life or the best way to live work marvellously well until someone takes a bite of the fruit of the tree of knowledge and realizes that there are many ways to live and many paths to happiness. As soon as that knowledge spread it became impossible to enforce social co-operation and knowledge sharing by appeal to a shared communal vision of the good life.

You may want to sit under the banyan tree and seek enlightenment, but your neighbour may be an anarchist socialist who thinks everyone should share all they have, including your banyan tree. You may be a Leafs fan (hard to believe, I know, but there are some, in a triumph of hope over experience) for whom a beer and nachos with your boyfriend on a Saturday night is the height of sophistication while your colleague at work listens to opera and is part of a secret BDSM society. Or you may be a petroleum engineer who believes that hydrocarbons are the elixir of life, while the skip of your curling team may be a Green New Dealer who believes they spell the end of life on Spaceship Earth. All this, and more, is to be found within the human heart.

But here is the rub: if you want others to make their knowledge freely available to you, so that you can do what you want, you can't at the same time be trying to tell them how to live. It makes people very uncooperative. You cannot tell them that they must live as Puritans in eighteenth-century Boston or as Savonarola wanted fifteenth-century Florentines to be. There cannot be a "right way to live." Sure, each of us will have our own vision of the right way to live and each of us may not like or even respect the choices of others. But the state, that one group beside the family whose membership is compulsory in society, must observe a strict neutrality between these competing visions. All visions (subject to some qualifications I will get to in a moment) are tolerated, none can be enforced on anyone against their will by the state, or by anyone else for that matter.

The way we achieve this in practice is by increasingly recognizing a protected sphere of conscience, choice and action that envelops each individual and within which individual choice and identity is sovereign. You get to decide who you are and no one in authority can second guess you, although that doesn't mean that your fellow citizens must like or endorse you or your choices, a distinction that seems to be lost on many people. Sauce for the goose and all that.

This protected sphere includes who you think you are, your identity, what you value, and protects the freedoms necessary for you to exercise your identity even in the face of disapproval by fellow citizens and the state: freedom of religion, association, assembly, conscience. Your freedom to express yourself and to make the case for your choices and against the choices of others is equally protected.

We buttress that sphere of individual freedom with institutions that extend our power to pursue a life built on our choices. Private property is one such institution whose practical effect is to allow the co-existence of many competing uses for ideas, land and things. A city block may contain a synagogue, a church and a mosque; a smartphone store, a bookshop and a crafts store; a diet centre, a dessert restaurant and a gymnasium. These people living cheek by jowl need agree on nothing, other than the need to let each other have the quiet enjoyment of their property. Co-existence here requires no administrative or coercive power, no political consensus, no extensive public consultations. People merely get on with things within the sphere of freedom that property creates for them. Nor do you need the capital to purchase what property you want outright, because property isn't a single concept but a bundle of related possibilities.[26] You can rent what you want to use or pay a fee to buy a licence.

The central point here is that property helps establish the tools you may rely on in pursuit of your choices. You may not take others' property, nor may they take yours. Your property (including the property of others to which you have negotiated access) is in fact an extension of you and your will that you may use freely within the limits of the law.

Contrary to the ravings of Marxist agitprop, even those who own no property benefit from its existence and the idea of an irreducible clash of interests between, say, the working class (assumed to be propertyless) and the "owners" is a destructive fiction.

You may not own a car, but Uber owners will rush to put theirs at your disposal for a few dollars. You don't own the cable that brings Netflix into your home, but the cable owner has paid a lot of money to connect it to your home and bring you Netflix in exchange for a monthly subscription. You don't own a pipeline, but you can gain access to the products that passed through one for a fraction of a cent a litre at the pump. You don't own your apartment but as long as you pay your rent you are entitled to act within it largely as you would within a home you owned yourself. In every case, the existence of property and the certainty it creates made it possible for others to invest in property *so that they could satisfy your needs*. And their urge to serve you does not depend on you owning any property whatsoever. The satisfaction of your needs, on the other hand, does require the existence of property, because without it the goals you pursue in life may be obstructed on a whim by others arbitrarily appropriating the tools you need and that you have acquired in accordance with the law.

If you doubt this proposition, simply ask yourself what the difference is between Canada, where money is effortlessly deployed in factories and apartments and homes and mobile phone networks and a thousand other things, and many developing countries that struggle to do the same. It is almost always down to the fact that here the owners of property may have reasonable confidence that their property will not be simply appropriated by prime ministerial cronies or brutal generals with the connivance of venal police and corrupt judges. That means that the owners of capital can invest with confidence in an effort to satisfy the needs of people. And as Peruvian economist Hernando de Soto has so richly documented, it is the inability of poor people in developing countries to get their property rights recognized and certified (in such things as the ownership of their dwelling) that causes their property to be "dead [in the sense of unusable for economic purposes] capital."[27]

When I said in Chapter I that many new Canadians come here because of the mainstream, because of our endowment of institutions and behaviours that create peace, order and good government, robust property rights would be an important such one. Many new Canadians are successful entrepreneurs, but that is not because coming to Canada taught them how to satisfy human wants and needs. They almost certainly possessed that knowledge before they got here. They became successful because in Canada their knowledge can safely be put in the service of others because the fruits of their efforts belong to them and cannot be stolen by thieves or unreasonably plundered by those in authority.

So property creates a beneficial certainty; you know what is yours and what you can use in the pursuit of your goals. That is also why society doesn't condone or allow theft or fraud: it destroys the certainty that is property's chief benefit. Theft is the unlawful transfer of property from one person to another. Fraud disqualifies the transaction to which it gave rise from the protection of the law of contract. Lying about the reasons why someone should transfer to you their property means the transaction is a form of theft. Both violate your protected sphere of action.

The law of contract is a similar institution. It extends your will and gives certainty in an uncertain world. You may not force others to bend to your will because that violates their protected sphere of autonomy. You may, however, agree with them in a mutually advantageous contract that each of you will perform specific services and you can know that the courts will enforce such promises. The existence of contract as an institution allows you to trade things you have in exchange for things you want. In fact, David Hume went so far as to argue that the three rules that underpin any truly just society were: 1) The stability of possession, in other words, property, including property in your own body; 2) Its transference by consent; and 3) The performance of promises (or contract).[28]

But we didn't arrange things this way to fit our society to some theory. For the longest time there was, for example, a state religion (established church) in the United Kingdom, the society from which our political, social and moral tradition chiefly emerged. Roman Catholics and Dissenters were at first severely discriminated against and then later came to be "tolerated," suffering important disadvantages compared to adherents of the Anglican Church. Jews, Muslims and atheists were beyond the pale and in the early days even subject to torture and death, later "improved" to mere intolerable discrimination.

After fighting a civil war and suffering a regicide over religious differences, however, Britons grew to appreciate as a practical, not a theoretical matter, that if the state could be used to impose a preferred way of life (in this case a religious orthodoxy) on all its citizens, political conflicts would become matters of life and death and social co-operation would be brought to a crashing halt.

Mutual agreement to leave people alone to pursue their own choices, leaving the state out of it, was the only way that civilized life and social peace could be preserved. From practical lived experiences like this emerged our concept of a protected sphere within which we make choices for ourselves, and no other person or group, including the state, may impose their will on us. The established church (like an official aristocracy) was an institution that didn't cross the Atlantic to Canada because it did not fit the ethos of a religiously diverse and deeply individualistic frontier society.

Now it so happens that this line of thought was given a compelling theoretical statement by Immanuel Kant. Indeed, since Kant, the touchstone principle of modern morality is always to treat other people not as inanimate objects whom you may force to act as you please, whom you may use as instruments of your will, but as subjects like yourself with a will of their own. And because we want others to respect our own will and choices for ourselves, we incur a reciprocal obligation to respect the choices of others.

Another way of thinking of this is that in modern western society we have learned that social co-operation is maximized when we don't tell people what to do but rather offer them reasons to want to do what is needed. *We are, therefore, chiefly a society of incentives rather than commands*, or at least we aspire to be and that vision is one that inspires gardeners everywhere. Even where we must issue commands, we have found they are most effective when expressed as negative prohibitions (whatever you decide to do in life, whatever your values, you may not steal from, coerce, or defraud others) that do not require you to *do* anything specific, only to *refrain* from the prohibited behaviour.

We were well launched on growing the practical institutions that embody such freedom before Kant, but Kant offers us a compelling account of their underlying logic. We would have got to the same place without Kant because our institutions, which mostly happen to reflect Kantian principles, also happen to be the ones that work. So if someone comes along and says, Kant was all wet and you should abandon Kantian principles to follow (pick one) Mao or Marx or Sartre or Kierkegaard or Fanon, the answer is that we are not followers of Kant and our institutions were not modelled on his thought or Edmund Burke's or Adam Smith's or anyone else's. They grew out of our day-to-day efforts to accommodate growing diversity of opinion about how to live and the bitter experiences we endured when that effort faltered.

Of course, that does not mean that grown social institutions do not provide the backdrop for other kinds of bitter experience. In particular, a social order that accepts that knowledge is scarce, that people are free and that lives are made up of choices is a society characterized by a certain kind of risk. You may not be forced to do anything, but you may exercise your freedom and make choices and life plans for yourself, and because knowledge is uncertain and subject to constant revision, you may make choices that ruin your life, your plans may not pan out, and you may fail.

My late roommate from my undergraduate days at McGill, the son of a rancher from Medicine Hat, Alberta, talked himself into believing that he needed to get away from the ranch and get a professional qualification. He went to the University of Alberta, met his future wife, got married and got an accounting degree.

He then got hired by one of the big national accounting firms and worked high up in a downtown office tower in Calgary.

He told me he spent the next couple of years working hard but also spending an inordinate amount of time staring longingly out the window at the beckoning prairie. Then one day he came to a realization about himself: *he was not an accountant.* He despised the life he was living. He walked out, took over his dad's ranch and loved every minute of the rest of his life with his family and his livestock and his land.

He spent a long time expensively acquiring a vital piece of knowledge about himself. Like every one of us, he took a risk on the basis of what he thought he knew about himself and his future. He failed. No one was at fault. He just misunderstood the choices he was making because he misunderstood himself.

Because knowledge is uncertain (including what we know about our-selves) and subject to revision, *no one knows with certainty what will work.* Hence the need for constant experimentation. Accountancy didn't work for my friend, but ranching did. Yet it is within this uncertainty that we are called to make our life plans and my friend invested a lot to discover that he was a rancher and not an accountant.

Fortunately, he recovered from his mistake. Other people make mistakes like this and much worse. Some don't recover. On this basis the critics of grown social institutions that give you freedom to choose but let people live with the consequences of their choices claim that the system is heartless and too risky.

This is exacerbated by the flip side of the gardener's approach, which is that reward must be proportionate to the benefit people feel they derive from the knowledge you put at their disposal. And if the benefit is huge, so too will be the reward. This is important not merely to get Steve Jobs to create the iPhone, but so that following generations can see that discovering or acquiring knowledge and putting it at the service of people can be richly rewarded. Since what each of us knows is not of equal value to our fellows, equality of outcome is not possible unless we want to eliminate the incentive for those with the most valuable knowledge to make it available to us.

The critics have a point that the costs of the ceaseless experimentation on which we rely to push back the frontiers of the unknown sometimes reveal to us that we have made poor choices and we alone bear the costs of that experimentation. Experimentation is indispensable. Failed experiments are a valuable source of knowledge. That is precisely why gardeners understand completely that some forms of social insurance are quite justified. Failure is a risk to which we are all exposed and yet we collectively benefit from the knowledge discovered (even if we don't know all the knowledge and don't know what we don't know). A great deal of the welfare state can be quite justified as a way of sharing the costs of the failure of experimentation, put-ting a floor under how far any of us can fall, with supplementary private insurance available for those who feel collective provision is inadequate. And the design of those welfare programs, as I will discuss in greater depth later, is properly the subject of vigorous political debate.

A society that wants to maximize the knowledge on which it operates has every interest in ensuring that the risk of the experimentation on which we depend is not prohibitive.

What we cannot do, however, is take away the rewards that come from successful experimentation, a taking away which designers often justify by arguing that success is just an accident, that it is unearned.

But remembering that we depend on knowledge to succeed in life and that that knowledge is dispersed, or unconscious, or not yet discovered, the process by which it is discovered is neither here nor there. Knowledge is almost always local, particular and time-bound. Opportunities are not permanent but fleeting. The person on the ground knows more about their circumstances than anyone else, and those circumstances include whatever knowledge they may have discovered by accident about themselves or the world. The point is that grown social institutions maximize the incentives for you to find a way to put your knowledge at the disposal of others, whatever that knowledge is and however you acquired it. Without those incentives, the knowledge will not be as forthcoming. And when the knowledge is not forthcoming, that makes us collectively stupider than we need to be.

Much more important than the social insurance that gardeners endorse is a different way that the state can reduce uncertainty and therefore the costs of the experimentation from which we all derive such benefit. I have already alluded to this in the idea of the creation of a protected sphere, and the protected tools that are conjoined to it, like property, freedom from theft and fraud, the ability to make contracts. The more the state can protect this sphere and these tools, the more certainty it creates for individuals and organizations trying to pursue their plans. The state cannot guarantee outcomes without distorting the knowledge-discovering action of grown social institutions, but it can guarantee the integrity of the tools we use in the pursuit of our plans.

This is obvious in the protection against force and fraud. But if government inflates away the value of your savings, that steals them just as surely as a thief in the night does, or a Bernie Madoff. And if the government makes the building of pipelines subject to onerous conditions, with the success of a project subject to high degrees of uncertainty, that diminishes the value of the property acquired lawfully by the project proponents and impoverishes us as a society by making it impossible for them to deploy their capital in order to supply the things people demonstrably want.

Gardeners are of the view that as tempting as it is in particular cases to override the protections offered by the law and tradition to the tools we need to pursue our plans, the social cost of doing so outweighs the momentary satisfaction that comes from twisting the law to get what you want. Property ought to be respected even when its owners don't want to do "the right thing" with it, because the value of property as an institution lies in the certainty it creates. If you only respect property insofar as its owners use it as you would use it, then its certainty is diminished if not destroyed. And on those rare occasions when political authorities conclude that some compelling public purpose requires the expropriation of property it is vital that the owner receive fair compensation for their disappointed legitimate expectations. This, too, maintains the integrity, certainty, and trustworthiness of property as an indispensable tool for pursuing our plans and allowing us to invest our time, our capital, and our knowledge with at least some modicum of certainty in a deeply uncertain world.

Part Two: Earning by sharing

I said earlier that the gardener's view is that the best way to get people to share their scarce knowledge (which is the basic aim of social co-operation) comes in two parts. The first, giving people freedom so they are motivated by what matters to them and tools like property and contract to underpin their plans, is explained in the preceding section.

The second part is to reward them for sharing voluntarily with others the knowledge they possess, so that they earn their way by being of service to others. This is the only arrangement worthy of a society of free men and women. It also happens to be the approach that works better than all the alternatives that have been tried.

Perhaps one way of getting at this principle is to try to imagine a society in which resources (i.e., money and other desired things) are handed out to people on some other basis. It is possible to imagine a society in which mullahs or priests distribute money, goods, services, and even spouses or permission to have children on the basis of piety, or one where they were handed out based on service to the Party, or as a reward for your "social credit" score in a surveillance state, or on the basis of your carbon-neutrality in Ecotopia.

It goes without saying that one defect of such distribution systems is that people aren't rewarded on the basis of what they know, but on the basis of what religious leaders or party apparatchiks or Big Brother or Greta Thunberg know or think they know. This in itself makes such societies less able to satisfy the needs and aspirations of their members than our society. Rewarding people on the basis of what rulers know makes entire societies stupid in the sense of not being able to use all the knowledge known by their members.

But let me draw your attention to a slightly different aspect of such approaches to distribution: they all depend on the *will* of at least one person. Or put another way, some other individual sits in judgment of you and what you do and decides what you are worth.

Now you may say, of course, *somebody* has to decide who gets what.

Well, not really. Under the systems I just described and others similar in principle, yes, someone does. Someone establishes what is important and rewards you based on their assessment of what *they* think is important. In that sense you are very much subject to the will of others and this violates the first part of what gardeners have learned about how to motivate people to share their knowledge. As John Stuart Mill wrote,

> A fixed rule, like that of equality, might be acquiesced in, and so might chance, or an external necessity; but that a handful of human beings should weigh everybody in the balance, and give more to one and less to another at their sole pleasure and judgment would not be *borne*, unless from persons believed to be more than men, and *backed by supernatural terrors.*[29]

But the objection I referred to a moment ago is that there is *no* system that does not rely on the will of another person or persons to determine the worth of what we do and the value of who we are. I beg to differ.

The grown order that has emerged in societies like Canada does not require some person or committee or authority to determine whether and to what extent what you are doing contributes to some values they think are important. Instead, a completely impersonal system *rewards you based on how much other people value what you do and the contribution you freely make to their own success, not on the basis of what you think or how you live.*

You may think that your boss determines how much you earn, yet your boss is probably aggrieved that she has to pay over the odds for someone who can do what you do. You may think lawyers are vermin, but if the police arrest you, you will pay the going rate to get one to represent you. And the worse the mess you're in, the more you're likely to be willing to pay for someone with a better chance of resolving it in your favour.

Pretty much everyone thinks *he or she* is underpaid. Most think *those who work for them* earn way too much. If someone was in charge of making these decisions, wouldn't he by definition think those decisions were correct?

But in a society of dispersed knowledge where employers want people who possess the knowledge they need, whether it be of accounting or systems analysis, or interior design, or how to teach geometry, and where each of us represents some more or less rare set of knowledge and skills, no party gets to set the terms of an employment relationship unilaterally.

Instead, the worth of any particular set of skills is determined by the state of play of completely impersonal forces of supply and demand. An employer who wants to underpay relative to the market price will only get less desirable candidates with inadequate skills or poor work records or no one at all.[30] A job seeker with unrealistic pay expectations will have to put water in their wine to get hired, not because the employer is a mean bastard, but because the vast array of information available in the job market will tell her that she can get someone with the necessary qualifications at a lower price.

It goes without saying that at the outset any employment relationship will be based on impersonal factors like market prices for the talent sought. This is because employers and employees at the beginning don't know each other very well. The longer the relationship continues, the more pay will be based on a knowledge of the specific skills and abilities of the employee and the desirability of the employer. In every profession and trade there are hard workers and slackers, people who keep current and those who let their knowledge erode, people who carry the team and those who are carried by it.

Of course, a few caveats are necessary. The first is that there is real-world evidence of discrimination against certain classes of people, such as racial and sexual minorities, women, and others. Our way of working requires that people have confidence that factors other than their knowledge, skills, competence and work record are not improperly influencing decisions such as whether they get a job and on what conditions, and so anti-discrimination laws have been instituted to ensure that these decisions really are based on these impersonal evaluations of the worth of what specific knowledge sets one brings to the job. I will have more to say about this in the chapter on identity and justice. For now, suffice it to say that once protections against discrimination against individuals are in place, we cannot then turn around and *infer* discrimination against individuals based on *group* representation in different jobs and professions. We cannot, for instance, say that basketball managers are biased against white players just because most basketball players are black and we cannot say the nursing profession is biased against men because most nurses are women.

Second caveat: there may be very specific circumstances in which employers enjoy superior negotiating power over workers, as in the case of, say, isolated company towns far from other jobs, but generally given the ability of workers to move, and even just to threaten moving, in a society like ours in practice this danger can easily be exaggerated. I think it is far more likely that employers will have to pay a premium to get workers to locate to remote communities. Indeed, a mining executive once told me that his company in northern Quebec had hired all the available local workers but were still short. They hit on the idea of paying for regular flights from Montreal so that workers from the city would consider coming north during the week and returning home at weekends. As a result, most of their local workforce moved to Montreal and then commuted on the free flights.

Third caveat: there may be a moral sentiment that no one should be expected to work for a wage below a certain level, which is the impulse behind minimum wages. There is nothing wrong in principle with minimum wages as long as we are all clear that their effect is not what most people think. Many people seem to think that raising the minimum wage leaves the number of people working unchanged and simply ensures that those at the bottom get paid more for what they were already doing. But since wages are not based on "the equal moral worth of individuals" (i.e., the justification for forcing employers to pay a "living wage") but on the impersonal question of whether the employee's work produces enough value to others to justify the wage, a decision to raise the minimum wage to, say, $15, is a decision that no one shall work who produces less than $15 of value with an hour of their labour.

This is a classic unintended consequence of a policy that sounds good but in fact harms those it is intended to help. Such a policy is not improper, just imprudent. It doesn't "make the rich pay"; it makes the poor pay. It doesn't require a Ph.D. in economics to connect the Ontario government's decision to raise the minimum wage quite precipitously with the subsequent emergence of far more widespread automated check-outs at stores across the province. The wage before was set at a level where it still paid to employ people rather than machines. Now the machines are the beneficiaries in that calculus. Well done, advocates for the poor!

Something similar happened in the case of sheltered workshops where, at one time, those with mental or cognitive disabilities could do work that was repetitive, but necessary, and earn some money doing it. The work wasn't worth the minimum wage, but it still needed to be done, and these people could do it and did it well – stuffing envelopes, putting stickers on flyers, etc. These organizations were exempted until relatively recently from minimum wage laws precisely because that wage was higher than the productivity that could reasonably be expected in the circumstances. Once sheltered workshops were required to pay the minimum wage, the result was not that those who worked there got a welcome boost in income, but that their possibility of working at all was utterly destroyed. The work was either not done, or mechanized, or outsourced overseas, or employers made some other provision. So these workers lost some of their dignity and independence – and the community sense that they got from working together.

Low incomes, just like high incomes, are based on an impersonal assessment of the value of what you can do as expressed by what all others in society are willing to pay for it. If you can't read or count and can't show up to work every day on time and in a presentable condition, you may not earn much. On the other hand, labour shortages can make employers who need workers awfully clever at making the unemployable employable.

You could see this at work in Canada, but even more so in the US, in the 1990s, where technological upheaval was accompanied by a huge social transformation: the end of welfare as we have known it, as President Bill Clinton liked to say. Just as huge economic opportunities were opening up, governments throughout the United States began pushing people out of the welfare trap and into labour markets. They began to demand that people get training and get into the labour market instead of merely being warehoused as "unemployable" in the welfare system.

The result was not impoverishment and misery, but rather a jump in the share of people seeking work, the application of new technologies to the problem of how to make people with little education productive, and the growth in both the employment and incomes of the bulk of the people who had previously been virtually totally excluded from the labour market, some of whom had been unemployed for generations.

As the labour supply began to dry up, it became more and more necessary to find ways to put people previously thought to be unemployable to work, and to do so quickly. Thus, for example, McDonald's invested a great deal of money in designing a cash register that could be worked by people who are illiterate. And since working provides tangible and immediate rewards (in terms of paycheques, self-esteem, and a sense of achievement), whereas going to school requires precisely that faith in long-term rewards that is absent in many cases, putting people to work is often a more realistic strategy than trying to force them to go to school.

So what looked like tough social policies turned out to be greatly empowering for hundreds of thousands of people. And the fact that the US labour market was able to draw so many new people into its labour pool was a big factor in its economic boom throughout the 1990s, the longest boom in postwar history. The best social program is still a labour shortage, where people have reasons to take advantage of the opportunities that a labour shortage creates and where there are immediate rewards and reinforcement for the cultural values and behaviours that allow people to succeed.

Of course wages are not the only way in which incomes are distributed. Drug-addled rock stars and preening actors and skirt-chasing sports stars earn their money from their fans who buy tickets to their performances. Lawyers and dentists and accountants charge their clientele fees for their services. Entrepreneurs offer products and services for sale. The gig economy, much demonized by designers for destroying traditional employment, does nothing of the sort. According to Philip Cross, former chief economic analyst at Statistics Canada, who analysed the tax data from the Canadian Revenue Agency about gig work,

> Despite the stereotype of youths being bullied by corporations into accepting precarious freelance work, a more typical gig person works a few hours a month in select years to top up their income, to allow for flexibility in parenting, or to stay busy in retirement. We should be encouraging people to choose the working arrangements that suit them best, not denigrating their choices.[31]

I could multiply the examples but I think the point is established that, contrary to those who subscribe to Marxist or feminist or intersectionalist dogma, employers do not enjoy the whip hand in negotiations with employees and the best friend of both employers and workers is a vigorous labour market with brisk competition between employers for people with valuable skills. High *and* low incomes are based on an impersonal evaluation of the worth of the knowledge possessed by the person earning the income and this evaluation is based on a vast network of individual transactions that, in the aggregate, establishes what it costs to buy anyone's willing contribution of their knowledge to our different activities.

Nor is it necessary to have knowledge of the value of Bill Gates's or Steve Jobs's or Jeff Bezos's. In fact, each of them, in pursuing the billions of dollars that consumers freely bestowed upon them for the valuable products and services they imagined, created thousands of jobs because they needed people with other skill sets they did not possess. And in seeking out those people they didn't say, "I am the mighty Jeff Bezos and you will come and work for me for a pittance." They said, "I need drivers and accountants and designers and builders and warehousemen" and people with those skills showed up and said, "I can work for you but this is what you'll have to pay to get me." Those who have billions do not get to dictate the outcome of the negotiation either. Believe me, Bill Gates and Warren Buffett pay the going rate when they need a plumber and they probably feel just as aggrieved about that rate as the rest of us.

It is worth remarking that while most people perhaps cannot articulate the way this works, they intuitively grasp its most important features. This is why most efforts to incite class hatred against the very rich are usually surprisingly unsuccessful. Some rich people deserve our opprobrium and contempt, and others deserve our support and admiration. What matters is not just the fact that they are rich, but *how they got rich*.

People don't mind the Gateses and the Jobses and the Bezoses, or the Madonnas, the Adeles, and the Pelés of the world getting rich from people freely parting with their money to buy something they value. We understand that these folks have enriched themselves by having an idea or a skill that bettered the lives of millions of people. No one *decided* these people would succeed; they did so by enriching the lives of others and put themselves at risk of failure to do so. Put another way, people are in favour of a system of "It's not who you know but what you know that matters" and they are opposed to one based on "It's not what you know but who you know that matters."

People's real ire tends to be directed against those who got rich by fraud or corruption or cosy sweetheart deals where the rules are fixed in their favour, so they didn't get rich the fair way, by taking risks and seeing them pay off; they got rich like Bernie Madoff by defrauding their clients or like corrupt companies that buy contracts by providing yachts and prostitutes to the children of dictators or by government officials handing out sweetheart contracts in return for backhanders or by government policy protecting favoured industries from "destructive" competition.

It is thus quite incorrect to say, as the designers do, that gardeners don't care about inequality. They care about it deeply and passionately. They have a different idea about which kind of inequality matters and why. For designers it is an aesthetic question; inequality created by traditional behaviours and grown institutions is offensive because, well, it doesn't conform to some nice tidy pattern like absolute equality (where everyone gets the same) or to some "pattern of distribution" they have chosen and want to impose because it makes sense to them and they are experts and we should defer to them.

Gardeners, as I have already said, don't care about the abstract pattern and how pleasing it is to their eye. They care about the kinds of behaviours that underpin one "distribution" or another. Nassim Nicholas Taleb, the author of black swan fame, was surely making a gardener's distinction when he noted that there are inequalities that people tolerate and ones that they find intolerable. The former are tolerated both because in their essence they represent the useful knowledge and abilities we have been discussing and the rewards that flow to them, as well as because people who have "skin in the game" run the risk of losing all if their knowledge ceases to be useful or relevant. The intolerable kinds of inequality would include those who get rich by rent-seeking, theft, coercion, corruption, and the like. Struggling against the second kind combats unjustified inequality but not by appealing to base emotions like envy or arbitrary "patterns" that are so pleasing to designers. As Taleb writes,

> [I]n countries where wealth comes from rent seeking, political patronage, or what is called regulatory capture (by which the powerful uses regulation to scam the public, or red tape to slow down competition), wealth is seen as zero-sum. What Peter gets is extracted from Paul. Someone getting rich is doing so at other people's expense. In countries such as the U.S., where wealth can come from destruction, people can easily see that someone getting rich is not taking dollars from your pocket; perhaps even putting some in yours.[32]

This, by the way, is why gardeners should be remorseless and enthusiastic in pursuing and prosecuting people who get rich the wrong way. Such a pursuit of the wrongly enriched protects gardeners from the charge that they are merely the hand puppets of rapacious capitalism or the "corporate agenda."

More importantly, that on-going pursuit serves as a reminder to everyone that wealth is and should be the fruit of service, not of corruption. Canada has a poor record in this regard, being notoriously complacent (and possibly complaisant) in the face of corporate welfare, corporate bribery, organized crime, money laundering, tobacco smuggling, regulatory capture and a host of other activities that have permitted and even encouraged people and organizations to grow rich through rent-seeking, force, fraud and corruption.

What gardeners learn from all of this is that we don't need political authority to co-ordinate or oversee or "correct" how we all play our role in society. We are all engaged in a ceaseless society-wide negotiation to find the terms on which people who know how to do what we need done will come and do it for us and vice versa. Because it is a negotiation, no one dictates the terms and the rich and famous are constrained by the society-wide outcome of these negotiations just as much as the poor and obscure.

And unlike systems for distributing people and incomes that rely on political authority, these grown impersonal institutions respect each person's protected sphere. We all share our knowledge with others because we have negotiated the terms on which we will do so and are free to seek better conditions at any time. No one determines what we earn because we think or live the "right" way.

The genius of the gardener's approach is that even though none of us may agree with anyone else on what we will do with the money we earn (such choices being our vision of the good life put into practice), we *do not need to agree* in order for this system to work reliably and without anyone being "in charge" of it. This is because people's income isn't determined, as the religious leaders and apparatchiks and others want to do it, based on *what you will do with that income*, it is based on *an impersonal, society-wide evaluation of how much what you know how to do contributes to the overall welfare*. In fact, in many cases, the transactions we are describing are completely anonymous. We may never meet face to face with the people who provide the goods and services we want, or they may be provided by corporations that employ thousands of people each of whom makes a tiny but necessary contribution to your satisfaction. You don't know them and don't need to know them – they may live in another country or countries. You certainly don't need to agree with their choices of how to live in order to co-operate with them effectively.

There will, of course, always be some people who will be indignant that Gates or Jobs or Bezos got rich supplying something people "should" not have needed or wanted in the first place, usually dismissively referred to as merely responding to people's frivolous "wants" as opposed to their genuine needs. (Apparently expert opinion can judge far better than us poor slobs doing the choosing, who may not even have a university education. The horror!). In other words the Starbucks-sipping, European-sports-car-driving, logo-branded-clothes-wearing, fancy-degree-bearing-experts should be able to sit in judgment on the Timmy's-drinking, pickup-driving, blue-jeans-wearing, Grade-Ten-drop-out's choices about what matters to them. Beer and popcorn anyone?[33]

But these critics miss the point. The vast network of social co-operation is quite indifferent to anyone's views about what others *should* want. It simply supplies what they demonstrably do want and does so with relentless efficiency. Decrying the choices people make when choosing for themselves what they want is exactly what gardeners have learned does not work. It expresses contempt for the free choices of free people and sets up those wanting to "correct" the choices as judges of how other people have chosen to live, using politics as a way to force people to make the "right" choices. This nearly always ends in populist tears.

There is a necessary qualification that comes in two parts. You cannot act on a desire that cheats, steals from, or coerces another person. You cannot reach inside the protected sphere that envelops each of us and the essential tools like property and contract that undergird the protected sphere. That is why, for example, the Criminal Code and various forms of justified regulation exist.

There are hard cases, like drug abuse, in which people's ability to choose for themselves is in fact degraded, or some kinds of mental illness, where the ability to choose is impaired, but these are exceptions (and therefore proper topics for political controversy) that prove the rule, not a justification for a full-scale assault on the principle of people choosing for themselves what they want.

The second part of the qualification is that you cannot demand things you are unwilling to pay for. Or more accurately, some grown institutions of social co-operation won't supply these things. Only volunteer organizations and families might, all of which represent various forms of voluntary burden-sharing that cannot be imposed on others without violating their protected sphere but which exist in profusion in the grown institutions of civil society.

Sometimes, though, the full cost of producing something is unknown. It may even be unknowable, at least in the sense that the true cost of things is often revealed only over long periods of time. The car was an environmental boon when it was introduced because it got huge piles of horse manure and its associated disease risk off city streets. Now a century later some fear that the internal combustion engine is also an engine of environmental destruction. But of course all human action contains both foreseeable and unforeseeable consequences for reasons we have already seen. Government action is no less subject to unforeseen consequences. When the full costs of making or doing something are not captured in the price, the fancy name for them is "externalities." Air pollution is an example of an externality. A factory that treats the atmosphere as free and therefore dumps pollutants into it is passing part of the cost of the production of its widgets on to the rest of us who breathe the air.

By and large, gardeners deal with the problem of unaccounted costs (externalities) in two ways.

First, they are dealt with through the courts. Since we cannot always know the effects our actions will have on others, the law provides that when our actions harm others, even when we could not reasonably have foreseen the harm but profited from it, we are required to pay compensation.

Second, they are handled through legislation, especially legislation that extends the logic of grown social institutions into new areas. The cap and trade system that eventually helped to eliminate the threat of chlorofluorocarbons (CFCs) is a good example. A carbon tax is similar in principle where greenhouse gases are concerned. So too are class action lawsuits that allow those harmed to act in concert and share the costs and risks of using the courts to seek redress. Forcing companies to be responsible for dealing with the packaging that their products come in, rather than expecting the consumer to put them in the garbage and foist the costs for that garbage disposal on municipal taxpayers is possibly another, although it is an example of a legitimate area of political controversy. Surely the person who buys the product, and pays the municipal taxes, is at least in theory paying the cost for the collection and disposal of the refuse he or she generates. A scheme to make the manufacturer pay may therefore be a strategy by municipalities to try to escape their responsibility to serve their citizens.

The social welfare problem

To this point we've been talking about people who are in a position to have, and profit from, knowledge that other people find useful. Any civilized society recognizes, however, that there are people who, for one reason or another – illness, disability, infirmity – are incapable of providing valued services. These people should be entitled to receive an income, the cost of which falls as a charge on the whole community.

The higher such an income, however, the greater the incentive for people to stop participating in the ceaseless struggle to offer valuable knowledge to others as the way of paying their way in the world. Instead, the incentive is for them to find a way to represent themselves as qualifying for the social welfare payment. The problem with this, in the gardener's logic, goes right back to the central idea that social co-operation (i.e., freely sharing our knowledge with others) happens best when *everybody* earns their living by serving the needs of others and then spends their income as they see fit, with nobody's choices getting preferential treatment.

But when you are capable of working and nevertheless expect others to pay your bills, you are in effect using the state to force others to subsidize your choices, to say that the way you want to live is worthy of them being forced to give up their own plans for their earnings. The greater the scale on which this is allowed to happen, the more widespread will be the resentment of those who conclude that some people are favoured by the system (they get what they want without working), while others are handed the bill.

A different way of saying this is that the recipients of such unwarranted social welfare are using the state as a mechanism to force others, both the willing and the unwilling, to hand over some of their earnings. In other words, the recipients use the unwilling contributors as objects or things to be used for their own purposes. It is only what the recipients want that matters, not what the people being taxed for this purpose want.

In practical terms people accept that no system is perfect and there will always be some abuse, and the possibility of such abuse must not be allowed to prevent care from being given to those who need it. But the more payments move away from this widely accepted principle to a system where some people capable of working can live at the expense of others, the more social co-operation will be imperilled.

It goes without saying that such directly financed social welfare schemes (including proposed guaranteed annual incomes) are quite different in principle from social insurance schemes like Employment Insurance (EI) or the Canada Pension Plan (CPP). The latter schemes recognize that old age and unemployment are universal risks and that while we work it makes perfect sense to set aside an insurance premium against the risk of unemployment or poor retirement planning. The universality of such programs may well be justified precisely so that the decisions of the improvident don't cause them to fall as a charge on the taxpayer.

Who is in charge around here, anyway?

Back to the main argument. One of the reasons that designers love to try to redesign the distribution of income is buried in the word "distribution" itself. A "distribution" implies a "distributor" or an active agent making decisions about who gets what. If income is "distributed" then someone must decide that the goodies are to be distributed this way rather than some other.

But in a society of gardeners, the "distribution" is determined by the actions of all and is simply the aggregate of their individual choices. We make decisions to buy and sell, volunteer and donate, relax and work, spend and save; each one of those actions shifts resources from one person or organization to another. The income each of us gets has not been "distributed" by anyone, or to be strictly accurate, *all* of us "distributed" tiny pieces of it but *no one* determined the final outcome.

Any decent gardener will tell you that as soon as you depart from a grown distribution based on the aggregate of people's actual choices, and move to one where rulers pick and choose who gets what, the vast field of voluntary social co-operation is transformed into a political battlefield, with various individuals, groups and organizations claiming that they too "should have" got more and complaining bitterly that those in charge have chosen others as more worthy than themselves. And the more we surrender to this impulse, the stupider we get as a society because we are deprived of the information that grown social institutions are trying to pass along to us about what we want and who is good at supplying it and what rewards are available to those who think they can do better.

This really gets to the heart of what I mean when, from time to time, I talk about people withdrawing from social co-operation. The very worst form of withdrawal from voluntary social co-operation is to shift over to a world of political competition. To repeat: the gardener's view of human nature is that most people will acquiesce in a distribution impersonally determined by grown social institutions that are not the will of anyone. As soon as people realize that desired things can be distributed by acts of political will based on choices approved by political elites, however, it distracts them from focusing on making maximum use of the knowledge they have available (and maximizing the discovery of new knowledge). Instead they focus on getting those in authority to transfer benefits to them. The fancy technical name for this is "rent-seeking." Elsewhere[34] I gave it a rather more accessible name: PUPPETRY or People Using Political Power to Enrich Themselves by Robbing You.

Gardeners don't say that political societies cannot designate some ways of life, some choices, as highly desirable. But gardeners would also say that as soon as you say political institutions may be used to support some people's goals with money taken from others through taxation, there is no way political authorities can limit who may make such claims. People whose choices politicians did not intend to support will rise up and demand that they be treated "fairly," meaning that their preferences should get the same support as others'. Instead of the freely entered into social co-operation made possible by grown social institutions, such policies cause people to divert their energies from responding to rewards for the sharing of what they know how to do, to lobbying politicians for benefits that may be coercively seized from others.

Thus you get the case where the bestowing of university research grants, which politicians originally intended should support "research excellence" at top universities, have led to loud demands from third and fourth rank universities for their "fair share." And you get the situation where regional development agencies, which were originally intended to support poor underperforming regions of the country, have become debased until even the richest regions of the country, like southern Ontario, get their "own" such agency. And you get wealthy corporations like Loblaw's seeking – and getting – the taxpayer to fund their new cold storage facilities using the argument that those facilities may combat climate change.

It isn't just about money

Of course the distribution of resources by the state need not involve only money; this is by no means a purely economic argument. Distribution of resources can include matters of recognition or prestige or power or authority. A classic example is our attempts in the eighties and nineties to amend the Constitution.

I was a negotiator of both the Meech Lake and Charlottetown Accords and saw them up close. To the designing mind, Meech Lake did justice to a "national minority" (the Quebecois), and so was justified. Quebec was entitled to constitutional recognition no one else was entitled to. But these fine distinctions cut no ice in St. John's or Prince Rupert or Thunder Bay. What many people across the country saw, rightly or wrongly, was the singling out of one aspect of national life, one aspect of one group's identity, and elevating it above all the rest.

The reaction was revulsion, a revulsion grounded in a fundamentally gardeneresque idea: that the State ought not to make distinctions or choices between individuals on the basis of their group identity. If we are all of equal moral worth, then our choices and allegiances are as well.

It may be true that we can make an intellectual distinction between the needs and aspirations of national cultural minorities like the Quebecois, and other kinds of minorities. Indeed, in earlier times countries like Canada and Britain were conceived of first and foremost as being composed of groups (French and English, or Welsh, Irish, Scottish, and English). But I am convinced that this era is ending as individual identity comes to stake out a far more powerful place for itself in our world. We can applaud or deplore the trend; we cannot deny it.

Does this mean that there can be no place for the accommodation of differences between groups? Of course not. No one, in those now distant constitutional debates, wanted to deny the very real differences that make Quebec different from the rest of the country, differences that revolve around language, culture and institutions. What many could not accept was that we can use political institutions to pick and choose which differences matter and which ones don't, which are "distinct" and which are merely ordinary. And nothing less than this is at stake in these kinds of decisions, for while Nova Scotia lobster fishermen and Jamaicans in Toronto and Alberta oil patch workers can accept that Quebeckers are different from them, they are also different (or "distinct") from each other and from many other groups.

Ironically, by the way, this is not an argument that Quebec shouldn't be different. Everyone accepts that it is different because people there make different choices and live a different way. But these constitutional packages all demanded that the rest of the country single out in some formal official way this difference as somehow more worthy of celebration or recognition than other differences held to be quite important by the people who lived them. Quebec doesn't need the rest of the country's permission to be different. Its difference wouldn't be *caused* by a symbolic constitutional recognition but *rather it exists today because of the will of Quebeckers to be different.* They don't need the rest of the country's permission to be different and setting things up so that Quebec must be "humiliated" as long as the rest of the country doesn't "recognize" their distinctiveness is a designer-inspired recipe for permanent and unresolvable discord.

Only two realistic alternatives are open. Either we recognize no group as "officially" different, set apart from the rest, or we recognize all groups as different, and therefore debase the constitutional recognition sought by the national minority. I seem to remember it was Allan Blakeney, then-premier of Saskatchewan, who made the gardener-like observation that Canada could either be a country of one culture, or one of many cultures. Two, however, was not the right number.

Anyone who participated in the Charlottetown negotiations, as I did, will know just how illusory is the hope that we can "draw the line" between those groups who deserve or warrant constitutional recognition and those who do not. Charlottetown tried to have it both ways, burying a recognition of Quebec's distinctiveness in a vast amount of bafflegab and Canada clauses, with various groups (including other provinces) essentially holding the process hostage until they got the "recognition" that they cared about, and with the groups who didn't achieve their recognition becoming bitter holdouts from the outside.

The country's resounding rejection of Charlottetown was, from a gardener's perspective, entirely foreseeable. If you think that this was anomalous and that more skilful leaders could have singled out a few groups for "special" recognition through elite negotiation, leaving the rest in some unrecognized "non-distinct" category, I am afraid that future prospects are not promising. Remember that pusillanimous politicians will always be the first line of defence of such distinctions, and final authority over changes is now almost certainly exercised by the whole electorate by referendum. Need I say more? Elite accommodation, much beloved of, well, the elites, is going to be ever harder to pull off.

There is another side to the Charlottetown experience which has received far too little attention, and its logic has now spread throughout the body politic. Those who defended Charlottetown were essentially making the case that resources should be transferred to privileged groups for cultural reasons. Another way of thinking of this is as a policy of subsidizing cultural difference. Now one of the cardinal rules of economics is that if you subsidize something, you will get more of it. If we as a society subsidize groups for being sufficiently different, then people will have an incentive to arrange their behaviour so as to qualify for the subsidy. It is no accident, then, that the explosion of group identification in Canada has followed hard on the heels of the Quebecois' growing self-awareness as a group and their demand for resources in recognition of that difference. Quebec's strategy has been wildly successful, and this has not been lost on others intent on getting a place on the gravy train.

The cost of intervention

Thus is created yet again the destructive dynamic that almost always accompanies government intervention, be it economic or cultural. A small intervention buys peace with the members of one group. Their success encourages further demands, and creates an incentive for others to ask for the principle of intervention to be extended to them. Soon those lucky enough to have won such privileges are battling with those who are outside the charmed circle asking to be admitted, who also want extra resources at someone else's expense.

Eventually it becomes clear that the only solution is the application, yet again, of one of two general principles. The first is that every group who has a claim to make has it recognized, breaking the bank and rendering the recognition worthless. Just think about a world in which every industry has achieved the same degree of tariff protection; no industry wins and all consumers lose. The other principle, the only truly defensible one, is that all activities or ways of life are equally valid (subject to the usual caveat about not reaching into the protected sphere of others) and the State will recognize this moral equality by adopting a studied neutrality between them. Only then can we find our way back to the gardener's world where people don't ask the State to take things from others in order to hand them over, but rather everyone is focused on what they already know, what new knowledge they can acquire and how they can put their knowledge at the service of others.

To avoid misunderstanding, let me be clear that this discussion of the dangers of using the state to hand out favours is no argument against taxation. It is a practical reality that gardeners recognize that gardens need gardeners and they must be paid for by a charge on everyone, although clearly gardeners and designers have very different views on how much help society needs to function. But gardeners would make the case that taxation should interfere as little as possible with the grown distribution (that is to say it should interfere as little as possible with the relative positions of people within the distribution) because the grown distribution itself is a massive piece of information about how people value different kinds of knowledge and therefore is telling young people, for example, what kind of knowledge they should cultivate and acquire if they want to succeed.

Incentives matter

There is also a practical limit to how much can be taken out of the grown distribution under designer redistribution. Designers will often make the case that they can pretty well mess as much as they like with the grown distribution at the top because people at the top derive satisfaction from their work and will continue to do it even if we tax away their "ill-gotten" (irony alert!) gains. (It is interesting that these folks don't think the same of the people at the bottom of the income distribution, and don't claim that they will work as hard as they possibly can no matter how little you pay them.)

But leaving that aside, this discussion gets to the issue of incentives. It is often said that if you want less of something, you should tax it (because by raising the price you get people to ask for less of it – the logic behind carbon pricing). This is the mirror image of the idea noticed earlier, that if you want more of something you should subsidize it.

What high taxes at the upper end of the income scale do is to tax effort and the use of valuable knowledge. People get rich legitimately thanks to the value that others place on what they know how to do. High taxes on their income discourage this valuable activity and reward them for other uses of their time that the rest of us find less useful. If the state takes one half of the value you create for people by investing an hour of your labour, but if you get to enjoy the entire value of an hour spent at leisure reading a book or golfing, then the incentives are for you to spend less time deploying your valuable knowledge and more reading or golfing. The signals that we are sending about what is valuable to us and the signals the tax system is sending are working at cross purposes.

Where exactly the point is when the tax burden flips from being a background noise that most people ignore to a strong signal that overwhelms the other signals that people are sending about the value of what you do is not something that can be definitively demonstrated, and so is a matter in politics of judgment and art. What can be said without fear of contradiction, however, is that designers would set the tax load higher than gardeners because they believe that they will produce better results for people by acting on expert knowledge and "what people told us they wanted," and they therefore have a superior claim to the money than those whose knowledge generated it.

As was the case for minimum wages, designers seem to believe that they can change the income distribution but everything else will remain exactly as it was, with people working just as hard as they were before at putting their knowledge at the service of others. Gardeners think that if you cut the reward for doing what individuals through their spending decisions voted most valuable to them, you will lower the level of satisfaction or happiness in society. People will get less of what they themselves have signalled they want. And that is before you even get to the question of what designers will then turn around and do with the money.

By the way, just as I showed that the existence of property benefits everybody, including those that don't have any, wealth benefits everyone, including those who don't have any, which is to say the poor.

The (purchasing) power of the poor

Critics of our grown income "distribution" focus exclusively on how much different people have, and in particular how much it varies from, say, equality of distribution. I've already pointed out that these critics don't spend nearly enough time thinking about *why* people have the share of income that they do. They also miss that our system *is* based on a moral equality, but it is the moral equality of our *choices*, or what we want in life. The rich and famous and powerful don't tell you how to live (well, ok, they do tell us what to do; happily they just have no authority or power to make us follow their absurd advice).

But I want to make a slightly different point here, which is that the wealth generated by our individual choices under grown social institutions creates an incentive for those with major resources to get more by satisfying more people.

Those people to be satisfied include the poor, whose well-being is measured not merely by how much money they have, but also by what they can get for that money. A dollar is only worth what it can buy. Because this is the case, when we get exercised over wide gaps in income between the better-off and the less well-off we miss a whole dimension of inequality that actually matters much more. If those at the bottom of the income scale are actually getting more for each dollar they spend, their standard of living is rising even though their cash income may not be.

The classic example is Moore's Law,[35] which states that the computing power of a silicon chip will double every two years. Moore didn't deal with price directly, yet the computer power available to the ordinary consumer has been rising roughly in accordance with his law, while prices have been falling. That's why I paid less last year for a replacement laptop far more powerful than its predecessor bought a few years before.

Households at every income level are stocked with electronics whose prices behave in the same way. People at the low end of the income scale are getting more and better technology and paying less than ever before for it. Consumers don't even need a lot of computing power at home; soon laptops will be as quaint as slide rules anyway. They can buy tablets and then use on-line software and data storage that are cheaper than owning this capability. Technological innovation is making computing ever more accessible to the technologically illiterate, who are often the least educated.

This rise in the purchasing power of the poor isn't only observable in consumer electronics. A revolution in logistics and retailing has contributed a great deal, too. Urban elites who like to shop at Whole Foods and

The Gap decry income inequality while sneering at Wal-Mart and Costco, which have dramatically cut the cost of a wide array of consumer items that their customers actually want to buy. And those retail giants are themselves under pressure from the Amazons and others who have got out of the costly bricks and mortar retailing business. Now low-income consumers can use their low-cost computing power to shop on-line and cut out the middle man. Along the way, they have enriched the Waltons and Jeff Bezos, not because their customers were being ripped off, but because these entrepreneurs made a major contribution to improving the quality of their lives. The wealth enjoyed by these entrepreneurs is a direct function of how much people value what they know how to do, and many of those people have very little money in absolute terms. But they see that the Waltons and the Bezoses enable them to get more for their money.

And before you trot out the tired meme that Amazon is ripping off everyone because they pay no taxes, first of all you are wrong and Amazon pays lots of taxes.[36] Second, one reason that Amazon enjoys a relatively low tax burden is not because the company cheats, but because it reinvests so heavily[37] in increasing its ability to do what it already does so well and in bringing that knowledge to more people (and in our system, we correctly don't tax reinvested profits).

This is exactly one of the key gardeners' arguments, that people vote with their money and signal both what they want and what they want more of. Amazon makes a lot of money providing a service people want and then invests a lot of that money in increasing its ability to do even more of it. The fact that we don't tax those reinvested profits is a gardener-inspired strength of our tax system, not a flaw.

People on low incomes don't need newspapers and flyers delivered by expensive low-tech delivery people and posties to get good special deals that stretch their dollar farther. They can just monitor Groupon or Ebates. In fact, Big Data is increasingly delivering direct to low-income consumers offers of low-cost goods and services specifically tailored to their incomes and buying patterns; the special offers will come to them.

Technology is increasingly allowing those on low incomes to escape the too-high cost of regulated services. They can't (yet) unplug from the electricity grid, but they can certainly dump their telephone landline in favour of a fixed-price cross-Canada calling package on their mobile phone. If developing countries are any guide, that mobile phone will also allow them to escape their reliance on expensive banking services, as the phone becomes a mobile wallet, complete with chequing account and credit card. Consumers can't (yet) escape the abusive supply management system that drives up the cost of their milk and poultry, but in many cities they can escape the local taxi monopoly in favour of Uber or Lyft. Indeed, if they have a car they might themselves become an Uber driver and supplement their income.

In fact, just as I argued earlier that property benefits even those (and perhaps *especially* those) who don't have any, this discussion of how competition and knowledge discovery drives down the cost of living underlines a key point: Grown social institutions are particularly beneficial to those with the least money. As the great economist Joseph Schumpeter once famously remarked, the strength of liberal capitalism is that it serves the poorest, not just the richest, who will be served under any system.

> The capitalist engine is first and last an engine of mass production which unavoidably also means production for the masses . . . It is the cheap cloth, the cheap cotton and rayon fabric, boots, motorcars and so on that are the typical achievements of capitalist production, and not as a rule improvements that would mean much to the rich man. Queen Elizabeth owned silk stockings. The capitalist achievement does not typically consist in providing more silk stockings for queens but in bringing them within reach of factory girls.[38]

Going back to cars, the moment is coming when they will be the shining example of how globalization increases the purchasing power of the poor. As places like China and India reach ever higher levels of income and technological sophistication, they are applying their impressive intellectual and entrepreneurial abilities to reducing the cost of consumer goods to the point that they are within reach of the millions of people in their home countries whose incomes are still tiny. As they achieve that goal, we will benefit from their innovations, none more so than those on low incomes here at home.

China's Geely brought out its IG car a few years ago to compete head to head with Indian car maker Tata's Nano. While the average new car price in the US is now over $30,000, these two cars each sell for less than $3000 in their home markets. *Forbes* writer Haydn Shaughnessy said a few years ago that when this innovation hits North America and meets our standards, these basic cars won't cost $3,000, but more likely $10,000.[39]

As economist Tyler Cowen notes in the *New York Times*, emerging economies are keeping down the costs of manufactured goods but they have a way to go before they are innovative enough to send us new products.[40] But if Japan and South Korea are any measure of what will happen when they do, markets and innovation will almost certainly continue to allow low-income people to get rising value out of their cash incomes – a rising value from which innovative business leaders derive big incomes, which they then turn around and reinvest in doing more of what brought them success to begin with.

So to sum up, gardeners are of the view that any particular state of things, including society, is only provisional and will be radically changed in unpredictable ways by unforeseeable knowledge discovery and that that knowledge will be discovered by individuals and organizations acting for their own purposes and under incentives that reward social co-operation (i.e., people pooling their knowledge for mutual benefit).

While we are all entitled to a protected sphere and certain tools in putting together a life that pleases or satisfies us, this is not done for reasons of some theoretical moral equality, but because it is successful in getting people to work together. The fact that others claim to have a superior moral theory is actually not very interesting and certainly not fatal to our social arrangements. The reaction of gardeners is always that your theory is very pretty but we want to know if and how it works in practice.

Gardening and conservatism

Those of you who have followed the argument to this point may be confused about something. "Gardening" sounds an awful lot like what we have come to call "conservatism," but the outcome of following the knowledge embodied in grown social institutions is not the conserving of a comfy status quo that changes at a glacial pace. On the contrary, the whole argument is that human beings learn (including things about themselves) and their behaviour and expectations and aims and ambitions constantly change as a result. Under grown social institutions, the social order that surrounds us responds immediately and effortlessly to people acting on new knowledge. So those grown social institutions make us smarter, in the sense of acting on the most information possible without us even having to know or master the knowledge in question.

But the price of being open to integrating new knowledge so effortlessly is that our efforts to organize our lives may turn out to have been mistaken in whole or in part. This makes gardening a radical enterprise. Everything is provisional and subject to revision because that is the price of being smart. Sometimes you have to let go of what you cared about because you learned it didn't work or someone else had a better idea. As John Maynard Keynes once sagely summarized a bit of gardener wisdom, "When the facts change, I change my mind."

Gardeners, therefore, care about methods, institutions, and rules, but accept that *outcomes* cannot be controlled except at the cost of making us stupider. Gardeners can set the rules of social co-operation and then let people and organizations navigate them, but we cannot control the final destination or outcome unless we want to use political authority to overwrite the desires and goals of individuals and their organizations and substitute for them the goals and desires of those with political power.

To revert to the example in the introductory chapter, we can make pretty footpaths on campus that look great from the air and then struggle to keep people from walking on the grass to get to where they want to go. Or we can let people show us where they want to walk and then make the official footpaths follow those routes, understanding that new routes may emerge at any time in response to new buildings and classes and old routes may fall into disuse or be shifted from being a means of getting somewhere to a smoker's haven or the perfect spot for lovers' assignations.

One gives an aesthetically pleasing result but at the cost of much effort in policing by designers and lost time and mounting resentment by people trying to get to class. The other accepts that people have their own plans and the purpose of pathways is to help them get there without judgment about whether this is the "right" path or not. But the price is that the pattern of pathways at the end will not be pretty – they will just do the job and there will be harmony between and among path makers and pedestrians.

The mirror image of the radicalness of gardening is the conservatism of politics, for politics is the realm of the designer, the people who think the *outcome* of social processes should be pretty and correspond to their aesthetic sense of what those outcomes should look like. They think that incomes are too skewed, groups too under-represented, the economy insufficiently green, Canadian culture too under-represented, dairy farmers too poorly paid. And they use the instruments of politics to try to "correct" these aesthetic failings. This they do, as I have already mentioned, by using politics to insulate some people from the effects of knowledge discovery.

Not only do such policies make us stupider (by giving us access to less knowledge than we would have without these barriers), but the policies designed to make social outcomes more pleasing become captured by organized interests in a way that is much more difficult to do under grown social institutions. What starts out being an effort to make society more pleasing to look at becomes an ugly privilege used by well-organized interests to make us serve them rather than the other way around. Some of these unjustified privileges gardeners have been able to remove, and the benefits to society have been incalculable: the abolition of state ownership of Petro-Canada, CN and Air Canada and the closing of the Wheat Board are just a few examples. There are many other dead men walking, however: supply management, the banking and mobile telephony cartels, the regional development agencies, Canadian content rules, the state monopoly on provision of health care and ever more progressive taxation are nothing more than this.

Of course sometimes compromise is necessary. As a practical matter gardeners see that sometimes social co-operation requires the conciliation of people and organizations that can use their power to obstruct experimentation and knowledge discovery or, more likely, harm the political prospects of parties that don't give in to their unjustified claims for privilege. The kind of poor policies I've mentioned often arose in just such circumstances. But it is always a deal with the devil, and the disruptions they cause in the social order always become deeper as what we know continues to evolve well past the point at which these "protections" were put in place. The price only rises. Most political battles between designers and gardeners are over whether to preserve or extend or abolish these anomalous designed exceptions to the operation of grown social institutions. Gardeners know which direction they want to go in, and would argue that every time they have succeeded society has benefited, but they equally accept that politics is the art of the possible.

For gardeners the chief role of government is to remove obstacles to the operation of grown social institutions by understanding and extending their logic, thus freeing all the knowledge in society. This is not "market fundamentalism." Of course governments may act to set social minimums and standards that arise from moral feelings of the population (e.g., minimum wages, guaranteed access to health care, minimum incomes, compulsory retirement savings) but these things can be done in such a way as to harness knowledge and creativity or obstruct it, and every such choice comes with unintended consequences.

For designers the chief role of government is to displace grown social institutions with designed alternatives, thus freeing the designers' aesthetic sense from the tyranny of the practical and useful, yet irredeemably messy.

Let the battle be joined.

CHAPTER IV

Designer's democracy or gardener's democracy?

ONE OF THE TRENDS SWEEPING the world is democratization in a powerful new sense – not the ever-greater collective provision of goods under formal political control by parliaments and political parties and bureaucrats, but on the contrary, the increasing empowerment of everyone, rich or poor, uneducated or well-schooled, to choose exactly what they want for themselves and not compromise with others. In fact, if anything, technological innovation means that the number of areas where we must rely on collective provision rather than individual choices is falling, not rising. If democracy means that people are getting what they want (as opposed to politicians telling them what they will get), then grown social institutions and maximum knowledge use are making that available to more people in more fields every day.

We see this in the marketplace all the time. People chose first Walkmen, then iPods, and then smartphone music apps (all innovations granting individuals total power over what they listen to) so they could control what they hear. Meanwhile, radio (which is collective provision; you must listen to what the station plays, not what you want to hear) listenership has declined. People bought first VHS, and then Blu-Ray players, and now Netflix subscriptions so they can control what they watch, and TV viewership (collective provision) has plummeted.

People choose houses over apartments, cars over buses, Wal-Mart and Amazon over Eaton's and Sears, because each such choice gives them greater control over the shape of their own lives. These are vast participatory decisions by billions of people who do not need to forge political coalitions, lobby politicians, or wrestle with established interests opposed to change. No ministry co-ordinates their choices. They simply spend their money in accordance with their own priorities in their efforts to make for themselves a life that appeals to them.

And yet what results is not chaos, but order, and an order that allows more of us to get what we want than any alternative, and certainly more than politics. Guiding and co-ordinating the efforts of individuals, communities and organizations are grown participatory institutions that have evolved and developed over time, and that embody more, and more certain knowledge, than governments can ever possess. These institutions – language, common law, the marketplace (including prices and money), tradition, civil society and the family, to pick six outstanding examples – enable human beings to co-operate successfully on the basis of vast knowledge without all of that knowledge needing to be "known" by everyone, or even anyone. When widely disparate human wishes and intentions and widely dispersed human knowledge work in tandem with such institutions, the result is a flowering of genuine diversity in which each person chooses for themselves what is important and builds a life for themselves following their own choices. This is in blessed contrast to a "democratic" system in which relatively small electoral minorities can seize political power and enforce their preferences on everyone through one-size-fits-all programs.

These grown institutions are a kind of informational gift from the past, derived from generations of gardening experience, acting not as instructions or commands but as kindly advice about what others in our circumstances have found works in solving similar problems; the guidance we get from such institutions is thus in distinct contrast to the compulsory orders from the top that are characteristic of designers and their schemes. I want to underline that the institutions we are talking about reach far beyond "markets," which are the main focus of economists. There are lots of grown participatory social institutions, like NGOs and other voluntary civil society groups, as well as tradition and language that are non-market but exhibit the same knowledge-rich complexity and voluntary nature.

As long, however, as we talk about "grown social institutions" as some kind of abstraction, as something outside ourselves, as something that "happens to" us, we misunderstand them entirely. The most extreme designers see spontaneously grown institutions like the market as some kind of alien "imposition" on long-suffering consumers who have no say in the matter. They thus propose to replace grown social institutions with a system of their own design, chosen by political parties engaged in competitive elections. They thus believe their "designs," when chosen by voters, are more "democratic."

From the gardener's perspective, this is a complete fiction. The energy behind grown social institutions is not that of plutocrats and one percenters and anonymous abusive corporations. The energy that drives these institutions is people, people who make choices every day about how to spend their limited money in pursuit of their own goals in life. Businesspeople who cater successfully to those choices succeed; those who don't fail. What we call "market outcomes" are thus simply the aggregate of our individual choices. The market is a vast participatory outgrowth of our individuality, far better attuned to and better at satisfying individual wants and needs than clumsy, inflexible and ignorant political systems can ever hope to be.

Every time you take a job or earn a raise, you participate in society's collective judgment about what your kind of work is worth, about the contribution it makes to others' wellbeing and what the supply of workers like you is versus the demand for people like you. Every time you choose Walmart over the local shop, or buy a car rather than take the bus, or live in the suburbs rather than the city centre, you make choices that shape our entire society's evaluation of things that matter and call forth more supply of the things you want and less of the things you don't.

The power of giant corporations, usually the subject of much handwringing by designers, is in fact entirely dependent on their ability to satisfy consumers. Indeed, if they have power, it is power conferred on them by all of us through the sum of our individual choices.

The one-time CEO of General Motors, Charles Wilson, is alleged to have said that what is good for General Motors is good for America. What he was really getting at was that obstructing GM's success hurt American consumers who voted for its cars in the marketplace every day. If GM's products had sat unsold on the dealers' lots across the country, the corporation's power would have been negligible.

The same might be said for the miners who supply the raw materials, the power companies that supply the energy, the entertainment companies that divert us, or the logistics companies that get intermediate products to manufacturers and final products to the people who buy them. In every case, their power does not derive in the first instance from how big they are. Rather how big they are is itself an index of their success in winning the votes of you and me and millions or even billions of others in these participatory grown social institutions. And as soon as that bond between producer and the people who buy what it sells is broken, the producer's power crumbles. You and I vote both positively and negatively with our money: positively in favour of those who supply what we want and negatively against those who do not. Each kind of vote has powerful consequences. And our choices are independent of the choices of others (although if you want something extraordinarily expensive and you are the only one who wants it you will need to be exceedingly rich!). I don't need anyone else's permission to buy exactly what I want.

Using these grown participatory institutions as the basis on which to organize our social life is profoundly democratic, but not in the way designers understand that term. Every time you use an ATM, you are "voting"; in this case, you are voting for more ATMs and fewer bricks-and-mortar bank branches with tellers in them. Every time you send a package via UPS or FedEx, you are voting for fewer posties and a smaller post office. Every time you use a self-service checkout you are voting for fewer cashiers. Every time you buy a suburban house you are voting against cramped apartment living and for space and comfort. Every time you take your car to work (and endure the traffic) you are voting for convenience and comfort and against the even longer travel times transit often requires. Every time you take your kid to soccer in preference to hockey, you are voting for more soccer fields and fewer rinks (and probably for the culture of soccer over that of hockey). Every time you buy a hybrid or electric car you are voting to take action on climate change. Every time you volunteer to help your church resettle a refugee family, you are voting for community action over remote bureaucracy.

Of course, the opposite choices are also available to you, with a different mix of costs and benefits, advantages and disadvantages. One choice does not need to triumph over the other. As long as people are willing to bear the cost of their choices, all of those choices can be catered to. And you cast these votes every day, not once every four years or so where a bunch of choices are jumbled together into a single vote for a local MP who may or may not want what you want. Under grown social institutions, choice is a positive sum game. That is, more choices make possible more satisfaction and the acquisition of more knowledge. Under political institutions, choice is a zero sum game: those with power choose. If you happen to agree with the choices, you're a winner and what you want gets acted on. If you don't, tough luck. Maybe you'll do better in four years' time. Or not.

That's why in a gardener's world we celebrate genuine diversity. In that world every possible combination of cost, service, economy, convenience, and so forth is catered to. The fact that you prefer a medium double-double at Timmy's for $1.79 does not mean someone else cannot get a grande skinny vanilla latte at Starbucks for $4.15. Or a fine Darjeeling at your local cafe for another price. In fact, if there is a taste not catered to in the existing mix, someone is bound to try an experiment to see if enough people share that taste and are willing to pay enough to make it happen.

Food is crucial to life (and to civilized living), but we do not therefore create a state monopoly ("Nourishment Canada" or "caloricare") to ensure that we all get exactly what officialdom thinks we should have ("scientifically necessary foodstuffs") and kid ourselves that everyone gets a great deal when the state buys in bulk. No, we have an incredible array of options and prices so that the food we want can be bought at a price we can afford, according to our own priorities. Those who have more time than money can join food co-ops or shop at food warehouses and they can download discount coupons on-line and stock up on sale items. Those for whom grocery shopping needs to be an "experience" and who can afford the priciest brands and (maybe) organic products can shop at Whole Foods. And there is everything in between. And if some people do not have enough income to buy the food they need, we have social programs that ensure no one falls below an appropriate standard. We can, of course, disagree about what that standard should be, but that is an argument about establishing a civilized minimum. It is not about restricting the wide range of choices above the minimum that ensures people get just what they want within the limits of what they are willing to pay.

The fact that someone else makes different choices than I do does not mean they are getting something at my expense. Grown social institutions allow a vast array of choices to co-exist happily. Yet the galaxy of choice I have described in many areas (coffee, homes, postal services, banking, welcoming refugees) is exactly what puritanical designers refer to dismissively as a "patchwork." A patchwork is exactly what you get when people have their own resources and use them to make their own choices. A patchwork is what you get when individuals and companies and not-for-profits are rewarded for identifying and answering a new need, or an old need on better terms than before. A patchwork is what you get when the highly individualized knowledge that each person possesses about what they want and need is matched with highly specialized and diverse knowledge about how to identify and satisfy those wants and needs.

An unresponsive monopoly is what you get when designers decide they (and their "experts") know better than you do what about you need, and supply it on their terms.

Progressive designers think this is all bunk. They might not object to your opinions and decisions too vociferously for things that "don't really matter," like your choice of coffee or supermarket. But where they have views about what you *should* want, what you actually *do* want becomes quite irrelevant. In child care, health care, pharmaceuticals, how you post your letters, how you buy your alcohol or your electricity, apparently the "patchwork" is evidence that some people are not getting what they "should" (either too much or not enough) and that this can be fixed, not by giving those with insufficient resources enough to be able to meet a decent standard, but by ensuring that everyone gets the same thing and turning the state into your agent to buy it on your behalf.

This is usually dressed up as "democracy," or what people "voted for," but as I've already mentioned, a once-every-four-years vote on everything as interpreted by the people who happen to win elections, often with a very small share of the support of the total electorate, is a very inferior form of democracy compared to your ability to vote every day on what matters to you, in the proportions that make sense to you, with the resources you have earned or been given.

Politicians who are progressive designers always like to aggrandize the importance of politics, as if these quadrennial elections were the sole decision point at which people get to express their preferences, perhaps accompanied by opinion polling and poorly attended and carefully stage-managed committee hearings in between.

But in fact evidence shows that people attach very little importance to politics. They often cannot name prominent politicians, have only the crudest sense of what the parties stand for and often express a rather defensive attitude about the possibility of state intervention in their lives. There is one exception, of course: when politicians offer to give people something they want at what appears to be a discount by offering to make someone else pick up the tab.

Yet politicians are always claiming that politics is "letting people have their say," as if the say they have been having every day through their actions was of no account.

In a sense the politicians are correct, of course. Politics is about people talking, although the politicians do a lot more of it than the rest of us, and then impute motives to our mute vote. But we all know in other fields of life that talk is cheap and that actions speak louder than words. We all know that leading by example is far more convincing than leading by pretty words and that "do as I say, not as I do" is simply a polite phrase for hypocrisy because we know that our actions reveal more about us than the words that come out of our mouths.

Politics is the domain of speech; grown social institutions are the field of play of actions. That's why gardeners attach far more importance to what we communicate with our actions every day (how we use what we have to build the life we want) than to the rhetorical flourishes that politics brings out (what we say we want when we think we can slip the bill to someone else). As the French philosopher Frederic Bastiat so aptly remarked, "The *state* is the great fictitious entity by which everyone seeks to *live at the expense* of everyone else. For today, as in the past, each of us, more or less, would like to profit from the labour of others."[41]

Is politics the best way to discover what people want?

Contrary to how things work in grown social institutions, in democratic elections most votes are "wasted." In Canada's 2019 federal election it only took the "winning" party roughly 33 percent of the vote (in an election where only 66 percent of those eligible voted and those eligible excluded everyone under eighteen and all non-citizen residents) to win the strongly dominant say in policy making.[42] The outcomes of the workings of grown social institutions are the aggregate of every single decision by every person. *No one's vote is wasted; every person spends their resources in the exact way they think will bring the best value to themselves and their family and the resources they command are in direct proportion to their contribution to society's wealth-creating efforts.*

Complaints by designers about this usually amount to them airily claiming that if only ignorant consumers knew everything wise designers knew, they would make "better" choices, by which they mean the choices designers like. Designers think their superior knowledge licenses them to use political institutions to make individuals comply with the designers' wisdom. But gardeners argue that this is backward. The knowledge that designers, including "democratic designers" claim to possess is in fact inferior, not superior, to that possessed by people doing the best they can in circumstances and with resources no one else knows as well as they do.

Politicians always like to put about the idea that they are just giving people what they want. But the gardener always wants to know, "How do you know what people want?" Politics starts out with a number of disabilities compared to grown social institutions as a way of discovering what people want. As a teacher of mine neatly summarized the problem: In participatory democracy one of two things happens. Either you have to be always at the assembly to defend your interests against plans by others to tax you to pay for things they want, or you can never get your plumbing fixed because the plumbers are always at the assembly defending *their* interests. You can never just be left alone to get on with your life and the things you want to do.

This little aphorism encapsulates important truths about politics as a way of discovering and then delivering what people want.

Party political democracy is terribly inefficient. It is an endless effort by politicians, political parties and bureaucrats to find out what people say they want. But the various means by which they do this involve serious flaws and take inordinate amounts of time. I was part of the vast effort to probe the consciousness of Canadians in advance of the Charlottetown constitutional negotiations. There were two major federal inquiries and numerous provincial ones (to one of which I was the secretary). Politicians spent endless time, effort and money trying to divine what people wanted. In the event, their attempt to produce just that was then vigorously repudiated by the electorate in the 1992 referendum on the Charlottetown Accord.[43]

Nor are those seeking the information disinterested in the answer. A political party that thinks that universal child care would be popular, for example, tends to consult people who agree and discount the importance of others ("they don't vote for us anyway"). But if put in place, a universal child care policy must be endured (and paid for) by *both* its supporters and its opponents.

If you have ever participated, as I have with distressing frequency, in parliamentary committee hearings, you will know how easy it is for the majority of the committee to limit the questions asked to those they feel happiest about, and to stack the witness list with people who will say what they want to hear, after which the committee will duly report what "most" of the witnesses told them. Ditto for "consultations" organized by the bureaucracy, which frequently end up being peopled by people remarkably like the bureaucrats: representatives of organized "stakeholder groups" who are usually the ones who called for the policies now being studied. In fact, often the heads of such organizations are themselves former civil servants. Shocking, I know.

Political coalitions are built (you support my child care scheme and I'll support your supply management) in which people "support" policies they care not one whit about because it buys them support for something they *do* care about. So even the people who profess to support policy A may not do so and if left in the privacy of their conscience to vote on it on its merits would not.

Then there is the problem of the Trotskyites. Trotskyites? Yes, the Trotskyites, named after a faction of the Soviet Communist Party led by Leon Trotsky. There are few genuine Trotskyites in Canada now, but their strategy for subverting democracy is alive and well. I am using the term here to talk generally about people who act in bad faith within a group or organisation, using its rules to subvert the organisation for their own purposes.

Most people who believe in the virtues of participatory democracy believe that people take part and get involved in good faith in a genuine search for the common good. But is this assumption justified?

Certainly the Trotskyites don't. In fact, they use the good will of others, and their commitment to the rules, to destroy participatory democracy from within. One classic Trotskyite strategy, for example, is to talk endlessly in the assembly until everyone of good faith has gone home in disgust. Then when there are only Trotskyites left, the vote is called, which is usually a vote to put the Trotskyites in charge and cancel all future elections.

The Troskyite strategy usually isn't taken to such extremes in Canada but readers can find their own examples of people swearing blind that they support all kinds of policies for one set of reasons ("they're good for the poor and vulnerable") when they usually mean something else entirely ("this program will necessitate the hiring of lots of my dues-paying members").

People using political power to enrich themselves

This necessarily leads to a discussion of the predatory nature of politics. Because it is relatively easy for determined and well-organized minorities to seize control of the political process, and because the political process allows you to make people pay for things they don't want but you do, the incentives to use politics to prey on others is almost irresistible.

This is in marked contrast to what occurs in grown social institutions. In these institutions you get to choose what you want without having to get anyone else's agreement (except maybe your spouse's or your bank manager's), *but* (and it is an important "but") you only get to choose what you can pay for. And the (non-criminally acquired) resources that you have at your disposal with which to choose are ones that you have earned by providing value to others or have been given to you as gifts (I will talk more about how we earn our way in the world in later chapters).

In politics, in other words, the conversation is often not about "what you would like" but "what you would like if you only had to pay a fraction of its true cost." It is true that *this* is a conversation that cannot take place under participatory grown social institutions, except where people want to volunteer their time and money to make it possible. People donating their own time and money is perfectly in order under such institutions, and indeed civil society (another name for all these non-governmental collective efforts) is often more efficient than government at providing the same services and serve their clientele more effectively[44], no doubt in part because they have a real constraint on what they can pay.

Never forget that what people say and how they act are often two quite different things. The choices people make in grown social institutions where they cannot pass the bill for their choices on to people who do not wish to pay, are, to the gardener's mind, a truer view of their real preferences, than what those same people *say* they want to politicians when the politicians labour mightily to obscure the cost of what they offer ("Vote for me and I will get you free drugs, free health care, free dentistry, free museum admissions, tax-free home heating fuel, 30 percent off your mobile phone bill, a tax credit for your child's music lesson, possibly even, yes, free summer camping"). Who wouldn't say "yes" to free (or subsidized) stuff if offered?

But that does not reveal people's true preferences, which only become clear in conditions of choice: do you want this or that, given that you have only so much money *and can't have both*? I might visit a museum if it's free,

but balk if it cost $20 and that's money I was planning on spending on din-
ner. I might *say* I want to reduce GHGs in the atmosphere, but reconsider
if I know it will cost me $2000 a year to do so when I have other plans for
the money. That last part is crucial: when politicians take our money and
spend it on their priorities (sorry, "what the voters told us they wanted")
they can only do so by taking money we had other plans for. If the purpose of
life is the unfolding of our character and personality through the choices we
make for ourselves, politics, to the extent it represents false choices, ones we
wouldn't have made ourselves if offered the chance, does not enrich our lives,
but impoverishes them. Politics does not reveal true knowledge about what
people want in the way that their own unfiltered and undistorted choices do.

Is politics necessary? Yes, of course it is. There are choices that are by
their nature collective and must be taken for the good of everyone. In such
choices there will be winners and losers and yet the choices must still be
made. Grown social institutions will not supply national defence. Volunteer
organizations cannot administer the border or police our streets or supervise
prisoners. Where to set welfare rates and how to design the social support
system will always be a subject of controversy since there will inevitably be
people who cannot support themselves on the one hand, and on the other
those who will be drawn into dependence on welfare if the benefits are too
generous or too easily available. Social insurance schemes like EI and CPP
can make eminent sense but their precise organization and cost are the subject of legitimate political controversy. Decisions about what to tax must be
made and rates must be set. Government must pay its way or borrow. These
are not matters that can be settled by appeal to principle; rather they are a
matter of patient, thoughtful, incremental adjustment and yes, they must
be based in large part on what the public will tolerate.

That said, there are many services currently offered by the state that
can and would be offered by private providers. Since politicians are always
reluctant to make people pay the full cost of services they consume, services
offered through the state tend to be cheap where people actually use or consume them. People being what they are, they therefore want to use more of
them than they would if they had to pay their true cost. Governments then
control their costs, not by charging the full value of their services, but by

making it hard to get them, particularly by making people wait. Now you know why you have to queue to get the surgery you need.

Gardeners, therefore, always tend to prefer private provision over public where the service is not of the necessarily collective nature that I referred to above. This is not "ideology"; they are simply acting on the practical insight that private provision reveals more about people's true preferences, and is therefore more "democratic" in the sense that it gives individual people what they actually want based on the choices they make when spending their own money and without it requiring that they compromise with anybody.

It is not about "making people rich at others' expense" or "people before [economic] profit," which is how the designers usually frame it. (The gardener's cry is "people before [political] profit," which is a call for the real needs of people to be served rather than the pursuit of votes). It is about what private producers must do *in order to get rich*, which is to satisfy people's genuinely expressed wants and desires. The income generated by private provision is not the *benefit* of such provision, it is the *reward* paid by consumers for private providers giving them what they want. And since private providers must cover all their costs or go under, each of us is fully informed about the real cost of what we propose to consume, unlike politicians who move heaven and earth to hide this very knowledge.

In the next chapter we'll get more deeply into the lessons gardeners have drawn from close observation of how participatory grown institutions work compared to the designed alternatives much beloved of politicians. At its most basic, private provision makes society smarter (because it is based on real, extensive knowledge and is instantly responsive to new knowledge); while politics make society stupider (because it is based on partial knowledge and false premises).

Competition

I can hear all my designer readers choking with rage. What do you mean private provision is based on real extensive knowledge and is more responsive than politics?

Thank you for this question, because it gets right to the heart of the gardener's case that humanity's problem is ignorance, not an abundance of knowledge, and that what knowledge we do possess (including about who we are and what we want as individuals) is unavoidably locked in the hearts and minds of billions of people. How do we assure ourselves that the greatest possible array of knowledge is effectively brought to bear on the solution of our most pressing issues?

Designers *want* the answer to be that we set a bunch of designer/experts loose on a particular problem and they give us *the* answer. But as I've already shown, our knowledge of pretty much everything is partial and provisional, subject to major revision tomorrow for reasons that are completely unpredictable today.

This all means that "*the*" expert answer makes society stupid, and we get stupider as time passes if we allow ourselves to be ruled by designers, because the designed solution is frozen in time (do you know how hard it is to get an established policy changed?) while more knowledge is acquired every day, both about how to provide the things people want, *and* about what people actually want. Never forget: the entire stock of human knowledge may now be doubling at least *daily*, yet we haven't been able to make real reform to medicare since it was introduced in the 1960s.

What is the alternative to *the* expert opinion? Well, since there is almost certainly more than one answer to both questions (What is the best way to provide what is wanted? What do we want?), the alternative is to allow widespread experimentation, with different entrepreneurs trying out what they know about how to provide what is wanted both cheaply and effectively *and* also offering things they think people *might* like to see if their intuitions line up with reality.

Since our operating assumption is ignorance about both questions (otherwise *the* expert answer might be the best we could do), and since practical, not theoretical knowledge is what is needed, and since we cannot know what will work in the human world (as opposed to the known operations of the physical world) in advance of actually trying it, this kind of society-wide experimentation is the only realistic alternative. We have a name for this. We call it competition.

Competition for many designers is an unpleasant concept. In our schools, for example, we frequently hear the cry that we should teach our kids co-operation, not competition. But gardeners know that this, too, is exactly backwards. If *the* expert opinion is bound to be wrong (if not now, then with time), how exactly are we to be guided in our co-operation? To what end are we to direct our efforts?

Sports teams are co-operative enterprises. Forwards and defensive players and goalies all have to play their part if the team is to function well. But no one knows whether they have learned their role well in the absence of their skill being put to the test by an opposing team. And the two teams are also engaged in a co-operative exercise. Certain moves are allowed, others are not, all with the objective of making play a tableau in which the skill and luck of players and teams is displayed for the fans. Team sports are at once competition and co-operation, but the co-operation would be damned boring and the games a flop if we took the competitive element out. Competition is what allows us to identify the highest standards of play for fans to admire and players to emulate.

South Africa used to dominate rugby. Then boycotts of the apartheid regime, including in sports, cut South Africa off from international competition. When apartheid ended and the Springboks returned to the world rugby scene, both the players and the fans were shocked to see that their admitted size and power, which used to enable them to dominate the game so effortlessly, were no longer enough. The style of world play had moved on, leaving South Africa behind. South African competitiveness had been damaged because they had been deprived of the co-operative aspect of play, learning from other players how to play the game to the highest standard *today*, not twenty years ago.

This metaphor applies to every kind of social activity. It applies in business, where knowledge entrepreneurs are constantly trying out new ways of offering consumers both old and new goods and services. These entrepreneurs sometimes displace well-established suppliers who cannot keep up with the times. Sometimes they crash and burn as the Edsels sit unsold on the lot or Blackberry and Nokia sales plummet.

The metaphor applies in other areas of civil society as well. Service clubs like the Shriners and Elks seem to be in decline, but Web-connected groups based on shared interests seem to be thriving. Volunteer groups like March of Dimes find their cause falters because of medical and public health innovation but animal shelters helping koalas injured in the Australian wildfires raise millions in just days. People don't show up to bowl with their neighbours but spend endless hours playing on-line games with people they have never met.

In all these cases, competition didn't "drive out" well-performing organizations that "deserved" to survive. Organizations deserve to survive because they serve human needs. What competition within the framework of social co-operation does is reveal who is doing precisely that. As Nobel prize-winning economist F.A. Hayek famously said, "competition is a discovery procedure." Competition reveals who, today, right now, has the knowledge that satisfies the needs of people as expressed by their willingness to part with their time and money. And part of what competition reveals is what we want that we didn't even know we wanted.

So the alleged opposition between co-operation (good) and competition (bad) is complete nonsense. Co-operation and competition are inextricably bound together. And competition under grown rules of social co-operation is exactly how the gardener knows we put the most knowledge to work while weeding out the efforts of individuals and groups that cease to meet our needs. And being "weeded out" is also valuable information. Bankruptcy, for example, signals that a business as currently organized and run couldn't convince people to part with enough of their hard-earned money to enable it to pay its way.

Monopoly is not just a game

Now contrast the social function of competition as a knowledge discovery procedure with the strong natural tendency on the part of designing political authorities to solve problems by coming up with the "best" solution, based, of course, on the most expert opinion, and then to take control and impose that solution on everyone, including those who know better. Of course, designers are offended by the notion that someone might know something better than they do. "We have consulted all the McKinseyites and Harvard PhDs we could find and they assured us that in theory this is the best solution!" Of course since it is the best solution, they insist that they are doing us all a favour if they put a stop to "wasteful" competition and make everyone fall in line with the "best" answer.

This explains why politicians so often resort to *monopoly* to supply the things they have "heard" that people want. Monopolies, by their nature, are resistant to change and technological innovation; once in place they become a technology backwater run by the authorities in the interests of the people responsible for them and who work there rather than the people who must use their product or service. Classic examples are the post office, the fixed-line telephone system, most urban transit, much of the old-style broadcasting system (premised on the mistaken technological assumption of spectrum scarcity), supply management, and public power monopolies. They also include numerous industries that shelter behind various forms of protection from takeover, new entrants, or other market pressures, and include banks, airlines, and telecommunications companies (which are oligopolies, which is to say clubs of providers shielded in various ways from the bracing winds of competition). It is no surprise that these protected organizations always top the list of poorly performing sectors of the Canadian economy in terms of innovation, no matter how profitable they may be. Gardeners are of the view that their profits come far more from their privileged legal status and protection from vigorous competition than from their service to the people who have little choice but to use their products.

Innovation (which is just a fancy word for one of the key benefits of competition), is an expression of human ingenuity directed toward solving practical problems while working under the constraint that people won't pay more for your solution to their problem than the cost of living with the problem. And that is why innovation hates a monopoly like nature abhors a vacuum. Monopolies, whether public or private, reverse the power relationship that exists in grown social institutions, which is subject to the discipline of competition and where most real innovation occurs. Grown institutions give power to people, who control resources and choose what they want.

Monopoly gives power to monopolists at the expense of consumers, who have to take what monopolists dish out regardless of its quality.

The classic example of monopoly run riot and its devastating effect on people's lives is the Soviet Union and its imitators. Under their five-year plans, state bureaucrats would determine in advance what people would get. Shoe factories and car manufacturers and steel mills and television makers would be told to produce a certain quantity of their product but did so with no feedback from consumers (who couldn't shop around, go to competing suppliers, or get the colours and styles they wanted unless they were lucky enough to want what those in charge of the Plan thought they should have). Even then, people were subject to the vagaries of the distribution system. The Soviet shoe factory might produce the colour you want in the style you want but if the store had already sold what you wanted good luck in getting more. You got what you were given and had to be happy about it. Thus was Soviet life an endless tale of gloomy queuing for whatever the shops had to offer.

The Soviet example may be extreme, but sometimes you have to push things to their logical conclusion to see where they lead. I've mentioned a number of analogous state-created monopolies in Canada. The comfortable (for owners) taxi monopoly in most cities is one, and ride-sharing services like Uber and Lyft are a classic case of how innovation even in the face of political and bureaucratic resistance is beating at the gates of privilege. I'll talk about Uber, ride sharing, taxis, and rapid transit in the chapter on life in the city.

Another is the monopoly often granted to bus operators to cover certain intercity routes. When Greyhound announced it was ending all its service in Western Canada, the predictable outcry was that rural regions were being abandoned by government. Yet what government, through regulation and the conferring of unjustified privilege on one company had instead done was to prevent smaller, nimbler, and more efficient operators arising to fill the gap. There is, in fact, a great deal of spare capacity to carry people around the country; just think of all the vans and cars and trucks sitting idle much of the day, or that are moving cargo around but are only partially filled. Information technology has made the costs of matching willing service providers and willing passengers more or less zero, blasting into oblivion the principal justification for collective provision through monopoly.

In the old days, we solved the knowledge problem of matching rides and riders by the terribly inefficient and wasteful means of having designated pick-up spots and fixed times of departure ("timetables") in relatively easily available form. But this is a crude and inconvenient system compared to one where competing small providers and widely dispersed potential riders can contact each other instantaneously and arrange pick-up times and locations that are mutually workable. Once technology solved the matching problem, the old government solution, like all solutions that rely on collective provision rather than individual choice and entrepreneurial response, became not the solution but the problem. By protecting one provider, the government made the decision that people who needed to get around and didn't own a car would have only one choice, in this case, Greyhound. The predictable result was rising prices and falling standards of service.

Now that Greyhound has pulled out of Western Canada, the problem, equally predictably, is not no service, but government regulatory obstruction of the solution. That solution is what designers call "illegal carpooling." By attempting to obstruct that solution designers force the people who are trying to fill the need for transport and their customers to act in defiance of the law just for the privilege of moving around. The solution is exactly the one adopted by many places with respect to Uber, namely, creating a new class of insurance so that such micro-operators are properly insured, thus discharging through private insurers the state's responsibility to ensure that the public does not run unreasonable risks in going about their business in the hands of operators about whom they can know relatively little.[45]

Careful readers will have noticed that there is something that unites these monopolistic protected interests. They are all *producers* of a product or service. Producers share some interesting characteristics, especially producers who have been around for a while.

Taxi drivers and owners, steel plant workers, auto workers, and dairy farmers, to mention just a few examples, derive in most cases their entire income from the industry they work in. They work together and know one another. The benefits they get from their work are highly concentrated and there are lots of them. That makes them politically powerful because the interests they share are easily identifiable, very large (and therefore motivating) and they are acutely aware of their interests and will organize politically and vote in support of them.

The people who are stuck with no choice about the good or service in question have completely different characteristics. They are dispersed. The interest they have in competitive provision of the producers' product is relatively small (in the case of dairy, for example, the average family in Canada is said to spend about $400 more each year for their groceries, especially dairy products, than they would in a competitive market with free entry for competitors).[46] They are often not even aware of the costs they are paying to protect producers from competition. So they are ill-organized and unmotivated. They are unlikely to vote for parties that promise to save them $400 on groceries, but producers are very likely indeed to vote for parties that promise to "stand up for Canadian jobs" like theirs.

Yet the purpose of the economy is to serve consumers. And the consumer interest is universal (we all have to buy cars and clothes and shelter) whereas the producer interest is narrow and concentrated. Steel workers don't have the same interests as dairy farmers who don't have the same interests as taxi drivers. In fact, steelworkers have an interest in cheaper dairy, and when dairy farmers need a ride they'd prefer it to cost less, not more.

So the consumer interest is universal (we are all consumers) and the producer interest is narrow. Politicians therefore have a moral duty to protect the consumer interest and not cave into the siren call of narrow protectionism, which is nothing more than the granting of unjustified privilege to a few. More importantly, *protectionism makes us stupid*, because the producers who clamour for protection are by definition those whose knowledge of what we want and how to satisfy it is less than the knowledge their competitors bring to the table. Otherwise they wouldn't need protection.

Gardeners, being deeply practical people, understand that this is a political dilemma that cannot be waved away by a magic wand. And angry workers displaced by technological change are not used tissues to be tossed on the scrapheap of history, but real human beings who are often blameless and powerless in the face of their industry's decline and the evolution of human knowledge that has brought that decline in its wake.

Indifference in these matters, or an airy dismissal of people's genuine fears, or phony empathy (a Clintonesque "I feel your pain") gets you a Trumpian populist backlash, as forgotten people and forgotten places[47] fall victim to ineluctable social forces that the experts assure them are for their own good. Ideology is no answer. Gardeners are of the view that more information is always better than less, and so tend to oppose hiding the cost of economic change in obscure subsidies and regulatory obstacles to change. If protectionism is necessary, it should always have a clear end point and decline over time. Compensation, including through generous social programs but also the buying out of old privileges (like supply management or taxi licences), are justified when the state drew people into an industry by misrepresenting to them the true state of demand for what they do. Perhaps most important of all, governments need to ask themselves what they do that prevents the emergence of alternatives. In rural areas, for example, supply management and inefficient bus service are often seen as evidence of the commitment of the rest of society to the continued existence of rural life. But at the same time, through ill-advised laws and regulatory regimes, we obstruct the emergence of a more vibrant rural economy.

In the agriculture and food sector, for example, as I have written elsewhere,[48] Canada's share of the world food market is declining despite rising demand and Canada's world-leading endowment of resources and capacity. Similarly, the government's ill-concealed hostility to the natural resource economy has placed a damper on the economic prospects of rural Canada. In both cases these are largely self-inflicted wounds. We as a society will find it easier to create opportunities that ease the transition from older industries when we stop obstructing the emergence of the new and the growth of the successful. Resistance to change will be less when people see there are realistic alternatives, not pie-in-the-sky green jobs that don't exist using technology that doesn't yet work.

As we discussed in Chapters II and III, the argument that planners and designers are inescapably ignorant is not changed by the fact that some people do not have enough money to be able to purchase the necessities of life and are therefore excluded from participating in the choices that participatory grown social institutions maximize. That some of us have an insufficient income is a problem of determining how to establish a minimum standard of living so that everyone has the wherewithal to participate, not a reason for junking choice-maximizing participatory grown social institutions.

So far I have been talking about how politically imposed monopolies reverse the power relationship between the monopolists and consumers of their products. Designers, however, often invoke the alleged "monopoly power" of private companies as a reason to get rid of them and put politically controlled suppliers in their place.

In one sense, they are on to something. Monopoly does indeed invert the power relationship between individuals consuming stuff (you and me) and producers providing it, and this is true whether the monopolist is owned by the state or by private interests. But as Confucius once remarked, when words lose their meaning, people lose their liberty. George Orwell mined this rich idea in both *Animal Farm* and *Nineteen Eighty-Four*, showing how political authorities crave to redefine inconvenient words, making them tools of ideology rather than enemies of obfuscation.

So when valuable words are misused, we have a responsibility to rebel. Monopoly is just one such word. In a classic case, PayPal co-founder Peter Thiel claimed that search-engine giant Google enjoys a monopoly in the Internet search business because it has not faced any serious competition since 2002.[49] Competitors like Yahoo! and Microsoft's Bing complain it is hard to make inroads against Google's dominance.

I mention Microsoft because of the irony that the firm complaining today was itself the target of numerous legal challenges in the 1990s because of its dominance of the operating system market. Similarly, IBM was repeatedly targeted by regulators and courts in an earlier era for its dominance of the computer industry.

In all these cases, the companies were frequently referred to as "monopolists" whose "monopoly power" needed to be whittled down to size. This was not true of Microsoft or IBM then, and it is not true of Google today.

It is wrong for an obvious reason: monopolists, by definition, are the only game in town. The absence of alternative suppliers is a key part of the definition of monopoly, and in all these cases the companies in question faced many competitors.

Take Google. Several years ago, according to US Internet data firm Comscore, "69.0 percent of [US] searches carried organic search results from Google . . . while 26.6 percent of searches were powered by Bing." By 2019 Google's dominance was even more pronounced, with nearly 89 percent of US searches being handled by Google.[50]

The fact that the competitors weren't as big as Google or IBM or Microsoft is not in itself evidence of their having done something wrong. On the contrary, as Google correctly observes, its competitors are only a click away. If Google doesn't provide value, the barriers to shifting to an alternative supplier are risible.

Google was born a mere twenty-one years ago[51] while founders Larry Page and Sergey Brin were working out of the proverbial friend's garage. As one observer notes, "Google's combination of clever algorithms, advanced search operators and sophisticated ad programs like AdWords quickly propelled it to the top of the search engine market."[52]

In other words, it was the value that Google created for consumers, despite the existence of competitive alternatives, that powered its rise. This is the very opposite of monopoly, which is not a synonym for "companies that got big because consumers really like what they do." It is this that Google has accomplished, as did Microsoft and IBM before it.

This idea of whether new providers face barriers if they want to challenge the dominant supplier is also key in assessing whether monopoly exists. To compete in the landline telephone business, the upfront capital cost to make your phone connect with every other phone is huge. Ditto if you want to supply natural gas, electricity, rail, or a few other such services. On the other hand, technology increasingly provides alternatives to many services, as mobile telephony does to landline telephony.

In information technology the barriers to entry are few and low. Just ask Blackberry, which went from dominating the smartphone industry to an also-ran in the blink of an eye because it failed to keep up with industry trends, driven by consumers hungry for what alternative suppliers offered.

Who rails today against Microsoft's "monopoly" in operating systems? Answering this question gives us insight into another part of understanding what really constitutes "monopoly." In an open market without insuperable barriers to entry, even a single dominant supplier does not enjoy monopoly power, in the sense of the power to charge what it likes for its services while preventing the emergence of competitors.

Indeed, the existence of a dominant and highly profitable supplier is a huge blinking billboard signalling a rich opportunity. Every David with a garage and some programming skills rightly sets his sights on getting a piece of the action by cutting Goliath down to size. This threat alone keeps dominant suppliers from charging whatever they want.

Technological change is the chief reason why the brilliant economist Joseph Schumpeter (of "creative destruction" fame) thought that anti-trust cases were a monumental waste of time. The moment of dominance enjoyed by one company is necessarily rendered fleeting by market incentives and technology's effervescence. History is littered with the corpses of companies that relied on their momentary market dominance to see them through and failed to respond to evolving technology and consumer preferences. Just remember what happened to the nineteenth century's oil, steel and rail "trusts," how GM's dominance of the North American car industry was brought low, and how Kodak was humbled by the smartphone camera.

Real monopolies are ones where privileged suppliers are insulated from competition, technological change, and having to respond to what people actually want. Sounds like the government-protected industries I mentioned earlier: health care, taxis, broadcasting, supply management and the post office. Despite having the punitive power of the state at their back, falling barriers to entry and technological change will fell these industries too. Time is on our side. But a lot of time, energy, and money will be wasted in the meantime. I will discuss a gardener's strategy for dealing with such unjustified privilege in later chapters.

Are there grounds for optimism that such undirected experimentation does not leave human beings worse off, that Adam Smith's Invisible Hand is in fact on balance benevolent rather than an Invisible Boot? After all, that is the belief driving much of today's public policy in areas such as the environment, or urban planning, or health care, to choose just three. In all these cases, the belief is firmly anchored, at least in the mind of governments and many others, that "unplanned" change is bad, and therefore that all human activity must be brought under the direction of a controlling mind that has an overview of what can and should happen as human society develops.

If you have been following the unfolding of my thinking so far, you will know that I believe this is not a formula for human flowering, but human wilting. I will apply the gardener's way of thinking to each of these three policy areas in turn in later chapters. Before we get there, however, I'd like to take a moment to look at the application of gardener ideas to a different public policy challenge, namely how to accommodate the vast explosion of diverse human identities that has been such a feature of our society in recent decades.

CHAPTER V

Identity, justice, and representation

DENTITY HAS ALWAYS MATTERED. At the time of Confederation, the identities that mattered most were Catholics and Protestants, English-speakers and French-speakers, Irish, Scots, English and *Canadiens*. Rural and urban, educated and non-educated, Habs fans vs. Leafs fans came later. Now we are focused on women and men, Indigenous and non-Indigenous, Caucasians and people of colour, newcomers versus Canadians *de vieille souche,* and LGBTQ(etc.) versus heterosexuals. As has always been the case, claims are made about what group identity means, what disadvantages group membership brings, and what benefits it confers.

Identity has become a particularly vigorous form of political weapon, with claims advanced on all sides about what Group X has suffered, needs, or is entitled to. In fact for designers, identities and their distribution in society have become a defining issue of our time. Entire social media platforms are aquiver with and millions of hashtags are conceived for the raging debates over whether or not different groups are well enough represented in parliament, the courts, the universities, advertising, and every other field of human activity.

On the vexed question of identity, however, as I said in Chapter I, gardeners view people not first and foremost as black or transgender or Chinese or Muslim or Irish or Indigenous. They are Canadians who enjoy the freedom to choose the identities that matter to them. And the identities that they *choose* will almost certainly be different from the identities that progressive designers think matter.

This can be true because identity can be thought of as an internal self-understanding, the way I as an individual decide to define and weigh the parts of my character and personality and genetic and ethnic endowment, what I put to the fore and what I consider to be secondary, what I invest time and effort in and what I leave in the dusty attic of memory. But identity can also be seen from the outside, without the benefit of the self-understandings that give identity meaning. Thus we can say that some percentage of the population "are" or "identify as" black or indigenous or bisexual or men or Sikhs or university graduates or parents or homeowners or suburbanites or soccer mums. These are objective, countable things. Either you live in the suburbs or you don't. Either you have children or you don't.

Where progressive designers get into trouble is in assuming that objectively observable characteristics define identity and therefore interests: that visible minorities have interests that distinguish them from whites; that women have interests that distinguish them from men; that Muslims have interests that distinguish them from Jews and Christians; or that the working class has interests that distinguish them from owners of capital.

The larger the objective countable group, the more political power ought to be exercised to promote their "interests." Similarly, the more vulnerable a group is thought to be, the greater the moral claim for political power to promote "their" interests. But the gardener believes that attributing interests to complex individuals based on their observable objective characteristics leaves out of account the single most important thing about any particular individual: what that person wants for themselves. A person is not merely the totality of their membership in various groups; there is at the core of each person a mind and a will and a character that decides what pieces of their identity matter. In fact gardeners deny that you can know much of anything important about people by totting up their externally observable characteristics.

The mystery of identity

This is best understood through concrete examples. Take a young man I know who is a fascinating study in the mystery of human identity. His father is a bi-sexual American of Italian descent, his mother a Quebecoise whose father was European. The young man's sister was born in the United States (where their mother was at the time an immigrant), but he himself was born and raised a member of the French-speaking minority in a western province.

Both his parents were immigrants there, although in different ways. He then lived for many years in the Maritimes, attending a French-language school. His identity draws on these (and many other) roots. In terms of his "group identification" he is by turns Italian (when the World Cup of soccer is on), bilingual Canadian (in outraged opposition to Quebec nationalism), American (he wants to visit every American state before he will even countenance the idea of visiting Europe), and Acadian (because of his shared experience with many pupils from that background).

He is heterosexual but sympathizes with sexual minorities because of his father. He is a man but cares deeply about the professional success of the women in his life. He is predominantly an English-speaker but cares about the French-speaking minorities in whose life he participated while simultaneously rejecting Quebec nationalism despite his mother's nationalist sympathies.

From an identity point of view, this young man is not exceptional. He is the rule, although perhaps slightly more complex than the average. And we have all known people like him. There are aristocratic left wingers (Enrico Berlinguer and Tony Benn), Protestant leaders of Irish Catholic nationalism (Grattan and Parnell), people of working class origin who went on to be wealthy businesspeople (Howard Schultz and J.K. Rowling), men who championed the rights of women (John Stuart Mill and Sir John A. Macdonald) and whites who led the fight to abolish slavery and establish equal rights for people of all races (Josiah Wedgewood and Abraham Lincoln).

Importantly, inside, each of us has an identity that is similarly complex to this young man's. Just like my former roommate who discovered he wasn't an urban accountant but a rural rancher.

I could multiply the examples, but the point is clear: identity is fluid, and group membership is something that shifts and changes according to the context in which we find ourselves and to our current state of knowledge about ourselves. Each of us occupies a series of overlapping and cross-cutting roles. The elements of our identity are drawn from the experiences that constitute our lives, but which experiences will be deeply integrated, and which superficial is precisely the mystery of human identity.

The point to underline here is that the young man in question is the person at the centre of those cross-cutting claims on his allegiance and identity. That is what it is to be a person; he makes order and meaning for himself out of the raw materials that the whirlwind of life is throwing his way. Others might not always agree with the choices that he makes in refining and fashioning those raw materials, but from a moral point of view that is irrelevant. It is irrelevant because the respect we owe him is not based on his choices, but on a recognition of our respective duties and responsibilities. I have a duty to honour his right to choose for himself because I claim such a right for myself. He and he alone must be responsible for his choices, and live with their consequences.

The political ramifications of this were brilliantly summed up for me by a Saatchi and Saatchi poster used by the Conservative Party during the 1983 British general election. It showed a photo of a black man. He was no caricature designed to stir up negative emotions, just an ordinary-looking bloke. The caption underneath read, "Labour says he's black. Tories say he's British." In other words, the message was that Labour saw him principally as a member of a group, one that had identifiable interests based on their shared skin colour, interests that set him apart from other citizens. The Tories, by contrast, saw someone who was British and therefore had the same rights and responsibilities as everyone else – a right to fair treatment and justice, for example, not because of a group identity that set him apart, but because of a shared identity that gave rise to mutual claims.

A different way of putting it is that the poster drew attention to two ways that group membership could be relevant to politics. It can either be I am different, it is my difference that entitles me to something, and my group is owed something by your group; or it can be we are the same in the ways that matter, what unites us both matters more than what divides us but it also gives us mutual claims against each other for respect for the choices that we make. One puts the accent on objective identifiers like race, on *difference*, the other puts the accent on subjective identity and the choosing character at the core of each person within society, on *commonality*.

The reason this matters is that there will always be differences between people and how they want to live and the groups they want to identify with. In making claims on other members of society, *the strategy that starts from difference is a dangerous one*. Here's why: if your argument is that you are different and treated differently than others and this differential treatment should stop, the response is quite likely to be, but I thought your argument was that you were different. The differential treatment you complain of is due to your difference. Who said that being different should only confer benefits?

Contrast this with an approach that says you and I are the same in the ways that matter. If you look at the way I am treated you will agree that you would not want to be treated this way and so what can justify the difference in treatment between us? The answer is far more likely to be, you are correct. Because we are the same in the ways that matter, differential treatment like this cannot be justified.

The mystery of identity is what makes the second approach possible. What we have in common is our humanity (our ability and even compulsion to learn who we are and what elements of our experience and person matter to us) and our membership in the state (citizenship). You may not agree with my choices of identity, but you agree that you and I both make choices and our choices are what define us (including deciding what groups we decide matter to us). We must respect and not impede each other's choices. And society is the framework within which we discuss and decide how equal and just treatment is to be conceived and put into practice for all our members. In other words, we focus on the chooser, not what is chosen.

It doesn't help to say that you don't "choose" to be a woman or black or gay. The thing to remember is we all choose what elements of our person and experience we give priority to, what matters to us, what groups we *feel* we belong to. We get to decide that for ourselves. It's a subjective choice.

Objective group membership doesn't define us. We choose what we care about. Put another way, you may not be able to choose whether you are a woman (although the transgender folks would assert vociferously that you *can* choose) or whether you are black or gay in some objective group identification sense, but you get to choose what being a woman or a black or a gay person *means to you.*

Andrea Dworkin, Anita Bryant, Germaine Greer, Helen Gurley Brown, Phyllis Schlafly, Maya Forstater, and Angela Merkel are all women, but would have wildly divergent views about what that means. George Elliott Clark, Walter Williams, Louis Farrakhan, Malcolm X, Martin Luther King, Ann Cools, Colin Powell, Shelby Steele and Thomas Sowell are all black but would vigorously debate the meaning of being black and how that can and should fit into a larger narrative of an individual life. Martin Luther King's dream was of a society where people would be judged, not on something as superficial as the colour of their skin (because of how little that fact tells you about the person inside the skin), but on "the content of their [individual] character."

Process or outcomes?

Choosing what groups we care about is part of the larger choice we make in life about who we become. The state, therefore, cannot be in the business of making sure that our choices succeed. That would be taking us into the territory of privileging certain choices over others, and while in the history of our political and social tradition we cannot claim that such privileged groups have not existed, what we can also say is that each time it has been allowed to happen it has quickly degenerated into a source of endless social friction. History is littered with societies riven with conflict because the members of some groups (ethnic, ideological, genealogical, caste, religious) were meted out preferred treatment because of their group membership. Lots of new Canadians have come here to escape such societies, just as previous generations of Canadians struggled hard to rid our society of the vestiges of such unmerited privilege handed down from the past.

What the state can and must do is to ensure procedural fairness for individuals. Discriminating against individual women or gays or Indigenous people or Jamaicans is not on. The state is justified in putting significant resources into this because equal treatment for citizens, equal protection for the protected sphere of choice that surrounds us, and equal opportunity are the promises of liberal-democratic societies like Canada.

In much of what will follow I will argue that there is in fact very little evidence nowadays of discrimination against individual members of identifiable minorities in the workplace in large part because of the effort we have made in recent decades to root out just such discrimination. I acknowledge, however, that the situation where women and minorities have a legally recognized and protected choice in the work that they can choose to do is a relatively recent one. Nothing that I am saying here is intended to deny that in the past women and minorities were indeed discriminated against in the workforce, often in a systematic way. The thing to bear in mind here, however, is that the data are in my view quite compelling that discrimination is *today* a vanishingly small factor in the labour market and the choices individuals make about what they want to do are of much greater importance.

Those instances of identifiable discrimination that surface, such as in the RCMP or the armed forces, are rightly the subject of political scandal and a great deal of effort is put into rooting them out. These are the exceptions that prove the rule. The knowledge you possess now matters a great deal more than your membership in objective groups. Just to pick one example, in 1990, women with postsecondary education were not as successful as men in finding work. Today, women with postsecondary education have pulled away from men without postsecondary education and are approaching the employment levels of men with such education levels.[53] We have established conditions where women now dominate many fields and outnumber men in postsecondary institutions. We don't need to deny that discrimination existed in the past to say that we don't allow it to operate any more and that where any vestiges are uncovered they are dealt with energetically and severely.

That said, what the state cannot do once procedural fair treatment for individuals is ensured is to see to it that your freedom to make your own choices about what matters to you will result in a pleasing pattern of outcomes for groups of which you happen, objectively, to be a member. There are three reasons for this. One, because only individuals, not groups, have claims to procedural fairness. Two, the outcome for groups, no matter what it is, is not evidence of the success or failure of the individuals who make up that group in pursuing their own choices. Finally, three, you cannot achieve "fairness" for groups without treating individuals unfairly.

Individuals are entitled to procedural fairness (equal treatment before the law, non-discrimination, etc.) because the purpose of society is to encompass and support the unfolding of individual human personality and character. That unfolding takes place through the choices we make for ourselves in a context of imperfect information about ourselves and the world. We learn who we are by living, and that includes the choices of the groups and interests we identify with.

Procedural fairness ensures that no one improperly interferes with your freedom to make these choices and particularly that the state does not dictate to you what to choose; nor does it reward or punish you for your choices. The state does not *protect your choices*, it protects *you the chooser*. What use you make of this ability is no one's concern but your own, largely because no one knows you as well as you know yourself. No one is in a position to choose better for you than you are, although that in itself is no guarantee of good or successful choices.

Once we have ensured procedural fairness for individuals, groups are not entitled to some extra protection on top of that afforded to those who choose to belong to those groups. Groups are not choosers; they are chosen. And nothing about the choices an individual might make is to be inferred from their objective membership in a group. As the earlier example of the young man with the complex identity shows, what groups people actually identify with is a not a clear or unambiguous process and identity must not be assumed or inferred by authorities based on objective group membership.

Second, then, what can we conclude if the members of some objective group are under-represented in the law or the media or the universities? Absolutely nothing at all. Simple objective group membership tells us nothing about what complex subjective individuals have done with their freedom to choose. There is no reason to think, for example, that all members of the black community would make the same choices for themselves in the same proportions as all members of the Chinese or Jewish or immigrant community. If preferences were identically distributed among objective groups, it would possibly be different, but they are not, and there are tremendous variations within groups as well as between groups.

Moreover, because resources (say, money and jobs) in a liberal-democratic society like ours are necessarily distributed among individuals based on an impersonal assessment of their unequal individual contribution to human satisfaction and not on the basis of their equal moral worth, resources will always appear arbitrarily distributed between both individuals and groups. Universal free education and a social safety net help to compensate to some degree, but a society that wants to use all of the knowledge so widely dispersed in the minds of its members has to let those members act freely in pursuit of their own goals while rewarding them based on the value of their service to others.

Once we establish that individuals will not be treated in a discriminatory manner, and that people may pursue their own goals with the share of society's resources their knowledge has earned for them, the place of each individual within society will be quite unpredictable. Rather, it will be based, importantly, on what the individual thinks matters most to them. The fact that this may produce different outcomes for people who happen to share certain arbitrary characteristics reveals very little and certainly is not evidence of "systemic" discrimination against all members of the group. In the absence of evidence of discrimination against identifiable individuals by identifiable other individuals (and the organisations they represent), the distribution of desired things like income, jobs and professional status is not the result chiefly of improper discrimination. Instead, it results from the choices that people make for themselves and society's impersonal evaluation of the worth of different kinds of knowledge.

Take the unshakable article of faith among progressives that there is a wage gap between men and women and that this gap is explained entirely by discrimination by men against women. This claim is ubiquitous. Then-President Obama said in 2012 that women are paid "77 cents on the dollar for *doing the same work as men,*" a claim rightly rated as "Mostly False" by *Politifact.*[54] Study after study has attempted to document this phenomenon. Alas, those studies consistently show that a very small part of the gap is potentially explicable by discrimination by men against women. The bulk of it is explicable by the different choices many women make compared to the choices that many men make. The outcomes for men and women who make similar choices are virtually indistinguishable.[55]

More women than men prefer, for example, the "caring professions" such as nursing and counselling which do not pay as well as a number of professions and trades where men predominate. But since wages are not set by men per se, but by an impersonal social process controlled by no one, this is no evidence of systemic discrimination against women, but rather is evidence of the relative availability of people wanting to pursue these different professions and the value people attach to the services offered by the practitioners of this or that profession or trade. Claiming that women "should" want to be more present in other lines of work is doing just what public authorities ought not to do, which is to make judgments about how people choose to live.

Similarly, more women than men prefer flexible and part-time work, possibly because they feel more responsible for children and aged parents. Public authorities can wring their hands and rail against the "pattern" of income distribution and promotions that this creates, but as long as these are the choices that people make for themselves in complex circumstances they know better than anyone else, it is not the state's business to second guess them. Even if, given different circumstances, some women might choose differently, the point is that this is how they *do* choose for themselves in the circumstances they have helped to create through their choices. We all might make different choices if our circumstances were different. We are interested in the actual choices people make in the real circumstances of their lives.

Other factors enter into the calculation. Women tend to marry men older than themselves and length of time in the workforce tends to lead to higher incomes. It may well therefore make sense within a family for a younger woman to take on child care responsibilities (which she may prefer to child care by strangers anyway), possibly accompanied by part-time work while allowing her husband to work full-time, thus maximizing the family's income *and* child care preferences.

An interesting piece of research emerged not too long ago that tested the reasons for income differentials between men and women in a situation where the sex of the subjects was demonstrably excluded as a determining factor. This study looked at the earnings of male and female Uber drivers.[56] The algorithm that offers rides to drivers takes no account of the sex of the driver, and so the people studying the incomes of drivers expected to find that there would be no significant difference between their earnings.

Instead, they found a seven percent difference. Discrimination? No. Part of the difference was due to the fact that men drive slightly faster than women (not a huge difference – we're not talking *The Fast and Furious* here). Men drove on average one percent faster than women (so if women drove on average 50 km/h, men on average drove 50.5 km/h); that's enough to account for one half of the earnings gap because over time a faster driver can take on more fares. The rest was down to where and when drivers chose to make themselves available, and how long they'd been driving for Uber (which gave them insight into how to make the Uber algorithm work in their favour).

Setting aside what the data show about the many factors that affect the earnings of individual men and women, there is a different way to come at this which is always met with silence by those who make the case that "systemic discrimination" explains wage gaps between groups. It has been illegal for many years, at both the federal and the provincial level, to pay different people differently for doing the same work. If such blatant discrimination against individuals was actually occurring on the kind of scale necessary to explain differential group outcomes, there would be a hue and cry in parliament and the media, class action suits would be launched and human rights commissions would have to hire new staff to keep up with the backlog. But none of this activity is to be seen.[57] Yet if we cannot establish that specific individuals have been discriminated against by specific employers, we cannot turn around and say that the pattern of income distribution to specific groups (like "all women") must be the result of discrimination.

One strategy for doing just that is to say that the problem is not a failure to offer equal pay for the same job (although that claim is often made too); rather the complaint is that women are not being paid equally for work of *equal value*, a completely different proposition.

This takes us right back to the way in which, in our society, the value of work is determined, which is to say by an impersonal process that takes account of the state of supply and demand of different kinds of knowledge. No one determines this, and employers are just as bound by this impersonal process as employees.

"Experts" who do studies alleging to show how Job A is actually of "equal value" to Job B but yields different pay, which therefore is evidence of discrimination, deserve a prize for fiction writing. Much as designers might like to kid themselves that such analytical comparisons are possible, in reality if there are many fewer people willing to do Job A than Job B and if those qualified to do Job B in fact possess the skills to do Job A, why don't they apply for Job A and get themselves a raise? And if the argument is not that the job involves the same skills but "comparable" skills, they are asking us to believe that their pitiful data set and analytical tools provide us with a conclusion more objective and more complete than the information gathered by the billions of transactions and choices made every day by real people, real organizations, and real firms facing real circumstances.

Making choices

Real identities are far too complex to be captured by individual objective group membership. But the decisions over employment relationships are equally complex and in real life hardly ever revolve around issues of the sex of the job applicant.

If you're a female job applicant,[58] you might look at a job and say, well, it's fifteen minutes less commuting time and that means I can pick my child up from school more reliably and still make it home in time to cook dinner on those days when my partner isn't cooking. I really like the location because it's close to a shopping centre and I can do my shopping over the lunch hour rather than taking up scarce time on the weekend. The other staff seem nicer than the other job farther away and I liked the fact that they seemed to care about work-life balance whereas the other employer made it clear that they were under some heavy-duty deadlines and needed people to be available when the job required it. The benefits and salary were a little better there though, and I am going to need a root canal soon, etc., etc., etc.

Employers go through a similarly complicated calculus: Betty seemed nice and would fit in here, which is important because Bob (whose specialist knowledge makes him irreplaceable) can be a pain sometimes and a sympathetic co-worker seems to help. She has good qualifications and has stayed a goodly period of time with each of her previous employers, so she might stay here, making it worthwhile to invest in some extra training. Frank's qualifications were a little more impressive, but he seemed way too interested in how much vacation time he could negotiate and seemed to feel that he knew more about the job than I did, but actually I did that job for ten years before being promoted. I am really desperate to fill this job. It's been vacant for two months and it is starting to affect our productivity. Are we paying enough these days for this kind of work? I wonder how much Doug across the road paid when he hired Martha last month? I should ask him.

Every such decision is driven not by abstract things like "what group do you belong to" but concrete and practical things like "how well do I think this person can do the job?" and "would this gig be a good fit for me given all the things I am trying to balance in my life?"

Since objective group membership is a tiny factor in the decisions about hiring, and given that discrimination against individuals is properly ruled out and carries heavy penalties, any after-the-fact calculation of how jobs are distributed across objective abstract groups is not compelling evidence of anything, let alone something so nefarious as a society-wide conspiracy to prevent women or blacks or gays or (insert your preferred group here) from getting "their share" of work or income or anything else. The fact is that no one individual or group is "entitled" to a fair share of anything, whatever a "fair share" might be, itself a matter of no widespread agreement. Individuals are entitled to fair non-discriminatory treatment, because ours is thankfully a system premised on procedural fairness, not on guarantees of outcomes.

Put differently, go back to my account of one potential employment agreement. The potential employee was a woman, but that was only one (and perhaps not a very important one) of the pieces of her identity she was weighing up in deciding which job to take. She was thinking of herself as a parent, a spouse, a commuter, a shopper, a time manager, someone who needs health care, someone who has expectations about the demands of the workplace and the quality of her colleagues. And every other woman (and man, and gay person, and racial minority, and members of any other objective group you care to think of) will go through a similar balancing of interests, ambitions, hopes, and practical limitations. It would be the rare job candidate indeed who asked themselves "Do I want this job because I am a woman?" The question is too abstract to be any help in actually making a choice. The question is going to be "Do I want this job as a person trying to balance up these ten competing priorities?"

The calculation on the employer's side will be similarly tightly bound to time and place and circumstance. It will hardly ever be "Do I want a woman?" Again, too abstract. It is much more likely to be "How many of the dozen qualifications the ideal candidate would possess does this person actually have and how do I weigh those different qualities and how likely is it that after further searching a better candidate will emerge?"

The key point to remember here is that on neither side was the predominant or even particularly important factor whether the candidate was a woman. If neither party attaches strong importance to this single factor, but each made their decision on a complex skein of factors *knowable only to them*, and if the fact that a deal was struck is *prima facie* evidence that the outcome was the best deal both parties thought they could come up with in their specific circumstances, and if any attempt to smuggle in irrelevant and discriminatory factors runs the very high risk of attracting the attention of human rights commissions, the courts and the media, and if every one of the millions of employment decisions made in a year look pretty much like that, why on earth would we feel that the aggregate of all such decisions "ought" to add up to a certain distribution of, say, men and women in different professions? The answer: there is no reason to have any expectations of what the distribution is among abstract groups, membership in which was a marginal factor in the original decision.

I can hear the howls of outrage already. On your own account, the critics will say, your female candidate was worried about looking after her kids during working hours, and in a perfect world there would be free universal daycare and it wouldn't be an issue. That's true. Doubtless people will also complain that she had to think about shopping and making meals when she has a husband who might do more. Also true. But only the person doing the choosing knows exactly what choices and trade-offs she has made to make up the entire life she is living. Only she knows exactly what her husband will and won't do and what other things he does for her or their children or their parents or the house or the community that compensate for his shortcomings. Only she knows how having a child may have (not "did"; only "may have") changed her from being focused on her career to being focused on what would be best for her child, the calculation of which may include maximum unharried and unhurried time with mum. Doubtless some trade-offs she has had to accept in life are less than ideal for her. But others may be more than she could have hoped for. This is hardly unique to women.

In any case, the less-than-ideal is the circumstance she finds herself in. If circumstances had been different, she might have chosen differently. Okay, but this is true of everyone. Comparing a person's real world choices against some theoretical set of ideal circumstances is really a thinly disguised way of saying that you don't respect and honour the choices she did make. If only she had chosen differently, more women would make it to the top of the legal profession, or break the glass ceiling in the executive office, or become astronauts, or rise up the ranks of the STEM professions. If only employers "hired more women" and therefore chose differently, more of these good things would happen too. But since these decisions aren't made on that basis by the parties, who are outside observers with no skin in the game to second guess the decisions made by any of the actual parties who take major risks each time they make such consequential choices? Remember the abstract designer's view of this isn't the real territory that is complex and messy, but the nice clean theoretical map. Nobody lives on a map.

Caveats anyone?

Given the storm of disapprobation that is likely to come my way for having the temerity to say that gardeners think women's choices ought to be respected whatever they are, whereas designers think that women's (and men's) choices are only to be respected when they produce an outcome that is pleasing to the designers, a few caveats may help to calm the storm slightly.

First, there is nothing wrong with thinking that the best outcome is one where men and women achieve the same results so that there are no statistical differences between the life outcomes for men and women. What matters to you just matters and no one is in a position to tell you that it is wrong to think the way you do (well, the designers will try but they are wrong to do so!). And if you and other like-minded people want to band together and proselytize for equal outcomes for men and women, and offer reasons to others why they should agree with you and act on those ideas, and you want to raise your children in a gender-role-blind household and you want to work to eliminate sex or gender stereotyping in textbooks and you want to sing the praises to girls of getting training in the STEM professions, that is your prerogative in a free society. I might even agree with much of your program.

And in a competitive world in which different individuals and organizations strive to satisfy human wants, needs and longings, if the people in your organization think that rigorous equality of outcome for male and female employees as statistical groups will confer on you an advantage, you are free to try it and see, *as long as you don't violate the principle of non-discrimination against individuals.* The whole argument I have been making is that the human condition is, among other things, often to know that things work in practice without knowing why. This is what places experimentation and innovation at the heart of human progress and why we cannot know in advance what the outcomes of different experiments will be. That's why they're called experiments.

If you think that rigorous equality of numbers of and outcomes for men and women will confer on your organization a competitive advantage in the ceaseless quest to satisfy human needs, go for it. If you want to market yourself on this basis, just as people market themselves on their environmental stewardship or their fair trade practices, or their commitment to the local community, your efforts will be watched with great interest by everyone else.

But remember that you don't get to decide whether this *in fact* confers an advantage on you. That is also the purpose of experiments: to discover what *doesn't* work. The principle underlying successful social co-operation is that we are more likely to achieve our goals when our efforts are based on real knowledge, but that real knowledge is unavoidably locked away in the minds of billions of people. Our experiments are designed to discover and then harness effectively our local, provisional and imperfect grasp of that knowledge.

If the effect of your experiment is to move your focus from *what individual people know how to do* (also called meritocracy) to *what objective groups they happen to belong to,* the likelihood (not the certainty, just the likelihood – try it and see) is that your experiment will not bring you success and will not be replicated by others.

Success will not be dictated by your theory of equality. It will be determined by the free choices of millions of people who compare what you have to offer to what others have to offer and who make their choices according to what *they* care about, not what you care about or what you think they *should* care about. If the result is not pleasing to you, the only way you can "fix" it is by saying that *other people's choices are wrong and not worthy of respect,* whereas yours are right and for the good of society they ought to be enforced on people who don't agree with them. It is on this central principle that gardeners and designers part company.

By the way, it may be worth spending just another moment on the business of knowledge. The reaction of many designers is that if the problem is an alleged differential distribution of knowledge, then education will clear that up. If, then, women are doing less well than men in the wider society, the way to fix that is through formal education. It is therefore to be celebrated that men are now under-represented compared to women in postsecondary education in Canada.[59] Surely if this continues, the problem will be resolved.

If you think this, then I have not explained myself clearly (or you may just not agree!). As Chapter II on the centrality of human ignorance tried to show, the "book-learnin'" we can acquire is actually a tiny share of the knowledge that human beings possess. Moreover, it is far from obvious that it is even the most important part. The world is littered with drop-outs (like Thomas Edison and Nick Mowbray[60]) who nonetheless succeed brilliantly. Einstein excelled at mathematics as a child, independent of his education; Mozart did the same with music. Many people trained in one area have excelled at something completely different (like my accountant/rancher roommate). Much of what we need to know to succeed cannot be taught in a classroom. And most of what you need to succeed in a profession is not taught in the professional schools you attend.

You can treat individuals or groups fairly, but not both

Many pages ago, I suggested that if all individuals are guaranteed procedural fairness and then left alone to make their own choices in their specific circumstances, the state cannot come along after the fact and "rearrange" the outcome for abstract and arbitrarily designated groups. I've already talked about the first two reasons why this is so, namely, that only individuals, not groups, have claims to procedural fairness *and* that the statistical outcome for groups is no evidence of the success or failure of the individuals who make up that group in getting the best outcome they could in their circumstances. Now we come to the third and final reason why we cannot "fix" the outcome for groups: because you cannot achieve "fairness" for groups without treating individuals unfairly, and the guarantee of procedural fairness for individuals is, in the gardener's mind, a bedrock principle of successful gardening.

There are two basic ways to fix a "maldistribution" of desired things (like jobs and income) among members of different abstract groups. One is to take it from the group in official disfavour and transfer it to the group in official favour. No one has yet had the courage to say what is likely in their heart, namely, that men or Caucasians or heterosexuals should be put out of their jobs in order to make way for the members of under-represented groups. The reason no one has suggested it, I imagine, is that everyone knows the outcry would reverberate from the Atlantic to the Pacific to the Arctic. And the outcry would be justified because such a policy would be plainly unjust and discriminatory and hugely disruptive of everyone affected. Since it would have to be a decision by those in authority, it would also have to involve a decision not just to favour one objective group but to punish the members of another objective group.

Yet those paying the price would not themselves be the authors of the "wrong" of systemic discrimination that the new policy was designed to correct; the wrong is by definition committed by "institutions" that have allowed "systemic discrimination" to take root. And gardeners are of the view that the logical deduction from successful social co-operation, both in Canada and abroad, is that individuals enjoy a protected sphere of action that entitles them to the value that their knowledge produces for others. This entitlement can only be taken away if you have wrongly obtained it. You cannot use force or fraud or theft to get it. But these forbidden behaviours cannot be practised on you either. If you have committed no wrongful act, you may not be punished in a society under the rule of law where individuals enjoy equal treatment before the law.

It is interesting to note that while the removal of innocent people from their jobs by public authority would be ruled out of court immediately by public opinion, the same is not true of income. Public opinion seems to regard the incomes of the higher earners to be endlessly pillageable, perhaps because "my income" seems rather more abstract than "my job." And yet legitimately earned income is even more obviously the result of the success-ful use of knowledge for the benefit of others than the simple occupying of a job. We can all admit the principle that there are public services that only the state can provide, that everyone should bear the cost of those services, and that the tax burden should be based on ability to pay. None of that commits one to the principle that just any old level of taxation is legitimate.

This is a practical matter of judgment, however, not one of principle; taxation levels are a continuing matter of experimentation by competing societies and this places practical limits on the levels of taxation that any society can impose without driving valuable people, organizations and capital to less heavily taxed jurisdictions. And public opinion seems to baulk at income tax rates over 50 percent, even for top earners. Everyone senses the unfairness of being asked to work more for the state than for yourself, even when the proceeds are used for purposes people might otherwise approve of, like income redistribution.

The real point I want to drive home is that even redistribution via taxation eventually runs up against both public resistance and the evidence of economic damage caused. So jobs cannot be redistributed at all, and income can be redistributed but only within certain practical bounds.

The rule of law and correcting "imbalances"

The other way to fix such a maldistribution between groups is to prevent disfavoured groups from getting certain jobs or certain benefits or advantages in the first place. Thus, for example, members of disfavoured groups could be "discouraged" from applying or even banned outright until the "imbalance" has been corrected.

Three problems here.

The rule of law and equality before the law and the requirement of equal respect owed by each of us to the choices made by others make this an extremely dangerous policy to pursue since it strikes at the very heart of social co-operation. The current distribution of jobs and income is based on the application of these principles and is widely acquiesced in, in large part because it treats all individuals fairly. Discrimination against individuals is outlawed. The value of knowledge is impersonally assessed and rewarded and employment and income are driven by knowledge possession (which includes skill and ability). No one is weighed in the balance and found wanting because of who they are.

As soon as we move away from this system, the consequences for fairness should be quite obvious. The only way one group can be favoured (beyond a relatively uncontroversial "between equal candidates prefer the member of the under-represented group" and "members of such groups are encouraged to apply") is by discriminating against the members of the disfavoured groups. The fact that such a policy might be pursued by a government with a "democratic mandate" or by companies pursuing "social justice" doesn't rewrite the far more fundamental rules of just treatment of morally equal individuals.

Nor can such policies be justified on the basis of them somehow compensating the group harmed by systemic discrimination. The specific individuals benefiting today from the new reverse discrimination would by definition not be the people harmed by the original discrimination. The people harmed were those who *didn't* get jobs or earn the appropriate income in the past. And the people paying the cost of the compensation (the ones disadvantaged by reverse discrimination) wouldn't be the ones who wronged the victims of earlier discrimination; that would be the people who set salaries and hired employees in the past.

It doesn't help, by the way, to say that no one is proposing active discrimination against disfavoured groups, but only a kind of gentle promotion of officially favoured groups. This is a polite fiction because the truth is too unpalatable. We now have policies and court decisions that recognize that the interests of under-represented groups may be promoted at the expense of others, and many organizations pursue unofficial discrimination for reasons of public relations. Far from seeing the impossibility of what they are asking, those promoting the theory of group underrepresentation see the failure of less coercive efforts as being only more evidence of how vicious and entrenched the systemic discrimination is. Each time the distribution among groups fails to improve as it "should," the greater the pressure on governments and organisations to "do better" or more Draconian measures will be "justified."

The second main objection to this way of "fixing" a maldistribution of desired things is that it would force us to abandon the pursuit of meritocracy in favour of the idealized representation of abstract groups. I have already shown why the current system focuses on knowledge as the *legitimate differentiator* of otherwise equal human beings. In fact, focusing on most objective group membership is rightly illegal.

Inescapably, then, handing out jobs and incomes based on objective group membership, *which is no indicator of knowledge possession*, will make us as a society stupider in that we will be employing, paying and promoting people, not on the basis of what their knowledge can accomplish for us, but on the basis of how the distribution of their objective characteristics pleases or displeases the aesthetic sense of designers and contempt for the choices that people on the ground made about how to make the best of their specific circumstances.

Believing three impossible things before breakfast

The third problem is one alluded to earlier. It asks us to achieve the impossible and, as the *code civil* wisely rules, *A l'impossible nul n'est tenu.*

So what is so impossible about achieving a "just" distribution of disadvantaged people across all jobs and professions? Leave aside all the arguments I have made about knowledge distribution and how both its general distribution and the value of specific knowledge are weakly if at all related to objective group membership.

Think instead about how *many* categories of under-represented groups there might be. Start with the groups that the Supreme Court says are particularly worthy of protection under the Charter's equality section, Section 15, namely, race (including national or ethnic origin), sex, colour, age, or mental or physical disability.[61] Even assuming the very generalized categories of race used by statisticians (things like Caucasian or Asian) and the number of potential disabilities (hearing, vision, cognitive impairment, illness, addiction and so forth) plus, say, all the sexual orientations implied in LGBTQQIP2SAA and remembering the idea of "intersectionality," that racialized and disabled women suffer far greater disadvantages than, say, "privileged" Caucasian women, how many categories are, in theory at least, subject to "underrepresentation"? It didn't take one analyst very long, nor did it require any improbable categories of potential discrimination, to arrive at the mathematical conclusion that there are more such potential categories than there are workers in the Canadian workforce — about

18 million.[62] In these circumstances no single employer could possible meet the standard of having a sufficiently inclusive workforce – not even the federal government with its hundreds of thousands of employees and contractors.

Social justice

What might all this mean for the way we think about social justice?

Ignorance is the basic human condition and knowledge is the great disruptor of social relations (especially of hierarchy and pattern) while also being the generator of progress of all kinds, if progress may be understood as an ever-increasing ability to realize our goals in life. If, therefore, we want progress, we must endure the constant upending of established social patterns and relations. The gardener's insight is that only a *procedural* philosophy of justice, one that concerns itself solely with judging the rightness or justice of *actions* is compatible with innovation and knowledge discovery's role as the central mechanism of progress. If the *individual* actions we perform are each just, if they violate no rule about how other individuals ought to be treated, then the aggregate *outcome* of those actions – in other words the state of society, including the relative positions of different groups – is also by definition just.

Concepts of social justice that appeal instead to ideas of *ideal outcomes, of patterns of distribution that are aesthetically pleasing,* must constantly seek to obstruct socially disruptive forces because they cause the pattern of distribution they admire constantly to be over-written with a new story. There is thus perfect harmony between progress and the gardener's procedural justice, and a constant tension between progress and social justice, to the extent that the latter rests on the premise that *outcomes* must be arranged in a way that is pleasing to our prejudices. *Progress upends patterns, no matter how much we may cherish those patterns.* Preventing progress, however, makes us stupid as a society because progress *is* the discovery and integration of new knowledge in human affairs. New knowledge changes the distribution of power, of income, of work, and much, much more; the knowledge of, say,

Aristotle, Isaac Newton, Michael Faraday and Isambard Kingdom Brunel was displaced in whole or in part by that of Rockefeller, the Wright brothers and Edison, which was displaced by that of Einstein, Bell, Packard, Gates, Walton, Zuckerberg, Jobs and Bezos.

But if the issue is that social justice disrupts progress, then surely the question must be, what is progress and why should we prefer it to the stately continuation of familiar and honoured patterns of social life, or to the newly engineered patterns of inter-group relations so beloved of latter-day social engineers? The answer, I believe, is that progress is all about beating back the frontiers of human ignorance, of extending the power of humanity to better its condition through the acquisition of new knowledge. I have already explained why ignorance is the default condition of humanity and the acquisition of new knowledge is the motor of progress.

To return to the theme of procedural justice versus social justice, we can perhaps see more clearly what is at issue. *If* human progress depends on the discovery of new knowledge, and *if* new knowledge on balance improves the quality of human life, and *if* new knowledge is irremediably linked to the disruption of known and enjoyed patterns of social life, then a philosophy of social justice that prizes patterned distribution – say a limit to how much the best paid can earn relative to the worst paid, or the distribution of jobs and parliamentary seats and incomes or even some version of that fanciful and unworkable Rawlsian will 'o the wisp, the maximin principle[63] – will worsen the condition of humanity, make us less able to solve our problems, less able to pursue our purposes with success. The very idea that public authorities could so arrange society that an overall pattern could not only be established *but maintained over time*, or that only progress that benefited certain groups would be permitted, or that all grievances could be erased for people whose identity is not a fixed and known quantity but something that is both variable and incompletely known or discoverable, flies in the face of this analysis of the depths of our ignorance and of the room that must always be made for the discovery of disruptive new knowledge.

What we must do and what we cannot do

Gardeners do not urge on us an indifference to the plight of the worst off. On the contrary, all they enjoin us to do is to pursue justice in our relations with individuals without worrying about the pattern of relations between groups that results, between the top and the bottom, or between, say, social classes, or men and women.

This philosophy is not one of envy; there is no levelling down to an equally shared burden of poverty and ignorance. It leads, for example, to establishing the social insurance system I have already discussed, including an income floor beneath which no one should be permitted to fall, guaranteed access to medical care regardless of ability to pay, universal and compulsory education and so forth. It leaves open the possibility of individuals and groups striving to improve the opportunities available to members of their preferred groups. It requires us to evaluate searchingly our protections of individuals against discrimination to ensure that forbidden grounds of choosing are not imported indirectly or surreptitiously.

What it can never accept or agree to is the elevation of abstract objective group membership above the equal protection and respect due to every individual and the choices they make for themselves.

What makes you think you can represent me?

This discussion about subjective and objective identity and how fundamentally different they are also leads us to consider a different aspect of social justice's preoccupations, namely, how well different groups are "represented" in our political institutions.

I'll not repeat the obvious ways in which the argument about the distribution of jobs and incomes applies to the issue of group representation in, say, parliament. There is absolutely no reason to think that preferences about whether or not to get into politics are equally distributed among members of different objective groups, since objective group membership is such a small part of how such decisions are made. It may be true that the legal protections against individual discrimination are weaker than in the employment market and more could be done here, but I also doubt that voters or political parties would like to see judges or bureaucrats, as opposed to party members, choosing candidates for election. That said, the way in which candidates are nominated for office by the different parties is notoriously open to abuse and manipulation and this is an area much in need of reform.[64]

The far bigger issue arising from the debate over group representation in politics is the meaning of representation itself which has, unsurprisingly, an objective and a subjective dimension.

Objective representation, of the kind much beloved of social justice warriors, is wholly consumed by the objective dimension of identity. Are there people who look like me (in that they share some objective characteristic like race or disability or sex or gender or ethnic origin) in parliament? If so, I am represented there. If not, I am not, despite the fact that I may have voted for someone who now sits in that august assembly. And if people who share characteristic X are a larger share of the population as a whole than they are of parliament, then group X is under-represented.

Let's leave aside the logical and mathematical impossibility of representing the complexity of all Canada's objective group composition in parliament, which is impossible for the same reason it is not possible in the job market.

Let's ask instead what it means to represent someone, literally to stand in their place and speak for them.

In determining whether someone "represents" me, I don't ask, "Do they look like me?" I don't ask whether they belong to the same racial or ethnic or sexual groups. I have been "represented" in parliament (in the sense of living in the constituency of an MP) by people of the same objective groups and felt ill-represented, while I have been represented by people from other "groups" and felt quite well represented. That's because objective group identification is a poor predictor of whether I agree with someone's ideas. *It is on the content of their mind (their subjective identity and beliefs) that I feel represented (or not), not on the basis of their group membership.*

Take a group much in the minds of politicians today: the middle class. The income definition of the middle class is people earning between

$45,000 and $119,000.[65] But a married Halifax plumber with two kids and a mortgage earning $90,000 a year would likely be hard pressed to see himself reflected in the circumstances of a single gay waiter cum Uber driver renting an apartment in Toronto on $60,000, or an Aboriginal woman in Red Deer with an extended family running a small on-line craft business bringing in $45,000 a year.

The same analysis can be made of any objective group you care to name. The people who actually share any particular characteristic will be tremendously diverse in other aspects of their identity. Lumping them together for "representation" purposes does nothing except to create an arbitrary statistical category of no practical relevance.

In fact, in all other areas of life, when you choose someone to "represent" you (as lawyers and accountants and physicians do all the time, for example), you don't ask yourself, "Do they look like me?" You ask yourself, "Do they possess the knowledge necessary so that they can act in my interest in an area where I am ignorant? And do they possess the sort of character that gives me confidence that I can trust them to represent my interests rather than their own when they are to act on my behalf?" I suspect that Vice-Admiral Mark Norman, a man, felt quite well represented by top lawyer Marie Heinen, a woman, when he was defending himself against breach of trust charges.[66]

Asking someone to represent you in parliament should be no different. One of the reasons that lawyers are traditionally over-represented in parliament, I suspect, is that they are professional advocates. They plead their clients' interests all the time and do so on the basis of their ability to use language persuasively. It would be unsurprising, then, for professional advocates to have a leg up in the "representation sweepstakes." They enjoy this advantage not because of their race or ethnicity or sex, but because people see in them effective advocates for their interests. And when people are choosing who represents them, *they get to decide who will do so effectively*.

To say that people who have themselves participated (through their vote) in the choosing of someone to represent them in parliament are nonetheless not represented there because the voter is white and the MP black, or the voter is a woman and the MP a man, is, yet again, to display breathtaking contempt for the actual decisions of complete and complex people making complex choices in real and complex circumstances. The fact that the person they voted for may represent a party that made promises and presented a program that was appealing, or represented the best hope of defeating the candidate of a party whose program they thought abhorrent and destructive, seems not to weigh in the balance at all.

Nor do the advocates for the "patterned outcome" so beloved of designers ever seem to put the question the other way around. If their theory is that only people who are objectively like me can represent me, then I as a male could never be represented by a woman, for this is the logical counterpart of the view that a woman cannot be represented by a man. And yet I would be delighted to be represented by, and would feel fully represented by, say, Angela Merkel or Nikki Haley or Lisa Raitt or Christie Clark or many other women – not because they are women but because we see the world in a similar way and they would be excellent advocates for what I believe in in the corridors of power.

Similarly, I would not feel represented by Bernie Sanders or Jeremy Corbyn or Jagmeet Singh any more than I would feel represented by Francoise David, Elizabeth Warren, or Kathleen Wynn. We do not see the world in the same way. I have doubts about their ideas and, in certain cases, their character. But in no case is this related to their membership in objective groups. It is solely based on what they think and feel and what they have revealed about their character.

When Justice Murray Sinclair tabled the report of the Truth and Reconciliation Commission and spoke out so eloquently about its findings, he spoke for (represented) many Canadians, including me, but he is Indigenous and I am Irish-Canadian.

When in 2015 Justice France Charbonneau tabled her report detailing corruption in Quebec's politics and construction industry,[67] she spoke for (represented) me and many Canadians who care about the rule of law and integrity in public life, but she is a woman and I am a man.

When Lincoln Alexander, a distinguished lawyer, spent his long parliamentary career speaking out eloquently for human rights, he spoke for me and many others, yet he was black and I am white.

The idea that women, as an objective group, can only be represented by other women is not just false, but pernicious. Once again it is redolent of the designer's contempt for the actual choices of complex people, dismissing the choices of women who disagree with them as either the products of false consciousness or, the crudest insult of all, "not really women." That last was an insult levelled at Margaret Thatcher,[68] for whom vast numbers of British women voted, presumably to represent them, not as a child care advocate or leader of take-back-the-night marches, but on other issues they cared about. And it is their right to choose what issues they care about and to vote on that basis.

I hope it is not necessary, but for reasons of self-protection please allow me to repeat myself. Nothing I have said here should be taken to suggest that it is wrong or improper to argue that there should be more members of Group X in politics for whatever reason you think valid. If you want to organize and raise money to help worthy Xs navigate the political process and get elected, more power to your wheel. When, however, you impugn the representativeness of the people actually chosen by voters on the grounds that they are not Xs or Ys or Zs, you are setting an impossible standard of representation and dismissing the actual choices made by people about whom they will accept as their representative.

Difference or commonality?

The issue of representation is, on the surface, a minor example of the struggle between gardeners and designers. In fact, however, it goes to the heart of what separates them.

If abstract group differences and patterns matter more than what we have in common, then the hope of liberal democracy is a vain one, for it means that men and women, Indigenous and non-Indigenous, gay and straight, black and white and yellow are fundamentally, essentially, irreconcilably different. Because they are different, they cannot represent each other, but only other group members like them.

Here is what's at stake in these two competing approaches. If Canada is merely an agglomeration of competing and irreconcilable interests thrown together by accident of history and geography, then there is no hope of using democracy and grown social institutions to reach mutual understanding and accommodation. In the designer's world where objective groups are what matters, policies can only be explained by power: one group or set of groups seizes political power and imposes their will on everyone else. Men impose their will on women, whites impose their will on other racial groups, straights impose their will on those of other sexual orientations. There are only permanent group interests that can either win or lose, either represent themselves successfully or unsuccessfully, either coerce or be coerced. Politics becomes a battleground, not a seeking of common ground.

In this designer world there can never be the extension of the franchise to women by men, the outlawing of slavery by white people, the creation of the welfare state by those who are called on to pay for it but never use it, the extension of marriage rights to gay people by straights, or the creation of truth and reconciliation commissions by those whose ancestors showed an indifference and complacency which allowed abuses to arise in the first place.

In a world in which only coercion can explain why those with power ever relinquish it these momentous social changes are inexplicable. But in fact, they didn't occur because a new group seized power and got the right to impose its will on the previously dominant group. Every one of these changes occurred because the powerful were brought to see that they were failing to uphold their own standards of justice and fairness. They were brought to see that they were treating morally equal human beings in ways they could not square with their conscience. The campaigns that abolished slavery, created the welfare state, or extended marriage rights to gays and lesbians didn't succeed because blacks and the poor and gays and lesbians seized power. They succeeded by convincing the powerful that unequal treatment of morally equal human beings was unacceptable. The weak simply had a better, more compelling argument based on our shared humanity.

For gardeners, it is only if there is something deeper, something underneath the group identities that are assigned to us by designers that there is hope. For that thing underneath the designed patterns of group symmetry is *us*, the real complex people who choose for ourselves what matters to us and the place we wish to seek in our society and the obligations we bear to one another.

What we share, then, is two things. First, we share a common humanity, a shared ability and will to shape a life for ourselves and to choose what matters to us. Second, we share a common citizenship that places on us a duty of care for our fellow citizens. In the gardener's world that is what creates common bonds of belonging and justice, of shared interests and mutual obligations beyond the objective groups that may or may not matter to us.

If the designers are correct, then democracy as we practise it is an illusion because society is nothing but a Hobbesian war of all groups against all other groups. Politics is the struggle among groups for dominance and so it is quite possible for the various objective groups that so preoccupy the designing mind to be under-represented in parliament.

If gardeners are right, then the preoccupation with objective groups is simply wrong-headed. The issue is not whether parliament "looks like Canada" as the designers always claim they want it to do; rather it is whether parliament *thinks* like Canada, which is what gardeners know matters most. The only way to guarantee that is to let people choose whoever they think best represents them, whatever their skin colour, ethnic origin, profession or sexual orientation.

PART TWO

Gardening in a Cold Climate: Examples of How Canadians Might Apply the Gardener's Creed

CHAPTER VI

Tending the urban garden

T USED TO BE SAID that the three most important things affecting the value of a home were location, location and location. But according to Sam Staley, a brilliant policy analyst at the DeVoe L. Moore Center at Florida State University who looks at the future of cities[69] and urban government, the three most important things now affecting the future prosperity and development of human communities are technology, technology, and technology. The choices people want to make for themselves are being empowered by technology just as much in city living as in every other field, which is turning cities into a battlefield between gardeners (who want to remove obstacles to people choosing what they want and living as they wish) and progressive designers (who want people to want what designers think is good for them). This chapter looks at how knowledge discovery (often embodied in technology but also in how people vote with their feet) is changing cities profoundly and how the rate of change is accelerating at a dizzying pace.

Technology is fundamentally changing the logic and nature of location. Where we choose to live is being determined ever less by commercial imperatives and ever more by our own individual preferences, so economic considerations are receding into the background when people make choices about where and how to live. Fewer and fewer people need to be in a specific location to do a specific sort of work.

This means that the attractiveness of a place rather than its economic function has become far more important in the urban geography now than it was in the past. Companies may still need or want to have a concentration of some workers (Silicon Valley still exists after all!), but the thresholds of concentration are much lower because products (and services) are becoming increasingly compartmentalized and specialized. More and more functions can be handled in remote offices and locations as long as mechanisms for accountability and quality control can keep pace. Individuals are now able to exercise much more choice and discretion in deciding where to locate their businesses and families.

In the old days, cities could count on natural advantages to help give them a competitive advantage (location at a port or a confluence of major rivers), or manmade ones (rail junctions, highway intersections, or physical concentrations of industries, such as automobiles in Detroit or southern Ontario, financial services in New York and Toronto). Now *people are more and more choosing locations rather than locations choosing them,* although I certainly recognize that there is a "hierarchy of place." Neighbourhood services and amenities are more important than ever, but it still matters where those neighbourhoods are. Technology has not abolished the importance of place, only lessened it. As we will see later in the discussion about what cities are *for,* I will talk about the most important economic role of cities, which is to bring together in one place lots and lots of opportunity. People living in cities still make themselves better off compared to their country cousins with similar levels of skill and knowledge, and that isn't even accounting for the greater cultural, social and other opportunities that exist in profusion in cities. Those benefits make cities magnets for people.

All of these opportunities create an environment for cities and city dwellers that is far more dynamic, fluid and difficult to understand than before. So, cities need to be adaptive and flexible, allowing for innovation to occur spontaneously. They need to be far more attuned to what makes people want to live in particular places than they ever were before. They also need to be attuned to the kind of people that they are trying to attract, which means following, among other things, demographic trends, fashion, taste and culture. And they need to remember that the technological changes and the ease of movement I've described not only mean that cities that get it right will enjoy substantial growth and development, but that cities that get it wrong will more quickly suffer the ills of urban decay, economic decline, population loss, falling property values, etc.

Moreover, the waves of change that wash over industry after industry around the world are going to continue accelerating, meaning that an industry that looks stable and prosperous today can quickly lose its sheen and its vitality. Look at how quickly Northern Telecom (Nortel) and Enron were transformed, how the mainframe computer industry disappeared with the development of the PC, how September 11 devastated the airline industry, how Canada's oil and gas industry was strangled in a few short years, to name just a very few. In other words, the only true constant in the economy is you and me – the people that make it up, and our ability to adjust to changes in our circumstances driven by natural events, economic adjustments, changing consumer tastes, technological change and a host of other factors.

Given what I've said about the footloose nature of much of the modern world's economic activity, the key thing those charged with authority over city development have to do is to think far more about how to create the conditions in which people will choose to live there. That will mean contributing to the creation of cities where people will want to choose to live. Gardeners and designers have very different visions of how to accomplish this.

In praise of suburbs

"Don't pull the plug on the suburbs yet . . ." That was the headline on an article I saw some time ago in the *Financial Post*. The piece, which reported on trends in Canada's real estate market, opened with this nugget: "The predicted death of the suburbs may be a little premature . . ."[70]

Premature is one word for it. Reports of the death of the suburbs have been greatly exaggerated and those reports have been coming in for decades.

This is not statistical nitpicking. Indeed, it is the fantasy of most progressive designers in Canada that our cities will be "densified" in the core, transit will replace the car as the chief means of getting around and the suburbs will rightly come to be seen as costly, unsightly and unnecessary.[71]

But while designers dream, Canadians have been voting with their feet, feet that are not carrying them chiefly to high density urban cores, but out to the greener pastures, bigger lots and larger (and cheaper) houses of suburbia and exurbia. One might almost say they have become gardeners.

Perhaps like many people your sense of our cities has been distorted by what is happening in the tiny areas right at the centre of the urban cores of Vancouver and Toronto. In those cores a blossoming of condominium developments and the stories about urban hipsters eschewing cars for bikes and living and working in the heart of the downtown have created the impression that this lifestyle is rapidly swamping the old suburban model. Nothing could be further from the truth.

Take the condo district in Toronto; it is concentrated in the area roughly covered by the old Trinity-Spadina and Toronto Centre electoral districts. Growth there has indeed been impressive, at 16 percent in the years between the 2006 and 2011 censuses. But the rest of the Toronto urban core grew at a mere 2 percent, while those suburban areas beyond the core grew by nearly 10 percent. And because the population in the suburbs was already so huge, the absolute numbers are overwhelming: the central core grew by a mere 38,000 people, but the outlying suburbs grew by 425,000, or over ten times as much. Yet it is the central core's growth which is somehow seen as the template for the future, at least in the central cities.

In BC's Lower Mainland, the single suburban municipality of Surrey may, in a few decades, have more people than the City of Vancouver.[72] Some have started to speculate whether we may have to start calling the Greater Vancouver area "Surrey-Vancouver."[73]

Suburbs, not cores, are where the vast majority of the action is.[74]

The story is similar in our other major cities. The central core is growing (and represents on average a mere 12-15 percent of the city's population), but the "near suburbs" are hardly budging. The density of the old central cities, taken as a whole, is thus declining, not rising. Even the Millennial hipsters know about the appeal of the 'burbs: A 2015 survey by TD found that while millennials preferred urban living over suburban living, *all* age groups – millennials to seniors – agreed that the suburbs were a better place to own a home and raise a family.[75]

Being sold a bill of goods about where and how Canadians want to live has real-world implications. Those who live in the fantasyland of compact urban cores put all their transport eggs in the urban transit basket. In the kind of centrifugal urban/suburban/exurban explosion in which we (and every other western society) are living, urban transit consistently ranks as a poor second best to building adequate road infrastructure in terms of efficiency, speed and convenience.

Ditto for policies designed to make suburban development more expensive in order to force people to live closer to town. The practical effect is to make people move, not inward, but outward, where gardeners are often in charge, land is still relatively cheap and they can afford the home they crave for their family even if it is at the cost of a long commute.

Saying this immediately causes the smug designer elites to wag their finger disapprovingly at these "ill advised" choices and intone darkly against the evils of the car, which is absolutely essential to the world Canadians clearly want to inhabit no matter what designers want. They trot out the paternalistic philosophy of centralized urban design that has infected city halls in many major cities in the country, as well as the regional development authorities and provincial governments in their role as ultimate authority over municipal government. Cars are bad, and the pejoratively-named "sprawl" that they give rise to is worse, a blight on the countryside that all *bien-pensants* abhor and wish to reverse.

Rubbish. The automobile is a wonder that rapid transit can never hope to replace, but can at best supplement to some minor degree, and at a cost greatly disproportionate to its benefit.

In praise of the car

Almost universally, as people's standard of living rises, one of the first things they buy is more space for themselves and their families. Those cities that anti-car proselytizers embrace with fervour, such as the centres of

Stockholm and Paris, have seen their population density *fall* over most of the last hundred years as people have fled their cramped inconvenience in favour of blossoming suburbs, where everything is bigger, including the building lots, and cars are the workhorse of city travel.[76] Even in those cases where central city populations have risen, the surrounding suburban areas have increased much more. Take New York. The population of the city is up about 400,000 since 1950, although much of that is concentrated in two boroughs (Staten Island and Queens) that had undeveloped land, not in the traditional centre like Manhattan, Brooklyn and the Bronx. By contrast, the suburbs have added at least 7 million people.

As a result, *people who don't live there* hold up the centre of Paris or Stockholm as examples of what we should do with our own cities, ignoring the fact that the French and the Swedes have left those centres and chosen to live in far greater numbers in suburbs that are basically quite indistinguishable from those of Toronto or Vancouver or Montreal.

What's this got to do with cars? Suburbs and space go hand in hand with the car. The car means people can reach affordable space. Instead of a balcony and a window box they can have a yard and a garden. What its opponents cavalierly dismiss as "urban sprawl" (and I think is better thought of as "growth on the edge") and the car have given people a higher standard of living and more freedom than ever before.

Cars put you literally in the driver's seat, including about when you travel, and what route you take (picking up the groceries on the way home from work or taking the kids to dance, hockey and music) without advance planning, transfers, or extra fares. You stay dry and warm no matter what the weather and travel time by car is in the vast majority of cases shorter than by transit, especially if you have to transfer. Cars carry more items than one can manage on bus, bike, or foot, allowing people to shop at supermarkets and discount stores farther from home. The car has been essential to the emergence of IKEA, Costco and Walmart, companies that raise our standard of living by improving choice and lowering prices.

Economic activity, and especially jobs, far from being concentrated in city centres is increasingly being dispersed across our cities, meaning that the way people move for work less and less matches urban mass transit, which largely moves people to the central core and back again, because it is assumed, incorrectly, that the core is where the jobs are. In fact, jobs are increasingly moving out of the core just as people are.

Access to jobs is one of the key functions of cities. Whether you can get to the jobs is therefore one of the key indicators of whether a city "works." This relationship is woefully understudied in Canada. While Canada is not the United States, the American data are illuminating and suggestive. In the US there has been important research on access to jobs by transit and cars. The standard is the percentage of jobs in a city (CMA) that can be reached by transit or cars within a thirty-minute period from the average home. The results are stunning.

For example, in the New York metropolitan area, with by far the largest and most developed transit system in North America, the average commuter can reach 6 times as many jobs in thirty minutes by car as by transit. Overall, in the US, the average is about *sixty times* as many jobs in thirty minutes by car over transit. Canadian numbers, if they existed, would almost certainly be less dramatic, but would still heavily favour access to work by car rather than transit. On the matter of the most valuable function of cities, the inescapable conclusion is that transit cannot compete with cars in the modern city. Transit can be quite competitive in a large, dense, downtown area, such as the old core areas of Toronto, Montreal and Vancouver. On the other hand, downtown employment shares are 15 percent or less of typical city (CMA) markets, and transit ridership to work locations outside the urban core is small.[77]

The biggest concentration of employment in the GTA now, for instance, is in Mississauga around Pearson airport, a part of the city largely inaccessible by transit unless you want to take the airport train downtown. If one of the key ways cities increase the standard of living of their residents is by the multiplication of jobs of all kinds easily available within reasonable travel time, and if they are characterized by the dispersal rather than the concentration of those job opportunities, this speaks eloquently to the role transit can play. Transit could never reproduce the blooming buzzing diversity of travel needs the car accommodates with ease. A fraction of commuter trips are made on mass transit. Even if we were to double the share of mass transit in major cities (in itself a huge, and hugely expensive, task), it would still barely affect congestion, while emissions per kilometre driven are now vanishingly small.

The incontrovertible and inescapable fact is the vast majority of people will continue to rely on their cars for transport. Mass transit is chiefly a poorly designed and very expensive social program for those who don't have a car and for the very modest share of metropolitan residents heading downtown during rush hour. Ten years ago we'd have been better off buying these people cars and spending the leftover money on well-designed roads, preferably where people were charged for every mile they drove including a premium at rush hour which would reduce congestion. Within ten years or so, Uber and the driverless car will make even that unnecessary, as we will see in a moment.

Many people talk in favour of urban transit, but what they really mean is that they wish the driver in front of them on the road would leave her car at home. This includes the allegedly anti-car young, who say they want to live downtown but in fact live in ever greater numbers in the suburbs. Pay no attention to what people say, because it is so unfashionable to be pro-car. Look instead at what people *do*; while city centres have grown, suburbs have grown hugely more, as people voted, not with their feet, but their steering wheels.

Of course relying on cars means relying on roads, and few ideas have proven more powerful in shaping Canadians' beliefs about cities than this: building roads is self-defeating. Like the famous South Sea Island cargo cults that built crude wharves thinking that it was the wharves that caused cargo ships to appear and unload valuable goods, the tenants of this view believe that building highways could never solve our transit woes because the mere existence of the roads would conjure up more cars.

This theory drives much of our preoccupation with building highly expensive urban transit – subways, light rail, dedicated bus and cycling lanes, and more – because, the argument goes, we break the cycle of dependence on the car and cut congestion by shifting resources away from road building and into transit.

Except it's not true. As urban geographer Wendell Cox likes to say, this idea that road construction only worsens congestion is like believing that building more maternity wards will cause more babies to be born.

In fact, looking at the choices people actually make as revealed by their actions, as gardeners are wont to do, it is clear that no transport policy will succeed that does not take as its starting point that the vast majority of people will rely on their cars for transport. If governments did their job of planning the development of transport corridors more quickly and effectively, giving people lots of advance warning about how the transport network was going to evolve, the choices of the buyers and sellers of property in the city would quickly produce a land use pattern that actually responded to the wishes of residents without the need for much of the cumbersome and wasteful planning process that currently dominates much thinking about urban development.

This was the experience of Houston, Texas,[78] a city that for almost all of the twentieth century had no land use regulations at all. Yet it ended up looking like most other cities, but with lower land costs and quicker turn-around times for changes in consumer preference for houses and the like. Ironically, Houston is one of the North American cities where density is rising the fastest. That suggests to me that the real reason why we struggle to get more people to live in the central cities is because of the political power of NIMBYists. These folks often say they want more people to live downtown, but like the driver who wants the person in front of them to take the bus, they don't want these new urban residents to move into *their* neighbourhood.

This connection between road construction and congestion has been most comprehensively studied, again, in the United States. There thirty years ago the Texas Transportation Institute at Texas A&M University created an annual Travel Time Index (TTI) that estimates how much time traffic congestion adds to commuting by comparing actual travel times of commuters in different cities with the time it would take to travel the same distances in the absence of congestion.

Over the decades of its existence the TTI has revealed some fascinating shifts. In the early days of the index, Phoenix, for example, had the tenth worse congestion among major urban areas in the US, despite being only thirty-fifth in population. It has more than doubled in size in the ensuing decades (it is now the twelfth largest urban area in the US), but its traffic congestion has fallen to thirty-seventh.

What explains this major improvement? A huge expansion of public transit? Hardly. Try a major road-building program. Something similar happened in Houston.

At the other end of the spectrum, Portland, Oregon, has pursued road-sceptical policies similar to those of many major Canadian cities. The result has been to worsen commuting times markedly. According to the TTI, over the last thirty years Portland has gone from having the forty-seventh worst congestion in the US to the sixth worst.

Now data are starting to emerge that enable us to compare commute times among similar rich-world industrialized countries in Western Europe, the US, Canada, Australia and New Zealand. The results are not encouraging for the anti-car crowd. The worst urban congestion in this group of countries is in New Zealand, followed by Australia, countries that have invested relatively little in urban highways.

Canada comes third, with the rankings showing that the average commute in Canada takes nearly a quarter longer than it needs to due to congestion. Vancouver takes the cake for the worst performance in North America (worse than Los Angeles!) and third worst among all the countries surveyed. Toronto has nothing to boast about with the sixth worst performance in North America.

Counter-intuitively for most Canadians, who believe American cities are largely highway-shaped parking lots, the US has the best performance overall, with the average commute lengthened by less than 20 percent by congestion. It also has only four cities in the list of twenty most congested, but fifteen out of the twenty least congested cities in all those studied.

Of course road-building isn't the only thing that distinguishes American cities from many of its international peers ranked in the data. Two other factors matter a great deal. One is that US cities tend to be *less* dense than cities elsewhere, and jobs are more widely dispersed throughout American cities.

This relationship between density and travel times is another counter-intuitive puzzler for designers who believe cars and roads are the problem rather than the solution to transit woes. How easy it is to assume that travel times must be shorter where cities are dense and people therefore have shorter distances to travel to work.

What the real world shows us, though, is that when people are a little more spread out in an urban area, and jobs are widely dispersed rather than concentrated in a city centre, commuter traffic is more widely scattered on the road network, *lowering* commuting times. This is a real challenge for the advocates of heavy investment in subways and light rail, which are reliant on that commuting pattern I spoke of earlier, focused on a hub-and-spoke model bringing workers downtown along densely developed transit corridors.

A good resolution for much of Canada's urban designer elite, then, is to remember that "urban sprawl" is not a problem to be solved, but part of the answer to how vast numbers of people can live together in big cities without life grinding to a halt in traffic. And I have barely touched on the ideas of road pricing and driverless cars, which would greatly increase the use we get out of our vehicles while cutting congestion even further.

In praise of the driverless car

Now is as good a time as any to talk about those things. Remember my argument that the gardener's philosophy aims to remove obstacles to people making their own choices, not throw up barriers to thwart them, and that one of the most powerful barriers that can be erected is monopoly, because monopoly reverses the power relationship between consumers and producers. Under grown social institutions, producers have to produce what people want or they go out of business, whereas monopolists have consumers just where they want them; as economists like to say, the best benefit of being a monopolist is that you get to live the quiet life, because the dissatisfaction of those pesky consumers can be safely ignored. Where are they going to take their business?

So in every field the power of the producer, no matter how big or dominant at any one moment, is being diminished by the growing power of the consumer – except where unjustified privilege is conferred on the producer at the expense of the consumer through bureaucratically created and innovation resistant monopoly. Little wonder then that monopoly is the designer's favourite response to people choosing products of which designers for whatever reason disapprove.

I remind you of this because car-sharing services like Uber and Lyft are a classic case of insurgent forces, backed by new knowledge, taking on the power of monopoly. Exponents of innovation have hailed Toronto's eventual grudging embrace of this innovative sharing-economy technology while conveniently forgetting that Toronto, like virtually every other city in the country, spent years fighting the threat it represents to the taxi industry, the rapid transit monopoly (for the carless), and their own regulatory power. Many municipalities now agree that ride-hailing companies can operate within their boundaries but a number of others are still fighting a rearguard action against the inevitable, raising considerably the cost of an innovation that will benefit consumers by costing less, providing better service, opening the market to new competitors and making more rational use of the cars already on the road.

Uber and Lyft are just giving us a taste of how disruptive technologies will transform the way we get around. Moreover, that transformation won't stop with the destruction of the old-style taxi industry. Uber's stock market evaluation indicates that the company may be worth as much as US$71-billion.[79] That means the market sees Uber, Lyft and their competitors as achieving far more than merely sweeping away the taxi industry, however desirable it is to see that regulatory dinosaur bite the dust.

Ride-hailing is the thin edge of a technological wedge that is going to transform the way we use the roads; it will make almost all urban rapid transit obsolete. Urban transit as we practise it has all the worst features of designerism. It is based on what benefits designers, not users, it creates huge shortages at times of highest demand, it goes where and when designers wish people wanted to go rather than where and when they actually want to go, it is often overbuilt relative to demand, it never pays its own costs, it is largely supported by government authorities creating perverse obstacles to what people actually want to do and it does little to nothing to relieve the congestion that is used to justify it in the first place.

Ride-hailing, by contrast, is the beginning of a shift in society from one in which the car is an individually owned capital good to one where transport becomes another "flowing service" where people buy the transport service they need at exactly the moment they need it and at the level of service they are willing to pay for. Once we reach the stage of the driverless car[80], which in cities is not far away, cars may well become like computing power – you won't need to own a car or a computer. You'll just buy the computing power you need online and you'll order the transport service you need when you need it. Cars will be able to work 24 hours a day rather than an hour or two every day, meaning there will need to be fewer of them and the shortage of automobile infrastructure we currently suffer in most major cities will ease somewhat, as will the demand for rapid transit with all its queuing, inconvenience, transfers and mismatch with the transport needs of modern city dwellers. Private car ownership will continue to exist for reasons of speed, convenience, and reliability.

Much of the picture I have painted here is dependent on public authorities not obstructing the emergence of these new services and the mobility that they promise, just as it is dependent on companies making autonomous cars available, not just in city centres, but in the far-flung suburban areas where 75 percent of Canadians live. Until that happens (and it will be a long transition), the individually owned car will remain indispensable.

To understand where urban mobility is going, consider these facts. According to environmental economist Ross McKitrick, "In 2005, 74% of Canadian adults reported going everywhere by car, up from 68% in 1992. In 2012, 82% of Canadians commuted to work by car, 12% took public transit, and 6% walked or cycled. Trips between cities are also mainly by car."[81] In other words, despite lots of spending on public transit, people travel predominantly by private car and that won't change anytime soon. The share of those travelling exclusively by car is rising, not falling.

Why? Speed, convenience and cost. The average door-to-door commute takes twice as long by transit as by car, and while cars go everywhere, buses and trains don't. Transit ridership isn't affected all that much by price, espe-cially when transit doesn't go where you want to go and travel times are longer than by car, just as rising gasoline prices have a rather minimal effect on the amount people drive.

Finally, the average car is parked twenty-three hours out of twenty-four.

What does all this add up to? A huge unused capacity to move people around by the means they prefer without it requiring much expenditure of scarce tax dollars on infrastructure, buses, trains and the like.

That spare capacity, however, could not be used effectively until technol-ogy emerged that allowed precise, real-time matching of travel needs and cars. That's what the sharing economy is all about: enabling those who have available capacity to share it instantaneously with those who need it. The sharing economy is a classic lesson in the perishable nature of opportunity – if I need a ride right now to an appointment in ten minutes and I don't find that ride, the opportunity is gone and I individually, and society collectively, have lost the value my appointment might have created. Perishable oppor-tunities are largely incompatible with spare capacity unless the matching can be virtually instantaneous. That's what the technology-enabled sharing economy makes possible.

Cars are just one example. You can now share your house,[82] your driveway,[83] your meals,[84] your office space,[85] and more with people who want to use the part you don't need. The Internet and smartphones have revolutionized sharing because before the costs of finding the person who had just what you needed just when you needed it were prohibitive. Now those costs are almost zero.

In this new world, many people will feel that owning a car may be less necessary than it once was. Before, if you wanted to buy just a piece of the transport services a car offered and not the whole car, your choices were expensive and inconvenient taxis and car rentals. Eventually you'll be able to buy car-time carefully calibrated to match not only your location and des-tination, but even the kind of car you want. You might want a cheap beater to get to work, but a van to move furniture and a BMW to go on a date.

Cars in the past could sit idle for twenty-three hours a day because the costs of finding others willing and able to pay to share its transport capacity were prohibitive. Now those costs have essentially fallen to nothing. As a result, we are very close to being able to increase the number of people moved without increasing our investment in rolling stock or infrastructure. Opportunities will soon open up for providers of fleets of cars offering different quality and price tailored to individual budgets.

And since people are willing to pay for "car-time" but are highly resistant to paying for "road-time" (i.e., tolls), the revolutionary changes about to be unleashed may allow us to get the next best thing to variable tolls, which encourage people to travel outside of peak times. Car-time can already be priced according to the time of travel (it's called surge pricing), thereby helping to smooth the peaks and valleys of traffic density.

This is only the first wave of change that is coming as the sharing economy meets urban transport. The second wave will be unleashed when the driverless car moves from experimental vehicle to urban fixture with computers managing the overall traffic flow more efficiently than individual drivers can.

When you need a car, it will come to you, on command. The privately-owned cars in many driveways will be amenities and back-ups. A large number of cars will not sit idle for hours every day but be out working much of the time. Brian Flemming, who chaired the 2001 Canada Transportation Act Review, now says, "so fast are these new technologies coming at us that no new subway, superhighway, or LRT should be built without doing an 'automated vehicle impact study' to ensure that projects that are supposed to last for decades are not overbuilt."[86]

So take a bus or hail a cab while you still can. To your grandchildren it will be like tales of typewriters, rotary telephones and vinyl records: quaint echoes of a long-ago age.

By their actions Canadians have spoken loud and clear about where they want to live and how they want to move around. Moreover, within a few short years the environmental case for transit will likewise have essentially vanished as emissions per kilometre travelled continue to fall and electric cars progressively displace the internal combustion engine.

The consequences of urban design

The reality I am describing (as opposed to the fantasies of downtown urban planners) has a series of consequences for housing policy, transit policy, and city governance.

To bring us full circle in this discussion, the burdensome land-use regulations (or zoning laws) that are part and parcel of the anti-sprawl agenda are the major impediment to making more homes available and keeping their cost down. And the impact is greatest for the least expensive homes, making housing affordability for those trying to break into the market a huge challenge.

In a series of papers, Harvard economist Edward Glaeser and his co-authors have demonstrated that such regulations are a critical determinant of housing prices. By affecting how intensively land can be used, strict zoning regulations create a wedge between construction costs (which tend to be similar across the market) and housing prices. Here are some key facts from their research and other studies.

- Approximately 50 percent of the price of a house can be attributed to restrictive land-use regulation.[87]
- Stricter and more onerous regulations are closely correlated with higher housing prices.[88]
- In California, housing prices and rents are higher in cities with stricter land-use regulations and new house construction is also lower.[89]
- In British Columbia's Lower Mainland, regulatory compliance costs for home builders can reach $40,000 per dwelling in some municipalities to say nothing of what it does to restrict supply.[90]
- It has recently been estimated that tight land regulation in America may have reduced GDP by more than 10 percent.[91]
- A study of London's housing market reaches the following conclusion: "Absent regulation, house prices would be lower by over a third and considerably less volatile. Young households are the obvious losers, yet macroeconomic stability is also impaired and productivity may suffer from constrained labour supply to the thriving cities where demand is highest."[92]

Remember that not living cheek-by-jowl with the neighbours and travel by car are things that many people want because they reflect a higher standard of living and more personal freedom, so the trends that fashionable planning philosophies are trying to reverse are a consequence of higher incomes. If the planners were to succeed in reversing these trends, the result would be, and would be seen to be, a lower standard of living for people who are forced out of their cars and pushed into more crowded living conditions than they find desirable. Only a land-use philosophy that recognizes these trends as an integral part of rising standards of living will have any hope of creating the conditions in which cities will thrive, because these are conditions that are in fact attractive to many people.

That is not to say that there will not be, in dynamic and growing cities, neighbourhoods where people will enjoy living closer together, or people who will get by without cars and walk or cycle to work. There is absolutely nothing wrong with these choices, just as there is nothing wrong with wanting to have a yard and a minivan. But these will be choices that people will make for themselves, and they will be only one part of a much richer and more diverse mix of land uses and approaches to transport. Just as they already drive the choices available in supermarkets and car lots, consumers can and will drive the extent to which people are called on to live close together or farther apart. Under grown social institutions, all of these choices can co-exist happily and we don't need bossy designers trying to put obstacles in the way of those who want to live as they wish rather than as designers wish they would.

And lest you think that this view has no support in the literature and that there is a settled consensus among those who study these matters that growth on the edge, or urban "sprawl," is an unmitigated evil that must be defeated, let me disabuse you. Randall Holcombe and Sam Staley note that "On an academic level, more than thirty years of research has failed to find consistent negative impacts of low-density residential and commercial development."[93]

The same authors then go on to cite a survey of more than 475 studies on urban sprawl and document the lack of consensus among the authors of these studies about the impacts of low density development and widespread automobile use.

You say infrastructure, I say boondoggle

Few words seem to have such magical connotations in Canadian politics as "infrastructure." No one seems to think that infrastructure is anything but an unalloyed good and that more infrastructure spending by governments is obviously good for everybody, justifying among other thing borrowing tens of billions of dollars annually on the federal credit card.

Yet much of what politicians call infrastructure is not genuine infrastructure but classic crude political pork barrelling of the "if it moves, pave it" variety. Not only do people not seem to notice that the way governments finance infrastructure is foolish and improvident, but they don't notice how politically-driven infrastructure decisions reinforce the designer prejudices against the way people actually want to live, favouring as these decisions do rapid transit, "green infrastructure" like bicycle paths, densification and other designer desiderata.

It cannot be said often enough (and those who study these things do say it): the way we pay for much of our local government infrastructure (parks, roads, water, sewers, transit and the like) is foolish and short-sighted. The way that the federal and provincial governments contribute to the cost is probably the main explanation for this failing. Specifically, many municipal services are improvidently provided to those who use them at considerably less than the real long-term cost, on the assumption that politicians at senior levels will pick up a significant part of the tab after the infrastructure's useful life is over. Why bother to set aside reserves to replace infrastructure before it is clapped out when Ottawa and the province will step in and bail you out when the time comes?

The totally predictable result is that infrastructure is overbuilt to begin with (because the people who use it don't have to pay the cost, so why not get the Cadillac version and at least get something back from the taxes you sent to Ottawa and the province), poorly maintained and overused (because everyone wants as much free stuff as they can get). Hence the fact that, for example, a great deal of municipal water in Canada is still unmetered and people pay a flat fee regardless of consumption. This formula is guaranteed to encourage heedless consumption of water, a resource allegedly so precious that even a hint that the Americans might buy some sends many environ-mentalists into paroxysms of moral outrage. This funding formula also goes a long way to explaining the overinvestment (relative to real public benefit as opposed to designers' fantasies) in rapid transit and the reason why fares usually don't even cover operating costs, let alone the cost of replacing or refurbishing the equipment when it reaches the end of its useful life.

In anywhere but the Canadian public sector, you would expect that infrastructure spending would be subject to a few basic requirements, like separate accounting for capital spending (as opposed to operating budgets) to make that spending more transparent and accountable. You might also expect a genuine, hard-headed analysis of the real cost versus the real ben-efit of projects so that money would only be spent where the benefit to be derived was demonstrably greater than the cost of building the infrastruc-ture. Instead you get politicians grabbing whatever "shovel-ready" project is to hand, regardless of whether it is the most useful to the local popula-tion compared to the alternatives. Politicians at all levels have also shown a preference for short-term rehabilitation and maintenance schemes even when longer-term projects might have delivered greater benefits because politicians prefer projects that will happen before the next election.

In New Zealand, where they do this stuff much more thoughtfully, these abuses are not tolerated. Every local government is required by law to have an infrastructure management plan in place that shows how each piece of infrastructure is to be managed so as to maximize its useful life and to ensure that reserves are set aside to replace it when the time comes.

New Zealand, which has a commendable gardener's mentality where infrastructure is concerned, has grappled successfully with the issue that Canadian politicians simply refuse to face up to: namely, that, in the words of one Canadian municipal finance expert, Harry Kitchen, "municipal infrastructure should be financed, as far as possible, by the residents who benefit from it, because this provides the surest guide to how much should be invested in what."[94] This is the true test of whether infrastructure serves a real need or useful purpose – or is motivated by politicians' need to attend ribbon-cutting ceremonies. If you tell people they are going to have to pay the real cost of their decisions, (the relative benefits in Toronto of, say, more subways or more thoughtful development of the roads) they are going to ask tough questions about what is being proposed.

Kitchen's recommendation, however sensible, butts up against the reality that local politicians regard it as a matter of commendable machismo that they can twist the arm of politicians at senior levels of government to pony up for their pet projects, with the result that the projects are often delayed by political wrangling and the final outcome is serious overbuilding of the wrong projects relative to what is really needed. Ottawa thus contributes to the economic irrationality of municipal infrastructure by: a) subsidizing the things that designers want (like overbuilt urban transit) rather than what people by their actions vote for every day (more of the right kind of road capacity in the right places); and b) essentially bailing out local governments who have failed to account properly for their infrastructure and failed to make people pay the real costs of their use of that infrastructure and now find themselves with their pockets empty when the infrastructure reaches the end of its useful life. As Kitchen so delicately observes in the same paper, "Economic arguments in support of capital grants are not strong. Their use should be conditional on recipient governments setting efficient user fees, prices, and local taxes for services provided. As well, recipients should have proper asset-management programs, along with requirements that asset replacement costs be included in the charge for services." New Zealand has shown it can be done and done well.

If confronted with the real costs of their infrastructure preferences, local voters would think more about matching their means to their ambitions and less about making politicians cough up the dough. If Ottawa really wanted to use infrastructure money to strengthen Canada and the quality of its infrastructure, it would make any infrastructure grants today conditional on showing how the new infrastructure will be run so that the federal government is never again asked to contribute. Because that would put the burden where it correctly belongs – on the people who are actually supposed to benefit from the spending – local voters might actually demand that local politicians listen to what they want rather than the three levels of government working together to give people what those designing governments think is good for them. And if all that was a bridge too far for politicians who cannot resist dishing out the lolly, a tiny step in the right direction would be tough objective tests of need and usefulness for municipal infrastructure rather than the political popularity and "shovel-readiness" that seem to be the measures that matter today. Just to be clear, the tough tests cannot consist of asking people if they would like expensive and overbuilt infrastructure as long as someone else picks up the tab.

Save me from your vision

Finally, in thinking about how to return control of cities to the people who actually live there or might want to do so, take a moment to savour the touching notion, so dear to designers, that the really important thing to know is what the current residents of a city (whether a municipality or a CMA or regional authority) think their city should look like in twenty, thirty, or fifty years, and that, once articulated, this vision should guide land use planning. Of the many fallacies that this view entails, let me underline just a few.

First, such politicized approaches to urban planning systematically neglect the preferences and desires of future residents, and give too much power to those people who happen to be resident in the city at any one time, and especially to the tiny minority of existing residents who are politically active, motivated and articulate. Yet in dynamic cities the wants and needs of future residents must be given significant weight, because the community's future depends on catering to the tastes and preferences of people who don't live there yet.

This can be done through grown social institutions guiding and buttressing individual choices, but not through politicized urban design. When builders and developers risk their own capital and livelihoods to identify land uses and population densities that they think are likely to find buyers, they are attempting to speak for future residents. If they are successful, they will sell their developments. If they are not, they will go out of business. Moreover, they can adjust their plans quickly in response to changing consumer preferences.

But when builders are obstructed in their work by cumbersome politicized planning processes and when current residents are given excessive power to block change and when the aesthetic preferences of elected officials and progressive designers predominate over those of people risking their money to satisfy the preferences of unknown future consumers, communities become stultified, costs increase and opportunities for growth and renewal are lost. Politics is a profoundly conservative force, because it privileges what is over what can be, and ignores that today's voters and governments have obligations to the future as well as to the present.

The second fallacy is that a city is somehow stable enough and its residents know enough that their preferences today should guide the city's development over decades. This gives rise to the famous "visioning exercises" with which we are all drearily familiar, in which politicized citizens, designers and elected officials determine a vision for their city and set out to achieve it through a comprehensive plan that governs land use for decades to come. But these planning processes are based on an unsustainable pretence of knowledge. In fact, we know remarkably little about what the world will be like in five years, let alone twenty or fifty. And the farther you get in time from the original plan, the more poorly it will fit rapidly evolving circumstances.

Take the case of one fast-growing community: Cary, North Carolina. In 1980, it had a population of 21,000. By 1997, it had ballooned to 83,000 and by 2017 it had reached 165,000. But no one in 1980 predicted this growth pattern (local planners thought the population would reach 235,000 in 2015), even though the forty years that have elapsed since then is a shorter period than many visioning exercises attempt.

Population change is only one factor that is hard to measure with any hope of accuracy. Remember, people in 1980 didn't know that within a decade the USSR would be no more. They didn't know what an MRI was, or CAT scans, or HTML, the World Wide Web, DVD, WMDs, NAFTA 2.0, the Belt and Road, Brexit, suicide bombing, the intifada, interferon, gene therapy, gene splicing, lap dancing, email, smoothies, AIDS, 9/11, Lehman Brothers, COVID-19, or Mad Cow disease. They didn't know much, if anything, about who Donald Trump, Vladimir Putin, Xi Jinping,

Pope Francis, Osama Bin Laden, Boris Johnson, Warren Buffett, or Justin Trudeau were. None of these names or acronyms would have meant anything to an ordinary person in the year 1980.[95] They wouldn't have known what you were talking about.

So no one can predict the world of 2050 or 2060, except perhaps by accident or dumb luck. Our models just project the present into the future. They're bound to be wrong. Everybody who gives it a moment's thought knows it. For example, in the 1960s no one knew how women's newfound control of their fertility would affect society, nor a decade later how the large-scale movement of those same women into the workforce would transform the workplace. Today we still have only a hazy grasp of how the Internet and mobile telephony will affect the workplace, commuting and home location. Already in the United States significantly more people telecommute than use mass transit. What will libraries be when books have long since ceased to be chiefly physical objects? What will the impact be on health and disease of the fact that we have now mapped the human genome?

In any case, as communities themselves change their character, their priorities change. New families move in, with children of different ages, and diverse experiences and expectations. A growing blue-collar suburb may have different priorities than a white collar one. Older empty nesters will have different priorities than they did when they were younger. Immigrants may wish to live differently than established local populations. Young single professionals will certainly have different ideas of the sort of priorities a city should have than the members of the yacht club. And yet the proportions of all these groups are constantly shifting. Cumbersome political and bureaucratic processes are slow to absorb and reflect these changes, and yet the time available to cities to adjust to new and changing conditions is shortening every day. Look how long it has taken Toronto just to resolve (badly) the problem of what to do with the city's waterfront, or the decades it took Halifax and Victoria to decide how to deal with untreated sewage dumped in their harbours. And the Boomer and Gen X designers doing much of the designing are themselves quite different from the Millennials and Gen Zs rising behind them, who are, for example, much more tech savvy.

The final contradiction is that the chosen instrument for the control of urban development by political authorities – land use planning – actually is a minor influence on the forces that drive change in the city. While regional planning may, at least in principle, be able to direct growth geographically, it cannot limit it overall, it cannot regulate migration into or out of the region, it cannot control business formation, expansion, or failure, it doesn't set interest rates or the movements of the TSX, and it cannot regulate the birth rate.

In fact, most of the factors that influence local communities are beyond the direct control of local governments. That doesn't mean that land use controls cannot wreak great damage, just that they are a blunt instrument and are used chiefly to stand in the way of the forces of change. Usually their most pernicious effect is to drive up the cost of land with little to show for it in terms of environmental improvement or enhanced urban amenities. In Vancouver, in the most egregious example, land use planning has contributed mightily to taking housing from very affordable (a house-price-to-income ratio of four in 1970) to its current very unaffordable ratio of twelve in 2019.[96] That planning has also led to some of the worst traffic congestion in North America and certainly worse that its population would justify. Land use planning in Vancouver has been regrettably quite successful in imposing designers' dystopian vision on people.

In such cases, however, self-correcting mechanisms are at work. The increased tax burden and housing costs drive some people outside the central municipalities, to areas such as the 905 or the Fraser Valley or Montreal's South Shore where houses are affordable and jobs accessible. When the Halifax Regional Municipality floated a particularly harsh anti-development plan, the mayor of Lunenburg said out loud what many people thought: that HRM may not want you if you want to invest in homes and buildings, but we do. More competition between local municipalities for growth opportunities will be an important constraint on the designing power of cities, even when amalgamation – the acme of designer-inspired policies – tries to extend the scale of municipal monopoly.

As for many of the planning and land use control activities that municipal and regional governments now engage in, they are increasingly out of step with our culture's transfer of more and more autonomy and choice to individuals. As I have argued throughout this book, in field after field the old paternalistic assumptions that people should simply take what designing professionals, authority figures and transitory political majorities dish out are crumbling. In a world in which you can order your own medications over the Internet without a prescription, in which you can choose your profession, your mate, your sex, your reproductive timetable, your home, your retirement plan, your job, your music, your car, your diet, your exercise regimen, your religion and your political philosophy, the notion is becoming increasingly anomalous that somebody can use political authority to dictate how big a lot you can have for your house or to tailor the downtown to fit their aesthetic preferences or force you out of your car and onto the bus.

The problem with comprehensive "visions" is that everybody likes the idea in principle *because they think their vision will prevail.* But in the event hardly anyone likes the concrete outcome because we do not, in fact, share a detailed concrete vision of what our communities should look like, except at the level of platitudinous generalities. Just look at the controversy that tiny decisions can arouse about mundane matters such as whether a tree should be taken down, a zoning variance allowed, or winter parking restrictions altered.

The real trick is not to design a comprehensive vision and then to impose it by authority from above, but rather to cultivate institutions that allow multiple visions to co-exist peaceably, which, as you have guessed, is the gardener's philosophy.

Gardeners see that what most dominates the regional urban landscape now is increasingly diverse individual choices of how to live, which are themselves empowered by technological change. Technology is upending traditional notions of urban geography because it is releasing people from the traditional constraints on location. With the Internet and World Wide Web, teleconferencing, video communications devices, mobile telephony, etc., people (and companies) have more freedom to choose how they want to be organized, where they want to be located, and who they want to be close to.

So successful cities will have to allow people more leeway to make their own choices about how they want to live. The days when urban planners and city councils could impose their tastes and preferences on their population are dying. Misguided efforts to contain the geographic spread of cities and to force people to live in higher densities and without cars will fail. But just as central planners did a lot of damage in Eastern Europe before the system was abandoned, so too the designer model of urban development based on patterns that designers find aesthetically pleasing can do us a lot of harm before people finally come around to see that it is incompatible with the direction our society and economy are headed.

The technological transformations I have already mentioned are also the explanation for why that economic activity, far from being concentrated in city centres, is increasingly dispersed across the city, meaning that the patterns of movement of people during the working day are less and less aligned with the needs of urban mass transit. And in any case the increasing wealth and falling population density of most modern cities militate against this solution as a viable means of transporting people around cities. People are widely and enthusiastically choosing ways of organizing their lives that express totally different preferences to those of many urban designers, and they're not likely to stop any time soon.

These are fighting words for designers who sincerely believe that urban sprawl, population growth and the automobile are an unholy troika that must be combated at every turn for the sake of the planet and the health of our populations. Nothing could be further from the truth. And if we surrender to these anti-growth prejudices, we will only end up driving away the prosperity that alone will allow us to attain a quality of life and a level of public services that will make our cities both successful and livable.

CHAPTER VII

Gardening for the planet

W HEN TALKING ABOUT THE environment there is an inescapable question: are human prosperity and well-being an illusion, bought at the expense of nature? To those who answer in the affirmative, human beings add nothing to the world and subtract everything. But, however much this answer may appeal to the apostles of environmental doom and gloom and the opponents of the oil sands and fish farming and pipelines and biotechnology, it is wrong.

There is something deeply rooted in the human psyche that believes that good fortune is the product of undeserved luck, and that we will be punished tomorrow for enjoyment and success today.

This belief has been particularly prevalent in the post-Enlightenment era, where it has advanced in lockstep with the very different reality that human intelligence and ingenuity have consistently and repeatedly unlocked technological and scientific wonders that have raised the standard of living of each generation compared to its predecessor while vastly increasing the ability of human society, in partnership with nature, to support larger numbers of people.

Yet Thomas Malthus earned economics the nickname "the dismal science" in the eighteenth century by arguing that the population was growing faster than the food supply. He predicted mass starvation.[97]

Again in the 1970s, the Club of Rome predicted massive shortages of natural resources due to overconsumption and overpopulation with disastrous effects on human health and material well-being.

In 1980, the *Global 2000 Report to the President* wrote: "If present trends continue, the world in 2000 will be more crowded, more polluted, less stable ecologically, and more vulnerable to disruption than the world we live in now . . . Despite greater material output, the world's people will be poorer in many ways than they are today."[98]

A few years ago, the front page of the *Halifax Herald* claimed that the resources of four more planets would be needed to maintain us at our current levels of consumption. We were exhorted to give up cars for bicycles.

And just last year Greta Thunberg cried out in anguish that we should "believe the scientists" who were predicting, according to her, that the planet would be unfit for human habitation within a few short years because of climate change.

Time and again, people have looked at growing human prosperity, improving health and population increase and told us that we were living in a fool's paradise, that it obviously couldn't continue, that our prosperity was at the cost of others, such as the poor or future generations, and that we would pay the price for our irresponsible wickedness.

We're still waiting.

The reason we're still waiting, why the ecosystem hasn't collapsed, why we are still successful in feeding ourselves, why incomes are rising and health status improving around the globe, is that the doomsayers have completely misunderstood the way the world works.

Of all their misunderstandings, two stand out. They don't understand what natural resources are. And they don't understand that the greatest natural resource of all is the human mind.

It may be popular, but it is quite incorrect to think of natural resources as exhaustible, as something of which there is only so much and when we use it up it is gone forever. If, for example, natural resources were actually getting scarcer, then the price would go up. That's part of what prices do: they signal shortages and availability.[99]

But the long-term trend in the price of natural resources has been stable or in decline for centuries. Remember the famous bet between ecologist Paul Ehrlich and economist Julian Simon? In 1980, Simon bet Ehrlich that the prices of any five natural resources Ehrlich chose would drop over a 10-year period, whereas Ehrlich, inspired by the Club of Rome, was convinced that we were on the cusp of huge shortages driven by overconsumption and population growth. Ehrlich paid up in 1990.

Ehrlich, like his many forerunners and successors, forgot that shortages and rising prices are an opportunity. Malthus didn't foresee that farmers, with the help of technology, could become much more productive in response to rising demand for food, eventually unleashing the last century's Green Revolution. Aquaculture, hydroponics and other technologies will allow us to keep feeding the world's population, probably at a declining real cost.[100]

Human prosperity and well-being are therefore no illusion, bought at the expense of the productive capital of nature. Human beings do not subtract everything and add nothing to the environment. They add something crucial. They add their intelligence to it. And the history of humanity has been one of the successful incremental application of human intelligence to the problems that arise in our relationship with nature. It is not that we do not face problems, such as the very real prospect of climate change (of which more in a moment). Of course we do. But we cannot stop with the identification of problems, *we must also look at the mechanism we have successfully used to solve every one of the significant challenges that humanity has faced since the dawn of time: our minds.*

Why nature is not enough

The wealth of humanity comes from mixing natural and human capital in differing proportions, and as natural capital becomes scarce in one context or another, we invent ways to sustain it, supplement it, or replace it. Thomas Malthus, the Club of Rome, Greta Thunberg and their ilk are not wrong in having identified challenges facing the human race at specific moments in our history – they have simply misunderstood how the grown social institutions that are our patrimony, such as private property, the rule of law, contract, incentives, and dispersed human intelligence all work together to reliably solve those problems, *even when the exact form the solution (or, more likely, solutions) will take cannot be known in advance.*

Thus, because of human ingenuity, the so-called "carrying capacity" of the planet (how many human beings may be sustained by the resources of the Earth) is not a fixed quantity, but a widely variable one, depending on how much of our intelligence we mix with the natural world.

We now require less and less land to feed each human being. We need less and less steel for each car, less copper for each telephone connection, and less gasoline for each mile travelled than ever before. Those resources are valuable, and it makes no sense to use more than the minimum necessary in each instance. And that minimum is falling all the time, because it pays to make it fall. When we are short of something we need, human ingenuity comes up with cheaper alternatives, or invests time and intelligence in increasing the supply, both of which ease the shortage.

Just one example: the telephone. Look at pictures of cities early in the last century and you'll see a forest of utility poles carrying hundreds of copper wires to connect telephones to each other. Copper is a non-renewable natural resource. If we had kept on connecting people to each other with copper wires, it is possible that we would by now have exhausted our planet's copper resources.

So, of course, now that billions of people are connected to each other by telephone, the price of copper has skyrocketed and the extension of telephone service to the billion plus people who have never made a telephone call has stopped, right?

Wrong. In fact, the price of copper, while it has risen in response to the urbanization of China and other Asian countries, has had a greater tendency to fall than to rise, overhead wires are largely a thing of the past, and those cables that do connect us are usually fibre-optic, made of cheap and plentiful materials like sand, and those materials carry literally millions more bits of data per second than the old copper wires.

Moreover, we have developed a whole system of wireless technology that is not connected to the network *by any physical object at all,* we can cram more data into nature's spectrum with each passing year and satellites carry many of the signals between cities and countries. We are vastly extending the reach of the telephone with fewer and fewer resources consumed per person.

Beyond the relatively trivial (but illustrative) matter of copper and the telephone, the state of humanity has improved over the course of the last two hundred years by almost any measure. Furthermore, human well-being has improved more in those two centuries than in the whole of the rest of human history, and this despite huge growth in humanity's numbers.

The improving state of humanity

Since 1800, the global population has increased about six-fold. Manufacturing output has increased seventy-five times in value. Total global economic product has risen more than fifty-fold. And this increase in human wealth has improved the state of humanity throughout the world.

For instance, the average person's life expectancy at birth has doubled, infant mortality is less than a third of what it used to be, and real income has grown 7-fold. Food is cheaper, children are less likely to go to bed hungry and women are far less likely to die in childbirth than ever before.

At the beginning of the twentieth century, average life expectancy in developing countries was about thirty years. By 1960 it had risen to forty-six, and by 1998, it had hit sixty-five. Longevity in developing countries is higher today than it was in the world's wealthiest economy, Britain, a century ago. People do still live longer in the developed world, but the developing world is closing the gap.

Children are likelier to be at school than at work. People are more educated and freer to choose their rulers and express their views, as measured by a number of human progress indexes (although there are of course ups and downs, particularly in the number of people living under genuine democracy). Work is less physically demanding and people work fewer hours than ever in the past.

Global inequality is declining, and that decline is accelerating. If we look only at the richest and poorest tenths of the population, inequality is growing, but if you look at the far more representative top and bottom fifths or thirds of the world's population, and control for the purchasing power of different currencies, the prosperity gap is closing. To use the economists' ugly language, the population-weighted Gini co-efficient for the entire world declined from a high of roughly .57 in 1962 to .50 in 1997 and .40 in 2018, a fall of nearly a fifth.[101]

We generate far fewer pollutants per unit of GDP than in the past. In fact, the richer countries become, generally the cleaner their environment.

In most major US cities in the 1970s, air quality was unhealthy for between 100 and 300 days a year. That has fallen to less than ten days a year, except for Los Angeles, where it is eighty days a year, but even that is a 50 percent improvement.[102] And remember that this has been achieved in the face of population and economic growth of sizeable proportions.

The benefits of wealth creation

Economic growth (or, if you prefer, wealth creation) is the key factor allowing us to reduce most of the problems facing humanity.[103] Prescriptions to fix the world's problems by restricting economic growth, such as suggested by David Suzuki[104] or the anti-pipeline ENGOs, are in fact a prescription for the exact opposite. It may be worth taking a moment to explain this, since for many people when they see the word "wealth" they incorrectly think that we are talking about the pointless further enrichment of the One Percent, or "the wealthy."

In this context, however, we are talking not about the wealth of individuals or corporations or social classes. We are talking about the wealth of our entire society and of the world. In this case, wealth is best thought of not as an accumulation of cash, but rather as the accumulation of the power to solve our problems by turning our ideas into reality. This is not abstract but deeply practical. Poor societies may possess the know-how to solve their problems, but lack the means (the wealth, and particularly the capital to invest) to act on that knowledge.

For instance, poor countries subject to flooding must endure an annual ritual in which everything they possess is wiped out, even though they may know exactly what should be done to control the flooding; possibly building dams and dykes, for example. *It is not the solution that is lacking; it is the wealth to make those ideas manifest.* Places like Holland, however, where around 40 percent of its land area is below sea level, had both the knowledge (properly engineered dykes to hold back the sea) and the wealth (capital) to do so. Even occasional but large-scale flooding such as that experienced from time to time in the Thames estuary in Britain can be controlled, provided society is wealthy enough to take the idea of the Thames Barrier and actually build it, as Britain did. A poorer society facing similar risks would know that a Thames Barrier could be built, but might lack the wealth to do so.

Societies with both water and agricultural land but no means to get the water to the land will struggle to feed their people even though they know in theory how to move the water. They lack the means to pay for an irrigation system (or more likely, they have created the conditions in their society where people with capital cannot afford to risk it by deploying it to solve this particular problem, for reasons explained in previous chapters).

Societies with water, agricultural land, *and capital or wealth* will be able to move the water to the land through investment when grown social institutions are allowed to work. Moreover, as water becomes scarcer, the means of delivering it will become ever more efficient. Less and less water will be necessary per unit of food produced, because people with ideas and access to capital will find it worthwhile to develop a way to grow more food with less water, such as using drip irrigation.[105]

In the context of apocalyptic claims about the impact (not the existence) of climate change, it might be worthwhile spending a moment on the likely impact of climate change on the world's ability to feed itself versus the impact of the availability of capital.

Today, thanks to human ingenuity, we produce more food than is needed to feed the world's population – about 25 percent more. Knowledgeable experts predict that our capacity to feed ourselves will continue to outstrip population growth.

The UN's Food and Agriculture Organization (FAO)[106] thinks that *even factoring in climate change*, we can reasonably expect crop yields to rise by nearly a third by 2050. And in the poorest parts of the world, like sub-Saharan Africa and other underdeveloped regions, the rise is expected to be more on the order of 80 to 90 percent (albeit from a low base). It is against this baseline that we must measure the impact of climate change on our ability to feed ourselves. For instance, one study looked at thirty different models and "found that yields would decline by 6% for every one degree Celsius increase in temperature.[107] Rates of future yield growth *depend far more on whether poor nations get access to tractors, irrigation, and fertilizer than on climate change*, says FAO."[108]

In other words, access to capital will have a much greater effect on the ability of the poor to feed themselves than the effects of climate change.

Access to capital and its intelligent deployment helps to explain why, at a time when the doomsayers among us are wringing their hands and crying apocalypse we are seeing a *decrease* in the number of people dying from natural disasters. And not a small or marginal fall, but a 99.7 percent *decline* in people dying in natural disasters since such deaths were at their peak.[109]

That peak occurred in 1931. That year, 3.7 million people died from natural disasters. In 2018, just 11,000 did. And as environmentalist Michael Schellenberg points out, that decline occurred at the same time as the number of people in the world increased fourfold.[110] Why this stunning reversal of the vulnerability of humanity to natural shocks? The deployment of both ideas and the capital to make those ideas manifest. Through human action in concert with grown social institutions, we have made the world safer for people.

In the context of the environment, then, wealth is not, as the Suzukis and Thunbergs of the world would have it, the cause of our problems, and the fruit of environmental destruction. It is rather the fruit of effective problem solving and the means to deal with problems awaiting solution. Wealth is capacity, it is resilience, it is creativity, it is the *means* of solving our problems. And as our level of wealth increases, all of these things – capacity, resilience, creativity, means – increase with it. Furthermore, from an environmental point of view, the means don't merely increase *in proportion to* the increase in wealth. On the contrary, *the richer a society becomes, the more its members are willing to demand that more be spent on environmental amenities, including through more costly environmental regulation which economic growth makes affordable.* This relationship has been extensively studied,[111] but two brief examples may help to illustrate the general point.

Air quality in the United States has been improving measurably at the same time as the economy has been growing. According to the US Environmental Protection Agency, "Nationally, concentrations of the criteria and hazardous air pollutants have dropped significantly since 1990."[112]

Similarly, forest cover is a good example of how economic growth correlates with environmental improvement. Forest cover often suffers at early stages of economic development, not least because wood provides a convenient fuel, but once a country reaches around $4,500 in GDP per capita, the forest area starts to rebound. This is called the "forest transition" or, more broadly, the "environmental Kuznets curve."[113]

Our changing relationship with nature

There can be little doubt that the human mind, as manifested in our increasing stock of knowledge and the power to act effectively in the world that our wealth represents, is changing fundamentally our relationship with nature, making us partners in the future development of the planet and human destiny rather than victims of forces beyond our ken or influence.

Take evolution or "natural selection." Contrary to the fashionable views in some quarters of the scientific community, natural selection has not ceased to operate, although its effects are doubtless more muted than at any time in human history. The reason that such natural biological processes are receding slowly into the background is that their main role has been superseded by human institutions. As in so many other fields, the things the human mind and human wealth together have created are being mixed in ever-larger proportions with nature, with results that are, on balance, very positive for humanity.

Remember that biological evolution is indifferent to the moral worth of each human being. Evolution is the ultimate collectivist: Individual human beings have no intrinsic value; they can carelessly be swept aside through illness and wretchedness for the greater long-term good (in other words, the survival of the evolutionarily adaptive) of the human race. It matters not if the child who dies from preventable illness might go on to be Mozart or Shakespeare or Pericles, or someone less exalted but no less valuable to their friends and families and colleagues.

The efforts of humanity, and particularly Western civilization, have allowed us to shelter one another from the ravages of natural selection through education, vaccination, sanitation, robust social programs, labour laws, agricultural innovation, and a whole host of other institutions that have softened the pitiless rigours of the natural world.

Today, multitudes of people survive whom nature would have discarded. They survive to pass on to their offspring and the larger society the fruits of their experience, their thoughts, their hopes and their creativity.

But that doesn't mean that nothing is changing. Natural selection was driven by the constant need of species to adjust to new circumstances: heat, cold, famine, drought, disease, predators, invaders and more. Whatever else characterizes our modern societies, change on a grand scale is a constant. But that change is so vast, and happening so quickly, that natural biological selection, which works over millennia, cannot possibly keep up.

That is why the brunt of adjustment to changing circumstances is no longer borne by biological evolution, but rather by the increase in human knowledge, the accumulation of wealth, and the evolution of human institutions. In the not-so-distant past, something like the AIDS virus would simply have devastated populations across the world over generations, much as leprosy or smallpox did, until homo sapiens was purged of people without a genetic resistance to the illness. Instead, within a few short years, we in the West learned to control, albeit imperfectly, this scourge of humanity. Deaths from HIV/AIDS declined from a high of fifteen per 100,000 people to about three or four after the introduction of the first effective drugs in 1995. Ultimately, we will learn to defeat this disease, and many others besides. And it will all be due to the application of human knowledge and energy and wealth aimed at mastering our rapidly changing circumstances through institutions such as research labs, charities, universities, pharmaceutical companies, governments and others.

We can go further: The natural selection that matters in the world today is not of individuals for their genetic endowment, but rather the selection of social institutions for the benefits they confer on us. The long Cold War was such a struggle, a struggle ultimately won by institutions that were built on the foundations of individual freedom, accountability and moral worth. Across the globe, similar struggles go on every day, and the institutions that seem to emerge and spread, however fitfully, are those based on values such as the primacy of the individual, universal education, equality of men and women and the rule of, and equality before, the law.

Evolution as nature has practised it isn't over. But increasingly, human intelligence is countering nature's attempts to weed out the genetically maladapted. And we are the richer for it.

So the wealth of humanity (and remember that this is a synonym for our capacity and our resilience and our ability to turn good ideas into effective solutions to our problems) comes from mixing natural and human capital in differing proportions according to circumstances, and as natural capital becomes scarce in one context or another, we invent ways to sustain it, supplement it, or replace it.

In environmental matters, like in all other areas, gardeners do not put their faith in designed solutions that try to impose a particular outcome on all of us. Rather, they turn to grown institutions that have proven robust, trustworthy, and above all more effective in solving our problems, provided we create the circumstances in which they work effectively. Those circumstances revolve around the acceptance of the irremediable decentralization of knowledge and the creation of institutions that protect knowledge holders and that reward and encourage the discovery of new knowledge and its application. This is a system that works, but not because some central designing mind is in control and issues orders. It works precisely because *no one is in charge.* If someone was in charge, we could only act on the knowledge of the person or group or authority telling us what to do.

Now, the pessimists among us claim that science and human intelligence backs up *their* view of humanity's place in nature. Indeed, modern civilization clings to few prejudices more tenaciously than the belief that nothing is beyond the grasp of human understanding and control, in the sense of someone being in charge because of their superior knowledge and expertise and then ordering the efforts of the rest of us. Indeed, science and reason, through their many apparent miracles, have given us little reason to doubt their power. The veil of scientific respectability in which the prophets of environmental doom like to drape themselves relies on the prestige of science for its credibility. Greta Thunberg summed it up beautifully: "Believe the scientists." These foretellers of apocalypse then propose to use science as a guide for re-ordering human activities in accordance with their understanding of the carrying capacity of the planet. They will become the greatest designers of them all.

And yet the burden of all that I have said to this point is that the power of science lies not merely in description, in the passive observation of what is; rather, science offers tools to the human imagination to discover ways of surmounting problems.

So, all our vast ability to satisfy human wants and needs is created by our knowledge of how to do an impressive range of things, but as the earlier chapters of this book laid out, that knowledge is – and must necessarily be – widely dispersed and locked in the minds and experiences of billions of individuals. With individual minds so limited, and knowledge so vast and variegated, so subject to radical revision and extension and incapable of comprehensive statement, we are condemned as individuals to becoming increasingly specialized and, the corollary of that, to becoming increasingly dependent on others similarly specialized in their field. No central authority can know enough to be able to tell us what to do without it hindering our efforts to solve our problems. Those in authority can help to concentrate our attention and our intelligence on problems to be solved, but they cannot know what form the solutions will take and therefore where specifically to direct resources in the pursuit of answers. They can provide suitable incentives to encourage people to turn their efforts to discovering new knowledge that will resolve pressing problems, but they cannot foresee what the most effective solutions will be that emerge from that effort.

Humanity's relationship to nature

What does this all mean in the context of the debate about sustainability and humanity's relationship with nature? That we should be deeply sceptical about the claims of people who refuse to see that humanity adds something to the world: its own imagination and intelligence and capital, and that that combination has repeatedly allowed it to surmount very significant challenges.

We should be less inclined to accept that our institutions are to be junked simply because someone with a specialist's view of an infinitesimal fraction of human knowledge cannot see solutions to a problem that he has identified. The solutions will come from unexpected quarters for unforeseeable reasons.

We should remember that those societies that have proven most adept at solving the problems that we have surmounted have been those that have grown institutions that maximize the use of the huge body of human knowledge that exists but of which we can have no comprehensive overview. They are societies where capital can be created and accumulated from the solution of humanity's problems and then redeployed to solve new ones, guided by the incentives we create. Societies based on centralized control by those purportedly possessing superior knowledge have consistently been less able to adapt and thrive.

The institutions that work best are the ones that decentralize power and authority, and leave people free to act on the knowledge that they possess; that is, knowledge of themselves, their particular circumstances and the resources (including capital as well as scientific and other forms of knowledge) at their disposal. Those people are then rewarded for producing goods, services and ideas that others find useful, including solutions to our environmental challenges. Our individual protected sphere, private property and the rule of law allow people to ensure that when your activities harm me, including environmentally, I am in a position to make you pay the cost of the damage to me, so that you have an interest in carrying out your activities in such a way that it is minimally bothersome to others. Price signals, private property, the rule of law, the accumulation of capital and the freedom to experiment and try out new things are the essential building blocks of a society in which we can have confidence – confidence that human ingenuity shall be given free rein to come up with the solutions we require to the challenges that we face.

Why should we have confidence in the ingenuity of humanity to interact with nature and science to solve our problems and move us up to a new level of prosperity and well-being without it costing, literally, the Earth?

Gardeners, for reasons laid out in detail in the preceding chapters, are largely unimpressed by claims that we need to junk our entire way of life on the grounds that our current state of knowledge does not seem to allow us to continue down our current path, or that the old, incremental, experimental approach is no longer up to the task and must be replaced by the techno-cratic rule of experts, who know better than everybody else how to live. And yet technical expertise almost always overestimates its own understandings and vastly underestimates humanity's ability to resolve its problems, given the right institutional framework and rewards for doing so.

Gardeners are of the view, therefore, that it is a startling and unjustified presumption to say, as Thomas Malthus did and his successors still happily do, that we can identify a looming problem but because we cannot see how to solve it with our current state of knowledge, we must abandon our way of life and adjust our expectations downward or we will destroy ourselves. These people remind me of the recording industry executive who, in the early 1960s, argued that the Beatles would not succeed in the US market. As the immortal advertisements for *The Economist* magazine so concisely put it: Have you ever wished you were better informed?

Climate change

Now let's put this discussion in the context of the greatest environmental challenge of our time: climate change.

For too long the debate has been monopolized by two parties. One has got religion, fervently believing in man-made climate change, and that only fundamental changes in human behaviour, as dictated by politicians guided by the advice of scientists, can stave off disaster. Their opponents argue that the science is uncertain, unsettled and inconclusive, and therefore that no action is warranted until we possess that missing certainty. Based on my scepticism about expert knowledge as the basis for imposing solutions from above, some readers will have concluded that I must be equally sceptical about the reality of climate change.

Gardeners, however, don't agree with *either* camp because this shrill, aggressive and divisive polar opposition is based on the idea that fervent belief and strident disbelief are only two views possible. Yet in most of life there is rarely such certainty; in most areas there is only ever certainty of uncertainty. In other words, both those who believe that certainty about human-made climate change has been achieved and those who say it has not share the same assumption: that certainty is what we are after and that it is possible to get it.

The reality is that long-range future energy, climate, economic, and other carbon-related environmental conditions are and will remain significantly uncertain, highly variable, and largely unpredictable. Scientists and mathematicians know that the systems involved in the various dimensions of climate change are in fact extremely complex and often chaotic, fraught with considerable irreducible uncertainty.

But contrary to the so-called sceptics, this uncertainty does not license inaction. The burden of my argument so far is that almost all human decisions (and certainly the most momentous ones) are made in conditions of imperfect and uncertain information. *We have to act even though we do not and cannot know everything.*

While it may not have been established that man-made climate change is an absolute certainty, it is undoubtedly a very serious risk. And thoughtful people act so as to manage serious risks, even when they cannot say with confidence exactly how great the risk is. The risk that any particular house will burn down is rather small. And yet fire insurance is almost universal. Most people sensibly believe that large risks, even if the probability they will occur is small, are still worth protecting against. And in the case of climate change the presumption now must be that the risk is real and substantial.

The key discussion, then, is not about whether climate change is occurring, but how great we think the risk is, and how big the insurance premium is we are willing to pay to mitigate the potential damage. That is a completely different conversation.

Another thread in that conversation will concern the climate itself. The earth's climate has changed continually and frequently throughout its 4-billion-year history and will continue to do so for as long as there is a climate. Moreover, natural forces have caused the climate to change suddenly and drastically many times in the past and are certain to do so again. Human activities are indeed contributing to climate change now. But more powerful, uncontrollable natural forces continue to operate. So policies that promise to prevent climate change are destined to fail and can only waste resources which can better be applied to improving human security and welfare, especially via strategies that will permit humanity and its natural environment to be more adaptable in the face of the potential impacts of climate change.

Yet a further thread is to take a cold hard look at what we know about the greatest factor that will affect the share of climate change that is likely caused by human activity; that factor is not the climate, but the behaviour of people. Any climate change policy that depends on transforming human nature is not a solution, because it will not work. Too much wishful thinking goes on that "science" should inform all our decisions, and yet we somehow think the findings of the physical sciences can and will trump what we know about how real people think and act. As a result, the policy "solutions" utopians promote (such as that we will give up cars and use buses and bicycles, a "solution" clearly never envisaged by someone living in most of Canada in February) assume a malleability of human attitudes and behaviour that has little or no basis in social science or historical precedent. We must act on the basis of how people actually behave, rather than how experts wish they would behave.

We should also dispense with the widely accepted but quite mistaken idea that small-scale experiments can always and easily be massively scaled up. This presumption runs counter to one of the broadest and most consistent scientific principles: that forces and phenomena observed at a small scale usually work quite differently at a larger scale, and vice versa. This is the reason, to choose one example, why giants are purely mythological: you cannot indefinitely increase the size of human beings because at some point the materials of which the human body is composed cannot stand the strain of the increased weight. Our physical size is not infinitely scalable.

To apply this insight to environmental issues, advocates of carbon cap-and-trade schemes claim that such "market-based" solutions worked to reduce power-plant sulfur oxide emissions and replace ozone-destroying chlorofluorocarbons with more benign products. But those industrial markets are orders of magnitude smaller than the global market for carbon-based fuels and other products. There is reason to doubt whether such policies would escape this scale effect.

The climate policy we need, therefore, is the one that hardly anyone is talking about. It would accept that manmade climate change is a real serious risk, but reject utopian and unworkable schemes to "stop" it or that assume that human nature can be abolished. We would concentrate our scarce resources where they would maximize human well-being: on policies, technologies, and infrastructure that allow humanity to adapt successfully to uncertain climate conditions in the future, including by reducing and where possible eliminating the effects of human activities that are thought to contribute to the risk of climate change.

Of one thing I am certain, however: trying to scare people out of their wits is a poor strategy for engaging them in the effort to respond to the challenges of climate change, not least because every time the outlandish claims of those who have climate religion are not borne out in the facts, they undermine the credibility of the whole effort. I am sure that this is one of the reasons why polling shows that while Canadians think that climate change is a problem that requires action, they say that they personally would be prepared to spend very little to solve the problem.[114] Furthermore, as Steven Pinker of Harvard has written, research in the field of psychology has shown that "people are likelier to accept the fact of global warming when they are told that the problem is solvable by innovations in policy and technology than when they are given dire warnings about how awful it will be,"[115] almost certainly because presenting it as an apocalyptic Manichean struggle makes it feel insurmountable and robs people of a sense that their actions can make a difference.

One environmental activist pulled together a selection of pronouncements by climate alarmists that makes the case eloquently[116]:

> Environmental journalists and advocates have in recent weeks made a number of apocalyptic predictions about the impact of climate change. Bill McKibben suggested climate-driven fires in Australia had made koalas "functionally extinct." Extinction Rebellion said "Billions will die" and "Life on Earth is dying." *Vice* claimed the "collapse of civilization may have already begun."
>
> Few have underscored the threat more than student climate activist Greta Thunberg and Green New Deal sponsor Rep. Alexandria Ocasio-Cortez. The latter said, "The world is going to end in twelve years if we don't address climate change." Says Thunberg in her new book, "Around 2030 we will be in a position to set off an irreversible chain reaction beyond human control that will lead to the end of our civilization as we know it."
>
> Sometimes, scientists themselves make apocalyptic claims. "It's difficult to see how we could accommodate a billion people or even half of that," if Earth warms four degrees, said one earlier this year. "The potential for multi-breadbasket failure is increasing," said another. If sea levels rise as much as the Intergovernmental Panel on Climate Change predicts, another scientist said, "It will be an unmanageable problem."

Greta Thunberg became *Time* magazine's Person of the Year largely on the basis of her grim-faced cry of anguish that her elders had brought humanity to the brink of extinction and that she and her generation have nothing to look forward to but ecological oblivion. The wildfires in Australia and in places like California and the Amazon are held up as proof positive that we must give up our illusions of progress and urgently reinvent society along "sustainable" lines.

Yet the scientists in whose name these dire analyses are being offered are themselves far more circumspect. The experts who are actually knowledgeable about wildfires have said repeatedly that while climate change may be a minor contributing factor, it is no more than that. In Australia, for example, drought has been a feature of that continent's eastern climate for many years and we happen to be in a rather dry period exacerbated by a great deal of dry and highly combustible fuel (particularly dead wood) in the forests. Beyond that, people have been building in ways that expose them needlessly to the risk of fire, just as people in parts of Canada have unwisely built in flood-prone areas and then profess to be surprised when their homes are flooded. Moreover, while climate change may be a minor contributing factor to these disasters, a much more immediate and tangible cause has been human stupidity and venality in the form of arson.[117]

One Australian authority says:

> Bushfire losses can be explained by the increasing exposure of dwellings to fire-prone bushlands. No other influences need be invoked. So even if climate change had played some small role in modulating recent bushfires, and we cannot rule this out, any such effects on risk to property are clearly swamped by the changes in exposure.[118]

Just to dwell for one more moment on the example of the state of the world's forests as a barometer of the health of the global environment, I note that NASA, which observes the earth's surface by satellite, says there has been a worldwide *decrease* in the number of square kilometres lost each year to forest fires. Between 2003 and 2019, that number has dropped by roughly 25 percent.[119]

Furthermore, according to new research published in 2017 in *Science*, "in 2015, 1327 million hectares of drylands had more than 10% tree-cover, and 1079 million hectares comprised forest . . . Our estimate is 40 to 47% higher than previous estimates, corresponding to 467 million hectares of forest that have never been reported before. This increases current estimates of global forest cover by at least 9%."[120] So not only are our forests not going up in smoke, total global forest cover is greater than previously estimated, and the extent of forest cover worldwide is increasing, not decreasing.

In fact, according to another recent NASA study, "global green leaf area has increased by 5 percent since the early 2000s, an area equivalent to all of the Amazon rainforests. At least 25 percent of that gain came in China. Overall, one-third of Earth's vegetated lands are greening, while 5 percent are growing browner.[121]

So, despite Greta Thunberg exhorting us to "listen to the scientists," she doesn't follow her own advice. Responsible and knowledgeable scientists do not endorse the alarmism of Thunberg and her fellow proponents of the "climate emergency."[122]

None of this is intended to say that climate change isn't happening, only that climate change is constantly invoked as the cause of every unpleasant or disastrous event now occurring anywhere, regardless of the actual evidence. This actually makes it harder for us to think calmly and dispassionately about climate change and how to manage intelligently the risk that it represents. Those who have climate change religion tend to regard anyone who says "Well, let's look at the evidence and take the actions that seem most likely to improve the situation" as insufficiently fervent. Like Naomi Klein, they think climate change "changes everything," in the sense that it will finally make people submit to the rule of their betters, those designers whose vast knowledge and insight entitles them to tell the rest of us how to live.[123] Yet based on their own behaviour, the climate change designers clearly think that the costs of the vast social transformation they profess to believe in, and that they find so aesthetically pleasing, will be borne by others.

Like the people who support urban transit because they hope that the driver in the car in front of them will take the bus and get out of their way, the designers want you to get out of your car or truck and onto the bus, out of your airplane and onto sailboats, out of your burger joint and into a locovore café, and out of your blue jeans and into unbleached jute. While many of them may have every intention of trying to put their principles into practice, many of them very publicly fail to do so as evidenced by outsized delegations to environmental conferences or award ceremonies to celebrate their environmental virtue.

More importantly, the alternative solutions they propose are almost always not as perfect and benign as the advocates would have us believe.

There are drawbacks to every policy proposal, from run-of-river electricity generation to nuclear power to electric cars to paper bags or drinking straws versus plastic ones. As always, the designers' besetting sin is to tell the rest of us what to do despite not being in possession of all the necessary knowledge and therefore often proposing solutions that are sometimes proven to be worse than the original so-called "problem."

Looking at the solutions

If, however, we *were* to look at the evidence and then apply a gardener's approach to climate change, what would that look like?

First, it would reject any solution that required us to make our society poorer rather than richer. That's for two reasons. When the economy is shrinking rather than growing, people will fight to protect what they have, so any resources spent on mitigating the effects of climate change have to be taken from people whose knowledge generated that wealth and who had other plans for the money. Climate policy becomes a zero-sum game, so deepening social conflict will be the inevitable result.

Paying for the costs of climate mitigation and improvement against a background of economic growth means that part of the growth can be used to pay the costs of climate change policy without it making anyone worse off. This is a far easier sell. Moreover, remember that wealth is a synonym for capacity and resilience and is perhaps the greatest means to solve problems; rich societies can afford to pay for the environmental and other improvements they value, whereas poorer ones cannot. Not only should we not make ourselves poorer, we should not stand in the way of developing countries seeking to raise their standard of living either. Our wealth is the only practical means available to deal with climate change by making our climate-improving ideas manifest in the world. Increasing the wealth of the developing world, therefore, makes a powerful contribution to confronting the challenge of climate change, not least because rising wealth is the most powerful birth control program ever invented. As wealth rises, birth rates fall, without it having been anyone's intention, a typical gardener outcome.[124] And since the climate change advocates are always making the case that humanity puts too great a burden on the planet,[125] and that economic growth and increased numbers of human beings are pushing us to the brink, it should be reassuring to discover that actually economic growth is the solution to climate change and that a side benefit (from their point of view) is that population growth will slow.

Second, the gardener would look at human society and human behaviour and conclude that any climate change solution that requires people to give up, say, the freedom and convenience of the automobile (not necessarily powered by internal combustion) or air travel or access to goods from all over the world is not a solution at all because people will not accept it. If they're not willing to accept having to pay less than $9 a month each to mitigate climate change effects, they are not going to accept a vast decline in their standard of living imposed from above either.

Politicians know this. It's why despite the evidence that the current carbon tax is set way too low to have real impact on human behaviour, even the carbon tax's greatest boosters refuse to admit that they will have to increase it substantially if it is to do the job they hope it will.[126] At $50 a tonne it is already a political liability. This suggests that technological fixes that allow humanity to continue to enjoy its current standard of living without so much resort to fossil fuels and with improved capacity to remove some of the carbon that already exists from the atmosphere while adapting to a slightly warmer world are much more likely to provide a path forward.

Third, humanity's solution to every earlier environmental challenge has been to rely on a mix of human intelligence, capital, and the natural environment. There is no reason to think that this is not the right approach to climate change, too. Contrary to Naomi Klein's view, climate change actually requires very few modifications in how we should organize ourselves. The designer's solution, which is to ban or obstruct activities that generate greenhouse gases while promoting green technologies that appeal to their aesthetic preferences, like solar and wind power or electric cars, may sound good because they promise immediate and energetic action.

For reasons I have laid out in detail elsewhere in the book, however, designers don't know enough to make this strategy work. They don't know which activities to ban and they don't know which activities to promote. That doesn't stop them, of course, from banning and promoting with abandon. They are busy obstructing pipelines, even though doing so indisputably makes Canada poorer than it needs to be and therefore degrades our ability to respond to climate change. They are busy promoting "green" energy to the point where Ontario now has a vast (and shockingly expensive) power surplus relative to its own consumption, a surplus that it has to sell at a considerable loss to American consumers with a resulting decline in the province's wealth-generating capacity and therefore its ability to take real effective action on climate change.[127] That's not even accounting for the billions wasted on the politically motivated cancellation of natural-gas-fired power plants.

The gardener, by contrast, knows that people in Ottawa or Queen's Park or Victoria or any other capital are never going to know enough about the complexity of the modern economy to be able to manage it (even for the most virtuous of environmentally motivated reasons) based on what politicians and bureaucrats know.

They also don't know what carbon-generating activities are central to the standard of living of Canadians and which could be phased out at little cost to us but to the benefit of the environment.

They don't know which technologies hold the greatest promise for reducing our greenhouse gas (GHG) footprint. Are the most effective technologies those that remove carbon from the atmosphere[128] or capture and store it at the point of generation, or improve our fuel systems to the point where our emissions are negligible, or increase dramatically our ability to store electricity or transmit it wirelessly over long distances, or capture solar power in space on a massive scale – or all of the above in unknowable proportions, or none of the above but something else that hasn't been thought of yet? They don't know what future technologies ("technology" being just a synonym for new climate-friendly ideas being turned into practical climate-improving applications) will be possible.

To repeat: this knowledge is widely distributed, not known in its entirety by anyone, and is subject to radical revision as new ideas and discoveries emerge. Put another way, the gardener focuses on process, on approach, on a way of working that has reliably solved problems for humanity, even though it cannot point to a specific solution as the "right" one, since solutions emerge unpredictably from the process and are often not singular but multiple and not revolutionary but incremental.[129] Designers focus not on process but on the solutions they think will work, and ordering everybody else to do what they say. They have the comfort of having definite answers. They have the disadvantage of having definite answers that in all likelihood won't solve our problems, or will rapidly be overtaken by better solutions they are unaware of, or will solve some of the problems but do so at a cost that is unreasonably high and therefore will not be accepted by people.

The question the gardener asks, then, is not how can I squeeze carbon out of human activity by giving orders about how to do so (including, for example, orders to make pipeline construction virtually impossible). The question is rather, how can I make the most effective use of the knowledge that exists about how to reduce carbon and how can I accelerate the discovery of more such knowledge when I will never possess all of that knowledge myself and therefore never be in a position to order people about with any hope of success in achieving our climate goals?

Incentives matter

The answer to that question, of course, is incentives. The incentives are not some poor second best to being a macho climate change warrior who lays down the law to polluters and turns down the screws on carbon production and makes people get rid of their cars and take the bus and returns global travel to the age of sail. *Rather, the answer is that incentives are the very best solution available to people and societies where knowledge is decentralized and authorities do not and cannot know enough to issue orders that have any hope of getting the results we want.*

Incentives can take many forms, but I will talk here about two: carbon pricing and tax incentives.

Carbon pricing is a gardener's tool, but the question is always whether it is the right tool for the job because, as I've said before, everything depends on the details.

In its favour, a carbon tax provides a generalized incentive to reduce carbon usage. It applies the logic mentioned elsewhere in this book that "if you tax something you'll get less of it," so raising the cost of using carbon gives people a reason (an incentive) to reduce their use of it. It makes no distinction between various uses of carbon, makes no claims that policy-makers know enough to favour some uses of carbon but not others (although exemptions or reductions for "large emitters" comes perilously close). It is predictable (assuming that it survives political and judicial challenges) and therefore allows people to plan their efforts around it.

On the other hand, carbon taxes have significant downsides that it is pointless to ignore. One such problem is that we don't know what the price of carbon "should" be. If human-made climate change is really an "externality" problem, the actions that are justified to make people take account of the costs of their carbon usage should be limited to the real damage caused. As I have already shown, there are lots of reasons to think, not that there is no damage, but that the extent of the damage is constantly being grossly overstated for political reasons. Some thoughtful and knowledgeable analysts have used scientific modelling and concluded that the actual cost of damage from carbon use is very low,[130] thus justifying rather modest policy responses. At the other extreme, Britain's Nicholas Stern published a report that reached the highly improbable conclusion that the damage from carbon was essentially incalculably high.[131] But measures that raise the price of carbon above the cost of the actual damage caused reduce our standard of living for no good purpose. And as I have already argued, measures that require us to lower our standard of living are not going to work because people won't accept them and because they reduce our capacity to respond to climate change.

Another difficulty with carbon taxes is the "leakage" problem. If the carbon price is not fairly uniform (as standard prices generally are) around the world, the incentive is not to reduce global carbon usage, but to shift your carbon generating activities out of Canada to untaxed jurisdictions in a kind of environmental arbitrage. If, as is the case with the vast majority of countries, their environmental standards are lower than ours, the result will not be lessened carbon emissions overall, but perhaps higher emissions in less well-controlled and regulated circumstances.

Additionally, carbon fuels are essential to our standard of living and wealth creation. If the best solution to greenhouse gas emissions is to harness technology to reduce and eventually eliminate them while still allowing people to benefit from the undoubted advantages of cheap energy, then the solution is not to reduce or eliminate fossil fuel use but rather to accelerate the search for the technologies that make their use more benign or that offer low-carbon alternatives that aren't damagingly expensive. The effort we as a society are already putting into reducing carbon usage demonstrates that this strategy works: the cost of green technologies like wind and solar has already fallen below the cost of carbon-based fuels in the US without the need for a carbon tax.[132] That doesn't mean we can't do more to accelerate the process as part of the insurance premium we are justified in paying against the risk of climate change. A gardener approach that assumes we don't have all the answers but can accelerate their discovery through incentives will get this job done more effectively and at lower cost compared to the designer approach that assumes we have the answers and all we have to do is to "listen to the scientists."

A different issue with a carbon tax that falls on the final consumer (who has relatively little control over the carbon production that goes into many of the products she consumes), is that the incentive for large-scale emitters to change their activities is blunted. And because the tax is relatively low (at the current level of roughly $50 a tonne) the incentive for final consumers to change their behaviour where it *would* make a difference (say in choosing the kind of car or truck to buy[133] or reducing the number of litres of fuel consumed) is also relatively small. According to some estimates, in order to get a major shift in people's use of carbon-based fuel, the tax would have to be about $2.30 a litre, well above its current level.[134]

The unwillingness to raise the carbon tax higher is surely why governments in Canada also rely heavily on a great deal of carbon-battling regulations and why they attempt to pick winning carbon-reducing technologies, which are precisely the command-and-control designer solutions that are costly and ineffectual. An approach that was truly willing to rely on gardener's logic would junk most of the command-and-control regulations so that the carbon tax's incentives would reward the rapid creation of new technologies that would reduce emitters' costs.

To get a sense of the scale of the issue of carbon reduction and why politicians shy away from setting the tax high enough to achieve their targets, consider Philip Cross's analysis:

> Overall emissions are a function of the carbon intensity of our economy (GHG emissions per dollar of GDP), real income (GDP per capita), and population. While carbon pricing works by reducing emissions intensity (which has been falling since 2005), real income and population growth are raising carbon consumption. Politicians of all stripes in Canada advocate for both income and population growth, which makes it more difficult to meet emissions targets. To achieve the promised 30 percent cut in emissions by 2030 requires an average annual decline of 1.4 percent in emissions. But if economic growth and population increases total 2.6 percent a year, about their recent average, then carbon intensity would have to fall by 3.8 percent a year . . . This represents a total drop of nearly 50 percent in carbon intensity, not the 30 percent drop most associate with achieving the Paris Accord targets for 2030. Halving emissions intensity in such a short period is unrealistic.[135]

Cross goes on to conclude that, "without revolutionary technological changes, making such advancements on this scale would require taxes so high that economic growth would be impaired significantly."

By the way, the carbon tax is not, as Ottawa would have it, "making polluters pay," as if the tax were a punishment. The purpose of a carbon tax is not to punish emitters, *but to reward emission-reducers.* The best carbon tax is the one you don't have to pay because you have reduced or eliminated your emissions. But designers just can't stop themselves from turning this into a mediaeval morality play.

As for the carbon tax's opponents, like the federal Conservative Party, they actually want to junk the carbon tax in favour of deepening their dependence on command-and-control measures. Don't ever let anyone tell you the Conservatives are gardeners.

Designers will mock the gardener's approach because gardeners say that the proper solution (or more likely solutions) is not yet known and we have to have faith in process. How comforting it is to be able to say "We have the solution! We know what must be done! We will lead the world!"

Ironically, designers, *on their own terms*, do not have the solutions despite all their smug talk. Canada is falling well short of its Paris Accord commitments and no expert that I have encountered thinks that the plans Ottawa and the provinces have put in place will get Canada there.[136] And Ottawa's signature policy, the carbon tax, is itself a gardener's incentive-based approach whose purpose is to encourage people to reduce their carbon usage and create technological solutions to do so although they cannot know what those solutions will be. To some degree, the federal government accepts that uncertainty is inescapable and it must rely on grown social processes to reduce carbon usage, processes that can be encouraged and possibly accelerated, but not controlled or directed. So even the climate-change enthusiasts have accepted the gardener's logic.

The chief problem with the government's approach is that if you listen to its rhetoric, it pretends to know what needs to happen and what the solutions are; it just thinks that people will not accept the damage that it would require to their way of life. But it still spends billions of dollars attempting to pick winners, like green electricity, the green economy, urban transit, etc., etc., when the whole burden of my argument is that government picking winners is a vain enterprise. *Nobody* can reliably pick winners. That's why experimentation and trial and error are so vital. Nobody knows what new idea will work until they try.

Sometimes governments can, by accident, pick winners, and they gleefully trot them out as if they prove that somehow governments can *systematically* pick winners. But they hardly mention their failures. As someone once said, if you give an infinite number of monkeys an infinite number of typewriters, eventually they will type the works of Shakespeare. But think of all the gibberish you'd have to sift through to find it.

Governments' attempts to pick winners are on balance ineffectual and costly because they have bureaucrats picking technologies and risking money taken compulsorily from taxpayers instead of given freely by savvy investors who have a good track record of knowing what a potentially successful investment looks like. Even the expert venture capitalists expect something like seven out of ten of their investments to fail, two perhaps to cover their costs, and one to be a big winner that will cover the costs of all the losses *and* make a pile of money to boot. They just cannot tell you in advance which will be which; that is why they have to invest in the ten to begin with. Unlike governments, however, the investors are taking these risks with their own money or that of people who know what they're doing and understand the risks. This makes them far more likely to be careful than government officials who are unlikely to be at the cutting edge of knowledge in any technical field and who get the same salary and pension whether their investments succeed or fail, who are using "free" money taken from the taxpayer who can expect no return and who are under pressure from politicians to ensure that regions and language groups and minorities get their "fair share" of the money.

So this gardener's assessment is that carbon tax enthusiasts have accepted the basic logic of the gardener's approach but have done so for the wrong reasons (such as "punishing polluters") and don't really believe in the efficacy of the approach (both because it is politically painful to use it properly *and* because behind the scenes they are still busy relying on designer solutions like command-and-control regulation and trying to pick technological winners).

For reasons I've already mentioned, it is entirely possible for gardeners to doubt that the carbon tax as designed is the right tool for *this* job, despite the fact that it is conceptually an incentive-based approach. If it rewards carbon leakage rather than overall carbon reduction, for example, it won't get the job done and may actually make it worse. If set too high, it will lower our standard of living while making no real contribution to improved human life in the future. On the other hand, my view is that a campaign to get rid of the carbon tax would be self-defeating, not least because all that such a campaign would achieve would be to get its supporters dismissed as cranks and climate-change deniers.

So the carbon tax as it stands is a gardener's tool, but has the drawbacks I've mentioned. At its current low level it is probably not doing too much harm and I suspect that it makes people feel like they are making a manageable contribution to the solution of a problem that worries them and that otherwise seems huge and insoluble. There is value in enlisting the public in specific doable actions that make them feel engaged and like there is something specific they can do to contribute to the solution of a problem they clearly care about. I've already laid out the evidence that you get more public support for taking action on climate change if you don't present it as an existential threat that seems insoluble but which requires you to upend your entire life in a futile struggle liable to end in defeat or impoverishment or both.

In this respect, the carbon tax is really a bit like recycling. Canadians seem quite committed to the principle of recycling, which is also a practical gesture people can make to the solution of a problem that otherwise seems overwhelming. The value of this sense of participation and personal efficacy is apparently not much diluted by the fact that much of what they so carefully sort, wash and set out in their blue bin isn't actually recycled, but ends up in the landfill anyway.[137] If you tried to cancel recycling programs because they don't accomplish much I am pretty sure you would quickly discover that public opinion was not on your side. People want to feel they are doing something.

I certainly wouldn't go to the wall in a fight to get rid of the carbon tax either, and for the same reasons. Gardeners, you may recall, are constrained by what Canadians feel and believe; unlike designers, they don't try to impose on people their own aesthetic preferences but try to find ways to make Canadians' genuine diversity of views co-exist reasonably peacefully. That suggests that carbon taxes should be left to the provinces, so that different parts of the country can tailor a carbon tax to their circumstances and preferences. Moreover, the existing carbon tax should be strictly revenue neutral, not a way to increase tax revenues by the back door, and low-income Canadians should be fully compensated for the tax's effect on the cost of living.

Overall, though, my own assessment of Canadians is that they are rather earnest, sincere and want to "do the right thing." In respect of climate change many of them want to feel that they are making a real tangible contribution to mitigating the dangers they hear so much about, but they clearly don't want to pay as big an insurance premium as the alarmists would love to impose. A relatively low carbon tax accomplishes this. Woe betide the politician who takes away people's sense of contributing and acting responsibly, even if the actual impact on the problem is relatively small. Gardeners must work with the raw material they are given and seek to supplement the carbon tax with other measures likely to make a more effective contribution to reducing the risks of climate change. If, however, I am wrong and people would acquiesce in the tax's elimination I wouldn't go to the wall to defend it either.

The point to remember is that a carbon tax on consumers cannot achieve what designers claim for it except at levels designers themselves are frightened to contemplate and even then, its contribution would be at best marginal.

So are there gardener's measures beyond the symbolically valuable but seemingly rather ineffectual carbon tax? I am sure there are many, but a couple of specific ones come to mind, including a redesigned carbon tax.

We need incentive-based approaches that reward the effective application of dispersed knowledge to the problem of accelerating carbon reduction without the risks of leakage and other drawbacks. We need approaches that don't punish those who use fossil fuels (many uses of which are essential to our standard of living and to wealth creation), but rather reward technologies that reduce carbon emissions or remove those emissions from the atmosphere.

Before I get to specific proposals, let me point out that it would be quite wrong to think that unless governments "tell us what to do" nothing will happen. In fact, inventive people and organizations are responding every day to the clear desire of lots of ordinary folks to lessen their carbon footprint. Inventors and entrepreneurs are doing so because many individuals and companies are willing to pay to see carbon emissions fall which in and of itself creates a strong incentive to innovate to give people what they want: ways to produce less carbon but not see their lives disrupted.

I mentioned earlier the evidence that the cost of solar and wind power capacity has already fallen substantially because it pays to make it fall. Other people are working on ways to transmit electricity wirelessly, ways to decarbonize natural gas and ways to make solar-powered flight practical among a thousand other technological innovations. So grown social institutions are already responding exactly as one would expect. Since those institutions respond to what people want and are willing to pay for, they are already smoothly moving toward decarbonzation and other technological solutions without anyone in authority telling them that they must do so. And the amount of carbon we emit for every new bit of economic growth is falling and the speed of that fall is accelerating.

The system works. Could it work faster? Of course. Part of the role of gardeners in our political institutions is to identify looming problems to which more attention could and should be paid and to create the incentives that make solving those problems more attractive. The improved incentives make it potentially more rewarding for those who might know something about solving, in this case, climate change, to put their efforts there rather than into solving some other problem people are also willing to pay to see overcome.

What follows therefore is not supposed to be an exhaustive list of measures gardeners should take. It is instead an *illustrative sample* of incentive measures that should appeal to gardeners in an effort to accelerate the knowledge discovery that grown social institutions are already producing.

Breaking the electricity monopoly

An example of a demand-side gardener's policy would look at that great enemy of innovation and experimentation: monopoly. Wherever Canadians live, with the partial exception of Alberta, they are forced to buy their electricity from a state-controlled monopoly (in Newfoundland and Labrador, distribution is in private hands but generation is in the hands of the public monopoly, exactly the reverse of what I am going to suggest). Those monopolies are controlled by "experts" under the direction of politicians and are notoriously run in the interests of the people who control them rather than in the interests of consumers.

In this monopolistic world, Canadians are prevented from expressing their preference for, say, clean green energy compared to GHG-heavy sources like coal or oil. This is analogous to the situation that prevailed in the old days with telephones, for instance. The inflexible old monopoly was justified on the grounds that it was so expensive to create the physical network that competition was impossible and inefficient and a regulated monopoly was the only practical (albeit second best) solution.

Next, competition was introduced by forcing the incumbents to resell capacity to competitors, and making the old monopoly separate its network construction and maintenance business from its selling of telephone services. Telecom prices started to come down and consumers had real choices.

After that, the physical-network-is-too-expensive-to-duplicate argument was eliminated entirely by bypassing the physical network altogether with wireless. And eventually every "pipe" entering your home (cable, gas, water, etc.) became a potential avenue for delivering telecom and other communications services. While government policy still unnecessarily shelters a number of these providers from full-throated competition, service is much better, prices are lower and consumers are more powerful than ever before in the history of communications.

Something similar happened in the US with so-called gas-on-gas competition, where ownership and responsibility for the physical infrastructure was separated from the ownership of the natural gas flowing through the network. The pipes became common carriers and anyone who could meet the standards could produce gas and feed it into the network, selling it on to final consumers wherever they were. Again the results were lower prices, improved service and empowered consumers.

In the electricity world in Canada we are basically still at the unreconstructed monopoly stage where we have to take what the monopoly provider thinks we should have. But what if consumers in Canada were prepared to pay directly for electricity that met their standards of cleanliness, carbon emissions and price? And what if the provincial electricity utility were converted to a common carrier that was obliged to allow qualified providers to connect to the network and sell, not to the utility, but directly to the consumer?

Canadians would be able to vote every day, directly and in detail, on the kind of power they wanted to consume. If Canadians wanted clean electricity (and remember that renewables now can compete directly on commercial terms with GHG-heavy providers), they would be able to take action directly and effectually, not indirectly and ineffectually through politicians. Artificially high feed-in tariffs such as the ones that have got Germany, Ontario and so many other jurisdictions in so much trouble, would be wholly unnecessary. Companies that consumed power would be able to market themselves to consumers: "produced entirely with GHG-free energy."

If recycling is any guide, Canadians would leap at the chance to choose the clean alternative and even be prepared to pay more. One reason Canadians are at once worried about ecological issues but reluctant to use the political system to address them is because they feel the issues are so huge that they overwhelm anything any individual can do and they don't trust politicians to do the right thing at the political level. Recycling, as noted above, is so popular because it feels like something doable that has an impact. Choosing the right kind of electricity and allowing renewables to compete freely and prove their commercial viability would restructure power markets in very short order.

If, moreover, we allowed Canada to get the full market value today of its energy resources, including oil and gas, we could, for example, use a major share of the wealth created to pay off the legacy debt burden created by the ill-advised decisions of the dinosaur electricity monopolists or to upgrade the infrastructure to allow it to support electric car recharging on a large scale.

If eventually the technology emerges to allow wireless transmission of electricity[138] on a commercial scale, the power of the old monopolies will be fatally undermined, just like wireless is sending landlines into the industrial museum alongside blacksmiths and slide rules.

The electricity industry would finally be free to adapt to what people want, rather than people having to adapt to what the monopoly provides. Already it is only stubborn monopolists and regulators and politicians that are preventing the transformation of the power supply into a consumer-driven model where no private provider would undertake the lunacy of Muskrat Falls and subsea cables to Nova Scotia, or ruinous feed-in tariffs in Ontario. Instead, big investments would be unlocked and directed toward local small-scale projects that are beneath the notice of the monopolists but hold out the promise of low-cost, low-risk, low environmental impact and low-carbon electricity for those who want it.

Gardening in the tax patch

A supply-side gardener's policy would ask how we could use the tax system to increase the rewards to carbon-reducing innovation more directly than the current carbon tax does and directs the incentives for innovation toward people more able to act on those incentives than consumers.

One such proposal, for clean tax cuts, has emerged from the think-tank world in the United States. This is not the place to get into a detailed discussion of tax policy, but it is at least conceptually possible to imagine a tax credit payable directly to companies and innovators who can demonstrate a documented technological ability to reduce carbon emissions by any legitimate means. Further, if the credits were tradeable, then under-capitalized companies could sell them to firms with large tax liabilities, helping to finance further R&D and deployment. This helps to avoid the problem that companies with good ideas but no taxable income may not be able to use the tax incentive themselves.

In other words, the clean tax cuts approach gives money rather than taking it away, as a carbon tax does. This is a cost to public budgets. Companies that spent money on legitimate carbon reduction technologies, including pure research and development, could claim such tax credits. Regrettably there would be some need for bureaucracy here to police this as companies would try to get tax rebates for silly things.

A different but complementary tax policy would require companies to calculate (by a defined method) how much carbon their product produces from manufacturing through consumer use and recycling. They would then be required to pay a tax on that carbon, with the tax burden reduced in accordance with the company's investment in technology to reduce their products' lifetime emissions.

Imputing emissions to the producer rather than the consumer would make less obvious the impact of carbon policies on costs borne by consumers. The cost of such a tax would, of course, still be built into the price paid by the consumer, but companies would be in a better position than consumers to respond to the carbon-reduction incentives the tax created and would be able to benefit themselves and consumers by improving their carbon performance, thus engaging the competitive pressures of the economy. Companies more successful at reducing their products' life-cycle emissions would have an advantage. Indeed, assuming that carbon life-cycle ratings were publicly available, companies could use them as marketing tools, again allowing people to vote for reduced carbon production everyday with their purchases.

Such a tax might have some fascinating effects. For example, electric cars, the darlings of the environmental movement, also have emissions associated with them[139] – the emissions required to generate the electricity that charging requires,[140] battery construction, parts manufacturing, recycling at the end of their life and so forth. A life-cycle carbon tax should apply to them, and to solar panels and windmills, as well. A genuine effort at carbon reduction doesn't leave anyone out of account.

Such tax measures can be supplemented with smart regulation that does not attempt to tell carbon emitters *how* to reduce their carbon emissions but simply requires them to do so on a predictable and reasonable timetable.[141] This forces companies to seek, and help to pay for, technologies that work best with the company's processes and existing technologies, relying on solutions driven by their detailed knowledge of their specific and unique circumstances rather than on regulators' necessarily partial and limited view.

Legitimate questions can be asked about whether this approach will be effective. Canada's leading tax thinker, Jack Mintz, has pointed out to me in private conversation that incentives can cause capital goods prices to rise, undermining the value of the incentives.[142]

On the other hand, one of the strengths of the kind of approach I am advocating here is that it pays cash for evidence of genuine technological progress in reducing carbon and removing it from the environment and does not therefore require profits in order to be effective.

Again, such schemes will be much easier to pay for if we permit new wealth creation, including the full development and commercialization of

Canada's oil and gas which, far from leading us to environmental destruction, could help to finance our transition to a low-carbon economy without it requiring that we give up the tremendous advantages of carbon-based fuels.

So the gardener's concluding message would be not to surrender lightly what has been bequeathed to us by previous generations: a rising standard of living for people throughout the world, higher levels of education, more and better food, better health, a cleaner environment and, more important than all of that, institutions that allow freedom and the human spirit to work together for the betterment of the human condition. Certainly we should not surrender these things to ill-informed doomsayers or peddlers of fantasies of rational centralized control. They claim knowledge they do not and cannot possibly possess.

Never forget that, as human beings, we do not know what we've got, we do not know what we know, we do not know where we're going and, most crucially, we do not know who we are. Within grown social institutions these aspects of our irremediable ignorance do not prevent us from putting all the knowledge enjoyed by humanity to work in the service of satisfying the full range of human wants, needs and desires, including reducing our carbon footprint. We do so in great abundance and we have proven ourselves equal to resolving all the problems that are created along the way. But those who do not understand how grown institutions co-ordinate human activity and knowledge are always soliciting us to abandon those institutions in favour of a social vision whose product cannot exceed the boundaries of designers' ignorance. I may not know much, but I know that that is not the path to progress and freedom for humanity.

CHAPTER VIII

Natural Resources, Indigenous Canadians and Social Licence

RELATIONS WITH INDIGENOUS PEOPLES in Canada pose one of the greatest challenges for the gardener's approach. This challenge is in large part due to the fact that it goes against the grain of the individualist inspiration that underlies much of what I have said thus far. Indigenous communities are nothing if not groups and putting group identity ahead of individual identity is at the root of much social conflict in the gardener's manual.

Set against this is the fact that the gardener's philosophy is an incrementalist one that proceeds on the basis of what works, not on the basis of what theory dictates in order to achieve "consistency." If this is a weakness, so be it, but I do not think it is.

The questions we ask ourselves as gardeners are these: How do we take the raw materials we have to hand today and, using the lessons we have learned about social co-operation, nudge Indigenous policy incrementally in the direction of individual empowerment and responsibility, of experimentation and innovation and of integration into the modern economy? How do we reward people for earning their way through their own efforts rather than being reliant on the state to transfer things to "compensate" for underdevelopment or past mistakes? How do we ensure that all people are brought under, and benefit from, the rule of law and the principles of justice? And how do we do all this while earning trust and engagement rather than resentment and obstruction?

With respect to Indigenous people these principles are put to the test because it is very difficult for Canada's institutions and policy makers to treat Indigenous people as individuals when this country's relationship with them is largely (but not exclusively) defined by group rights under treaties and Indigenous rights and title, all of them protected under the Constitution since 1982 and subsequently given vigorous new life through judicial interpretation. In addition, Indigenous people are the only group ("Indians and Indian lands") singled out in the Constitution as being an exclusive preserve of the federal government (although this emphasis is shifting as provincial and territorial governments are increasingly brought into the relationship).

This unique status within Canada has been both a blessing and a curse for Indigenous people. The blessing is that it gives them unique tools, emerging only in the past forty years or so, to protect their culture and traditional way of life and, under the new Constitutional dispensation, considerable power with which to negotiate with the rest of Canadian society.

The curse is that being so egregiously singled out as a group has, since the beginning, made them the target of well-meaning designer intervention, with "experts" champing at the bit to "fix" the ills and problems of Indigenous society. Designers now see the narrative around Indigenous people as largely one of group victimhood, something to be put right by self-flagellation and inquisitions into the past that will underline yet again the poor treatment meted out to Indigenous Canadians. To designers, the solution consists of compensation, apologies, increased financial transfers and especially more well-meaning but paternalistic attempts to "fix" Indigenous people's problems. They forget that earlier attempts to solve Indigenous challenges led to such "designer" measures as residential schools, the Indian Act, reserves and welfare. One flinches at the thought that government designers are working up the next set of state interventions, in the faint hope that solutions imposed from without will somehow work better this time around.

I'll explain in a moment why I think that, far from being the solution, this is embracing the causes of the immiseration of Indigenous society. It empowers policy-makers who know little about the lives of Indigenous people, and disempowers those same Indigenous people by denying them key instruments of control over their lives, instruments the rest of us take for granted. Over the years those instruments have passed progressively into the hands of distant experts and bureaucrats. The designer approach today will only dig ever-deeper the hole we have dug for Indigenous people.

A gardener's narrative would take an entirely different tack, noting that victimhood focuses on the past, which cannot be changed, and takes power from the victims, who must go cap in hand to the authorities for restitution or the resources to "catch up" with the rest of Canadian society. In its place we can put a narrative of opportunity and legitimate Indigenous power that must now be accommodated in modern Canada.

I say that a gardener's narrative "would" take a different tack because it has not yet happened. That's because many gardeners in Canada, while grudgingly admitting that Indigenous people have gained power thanks to the courts and the revitalization treaties and Indigenous rights in 1982 through constitution-alization, feel in their hearts that this power is somehow illegitimate and cannot be embraced precisely because it is based on collective rights and not individual equality under and before the law or, in yet another instance of old-style paternalism, because Indigenous governments are not "ready."

I know it is hard for gardeners in this country, *but it is time to let this narrative go.* It has been overtaken by events. The courts have spoken, and done so soundly, repeatedly and correctly, summoning Canadians to honour the commitments made to Indigenous people, commitments now given constitutional protection. Just as importantly, the rising generation of young Indigenous Canadians wants jobs and opportunity on the reserve as well as in the cities, and the natural resource frontier continues to run through many of those communities, juxtaposing legitimate Aboriginal power and real opportunity in a way not seen before in our history since the decline of the fur trade in the late nineteenth century. It is my view that the leading edge of reconciliation with Indigenous people in this country once again runs along the natural resource frontier and it is natural resource companies and Indigenous Canadians who are striking the deals that are making reconciliation a reality on the ground.

I do not say it will be easy for gardeners to come to terms with these questions of Indigenous autonomy and empowerment. On the other hand, gardeners can sometimes get a bum rap for being cold and heartless, relying on pitiless social forces rather than the warm helping hand of government compassion. I think this is the exact opposite of the truth, but one cannot ignore the reality of how the gardener philosophy can be caricatured. Gardeners wishing to burnish their philosophy's compassion credentials might well want to start with a burning social issue that most Canadians regard as a stain on the conscience of the country, namely the shocking conditions in which far too many Indigenous citizens live. Especially in the wake of the Truth and Reconciliation Commission, reconciliation with Indigenous people is now properly a major national preoccupation. Gardeners cannot permit themselves to have nothing to say on the topic, or worse, to be grumbling dissenters with no real alternative on offer. Opposition to Indigenous rights disrespects history and the law and is simply unrealistic. These ideas have no place in the gardener's toolbox.

I would remind my fellow gardeners that they do not reject federalism, and yet it allows different communities within Canada to pursue different and sometimes opposed policies (such as toward education or health care or pipelines or reasonable accommodation), so the group rights approach to Indigenous issues has some analogue in institutions we gardeners already embrace.

It is true that there is a fundamental difference between provinces under federalism on the one hand and self-governing Aboriginal communities on the other in that other Canadians cannot move to Indigenous communities and automatically become full members as they can by moving from province to province. This is a derogation from equal rights and equal citizenship, but it is one that history, the Constitution and the courts have bequeathed to us. We must make it work while insisting that it is an exception that must not become a rule.

Always mindful of the potential for governments to abuse their power over their citizens, gardeners might be concerned about a different problem, that of ensuring that Indigenous Canadians do not become prisoners of unaccountable governments in their communities. Saying that Indigenous communities must be empowered to solve their own problems cannot mean that other Canadians therefore become indifferent to their fate.

It may be helpful to remember that one of the key freedoms enjoyed by individual First Nations, Métis and Inuit people is that they have free entry into the rest of Canadian society. They can vote with their feet and this is a real constraint on the power of their governments. To that may be added the fact the power of the federal and provincial governments, the courts, the Charter, etc., continue to apply in Indigenous communities. Equally, First Nations people can move off the reserve and still be politically engaged in community, political and administrative affairs. Under Canadian and international law Indigenous people are Canadian citizens, not tiny sovereign nations like Britain or France or Japan, carved out of Canada. When Indigenous people want their rights recognized they turn to Canadian courts, not international tribunals. As then Chief Justice of the Supreme Court, Antonio Lamer, once wisely remarked, "Let us face it, we are all here to stay."[143] We are now grappling with how to make this unique form of legal and political togetherness (not yet fully reflected in social and economic relations) work for all parties.

Ironically, and perhaps surprisingly to many, how Indigenous and non-Indigenous people should engage with each other is an issue that lends itself increasingly well to a gardener narrative. In fact, instead of the old veiled hostility, a different way for gardeners to conceive of the place of Indigenous people within Canada is as an object lesson in why the designer's approach does not work, and in fact actively harms those it is intended to help.

Take the origins of that same sorry state of much of Canada's Indigenous population to which I referred earlier. Designers will tell you that it is attributable to a history of racism, exclusion and discrimination that goes right back to the arrival of Europeans on the shores of what was to become Canada. While no one can deny that racism has existed and still does exist, the reality is that the position of Indigenous people has worsened considerably since the post-World War II years when designers came to think of that situation as a "problem" to be "solved" by designer measures. Much of the anger and hostility that Indigenous communities clearly feel is directed against institutions and practices that has left them disempowered wards of the state.

The objective of Indigenous people is to wrest back control over their lives, to become self-sufficient and autonomous, to connect with the modern economy and to generate the "own source" resources that will allow them to do what the rest of us take for granted: make decisions about how to live without those decisions having to be approved by those in authority. One of the greatest motivations behind Indigenous action is to build incremental access to income and capital generated by and belonging to Indigenous governments that is not subject to federal government control. This is unequivocally a gardener's agenda.

Government control of Indigenous lives

As First Nations know well, the period after World War II saw the rapid expansion of the presence and impact of the government of Canada on their communities. Motivated by a desire to see marked improvements in Indigenous lives, economies and conditions, the government launched a wave of interventionist programs. Ottawa required Indigenous children to go to school, with many going to one of the country's growing list of residential schools. The government encouraged (a euphemism for required) First Nations people to live on reserves, built houses, expanded social and economic programs – and installed a culture of welfare dependency that undercut Indigenous independence and established the dominance of federal authorities.

Who would have thought that one of the most interventionist tools in the hands of the post-WWII government would be the Family Allowance, seemingly one of the most harmless and innocuous government programs? The FA provided monthly payments to all Indigenous mothers, designed to support children and families. But the government added a requirement: for mothers to get the money, their children had to attend school, which then led to a shift to living in reserve-based communities.[144] Northern

Indigenous people were not given cheques like almost all other Canadian families. Instead, the government produced a list of "acceptable" purchases, which Indigenous mothers could collect from government authorized stores and charge against their allowance.

As First Nations in the northern parts of the Prairies remember, Indigenous ways of living remained strong through the 1950s and 1960s. Hunting, fishing, trapping and other harvesting activities continued. Many First Nations people lived in homes they built for themselves and spent much of their time travelling in their territories. They made decent incomes from their harvesting, fed their families and worked in mining, forestry, and other industries when seasonal opportunities existed and when they sought or needed work. While the prevailing Canadian view of this period is that Indigenous peoples and communities were suffering from extreme poverty and social challenges, the reality was different in many parts of the country. First Nations language use was strong, the elders had clear and valued roles in their communities, and alcohol and drug abuse were little known. There were undeniable problems to be addressed, including health issues, high rates of infant mortality, low incomes, and major shortcomings with services on reserves (especially water, sewage, electricity, and roads).[145]

Beyond those recognized problems, however, the new culture of imposed welfare dependency, intended to raise the Indigenous standard of living, took a toll of its own. The Canadian government made all major decisions about First Nations issues itself. Meaningful consultations were rare and resource projects and infrastructure were built without reference to Indigenous interests and traditional activities. Development often ran roughshod over them, and either generated no income for communities or that income disappeared into the maw of "Indian Affairs" and its trust accounts, never to be heard from again.

The welfare payments interfered with traditional family support systems and economic activities. Relations between men and women were disrupted by the availability of housing and funding for child support, food and other supplies.[146] In the vernacular of that age, social assistance meant that, for Indigenous women, the government became their "old man," a stunning state of affairs that underlies the degree to which state intervention upset the fundamentals of Indigenous life.[147] The Family Allowance requirement that students attend school either resulted in young people being relocated to residential schools, often for years, or convinced parents to remain in the reserve communities so that the children could go to school close to home. In a variety of ways, growing levels of government intervention caused widespread disruptions within First Nations lives, families and communities.

First Nations took out their frustrations in different ways, from direct protests to the federal government or the local Indian agent through to various acts of self-destruction. Communities suffered, revealing aspects of socio-cultural distress that were not evident in earlier decades. Residential schools and aggressive assimilationist efforts in provincial and territorial schools eroded language use and upset centuries-old traditions. Harvesting activity slowed substantially and a wide generational divide emerged. A growing number of members relocated from the reserves to towns and cities, drawn by employment or educational activities. Government policies, introduced in the designer's misguided belief that federal authorities knew what was best for First Nations, proved to be extremely disruptive, setting off crises within First Nations that have reverberated across the subsequent generations.

Now the tide is turning and newly-empowered First Nations are demanding that the paternalism be swept away. They insist that First Nations people get the same resources as other Canadians do for public services, hardly a radical expectation, but one that is far from being met despite the widespread prejudice that Indigenous Canadians are somehow getting far more than other Canadians.[148] They are demanding not just that they get the same as other Canadians, but that they control those resources so that they can spend them in accordance with community priorities. They are demanding control over their lands, their housing, their education and their persons – the same kind of community control and respected sphere of individual autonomy that other Canadians enjoy – much greater control over the community's property and the same right to use what they have, including treaty and Indigenous rights, to negotiate their way to a better standard of living based on what they own, on the opportunities available to them[149] and on what they know how to do. Such full participation in the economic mainstream, in accordance with Indigenous beliefs and values, will do more to achieve genuine reconciliation and healing than all the government consultations and new programs you can imagine.

How the natural resource economy fits in

Where their communities are located near cities and towns – like the Musqueam, Squamish, and Tsawwassen First Nations in the Great Vancouver area, the Mi'kmaq in Sydney, Nova Scotia, and the Muskeg Lake First Nation in Saskatoon, for example – First Nations are using the new tools provided by constitutional recognition and supportive court decisions to good effect. Many other Indigenous communities do not enjoy the opportunities afforded by proximity to cities; because of where they are located, the greatest opportunities that are available to them are in the natural resource economy. That puts First Nations' issues right at the heart of one of the greatest debates racking Canadian society: how do we feel about our natural resource endowment?

Prime Minister Justin Trudeau has said that Canadians want to be known not for their resources but for their resourcefulness. Some environmental groups believe that our petroleum resources need to be left in the ground. Ordinary Canadians wonder if natural resource development can be done responsibly and in a way that is compatible with the highest environmental standards, including the global struggle against climate change.

In an earlier chapter I nailed my colours to the mast: it is foolish and self-defeating for Canada to deny itself the full value of its natural resource endowment, especially in the context of dealing with the risks of climate change. Wealth is our ability to respond to challenges, and increased wealth is increased capacity, a realization that many Indigenous communities are embracing with enthusiasm.

Successful natural resource development, however, is inextricably bound up with gardener values. Let me take a moment to explain why, and then to tell you about the challenges that Indigenous people are wrestling with in their engagement with just this kind of development.

We Canadians are a people who have earned our way in the world by exploiting the bounteous fruits of the earth, whether agricultural commodities, minerals, or oil and gas, and then transporting them to those who need them in every corner of the globe. This vocation of developing and adding value to the wealth implicit in the earth is something of which we should all be inordinately proud, for it is a calumny on the Canadian character and our history to say that we are mere hewers of wood and drawers of water, as if knowing how to develop, enrich and move the earth's riches well and intelligently were an inferior occupation. Nothing could be further from the truth.

But too often we misunderstand or are unaware of why we are so good at this, and because we do not understand our success, there are important dangers that hover over us. Let me try to illustrate what I think the issue is with a non-Canadian example.

During my time working for the UN in the Democratic Republic of Congo (or Zaire as it then was), I became good friends with a successful Ismaili businessman who had built a lovely home in the hills overlooking a mist-covered lake in the east of the country.

One day a Zairean army general drove up to the house and looked around appreciatively at the view, the grounds and the house. He knocked on the door and said to my friend, "You have a beautiful home here. You have twenty-four hours to get out. It's mine now."

This appalling story isn't merely about arbitrary abuse of power in lawless lands. It is an object lesson in the incredible power of property rights, regulatory certainty and the rule of law to unlock prosperity – and conversely how their absence is so frequently the cause of the impoverishment of entire societies.

My friend had title to his land and had honestly earned the money with which he built his house. But he lived in a society without the machinery to give his rights solidity. Men with guns could override deeds and contracts with impunity. Thus, few people could risk investing in mines and pipelines, power plants and apartment buildings, dams and railways. Only big international players who could afford their own armed men and could bribe governments to leave them alone could afford to invest, and even those ventures were highly risky because who knew what would happen if the government fell or the president died?

In fact, it is the weakness of property rights and regulatory certainty in such societies that is at the root, for example, of the environmental degradation that too often accompanies development in these countries. Why? Because in the absence of reliable and enforceable rights, if your tenure can be yanked out from under you on a whim, as a rational risk manager you have to assume that if it *can* happen that it *will* happen. The incentives then are to pillage the earth to recover your investment as quickly as you can. Only in circumstances where you can be confident that your tenure is secure can you take the time and invest the money that allows responsible development to occur.

In other words, the value of our natural resources doesn't come solely from the resources themselves. Otherwise, places like Russia and Congo (Zaire) and Angola and Indonesia, with fine natural resource endowments, would be rich like Canada. Instead, what we have and they don't is a natural resource endowment nested within a much more important endowment of institutions, rules, laws and behaviours that are the gardener's pride and joy and that create the certainty that unlocks the investment on which the natural resource economy depends. I have mentioned what these grown social institutions consist of elsewhere, but just to remind you of a few key ones, they include the rule of law, democracy, judicial independence, robust property rights, respect of contracts, speedy and authoritative dispute resolution, non-corrupt police and bureaucracy, a relatively stable regulatory and tax burden, non-violent resolution of disagreements, a strong work ethic and more.

The natural resource economy is thus heavily reliant on the certainty that grown social institutions create. That is both why we have been so successful, compared to other places, in developing that endowment, and why recent developments that call that certainty into question, including the delay in the Trans Mountain Extension approval and opposition to the already-approved Coastal GasLink pipeline, as will be discussed in much greater depth later on, are so troubling. The new uncertainty gnaws at the very root of our success.

Think for a moment about this. Why is it that the natural resource economy represents only about 12 to 13 percent of the national economy, *but about one half of the business investment intentions?* Because natural resources require huge investments up front, with a payback period measured in decades. In order to play in this game you have to spend billions and billions up front on a mine, oil sands plant, LNG terminal ($40 billion for the west coast's LNG Canada project alone), or pipeline, and then hope that the price of the commodity and all the other uncontrollable variables come together over thirty years to allow you to recoup your investment. That's why uncertainty in our institutions is so devastating to the natural resource economy in particular, because the decision to invest the money upfront is highly sensitive to the conditions of the day. Investment won't be made in a place where local conditions make payback over thirty years more risky than it already is globally.

The next concept I want to introduce is what I call the perishable nature of opportunity. The natural resource opportunities facing the world are huge and will last for many years, regardless of short-term price movements. But the opportunities for specific projects are extremely dependent on the circumstances at any given moment.

For example, Japan is closing down a major part of its nuclear power industry. That opens a window for the suppliers of natural gas who can build the infrastructure and make long-term contractual commitments to get that gas to Japan to fuel the natural gas fired plants that will take nuclear power's place. In this race there will be winners and losers. Those who cannot deliver on time and on budget will lose, and that opportunity will be gone for a very, very long time. This was certainly the case in the Mackenzie Valley where it took a decade to get approval for a proposed natural gas pipeline. By the time the approval was forthcoming, market conditions had shifted and the window had closed, to the immense frustration of many Northerners, including the Aboriginal Pipeline Group, representing many Indigenous communities who stood to acquire a one-third interest in the project. That is an object lesson in the perishable nature of opportunity and in how local enthusiasm is no guarantee of a project's success.

Having a great natural resource endowment is not enough if you don't have reliable and predictable institutions that give us access to the minerals and other resources to be developed.

This brings us back to the relationship between Indigenous people and natural resource development.

First Nations, Métis and Inuit are now striking deals for development of those resources with hundreds of developers and realizing major opportunities as a result. I know that many Canadians might be unaware of these developments, particularly if they share the widespread view that the "Indigenous problem" is an intractable and insoluble one that sucks up billions of dollars but never shows any sign of improving. Moreover, Indigenous people, at least as they are portrayed in the media, appear to be resolute opponents of natural resource development, with the poster child for this attitude being the apparent decision by one First Nation to turn down over $1 billion in return for permission to put an LNG plant on their territory on the BC coast.

Let me offer you specific examples of why I think this storyline is not merely a distortion but has become an obstacle to the reconciliation or partnership I am calling for between gardeners and Indigenous Canadians.

Let's go straight to the hard case: the Lax Kw'alaams' alleged decision to turn down $1 billion they were offered from Pacific Northwest to put an LNG terminal on Lelu Island south of Prince Rupert off the BC coast. As one might expect, the media, who feed on conflict, gleefully reported the refusal. What got far less attention was the fact that the Lax Kw'alaams themselves explained that the proposed site was unacceptable for conservation and cultural reasons, but that there were several other sites on their traditional territory that they thought would be suitable and they would support.

Further, the media paid no attention to the fact that the Nisga'a, in the next valley over, the Nass, saw the opportunity that had opened up and spent their own money to survey and identify seven sites that they said would be suitable and where they would be interested in becoming partners in development and seeing the pipeline and plant built on their territory.

Just a few years ago in Saskatchewan, the Muskowekwan voted almost four-to-one in a referendum in favour of developing a potash mine on their territory in partnership with Encanto Potash Corp.

Also in Saskatchewan, the Muskeg Lake First Nation took a Treaty Land Entitlement settlement and used the money to buy a piece of the city of Saskatoon, turn it into a reserve, and create an industrial park there.[150] This has been a very successful venture that now employs many Indigenous and non-Indigenous people but was opposed at the time by some in the non-Indigenous business community on the grounds that it would be unfair competition. Now all sides recognize the contribution that this initiative has made and they can see that this First Nation has supplied important and welcome business leadership to the city.

In the Northwest Territories several Indigenous communities abandoned their earlier opposition and became some of the most fervent advocates for the Mackenzie Valley gas pipeline once they had negotiated the right to purchase a 30 percent equity stake in it. No one was more disappointed than these local Indigenous communities when the pipeline failed and they ended up with 30 percent of nothing thanks, in part, to a long and drawn-out approval process that couldn't reach a timely decision. Many people do not realize that the much-criticized reforms to the pipeline approval process (reforms that streamlined and reduced the time the process took) that were carried out by the Harper government were partly a response to Indigenous pleas to reduce the regulatory obstacles to their success in the natural resource economy.

Today three different Indigenous-led groups, each representing many First Nations and Métis communities, are seeking to buy the Trans Mountain expansion project either in its entirety or as a significant partner, so they now have a major interest in seeing that project completed. Other Indigenous-led and -owned major infrastructure projects are under active development.

Other new pro-development alliances are forming and will give the lie to the widespread narrative that Indigenous Canada is anti-development. Another good example is the First Nations Major Projects Coalition. The Coalition was conceived to respond to the capacity issues faced by many First Nations, Métis, and Inuit communities whose relatively small number of residents and limited financial resources make it hard for them to possess all the information, expertise, and capital needed to develop their economic opportunities. The Coalition offers a framework for nearly fifty First Nations to work collaboratively, sharing resources on a case-by-case basis. More communities are asking to join the coalition.

This is no pie in the sky. Hundreds of acts of Indigenous self-empowerment are happening right now. There have been a record number of deals done in recent years with First Nations over resource development across Canada. If we focus more on the opportunities that bind us together than the obstacles we all face to developing those opportunities, we will get through this together and that when we do we will have created pathways that bring Indigenous people into a level of participation in Canadian society and the economy that meets their needs and that honours their communities. That will be no mean achievement.

Having skin in the game has made Indigenous people acutely aware of the perishable nature of opportunity. The Mackenzie Valley pipeline will not be built for decades now, if ever. A similar evolution has occurred in British Columbia, where one First Nation had opposed natural resource development on its territory for years, but then came to see that they were forgoing economic opportunities available to other Indigenous communities. They responded to the suggestions from the business community for certainty on the rules by agreeing to put in place a natural resource development law governing their territory rather than negotiating with individual developers on a case-by-case basis – showing that Indigenous communities are increasingly understanding the needs of the business community and showing a willingness to respond in a constructive way.[151]

These are all good examples of how some First Nations communities have seized opportunities and improved their prosperity and power to solve their own problems. They are helping to create a slowly widening virtuous circle of prosperity. Communities that have been holding back from engagement increasingly see their more successful brethren and ask, "Why not us?" Within a few years several Indigenous development corporations could well be among the largest corporations in Canada, with billions of dollars in assets. Indigenous communities are collaborating, as I've already noted, through organizations like the First Nations Major Projects Coalition, First Nations LNG, and the First Nations Financial Management Board, to overcome the disadvantages of small size and isolation to participate in new economic initiatives. New Indigenous-controlled partnerships are emerging to allow successful Indigenous communities to invest in less-developed communities that have opportunities but no access to capital. The evidence shows that when Indigenous communities negotiate benefits with developers, those benefits stay in the local community and region, benefiting Indigenous and non-Indigenous alike.[152]

Now, it would be foolish to assert that there have been no uncertainties created along the way as the country integrates Indigenous rights into the regulatory edifice surrounding the natural resource economy. The confusion arising over the Coastal GasLink natural gas pipeline project is a good case in point. The project's proponents have signed agreements with the duly elected band councils of every one of the twenty First Nations along the 670 kilometre route. Nevertheless, a power struggle has erupted *within* one of those First Nations between the elected band council and most of its hereditary chiefs. The result has been a national campaign – supported by non-Indigenous organizations, environmentalists and non-Indigenous protestors, many of them not Canadian – complete with barricades, injunctions, conflict, and yet more media reports highlighting Indigenous "opposition" to natural resource development. These counter-examples undeniably exist, but I would say that, contrary to a widespread view, we have made great progress – and more is on the horizon.

The thing to remember, and the evidence bears this out, is that Indigenous communities (like virtually every other community in Canada) have their vocal minorities opposed to development. These expressions of their dissatisfaction are fodder for the media. But these vocal minorities are no more representative of Indigenous Canada than non-Indigenous protesters are of the country as a whole. When we treat the aggressive and vocal minorities as though they are speaking for the mainstream of the Indigenous world, those of us who believe that jobs and wealth creation hold the key to the country's advancement abandon our natural allies and help reinforce a narrative of conflict that is holding a major part of the economy to ransom.

This is a microcosm of a larger issue. Many Canadians simplify First Nations affairs and, in particular, they see policy and legal options from non-Indigenous perspectives. Canadians broadly agree that we must break the cycles of poverty that disempower Indigenous communities, but there is no broad consensus on how to do so. Some demand that Indian reserves be dismantled. Others argue for more programs, more policies and more money (the latter is urgently needed in some areas, particularly social services, on the basis of simple equity and to address serious and immediate challenges). Many favour some form of Indigenous self-government without recognizing that empowered Indigenous communities will have a lot of power and influence over the future of whole regions of the country, not just over issues that affect their own poverty and despair. The courts have added dramatically to Indigenous power in recent years, offering decisions that typically alarm non-Indigenous people while leaving Indigenous people with Pyrrhic victories that rarely convey the power, clarity, or resources needed to enact the desired and necessary changes. And so Canada limps and stumbles forward, oblivious to the fact that delays and half-steps add to the burdens and challenges facing Indigenous communities.

Clearly, there is no easy or obvious path forward. Hundreds of years of marginalization, mistrust, and paternalism cannot be set right overnight. Many critical issues – building prosperity, addressing infrastructure needs, revitalizing language and culture, sustaining autonomous Indigenous governments, and protecting traditional lands – require urgent attention. In particular, strengthening individual and family lives, and overcoming the legacies of colonialism and eliminating the scourges of teenage suicide, alcohol and substance abuse, massive over-incarceration, and related social and health issues, remain absolute priorities.

In this context and given the small size and geographic isolation of most First Nations reserves and Inuit communities, it is hardly surprising that there is no consensus among Indigenous people themselves about how best to proceed. Remember, too, that these often-tiny Indigenous communities spend an inordinate amount of time and effort applying for government funding, reporting to Ottawa, and consulting with municipal, provincial or territorial and federal authorities. The administrative chaos within which Indigenous governments and peoples are called upon to operate – a reference to other levels of government and not Indigenous authorities – although they are well-meant by the current generation of government officials and designers, causes enormous and continuing difficulties for Indigenous leaders and governments.

Internal tensions within and between Indigenous communities, therefore, is a reality. Indigenous governments are typically intensely democratic, with high levels of internal consultation and approval. Most of the communities have strong traditions of accountability and transparency – ranking openness to their membership over complex and seemingly endless reporting to the government.[153] These communities are routinely challenged to make major and difficult decisions: to participate (or not) in a resource project, to accept a settlement of a legal claim, to launch an expensive, time-consuming and unpredictable court case, to determine how to use their own revenues, to participate in multi-community Indigenous collaborations, and many others. These are difficult choices, often carrying considerable risk.

Not surprisingly, there are occasional disputes. Indigenous leaders often struggle to get consensus or even strong majority support from their membership on major decisions. On high profile issues like pipeline construction, external commentators (such as the environmental movement, of which more in a moment) often intervene in community affairs, adding to the complexity and intensity of the issues. The debates can be extended and complex. They flow over into community elections and regional politics. For communities determined to break away from the federal government and end systemic poverty, opportunities such as natural resource or construction projects or the establishment of a casino are highly emotional decisions and far from easy to resolve.

These divisions typically play out in the privacy of community meetings and without external media coverage. When an Indigenous community makes a decision to support a major project, or to make a major investment, these judgements typically come after intense local debate, extended consultations, and painful concessions by all sides. That Indigenous governments have made many major decisions and achieved a community understanding of the importance of key issues is a testament to their ability and willingness to work through profoundly challenging decision-making. It is this chaotic, intensely challenging world that we are seeking to coordinate with the larger

Canadian society and to bring some certainty to their use of their newfound power. I never said it was going to be easy.

But we cannot be dissuaded by the fact that it will be hard to do this right. It is necessary for the cultural vitality, future success and prosperity of Indigenous people, but as I have been arguing throughout this chapter, it also has major implications for the rest of us.

We must never forget the point I made earlier, that while the natural resource economy may only represent around 12 to 13 percent of the economy as a whole, it represents roughly half of the business investment intentions. Those investment intentions represent future jobs, future capital accumulation (remember: that is future problem-solving capacity) and future prosperity.

Getting the relationship with Indigenous people right on the resource frontier will unlock a great deal of value for all Canadians. It is only right that Indigenous Canadians use their hard-won and legitimate power to win a share of that action. We should welcome that growing spirit of enterprise and entrepreneurialism that seeks opportunity for Indigenous people, respect for their rights, and control over their own lives. These values are what gardeners believe lies at the base of Canadians' great success in the world. Why not embrace and celebrate them when we see ever larger harvests from their re-emergence in the Indigenous world?

By the way, the embrace of Indigenous treaties, rights and title as the basis for the creation of a much-needed Indigenous prosperity need not imply the abandonment of the search for accountability and transparency in Indigenous government. It does imply, however, a change in strategy and tactics – basically abandoning the stick that has traditionally appealed to so many of a gardening bent in favour of the carrot.

Two points here. One: No one, including First Nations, can play in the high stakes business world, where billions are at stake and companies face unprecedented scrutiny through stock exchanges, audits, Foreign Corrupt Practices Acts, etc., without adopting appropriate standards of transparency and accountability. That the Membertou First Nation, in one of their early acts of economic revitalization, became the first Indigenous community to secure ISO certification is an example of an Indigenous community acting on this necessity. Being at the table as a partner, equity stakeholder, or board member, brings responsibility as well as power.

Two: The need for responsibility means that accountability comes progressively with success. This is not a theory, but is already happening in practice. For example, financing mechanisms for Indigenous communities to acquire equity stakes in resource development require suitable levels of transparency and accountability and high quality business practices in return. First Nations make these choices for themselves because of the benefits it creates for them, not as something imposed on them by hostile outsiders or by Ottawa. This approach works, as the path-breaking work of the First Nations Financial Management Board attests.

The challenge we, Indigenous and non-Indigenous Canadians together, have before us then, is how do we fully integrate the power and authority Indigenous people now enjoy over natural resource development in a way that makes them full partners in development and decision-making, while unlocking perishable opportunities when they are ripe? How do we make their newfound power and authority an integral part of the endowment of institutions that I referred to earlier, making Indigenous authority a matter of certainty rather than uncertainty, of collective pride rather than conflict?

Companies more and more understand that establishing and nurturing positive relationships with Indigenous people helps them get their jobs done, just as failing to establish such a relationship virtually guarantees a pipeline full of headaches and opposition.

Make no mistake: Indigenous communities are asking themselves these very questions. Let me quote from a recent commentary by Stephen Buffalo, the head of the Indian Resource Council. Buffalo had this to say about the debate over the Trans Mountain pipeline expansion:

> When pipeline opponents use the courts to slow or stop pipelines, they undermine our businesses, eliminate jobs in our communities and reduce the amount of money flowing to our governments.
>
> But there are lessons for all Canadians in the Trans Mountain decision. Indigenous rights mean something. Consultation has to be real, robust and meaningful. This does not mean that every Indigenous

community will get everything they want out of every development project. We understand and respect the authority of the Government of Canada and its mandate to address the needs of other Canadians.

But our rights are meaningful and powerful. There are no shortcuts around the duty to consult and accommodate. We have the right to be heard. We have the right to be part of the solution to the challenges facing Canadian resource developers. This works. Our communities are partners with hundreds of oil, gas and transmission companies across the country. Our resource-active communities are gaining autonomy from government and are showing that we will be an active and progressive part of this country's economic future.

Please do not hold Indigenous peoples to a double standard, as Canadians have often done in the past. Some First Nations oppose oil and gas development and others do not, just like other Canadians. After all, it was opposition by the City of Montreal, not Indigenous groups, that helped kill the Energy East pipeline project.[154]

Buffalo went on to say: "Indigenous peoples are sick and tired of being seen as a problem for Canada. We understand that Canada's prosperity can and should be good for Indigenous peoples. Canadians need to appreciate that our prosperity is good for Canada, too."

Let me build on what Buffalo said about the case of Trans Mountain, but which I believe is increasingly true of Indigenous involvement in the natural resource economy generally. Forward-looking Indigenous communities will soon be the indispensable allies of the natural resource industry. I say this in part because I have seen recent polling data that says that while the credibility and authority of politicians and regulators is at a low ebb in the minds of the public, when it comes to convincing them that development is environmentally responsible, Indigenous support is viewed more favourably.[155]

When Indigenous communities do their due diligence and support natural resource projects because they are both environmentally responsible and unlock opportunity, the public tends to be highly supportive. That means that Indigenous people now occupy a strategic political ground. If they side with those opposed to a particular development, the project will face almost insurmountable odds. When Indigenous people exercise their rights to full involvement in a development and lend their voice to support the important opportunities it brings, the chances of overcoming other forms of opposition are vastly increased.

Put another way, for the first time in modern history, First Nations don't just have the power to say "no." They now also have the power to say "yes," which they are exercising more frequently than you may imagine, and that they are doing so under the rule of law by exercising the rights that the Supreme Court has recognized, including that the Crown has a duty to consult and accommodate Indigenous interests where they are engaged by decisions of the Crown.

Think about this in the context of the recent announcement by the federal government, without consultation, without study and without the support of experts knowledgeable in the field, to ban oil tanker traffic off the northern BC coast. Given the economic stakes and the number of Indigenous communities already engaged in various pipeline and other projects that require access to such shipping, I was not in the least surprised to learn that First Nations are contemplating dragging the federal government to court for having so egregiously trampled on their rights and opportunities.

This cavalier dismissal by Ottawa of Indigenous interests on one issue (tanker traffic and its associated economic opportunities) highlights a more general problem. Canadians struggle to separate out Indigenous politics and rights from larger public debates, in large measure because many different groups use First Nations interests as vehicles for their own agendas. But those interests are too often tossed aside once they've served their purpose of getting the attention of non-Indigenous Canadians for the issue *du jour*.

People who want to berate the Canadian government for failing to deal with inequality and injustice, for example, routinely highlight Indigenous affairs as example number one. Those who favour judicial engagement over political problem-solving support Indigenous recourse to the courts on major issues. Those in favour of activist government demand state intervention on behalf of Indigenous communities – despite the considerable evidence (residential schools, the Indian Act, welfare dependency) that Ottawa's intervention in Indigenous lives is more the root of the problem than a realistic solution. And, particularly in the twenty-first century, non-Indigenous people who favour aggressive action on climate change and oppose oil and gas development rarely hesitate to invoke Indigenous spokespeople, values and rights as a centrepiece of their arguments.

To a substantial degree, non-Indigenous Canadians insist on portraying Indigenous aspirations, values and goals in ways that support their own perspectives rather than understanding Indigenous points of view and this is nowhere truer than in environmental matters. On many fronts, the country's activists continue to "use" Indigenous people to achieve their own ends rather than respecting the right of Indigenous people and their governments to control their own destinies.

Most Canadians know that some Indigenous people oppose the Trans Mountain Expansion Project, for example. Few realize that the majority of First Nations governments in the affected regions support the project. There has been global attention to the actions of a small number of Wet'suwet'en hereditary chiefs in opposing the Coastal GasLink pipeline to Kitimat, BC. Much less attention is given to the overwhelming support among all the elected chiefs, councils and other First Nations community members in the region for the project and for the economy and society-building opportunities associated with prosperity and opportunity.

Blaine Favel, an Indigenous business leader from Western Canada and former Grand Chief of the Saskatchewan Federation of Indigenous Nations, said what was in the mind of many Indigenous leaders recently when he described the intervention of non-Indigenous environmentalists on major resource projects as "eco-colonialism."[156] Favel went on to liken the role played by the environmental movement today to that played by nineteenth century Christian missionaries in Indigenous communities. We all know that out of that grew the massive effort by well-meaning authorities, churches and others to "fix" First Nations people through a massive program of re-education and community disruption.

To Favel, the environmentalists do not support Indigenous people; they only capitalize on those Indigenous people who share their agenda – which is mostly opposition to pipelines and energy development – and ignore, criticize and even, regrettably, intimidate those who adopt a different perspective.[157] Climate change activists do not find pro-development First Nations "usable." Those who oppose energy projects, by contrast, are very helpful.

I hardly need to point out that this is paternalism at its most egregious. Environmentalists show up, fervently convinced they know what is "good" for everyone, including Indigenous people, despite knowing little about the history or the current conditions and aspirations of these communities. Then by their actions they reveal their true agenda. This can be summarized as, "we will tell you what your interests are and the right thing to do to defend them and we will be there for you if, and only if, you agree."

Perhaps the most extreme example of the paternalistic "We know what's best for you and we don't need to ask you to know" kind of thinking occurred in December 2019, when the United Nations Committee on the Elimination of Racial Discrimination (CERD) released a directive calling for three large-scale natural resource projects in British Columbia to be "immediately" shut down, including the Coastal GasLink pipeline. When Reuters asked CERD chair Noureddine Amir about it, he admitted that the committee did not study First Nations views on the project, saying, "I did not know that most First Nations agree on that. This is something new that comes to my understanding."[158] Thank God those fervent anti-colonialist advocates for Indigenous people at the UN are on the case!

The eco-colonialists rightly denounced by Favel do not, it seems, really support Indigenous rights and the ability of First Nations, Métis and Inuit communities to plan their own futures. Rather, they push Indigenous communities to adopt the twenty-first century's religion of ecological action or be condemned and punished for their sins. *Plus ça change* in the Indigenous world *plus c'est la même chose.*

Southern, urban and other outside activists have every right to their opinions, which are clearly deeply held. They have every right to try to convince Indigenous communities to share them, although it would be good if they did their homework first and abjured intimidation and coercion as tactics. By contrast, the cynical manipulation of the social, economic and cultural vulnerabilities of Indigenous peoples and the lack of respect for their autonomy and decision-making are simply inconsistent with full partnership and respect for Indigenous peoples and their rights.

The major changes in the law and political arrangements that I have talked about in this chapter have re-empowered Indigenous peoples. A fair bit of work remains to be done, and it will be achieved either through major court cases or negotiated accords. But if we truly respect the right and ability of Indigenous peoples to make their own decisions to protect their lands and cultures *as they choose to*, and if we listen with openness and compassion to Indigenous perspectives, we will quickly conclude that the eco-colonialism of the present-day environmental movement has to be called out for the paternalistic manipulation that it is. Imposing others' values on Indigenous peoples did not work in the past; it will not be any less destructive today because it is hip and enlightened designer values that are the justification for "fixing things." Indigenous people don't need to be "fixed." They need to have the same resources other Canadians do and the same room to make their own decisions, including their own mistakes and their own successes. Nobody knows who Indigenous people are, what they are, and what they want better than Indigenous people themselves.

May I see your social licence, please?

I earlier identified an emerging confluence of interests between Indigenous and non-Indigenous Canadians in the full development and responsible exploitation of our natural resource endowment. I now want to suggest that this potential alliance of interests extends further. It extends to managing and ultimately defeating a great challenge to our continued success as a natural resource power: the social licence movement.

Wherever there is organized opposition to new pipelines, mines,[159] railroads, electricity generation and transmission,[160] manufacturing plants, container terminals, tree cutting,[161] or even agricultural practices, to mention just a few examples, the opponents repeat the mantra that such projects must obtain "social licence" or they must not be allowed.

The social licence movement, which ironically arose in the natural resource sector, matters because it goes right to the heart of the certainty about rules that the natural resource industry needs in order to invest in Canada. This certainty is just as essential if you are part of an Indigenous community that hopes to develop, and benefit from, resource opportunities on or near your traditional lands as it is if you are part of an international resource consortium.

It used to be that the framework for natural resource development in Canada was pretty clear. Governments generally owned the resources and they set a regulatory and tax framework that was relatively clear and stable. Developers knew in advance the rules that had to be satisfied in order to be granted permission to proceed with the project. Regulatory proceedings were not intended to be a place where the desirability of development *per se* was to be debated; they were instead an evidence-based technical inquiry about whether project proponents had satisfied the regulatory requirements and so could be given a green light. And all of this occurred within a climate of public opinion that generally held that well-designed and run natural resource development was in the public interest.

The evidence, however, is that the longstanding political consensus is breaking down all around us, and with it the confidence in and deference toward our generally excellent regulatory proceedings.

And while this breakdown is most visible in the oil and gas sector (think of the vehement opposition to pipelines, oil sands development, LNG facilities and so forth and the political circuses that many regulatory proceedings have become[162]), the rest of the natural resource sector is *not* immune. The obstacles to reasoned development of our resources, including forests, hydro power and minerals and their attendant infrastructure, are becoming ever more daunting and I think it is safe to predict that the sector's opponents will continue their slow ratcheting up of opposition to development on an increasingly broad front.

This is not to say that the natural resource sector has stopped working, because it hasn't. The mining sector continues to enjoy considerable success, both in securing regulatory permission and gaining Indigenous support. But the legal framework we have created to ensure that these activities are compatible with the public interest are increasingly and vocally con-tested. This type of opposition greatly increases the cost of these projects and decreases the certainty that they will succeed. This connects with the argument I have already made that one half of all the business investment intentions in Canada rise from the natural resource sector, and that invest-ment is falling precipitously.[163] It is not that, once established, these projects do not run successfully (even the existing pipelines in Canada are allowed to function, although there is concern about the rising number of efforts to interfere with their operation[164]). It is rather that confidence in Canada's ability to get major *new* projects done is in peril.

I would go further and make the case that the old consensus is break-ing down largely due to increasingly vocal minorities who are opposed to natural resource development *per se*. They are now using the institutions we created to ensure an orderly and thoughtful approval process to ensure a disorderly and emotional one. One of the most devastating pieces of federal legislation came at the end of the last parliament and took aim at energy project approval. Bill C-69 licensed a large increase in the scope of the geography, the topics and the interests on which consultation was to be made mandatory and legitimized an endless and limitless consultative process as, in effect, not a way to win approval for projects, but a way to obstruct them almost without limitation.

One of the greatest challenges we face in continuing our great tradition of success in the natural resource sector is the undermining of the institu-tions that surround decisions about development. As long as we continue to fight a rear-guard action in defence of individual projects those who support natural resource development will always be on the defensive and will increasingly see projects fail as a result. Unless this changes there will be many more Energy East and Northern Gateway pipeline projects and Teck Frontier mines in our future.

Social licence is the phrase that now captures the central idea that natural resource development shouldn't be carried out under objective tests estab-lished by lawmakers to determine if they are in the public interest. Over and above those tests there is allegedly a form of permission that must be obtained from "society" and especially local people directly affected by development. In the process, depth of feeling in opposition to projects becomes a major obstacle to their success. Justin Trudeau, before he became prime minister, gave his imprimatur to this trend when he repeated the mantra of the social licence movement, that governments issue permits but only communities can give permission. He has never officially backed away from that view.

It has been suggested by some, however, that the social licence movement has had its day, done in by public rejection of its intransigence. In particular, Prime Minister Trudeau and then Alberta premier Rachel Notley hitched their wagon to the social licence movement, thinking it was a bona fide request by a popular movement to take account of their opposition to the further development of Canada's oil and gas industry. Trudeau and Notley, thinking that there was a deal to be struck to get new pipeline capacity to tidewater, brought in emissions caps in the oil sands, a carbon tax, the cancellation of the Northern Gateway pipeline, the failure (in the face of intense political hostility, particularly in Quebec) of the Energy East project and much tougher requirements for future projects in exchange, or so they thought, for acquiescence on the expansion of the existing Trans Mountain pipeline (TMX).

Predictably, the opposition to TMX continued unabated, the concessions regarded, not as a good faith negotiation, but as a sign of weakness presaging even more concessions if only the pressure was kept up. I am personally persuaded that even now that construction has actually begun on TMX that its opponents will engage in further civil disobedience along the route in the not unreasonable hope that those who favour the project will eventually find that the price of success is just too high. And the protesters will do this in the name of social licence. Critically, the bar for achieving social licence is deemed, in the new formulation, not to be substantial, majority support, but the agreement of project opponents, no matter how small a minority they may represent. The pursuit of social licence is, clearly, an unwinnable race. Ironically, despite the Wet'suwet'en debacle, it is mostly Indigenous communities in Canada now who have clear procedures for ensuring widespread and documented support for a major project.

Even if I am wrong and TMX is successfully completed, that does not mean that the social licence movement has lost its vigour. It has just too powerful a rhetorical appeal, claiming that "ordinary people" oppose these projects and that as long as they do, the projects themselves are just the brainchild of greedy corporate interests trying to impose their will on communities that don't want them. Even if it does turn out that "social licence" as a term has been damaged, we can be confident that the concept it embodies will continue to be invoked by opponents of natural resource development. It is therefore worth digging into the idea, regardless of what name will be attached to it in the future.

Even among those who believe that social licence is the indispensable precondition of a legitimate project, no one seems to be able to answer a few basic questions about such licence.

What, for instance, is the address to which you need to write to obtain it? What form must you fill out? Who are the authorities who decide if your application meets the rules and to whom are they accountable? In fact, what are the rules? What are the procedures followed in determining if you satisfy them? What appeal procedures exist if a project proponent feels their project has not been fairly assessed?

If you're like most people, these questions will make you smile, because we all know that they have no answers.

And yet these are not silly questions. On the contrary, they go right to the heart of how a democratic society that lives under the rule of law operates. They are, in fact, gardener's questions.

The very vagueness of the term social licence means we cannot know what the rules are, when we're in compliance, or whether we've still got work to do. And project opponents like that vagueness just fine because it gives them unilateral authority to claim that the need for social licence has not been met. How can they be proven wrong since no one knows the tests that must be satisfied?

Change always creates winners and losers. That is why we surround economic development with many restrictions and requirements, including the need to consult and compensate people whose legitimate interests may be damaged, including Indigenous peoples. We must minimize any unavoidable harms to the greatest extent possible. We also must meet the highest environmental standards while seeking to maintain the consent of the population.

But we also have to balance the costs against the benefits that development may create in terms of jobs, business, government revenue, investment and opportunity. Whether we want to recognize it or not, we are embarking on a conversation about whether we as a society will confront our future challenges with more resources and wealth, or less, and therefore with more capacity to turn our ideas into reality, or less. The stakes are enormous.

In a civilized society we create numerous institutions that are domiciled at known addresses that are given specific authority to examine impartially the issues that development raises according to known rules – outfits like the National Energy Board (NEB) or various federal and provincial environmental assessment agencies.

The purpose of these regulatory and administrative proceedings is precisely to create a fair setting where all relevant information is gathered and where independent and disinterested commissioners ask themselves what a reasonable person would conclude about the balance between the costs and benefits of the project before them.

Moreover, administrative tribunals such as the NEB, the Canadian Nuclear Safety Commission (CNSC), environmental assessment panels and others are accountable to the governments that appoint them as well as to the courts, to whom aggrieved parties may appeal when they think the rules have been broken. The legislators who pass the laws creating these agencies must submit themselves periodically to the verdict of the voters.

The rules generally require public consultations of some kind and compensation for damaged interests. As an example, after a detailed and extensive consultation process, in June 2014 the NEB granted a permit to the Northern Gateway pipeline to proceed, subject to 209 conditions designed to respond to Canadians' rising expectations around the stringency of approvals for such major developments.

Smart developers want local support for their plans. Politicians want development that wins public support rather than alienates voters. These institutions I am describing help to achieve this.

If this is what is meant by social licence, who can object? Reasonable people want to be reassured that the properly constituted authorities – including companies – are applying reasonable standards to momentous decisions that one way or another affect us all. The people who make it through these onerous, demanding and internationally admired regulatory processes put in place by our democratically elected governments are the ones who legitimately *do* have social licence.

Extreme social licence advocates have been working overtime in recent years to undermine the credibility of the institutions we have created democratically to manage these decisions on behalf of Canadians. Yet despite what you may have heard, these institutions have not been turned into pushovers, toadying up to project proponents and ignoring the rising expectations of Canadians with respect to environmental protection and other standards. On the contrary.

Despite rhetoric deployed in the 2015 federal election, for example, there is little objective evidence that Canada's regulatory system has failed or needs to be tougher. Energy installations, mines, hydro transmission facilities, some decades old, work day in and day out without incident, including the original Kinder-Morgan pipeline, which was approved in one day of hearings by the NEB in the 1950s and is still operating safely and highly successfully today decades later. Other countries hold up our regulatory institutions as models to emulate.

The proponents of full-blooded social licence dismiss this sort of defence of our institutions as mere legalism. According to them, some abstract and ill-defined entity called "society," independent of legislatures, regulators, or courts, must be satisfied or else it is illegitimate to build the mine or the pipeline or the plant or the road or the railway.

But as I hope I have made clear, these claims constitute an attack on the gardener-inspired institutions and behaviours that are Canada's greatest endowment. The uncertainty thus created is undermining the value of our natural resources and is causing us to forgo opportunities, which in turn undermines our prosperity.

These claims do more than constitute an attack on the rule of law thanks to their lack of due process and natural justice, for example. They also constitute an attack on democracy because they don't just attempt to intimidate legitimate political and regulatory institutions which operate within the democratically established rules of our society to help governments make such difficult decisions. Opponents refuse to recognize the fundamental legitimacy of those institutions. Unless those institutions come to the same conclusion that the objectors do about individual projects, the work of those institutions is to be discarded and indeed denigrated as obviously the work of the hand puppets of rapacious capitalism.

There is nothing undemocratic about saying that you think the processes used to make such decisions ought to be changed, and submitting your ideas to political parties and the voters. It is entirely legitimate to go to court to question whether the law is being correctly, fairly and properly applied. It is equally democratic to voice your displeasure about proposed projects, to demonstrate against them, to threaten politicians with a loss of support if they go ahead. That is fair game. That is part of the process by which politicians get feedback about how the rules should be framed and what is publicly acceptable.

It is wholly undemocratic, however, to say that you simply disregard the decisions of duly constituted constitutional and democratic authority as without merit or foundation, as if your views are the only ones that deserve to be heard or respected.

Sometimes social licence takes the rather different form of claiming that people far away shouldn't have an important say on decisions that have a differential impact on locals, and therefore that social licence is something that must be conferred by those who have the most at stake. Moreover, if the economic benefits are to be enjoyed more by the "far away" than by the locals, that authorizes extortion of the far-away interests. Failure to do so means "social licence" will not be forthcoming.

If the argument is that those who benefit must pay all the costs of their projects, including of the highest standards of environmental protection and of any clean-up required by a failure of those protections, and compensation for legitimate interests damaged, I scarcely need to say that such things are the hallmarks of a civilized and gardener-inspired society and can and must be done. But again, these things must be determined by an independent and evidence-based process, not on the basis of orchestrated and exaggerated fear and emotion. Indeed, in the case of Northern Gateway, to return to that example, that is precisely what many of the 209 conditions I mentioned were designed to ensure: that the project had confronted all these issues and had offered reasoned and reasonable answers to the foreseeable risks and dangers the project gives rise to.

Once these legitimate claims are recognized and honoured, however, vital projects cannot be held hostage to every grasping local interest. The St. Lawrence Seaway benefits some communities hugely, others not at all. For yet others who were flooded to make it possible, it was a death sentence. Railways pass through hundreds of communities in Canada where they never stop, and yet those communities run the risk of noise pollution, collisions and catastrophic spills of chemicals and other toxic substances. People who live next to airports are surely inconvenienced by the noise and traffic.

But we don't allow provinces or communities or disaffected groups to throw up customs booths at their borders and collect taxes to allow them to get what they judge to be their "fair share" of other people's goods as they pass through or to prevent them from carrying on their lawful activities.

That's what countries too often do to each other and the result is the collective impoverishment of the world. We are busily engaged in a massive effort to try to tear down those barriers so that other countries cannot object to the importation of our goods and services on the grounds that such transactions benefit Canadians more than the citizens of those other places. We rightly regard it as a great victory for Canada that we have just negotiated a free trade agreement with the European Union (EU) and renewed North American Free Trade Agreement (NAFTA) with the US and Mexico, for example, which will prevent local European and American industries and politicians from obstructing access to their markets for Canadian products, claiming that Canadians have not been granted "social licence" to threaten local livelihoods.

Some may want to make the case that specific communities or provinces get shortchanged in the benefits generated by individual projects. That is a legitimate political position. But holding up projects that benefit the whole province or country simply because you think you haven't got your "fair share," whatever that is, is the precise logic of protectionists and NIMBYists everywhere: unless each transaction can demonstrably be shown to benefit them more than other parties to the transaction, they will block it – not because blocking will help them, but because they would rather all be poor together than to see others get ahead.

What the proponents of the mob rule version of social licence mean to say is that change must be approved by its opponents, who will be the ones to decide whether social licence has been achieved. Its alleged absence will be established by angry media releases or hand-lettered signs waved on the evening news.

Even the idea that endless talk is helpful in the search for the elusive social licence is in my view quite wrong-headed. One of the features of designerism seems to be that if only we talk enough, people of good will invariably find that deep agreement underlies their superficial disagreements. More consultation is therefore always better than less.

Like me, you may feel that this is ironic given that the current aesthetic theory to which designers pay court is that of group representation, as outlined in Chapter V. Note that there, however, the underlying theory is that it is politically privileged objective groups that have irreconcilable interests. Women cannot be represented by men, nor blacks by whites, nor gays by straights because their interests are opposed and irreconcilable. But individuals who just have different ideas from one another, well, that's small beer.

The gardener's view, however, is that the alleged irreconcilable interests of groups are in reality the irreconcilable *ideas* held by *some* members of these objective groups, ideas they are seeking to promote by making the argument that they can define the "true" interests of the entire group, whether the group's "members" recognize it or not. This allows the people who believe in these ideas to make them appear to have far more support than they in fact do and they buttress their political power by claiming to be the only ones who can represent these antagonistic interests.

Gardenerism, by contrast, doesn't care about the alleged interests of groups. It cares about and respects the choices identifiable individuals have made about how they want to live. It further believes that many disagreements about what is good or desirable in life are irresolvable. Just as you cannot argue someone into loving you, you cannot argue someone into loving how you want to live and the way you want the world to work. Unlimited talking is no solution to such conflicts of beliefs and values.

Of course, some disagreements are based on misunderstandings and can be resolved. Many, however, are based on incompatible values and gardeners accept that we will not all get what we want. Instead, gardener institutions like those described in earlier chapters (such as your protected sphere of autonomy and action, the impersonal assessment of the social value of what you know how to do, the private property that is the extension of your will) all allow us to pursue our own objectives without us having to agree on what the right objectives are.

The outcome of the heedless pursuit by designers of social licence offers ample evidence that the limitless search for agreement between people holding opposing beliefs is only a recipe for entrenching conflict. Designer politicians have come to see this and that is why they speak ever less about social licence; they have in their heart of hearts reached the gardneresque conclusion that the debate over, say, pipelines is one of those irreconcilable conflicts of values that cannot be resolved by endless talking.

On the contrary, if the irreconcilable opponents of pipelines see that the social licence idea gives them endless ways to obstruct something they will never agree to, they, like their Trotskyite antecedents I talked about in an earlier chapter, will just keep talking and demonstrating until project proponents give up and go home. For proponents, time is money and opportunities fleeting. For opponents, talk is the currency of time and if they spend enough of it they will win the day.

Increasingly, therefore, "social licence" ought properly to be called "opponents' permission." And a moment's thought reveals why such open-ended, undefined, biased, undemocratic and unaccountable tests can never be the basis on which civilized societies make such crucial decisions.

Now there are gardener's approaches to reducing social conflict over resource development, and at least some of these approaches used to be the bedrock on which project approvals rested. For example, gardeners would be of the view that it is precisely because of the irreconcilable nature of visions of how we should live and what the good life looks like that social institutions are required to keep such discussions out of public policy as much as possible. Social co-operation works best when we create the space that allows different visions of the good life to go forward in parallel, to co-exist but not require mutual agreement or endorsement. All that is required is forbearance.

I pointed out in earlier chapters that there is, for example, no agreement in our society about whether we should live in dense neighbourhoods and walk or cycle to work, or whether we should live in suburban communities and drive to our workplace. But in a gardener society we don't need to agree. We need to offer choices and use the wisdom embodied in grown social institutions (like the rule of law, our protected sphere, and private property) to ensure that these different choices can co-exist peacefully.

Similarly, there would be no agreement among us if we had to distribute income by public policy as opposed to allowing it to be done by impersonal social institutions (backstopped by a state-guaranteed minimum), not under anyone's control or direction. There would be huge and fundamental disagreement about which objective groups are entitled to political privilege, but we can all rub along on the basis that every individual's right to choose their group membership(s) is protected, and *no* group gets any extra resources or special recognition for the ones they happen to choose.

Gardeners apply this logic to, say, pipelines and mines and forestry. There are many divergent views about the desirability of these things, and if we are required to reach agreement across these many divergent and often irreconcilable views, the change, the innovation, the experimentation, and the application of new knowledge from which we all benefit would grind to a halt.

The gardener, therefore, proposes that the rule of law and the tools of the protected sphere, particularly private property, form the basis for determining if projects should proceed. That would mean that individual projects would not be subject to arbitrary decisions based on the political climate of the day. Rather, the technical tests that projects must meet in order to be approved must be laid out in the law for *all* projects, and regulatory processes should again become what they once were: an evidence-based inquiry into whether the tests had been met. If the tests are met, approval should be automatic. If politicians don't like the projects that are approved, they should change the rules, not obstruct and veto projects piecemeal.

Furthermore, no requirement for public approval of any kind should be among the tests. Turning regulatory hearings into places for opponents to come and repeat *ad nauseam* their opposition is pointless. *The place for public participation is in the setting of the rules, not in determining if the rules have been followed.* If policy-makers in Ottawa want no pipelines, let them have the courage to say so and pass a law outlawing them. Otherwise Ottawa needs to set the general rules and then butt out and let the approval process play out. Anything else is an arbitrary exercise of political power incompatible with the rule of law.

It is perhaps also worth observing that the solution for politicians will not be hypocrisy, for which the poster child is BC Premier John Horgan. Horgan made a lot of political capital out of opposing the TMX pipeline project on the grounds that people in BC, on his reading, were opposed to it and he needed to stand up for what the people of BC wanted regardless of how many times the court told him that he had no jurisdiction under the law. This was nothing more or less than a demand for social licence from the people of BC, with Premier Horgan the only judge of whether it had been achieved or not.

And yet is that not Premier Horgan I see now trying to face down the opposition of the Wet'suwet'en traditional chiefs to his cherished Coastal GasLink project, and doing so on the ground that the rule of law must be protected at all costs?[165] Politicians availing themselves of the social licence argument and then sweeping it aside when others try to do the same is just further evidence that social licence is not a genuine attempt to come up with an objective rule that could be enshrined in law and take its rightful place as a contribution to the rule of law in Canada. It is just a convenient rhetorical device for opponents of particular projects. It has no place in the institutions of Canada. Yet we will be unable to drive an oaken stake through its heart until politicians themselves stop appealing to it and actually disavow it as an acceptable standard by which to judge projects.

Now some people see in the enormous political, judicial and constitutional success of Indigenous people in asserting their treaty and Indigenous rights a threat similar to the uncertainty created by the social licence movement. I hope I have made it crystal clear that these two things are not similar at all. Indigenous rights in Canada are recognized in the Constitution, in treaties (both historic and modern) and in Indigenous rights and title as recognized by the courts. These are not outside the law, but are rather at the heart of the law as it has been developing in Canada for centuries and particularly in the last forty years.

I hope I have headed off at the pass any impression that in criticizing the extreme social licence movement I am taking aim at increased Indigenous authority in natural resource decision-making. That is the precise opposite of my point.

My criticism of the social licence movement is not directed at the legitimate exercise of lawful requirements that Indigenous people's interests be consulted and accommodated. Indeed, my focus here has been on exactly how that can be made to happen in a way that benefits Indigenous and non-Indigenous people together, so that the natural resource economy becomes a platform for reconciliation, not division.

That does not mean that there are not occasions when Indigenous people have appealed to the concept of social licence in attempts to derail certain projects. As Dwight Newman, Canada Research Chair in the law faculty at the University of Saskatchewan and an expert on the evolving state of Indigenous-focused law in Canada has argued to great effect, this is likely a strategic and tactical mistake.[166] Minorities in Indigenous communities are already using calls for social licence to thwart natural resource developments approved and supported by those communities. I am arguing that the wrong kind of social licence is just as harmful to the legitimate aspirations of Indigenous communities as it is to the larger economy, and Indigenous people make an important error when they base their claims to full consultation on the extra-legal concept of social licence as opposed to their completely legitimate rights and authorities under the Constitution, the law and the treaties.

Conclusion

Pipelines provide the great test case of whether we have got Indigenous rights, the rule of law, the regulatory environment and social licence issues right. So let me conclude this chapter with a quick review of the gardener's view on pipelines and how they should fit under the rules.

Let's start with whether or not we should strive to bring Canada's energy resources to market. I think this is quite straightforward. It does not require us to agree on the level of risk attached to climate change. If Canada does not develop its energy resources, other petroleum-producing nations that have lots of spare capacity will simply step in and fill the gap. There is no way we can prevent this. That means that despite depriving itself of the value of those resources, Canada will not contribute one jot or tittle to reducing GHG emissions, especially since the newest oil sands production facilities have quite enviable GHG records.[167]

Moreover, if I am correct in my earlier argument that no solution to climate change will work if it requires us to abolish human nature, the idea that we will force change on a reluctant humanity by turning down the taps on oil production (even if Canada could do it unilaterally, which it cannot) is merely fanciful.

Finally, remembering the link I drew between wealth creation and the technological change that holds out our only real hope of dealing with climate change (real because actually usable), it becomes apparent that a policy that denies us the full wealth-creating value of our most valuable endowment of natural capital and our most valuable export is a policy guaranteed to weaken, not strengthen, our ability to combat this environmental scourge.

You can vote every day in favour of a carbon free future by not using internal combustion engines, biking to work, buying emissions-free vehicles and making a thousand other decisions that express your support for this vision and that are available to you right now. More are emerging all the time. In another chapter I have suggested that there are ways to make even more opportunities to vote every day in this regard, such as enabling you to specify that you want to use only green electricity. You are free (because of your protected sphere of individual autonomy) to make the case to others to follow your example.

Indeed, such a transition, led by the idealistic, is making important changes in industry after industry as people experiment with ways to satisfy this ever more strongly expressed desire. The fact that this shift is being driven by individual choices means that people who disagree need not be consulted, nor is their permission needed. These differing visions co-exist quite happily as cyclists and SUV owners, wind power workers and oil-patch roughnecks, environmental activists and oil executives all get to do what they want to do under the law as long as they can convince enough people to pay the freight.

This is exactly what the gardener would predict from grown social institutions left free to work their magic.

If, in addition, we capture and apply an important share of the wealth created from the petroleum industry to the development of the new technologies that are the solution to climate change risk, we have a virtuous circle that deserves widespread public support.

Indeed, judging by the shifts in how people behave and the things they want, the advocates of action on climate change are winning the argument for people to make different choices. Companies are investing billions of dollars in the constant pursuit of new technologies, not chiefly because governments are forcing them to do so, but because they believe climate-change-combatting innovation wins the support of consumers.[168]

Even Saudi Arabia, the world's top oil producer, sees which way the wind is blowing and has started to sell off its state-owned oil corporation in order to free up the capital to help Saudi society make the shift to a post-oil world. More power to the wheel of those advocating climate-preserving change – as long as they are convincing people to do so freely, rather than by using government to force their preferences on unwilling people who have different ideas about how to live. Sometimes you have to learn to take yes for an answer.

On the other hand, those who defend the oil and gas industry haven't exactly lost the argument either. All the knowledgeable observers predict continued and even increasing demand for petroleum products for decades before technological change and other factors may turn the tide away from fossil fuels definitively. And when the small slice of the Saudi state-owned oil company, Aramco, was sold, it became the largest publicly traded company in the world overnight,[169] meaning a lot of knowledgeable people were willing to risk a lot of their money that there is significant life left in the oil industry.

As long as they obey the rules and carry out their activities within Canada under the law, those in that industry in Canada have a right to expect that their activities will be neither promoted nor hampered by government, any more than the government should promote or hamper the activities of those seeking to make fossil fuels a thing of the past.

What I take away from the preceding few paragraphs is that we can choose to remain true to ourselves as a society that prefers to act by accommodation and negotiation than by authority and command, in which people who believe diametrically different things can nonetheless be respected and act on their beliefs without preventing others from doing the same. Because Canada is still essentially that kind of society, we are navigating the climate change issue with some success while respecting our fundamental values, including genuine and deeply felt diversity of opinion. Yes, it is too fast for some and not fast enough for others, but that is to be expected. Where we are failing to get it right is chiefly in the development of our energy resources.

It is important not to lose sight of the fact that whether we build pipelines or not (and pipelines are a proxy for the whole industry in the public policy debate) is a matter of differing visions of the right way to live, of what is good and desirable. Designers always think that where such conflicts exist there must be a "right" answer, which will be revealed to us by technical expertise (ideally a "consensus" among the experts), and all opinions that dissent from this view are to be dismissed as ill-informed and therefore not worthy of respect or legitimacy.

Gardeners are of the view that *conflicts over such values are facts to be accommodated in a social order of free people*; they always seek ways to make legitimate differences co-exist, not to overrule one side by means of the political victory of one "vision" over another. Indeed, they think it is not the business of government to favour one vision over another because to do so means picking favourites among visions of the good life. This is just what governments ought not to do if they do not want to damage the prosperity and goodwill that comes from successful social co-operation in which people put their efforts into sharing freely what they know with everyone else.

Our views about how to live are not valid only when approved by governments or verified by experts; they are self-validating because we have chosen them. The primary role of governments in societies like Canada is to protect our integrity and autonomy as individuals. You are just as entitled to be a flat-earther, a conspiracy theorist, or a druid dancing around Stonehenge in a white robe at the solstice as you are to be a professor of philosophy, a deputy minister of industry, or a Nobel-prize-winning chemist. The government does not get to dismiss the choices of some of their citizens just because policy-makers would not choose to live that way themselves. Your professional status or education or opinions do not trump the protected sphere of individuals or the duty of respect we owe each other as people seeking to live the good life according to our lights while co-operating with one another despite our differences.

Those in authority in Ottawa would be less mystified by their angry rejection by the people of most of the West except for Winnipeg and the Lower Mainland if they could understand that rejection as Westerners do: the perfectly intelligible moral outrage of people whose government has said to them that their choices of how to live are not worthy of respect. That disrespect is made doubly offensive by the fact that the government then airily asserts that everything would be fine if Westerners made the transition to the Green Economy (which is in its infancy to say the least) *and* the fact that these arrogant pronouncements are made by hypocrites who clearly have no intention of depriving themselves of the benefits of fossil fuels (see, for example, massive delegations jetting off to climate change conferences, the prime minister hiring not one but two planes for his 2019 electoral campaign, state support for struggling aviation company Bombardier and a thousand other examples) but expect others, whose way of life they again do not respect, to live as those in authority wish they would.

Under the gardener's dispensation, governments have two choices about pipelines. They can ban the oil and gas industry outright if they think the evidence is such that its success is actually being bought at the expense of everyone else. If that was the case it would be an externality problem; the industry would only exist by passing on some of their costs to everyone else in the form of environmental degradation. No one has made this case successfully to date, although a number of people think they have. In any case, because this involves banning activities that are freely supported by many people in our society (including many technical experts, and the many people who vote every day with their pocketbook by buying carbon-based fuels or the fruits of the use of such fuels), the standard of proof to justify a complete ban would properly be very high.

The alternative is to do what we do with all other industries, which is to subject them to rules about how they carry out their activities to ensure that our society's standards are upheld. We get to say, for example, that minimum wages shall be paid, that there will be no discrimination against individuals, that taxes shall be paid and that all activities shall be carried on to the highest environmental standards. The rules would of course vary according to the circumstances of the industry, but all would be treated equally under the law.

Sometimes the law is so complex and the circumstances of projects or other activities so unique that it is necessary to have regulatory proceedings to ensure that the unique circumstances of a project can demonstrably meet the abstract tests laid out in the law. That's what we do with pipeline projects, for example, but with lots of other things as well, such as road-building, power plant construction, nuclear waste disposal, siting of solar panel farms, and so forth.

Under the rule of law, however, regulatory proceedings ought not to become a thinly disguised but deliberately insurmountable barrier to actual projects. Indeed, contrary to what a lot of people seem to think, the purpose of regulatory proceedings is to help create certainty, not uncertainty. The purpose of laws and regulations is to let people know what they must do to get approval. Going into the proceedings, proponents should actually be fairly certain they will get approved because they have spent a lot of time and money ensuring that they have good answers to the questions regulators should ask about how they plan to conform to the law.

Such questions might include, "Are you able to demonstrate that you will meet all applicable environmental standards? That you can return disturbed nature to something very close to its original undisturbed state when the project is over? That you will mitigate harms to wildlife? That you have made every effort to consult affected Indigenous people and to accommodate their legitimate concerns? Ditto for local communities?" These are reasonable tests and similar requirements can be placed on any and every industry, ensuring that the law treats everyone's activities on a reasonably comparable basis and the law is not improperly used to place an unfair advantage or disadvantage on any particular group or individual.

In a society of free individuals under the rule of law, however, one of the tests cannot be "Everybody should be in happy agreement and there can be no protesters." The interests of all Canadians, including Indigenous Canadians, require that we be much tougher-minded than that and that we stand up for clarity of the law and equal treatment under the law. Our failure to do so isn't just causing us to forgo valuable projects that would offer genuine economic opportunity to Canadians and genuine opportunities for reconciliation with Indigenous people. Our failure to be tough-minded is also causing us to forget the duty of respect governments under the rule of law owe to the tremendous diversity of views and ideas which is our real strength.

CHAPTER IX

Health care for gardeners

ONE OF THIS BOOK'S ARGUMENTS is that command-and-control designer-inspired systems based on alleged expert knowledge make us stupid. Similarly, monopoly is the designers' favourite tool for making us take what experts think we *should* have because monopoly responds to the interests of those in charge rather than the interests of those it is allegedly intended to serve. Medicare is a command-and-control designer-inspired monopoly provider of health care to Canadians. This will not end well.

Medicare started from an idea that gardeners and designers could all get behind: that no one in a society like Canada's should go without needed medical care because they cannot afford it. But while gardeners would simply have sought to fill the gaps in an existing and well-functioning system that covered the vast majority of Canadians (I hope no one thinks that nobody got medical care before medicare, or that it was the exclusive preserve of the rich), that was not good enough for designers.

The designing urge to bring everyone under a uniform system that produces outcomes that are aesthetically pleasing to the designers is a powerful one, however, and the system is now based on a completely different (and much more contestable) principle that no one should get health care without waiting their turn in a monopolistic public system which has displaced and largely destroyed the perfectly well-functioning system of multiple competing providers that used to serve the vast majority of Canadians quite well. The system that has replaced it is expensive, performs poorly, gives us inferior service compared to our international peers and, according to the Supreme Court, violates our rights when it puts us on waiting lists rather than supplying health care when we need it.

Yet it is hugely popular.

It is possible to reconcile these things, but only when we realize that the public's support for the system is based on a designer-like faith in good intentions and the superior knowledge of our betters. The key to sensible reform lies in convincing Canadians that they have been sold a bill of goods about how to act effectively on those good intentions and who knows best what is good for us.

Let's start with what the evidence tells us about how Canadian medicare performs relative to its peers. After all, if there's nothing wrong, or at least nothing egregiously out of step with other similar countries, what is there to talk about?

Canada's public service unions, easily the most enthusiastic cheerleaders for medicare and public provision of services generally, gleefully embraced a 2017 international ranking by Oxford University and the Institute for Government that placed us number one in the world for "civil service effectiveness."[170]

Perhaps understandably intoxicated by this success, those same unions were curiously silent when the prestigious Commonwealth Fund in the US brought out its 2017[171] report card comparing health care systems in the rich industrialized world. This report card showed our health care system, run virtually in its entirety by these self-same effective Canadian public servants, not just below average, but nearly at the bottom of the heap, barely outperforming our health care system's arch-enemy, the US.

On measure after measure that the medicare apologists tout as proving we have the best health care system in the world, the data from the Commonwealth Fund report belie this boast. When measuring the "equity" of our system against the others, we come out a pitiful ninth out of eleven, despite the fact that "fairness" is the argument that is most often trotted out to defend the status quo. Turns out Canadian health care isn't all that fair.

Ditto for health care outcomes. Despite being a fairly high spender, we are not able to turn that money into better outcomes for Canadians. Again, we rank ninth out of eleven.

Even worse, as other international comparisons have repeatedly shown, not only is Canada's actual performance only mediocre when compared to many other western industrialized democracies, in terms of other measures like waiting times, access to the latest technologies, access to physicians, paraprofessionals and specialists, and coverage of health services beyond hospital and physician care, we pay over the odds for this under-performing system, especially when adjusted for the age of our population, which is still relatively young compared to most of Europe and Japan.[172]

But in what must be the bitterest pill for Canadian medicare's supporters, we come tenth in access. That means that among the eleven systems studied, *every one of them gives their citizens better access to health care services than Canada does with one single exception: the United States.* Gives a whole new meaning to the sentiment that we don't want American-style health care here, doesn't it? Of course we don't, but it is a wonder that people think Canadian-style care is somehow overwhelmingly superior. It is barely better than the US on some measures, so why compare ourselves to those doing worse than us and indeed congratulate ourselves effusively that at least we are better than the only country behind us? Surely we should aspire to better.

The reason why the defenders of the status quo want to keep Canadians fixated on America's failings is that the top performers in this survey put the lie to every one of the myths trotted out to defend the status quo in Canadian health care.

Take the much-loved "single payer" principle whereby a public sector monopoly (of which more in a moment) in each province determines what health services shall be insured, how much the government will pay for it, how it will be delivered, and what quality of service is acceptable. In most cases, private providers are forbidden by law to provide publicly insured services that are deemed medically necessary.

Yet none of the national systems that outperform Canada approach health care provision as we do. Look at the top three performers in the Commonwealth Fund rankings for proof. Second place Australia offers both public sector insurance and competing private sector plans. Many hospitals are privately owned. Third place Netherlands has competing social insurance funds.

Even first place UK, closest to the Canadian system, has a parallel private health care system that allows people to opt out of the public system and purchase private insurance. When the Labour government of Tony Blair sought to shorten endemic queues in the public system (the NHS), it was able to contract with a flexible private sector to purchase the services it could not get the public system to provide. In Canada, by contrast, Saskatchewan's highly successful experiments with private clinics providing services[173] earned it a tussle with Health Canada, which was trying to stamp out the practice.

While the UK doesn't allow user fees for most health care services, there are charges for some, and people using the private system must pay the full shot. User fees or co-payments are standard in both Australia and the Netherlands, not to mention the other countries with proud traditions of quality public health care that also outperform us in these rankings, like Sweden. In many cases, doctors and other health care professionals may practise outside the public system and yet that system is quite able to recruit the professionals it needs. Yet access, equity and outcomes in these systems are superior to what we enjoy here in Canada, disproving the oft-heard argument that any compromise on these "principles" would signal the end of a Canada committed to a fair and high-quality system in which no one suffered economic hardship through illness or disease.

In fact, the reverse is true. Even the best civil service in the world cannot save a system whose design is flawed at its heart and which no other country committed to similar principles holds up as a model despite Canada being seen internationally as having the "most positive influence globally," according to yet a third international ranking.[174] A former minister in the Swedish government has told me, not entirely tongue-in-cheek, that Swedes like to visit Canada to remind themselves of the bad old ways in which they used to run their health care system before they understood those ways didn't work. In fact it is the defenders of the status quo who are denying to Canadians the kind of experimentation and reform that provide superior equity and outcomes in our (non-American!) peer countries every day.

The fall of the Berlin Wall is the great unlearned lesson of our health care system. The Wall fell for a reason, and until we learn that reason and apply it to health care, we are doomed to repeat the cycles of pretty sentiments and squandered money. The lesson in question is the impossibility of the designer's "progressive" ambition to replace the messy, flawed, "patchworky" and inconsistent past with a shiny, fully rational model that offers the same thing to everyone and confers only benefits and has no unintended consequences. Eastern Europe and others who tried to foist such systems on their people learned there are systemic reasons why it fails. It fails because of its inherent contradictions and flaws, no matter how beautiful the theory or good the planners' intentions.

Designed economies couldn't feed, clothe, or house themselves. Why? Because they made impossible demands on the designers in charge.

Such economies demanded that they know how many shoes people would want, in what styles and sizes and where they would need them. They demanded that designers know whether people would prefer more shoes or fewer if they had to make a choice between them and, say, coats or cars or food or houses or computers. This is unknown and unknowable. Command-and-control design fails because it can only operate on the basis of what distant and remote designers know, which is always much less than what people know about their own circumstances and needs.

By contrast, gardeners urge an approach based on the ideas of decentralized information and control, of the rule of law, individual decision-making and competition. Where we don't interfere through ill-advised policies and instead allow ourselves to be guided by the ever-useful grown social institutions bequeathed to us by the past, our society operates on more information than any individual or committee or ministry can gather and analyse and act on. Our society works *because, not in spite, of no planning ministry being in charge.*

Gardeners celebrate this, not because it is some form of devil-take-the-hindmost social Darwinism, but because it ensures that many people in many places in many circumstances are rewarded for trying experiments to discover what works best and then offering those improvements to people looking for the best solution to their problems. Our society, and the various industries and activities within it, operates on more information than any individual or committee or ministry can gather and analyse and act on.

That is the secret of the west's prosperity: we have discovered the key to making use of the information in the heads of all our people. The chief difference between the old-style Soviet central planners and us is our ability to integrate more information in our decisions, even though no one in authority possesses all the information at some central point and sends us instructions on how to act. The idea that such a fully informed control centre can exist and direct our activities successfully is what economists and information theorists call the "synoptic delusion," and it was this delusion that killed central planning.

While for the most part in Canada we have escaped the delusion of such progressive designers' ambitions, medicare remains a lonely outpost of its logic. It can only be kept precariously afloat by ever-increasing cash infusions. But as Margaret Thatcher once observed, the problem is that eventually you run out of other people's money.

Is medicare a lonely holdover of the pre-fall-of-the-Wall mentality? Consider: provincial ministries of health govern, administer and evaluate the health services that their system provides and pays for. They define "medically necessary services" and then pay for all such services. They forbid private insurance for those services. They negotiate pay with all the powerful provider groups. They often set the budgets for nominally private health care institutions, appoint most of their board members, and may override management decisions, a power that they employ freely, especially when political controversy looms.

In a provincial election in a western province a few years ago, *the quality of toast in hospitals* was a major issue. The parties thought that they could and should be able to affect this matter, and the electorate did not laugh them out of court. That's the designer mentality. Everything may be planned and co-ordinated by wise and disinterested experts, right down to the finest detail.

Design from above encourages delusions of grandeur in which officials come to believe that there is a right solution to every problem (how many doctors should there be, how should they be paid and their practice organized, how should paraprofessionals be integrated into medical practice, etc.) which it is up to them to find and then impose on everyone from above, regardless of local circumstances. Alas, though, *there is no one right answer to most such questions* because everything depends on circumstances known only to people on the ground. The system cannot be run successfully from the centre no matter how many billions you lavish on it to buy the illusion of it working in the short run.

Just consider how fast knowledge is expanding in the health care world, and the incredible balancing acts that need to be undertaken to make the system work. We have to think about innovation, new technologies, orphan drugs, insured services, gene therapy, doctor shortages, how to organise practices, how the pie should be cut up between doctors and nurses and others, how to balance surgery versus managing chronic conditions, etc., etc.

Consider something I mentioned in an earlier chapter, namely, that the whole stock of human knowledge is now generally judged to be doubling perhaps every 12 hours or so. I would suggest that the doubling period is even shorter in dynamic areas as diverse as management, genetics, insurance, IT, pharmaceuticals, gerontology, nanotechnology, "personalized medicine" (designing drugs based on your genome) proteomics, metabolomics, genomics, etc. How credible is it that provincial bureaucrats can acquire all this information in a timely way, assess it and then thoughtfully integrate into their decision-making given the institutional constraints I've described?

We never talk about this and yet I believe it is the single biggest problem facing the Canadian health care system, and it is by definition going to get worse. It will get worse because, as the body of knowledge relevant to health care expands exponentially but the capacity of the managers of the system and the incentives that surround them remain those of progressive design, the system can only respond to the knowledge of the people in charge, no matter how good their intentions. This makes for a health care system singularly and systemically resistant to innovation.

Innovation is one of those words to conjure with in the political lexicon. In Ottawa for at least the past thirty years or so, there is a firmly anchored belief that "innovation" is a recipe for Canadian success and we don't have nearly enough of it. Scarcely a day goes by without some minister patronizingly explaining why business needs to do more to innovate and how the feds will be there to help.

Instead of officials telling business how to run itself, however, perhaps they might ask themselves what obstacles governments create to innovation and then dedicate themselves to removing those obstacles.

The response will be hurt protestations of innocence. But this charade of innocence can only be sustained by hiding behind the obfuscation of an abstract word – innovation – that sounds warm and cuddly but means nothing specific. Innovation is just an impressive-sounding word for doing new things or doing old things in a new way. And as soon as you put it that way, you realize that all too often a synonym for innovation is "disruption." And there is nothing politicians hate more than something that upends a world their constituents find quite comfortable – and what politicians hate, their officials avoid if they wish their career to advance.

Uber is a classic example I used in an earlier chapter. Officialdom should have welcomed ride-hailing with open arms. Instead, they stood po-faced at the city gates, egged on by a tiny but well-organized band of taxi owners and drivers, loudly crying "stop" to the march of history. Most of them are still there. Innovation-friendly indeed.

Now let's talk about innovation (for which read "disruption") in health care.

Health care is one of the largest sectors of the economy and with our rapidly ageing population it is going to expand enormously in coming years. Worldwide it is the focal point for almost every innovative technical field there is.

Essentially, the system in Canada is run, however, by the powerful established interests within it, like doctors and nurses, and it is administered by bureaucrats for whom Rule Number One is never do anything that will embarrass the minister.

Yet every important innovation in health care threatens some powerful vested interest in the system. That's one reason why international comparisons of health care systems consistently show that Canadians have poor access to the latest technologies. We try in vain to keep costs low and vested interests quiescent by short-changing patients, who are far less well-organized than the health professions.

Ironically, this is expensive. If we develop innovative drugs to manage conditions that previously could only be treated through surgery, you can be sure that ministers will complain bitterly about the cost of the drug, but surgeons will still get the same or a growing share of the health care pie at the negotiating table where that pie is divvied up.[175]

In fact, innovative technologies are so feared as a cost-driver within the health care system that one background study for the Romanow Commission some years ago came up with the perfect solution based on our history to date. The author opined that the simplest way to control the cost of new technologies was not to use them. If you were a patient who might have benefited, too bad.[176]

In Canadian health care, *which will soon represent nearly a fifth of the economy*, innovation must go cap in hand and beg to be allowed to help patients. And in doing so it will meet at least some opposition by those in the system whose power and livelihood might be threatened, just like those taxi owners fighting Uber.

There are a couple of reasons why this is so. One modestly important one is that our system is one where the amount of money available is determined in advance through government budgets. Every innovation accepted is a charge against a fixed pie, meaning that established interests may be damaged to accommodate the innovation. And it is those established interests who are the system's gatekeepers. The only way to accommodate innovation is to increase the health care budget so that old practices can be maintained unchanged and new ones paid for out of the increase. Thus while doctors may be attracted by the easing of their workload that new technology makes possible, they are also mindful that, ultimately, their incomes come out of the same fixed pie that pays for technology, no matter how governments try to obscure this by "structuring" their budgets one way or another.

Much more importantly, we need to think about governments' preoccupation with keeping costs under control, lest health care eat up everything else. This means that far from being focused on ensuring the best quality of care possible for patients, governments look for ways to keep costs down without saying that that is what they are doing. Since government controls the amount of equipment of every kind in the system (ranging all the way from hospitals, operating rooms, and clinics down to MRIs, CAT scanners, lithotripters, and (insert your favourite medical technology here), government health planners keep costs down by limiting the capacity of the system actually to deliver the number of individual services that the system is called upon to pay for. Queueing and poor access to services are thus not a bug in our system, but one of its features, and it is a feature because health care bureaucrats are rewarded for turning down the screws on the supply of needed technology and personnel.

There are other ways to keep costs down – for example using a fund-holding approach, under which doctors decide on which patients to spend a fixed budget for medical tests – but from the point of view of the government officials running the system, just not making things like equipment and operating rooms available is easier to understand and easier to implement and manage than the alternatives. It is not in the interests of patients? See my earlier comments about the nature of monopoly and how it inverts the power of suppliers and consumers.

It might be worth opening a small parenthesis and point out that one of the main justifications offered for the Canadian health care system is its superior ability to keep costs down. Officials look down their nose at the American system, which is undoubtedly more expensive than it needs to be, and hold up our lower share of the economy spent on health care as evidence of our clear superiority.

The mythology that has grown up about the superiority of our system to control costs traces its roots to the fact that, until the introduction of medicare in the late 1960s, our health care costs tracked those of the US. After the introduction of medicare, however, our growth in costs, and especially physician costs, dropped significantly after the predictable short term rise.

Examine these numbers a little more carefully, however, and a wholly different picture emerges.

Yes, we see the spike in spending associated with the introduction of medicare, and the slowing of that growth as the adjustment to universal coverage worked itself through. But by the late 1970s, Canada's and America's rate of spending on health care was back in sync – in fact they were more closely aligned in that period than they were in any previous period. They diverge again only in the mid- to late-1980s, when, arguably, Canadian governments became really serious about controlling spending.

So while we can identify short-term transitional effects from the introduction of medicare, it is not possible to identify a lasting effect on spending on physician services. Basically, the introduction of medicare had no effect on the rate of growth of spending, and the reason the share of Canada's national income spent on health care fell below the US's share was not because of differences in the rate of growth of expenditure *but rather because Canada happened to have the good fortune to bring medicare in during a period in which real growth in the Canadian economy outdid that in the US.*

Had our economic growth been as weak as it was in the US through the 1970s and '80s, and had our health spending nonetheless remained unchanged, for two decades our share of GDP devoted to health care would have been higher than the actual US GDP share. Canada, in other words, would have had the most expensive health care system in the world, a situation that would have changed only in the 1990s.

Why, given Canada's apparent success at controlling health care costs through the '70s and '80s, at least as judged by the GDP share evidence, have more recent efforts at cost control not been handled with less disruption?

The answer now seems to be not that we are inexplicably poor performers now, but rather that our earlier "success" at bringing costs "down" was illusory. Simply put, the introduction of medicare did not introduce a period of, or efficient mechanism for, health care cost control. When it came to the question of how much of our national income we were spending on health, we weren't particularly good, we were just lucky.[177]

And one might say that our luck has run out as we get more and more ham-fisted and desperate to control costs without any real mechanism to do so within the government monopoly designer status quo except by cutting services without saying that's what we're doing. In other words, our main cost control mechanism is hypocrisy.

Returning to the main thread, in most industries technological innovation is a cost reducer, not a cost driver. Surely, then, cost-conscious bureaucrats should embrace new technologies as their friend, not their adversary. My impression is that, aside from the ease of understanding and managing the squeezing of the supply of services as a bureaucratic management technique, there are a couple of further factors at work.

In many cases, new technologies are not substitutes for existing techniques, but are additive – solving problems that we were unable to solve before, and yet not allowing us to dispense with already existing techniques and technologies. Second, innovation only helps to reduce costs when you can shift activities from old, less technology-intensive approaches to new, more technology-intensive ones. But in a politicized designer-inspired health care system, this shifting of resources out of old approaches and institutions and into new ones is severely hampered, despite what I said in an earlier chapter about the half-life of knowledge.

Finally, there is the fact that much of the system is driven by what governments are willing to pay for. Just to pick an example, if government is willing to pay for heart surgery, but patients must pay for drugs, there will be tremendous pressure to keep heart surgery facilities open and resistance to moving to drug-based therapies that might manage heart disease as a chronic condition rather than one requiring surgery.

So what is to be done?

To repeat, the gardener's view is that the important decisions about our health care are not the macro ones taken by distant bureaucrats in office towers in our provincial capitals. It is the micro ones taken by patients and doctors and other professionals about what is good right now for the flesh-and-blood person before them who is sick and needs care. Empowering patients to get the best care and giving them incentives to do so in the most cost-effective way possible *is* applying the lessons of the west's success and rejecting designers' ineffectual but well-intentioned pretensions to knowledge.

Interestingly, there is actually widespread acceptance of this analysis of medicare's failings. What is not widely accepted, however, is the prescription for alleviating those ills. To the gardener, the solution is obvious. You have to find the way to harness all we have learned about knowledge scarcity, the discipline of competition, personal responsibility, accountability and all the rest.

While there are many gardener-inspired systems, one that would be completely compatible with Canadians' commitment to fairness and high-quality care would have the following elements. The government would not just allow but encourage competing regulated public and private providers to offer their services to patients who need them. *The government would continue to fund all such services out of its budget,* but instead of giving, say, block grants to public hospitals, it would let the patient choose where they wanted to get the service they need, based on their own assessment of timeliness, comfort, quality and so forth. The money would then follow patients as they chose between competing providers.

In those circumstances, every patient coming through the door would be seen as new revenue, not a cost, which is to say the reversal of the status quo. Institutions would be actively trying to get patients in the door, rather than actively making them queue until they (the providers) were good and ready to do something for them, and the incentives to keep costs low and have them driven by patient needs rather than supplier interests would be improved. If existing hospitals found they couldn't maintain their services levels because they weren't attracting enough patients, that would be a signal that they needed new management.

Note that this system would still permit the government to try to keep costs down by restricting the number of services that it would pay for. But now this cost-control at the patients' expense would be completely transparent instead of obscured as benign-sounding "waiting lists": when the government ran out of money for Service X, the patient would show up at the door empty-handed.

On the other hand, if competing suppliers could demonstrate that they could keep costs down while maintaining quality care, the government could give incentives to people to choose the more efficient providers. The money would go further.

Is federal "leadership" the solution?

I scarcely need say that this is not the solution that appeals to those who benefit from the status quo. For example, a few years ago I attended a speech by a leading advocate for that status quo, the outgoing chairman of a lobbying group for that status quo who was himself the CEO of a large hospital in a major Canadian city. And like many observers of the system, he accepted that the data about our health care system completely contradict many of our cherished beliefs.

Topping the list of cherished beliefs is that we have "the best health care system in the world."[178] This belief of Canadians is remarkably resistant to the kind of evidence I presented at the beginning of this chapter; but what I have come to understand about our commitment to the Canadian health care system is that it is resistant to facts because the statement about it being the best system in the world *isn't actually a statement about facts.*

It is a statement about morals, beliefs and desires. It encapsulates a belief fervently held by many Canadians that *there is something especially morally worthy about our system that elevates it beyond mere criticism of outcomes.* Canadians' support for our system is based on "values" and especially the values of equity and fairness that apparently transcend any concern for the quality of care actually received. What is great about our system, if my reading is correct, is that its intentions are good and pure and any falling short in practice, while deplorable, is only an accident caused by insufficient reverence for good intentions. Oh, and of course an inexplicable unwillingness by governments, and especially Ottawa, to fund the system adequately.

Indeed I was quite struck by the reaction of the audience to the talk I referred to a moment ago. The room was full of the great and the good of the Canadian health care establishment, the heads of most of the professional associations and other health care lobby groups. Heads nodded all around the room when our speaker lamented the lack of "leadership" by

Ottawa on the health care file, and even though he did not explicitly say that Ottawa should put more money into the system, it was clear from the softball questions thrown to him from around the room that almost everyone there shared the analysis of the Romanow Commission, lo these many years ago, that there is nothing wrong with the Canadian health care system that more money wouldn't fix. Ottawa's job was, through this vague and unspecified "leadership" role, to rescue the health care system from its torpor and decline and to make the reality of the system equal to its designers' moral intentions.

Sadly, the reaction of the audience was roughly equivalent to Dorothy believing she could close her eyes and wish really hard to be home in Kansas and the ruby slippers of good intentions – federal leadership and more money – would magically take her there.

At my table at the luncheon talk one of the other guests was the chief of staff to the premier of a small province. He nodded sagely at the speaker's suggestion that what was missing from the system was federal targets, federal objectives, federal goals and just good old federal leadership generally.

So I said to him, "Let me see if I understand. Your position is that the folks who run the post office, Aboriginal affairs, and military procurement should be leading the health care system because they know more about what the residents of your province need than the premier does." He assured me that wasn't the case. What he really meant, although he was reluctant to say so in so many words, is that federal leadership is exercised through more federal money. And by the way, since one of the main justifications for government control of the health care system (and possibly soon the pharmaceutical system as well) is government's alleged power to negotiate lower prices through bulk purchasing, I cannot prevent myself from noting that if governments really could save money through bulk purchasing, military equipment would be dirt cheap. More magical thinking.

But magical thinking is not going to make disappear the gardener-inspired factors that will re-shape the Canadian health care system, the same factors that, decades after the Romanow Commission, after successive federal health accords and after record high levels of federal cash contributions to health care, were supposed to buy us reform. After all that, the system is essentially what it was, except it is decades older, more expensive than ever and the money got us almost nothing in the way of reform. It is a positive triumph of designerism.

Federal leadership that works

Gardeners learned some valuable lessons about the nature of true federal "leadership" in areas of provincial responsibility when Ottawa fixed its fiscal problems in the 1990s. One such lesson, I believe, is what works in fixing large, out-of-control public entitlement programs.

My favourite example is social welfare,[179] and I believe those lessons are directly relevant to health care. In the decades prior to the 1990s, welfare spending was out of control, in large part because of the way we paid for it. Ottawa used its spending power to entice the provinces into what was essentially a poorly designed one-size-fits-all national welfare system. The system was very effective at making people dependent on welfare and was consequently very expensive not just in money, but in lost productivity and in lives blighted by being trapped behind the welfare wall. We saw the number of people on welfare rise in each recession, but never drop in subsequent recoveries. Welfare was an escalator, not a roller coaster.

The provinces had little incentive to enact reforms because they could pass a lot of the cost along to Ottawa. As a result, by the mid-'90s, well over ten percent of the Canadian population was receiving welfare benefits, including in our then-wealthiest province, Ontario. This lovely system was the fruit, in other words, of one kind of federal "leadership."

As everyone knows, when Ottawa decided to fix its deficit problem, it did so in part by cutting transfers to the provinces. This has become known as "downloading" and every provincial politician decries it. This is wrong – "downloading" gets a bum rap and is actually an example of the right kind of federal leadership at work.

It gets a bum rap because cutting transfers was only one half of what Ottawa did with respect to welfare, and that's why welfare reform worked. On the other hand, cutting transfers to the provinces was *all* that Ottawa did with respect to health care, and that's why reform failed that time round.

What was the other half of reform with respect to welfare? Ottawa said to the provinces, in exchange for you accepting less money, that money will come as a block grant with no strings attached. We are getting out of the business of using the federal spending power to try to design and impose a uniform national welfare system. And while they didn't say it, if a gardener had been writing the media release, she would have written, "This is being done in recognition of the fact that Ottawa knows a lot less about the circumstances in each province than the provincial government does. We are happy to let the provinces act on what they know about local circumstances without paternalistic and ill-informed second-guessing by us."

This combination of reduced transfers plus the freedom for the provinces to design their own welfare system unleashed a wave of exceptionally innovative welfare reforms across the country. Many of the reforms were ultimately adopted by all the provinces, but there were also important differences in focus. British Columbia, for example, emphasized time limits for welfare. Alberta's priority was getting employable young people into work. Ontario focused on workfare. The provinces chose different policies because of what they judged were the most important aspects of their local circumstances, what the advocates of "federal leadership" usually refer to as a "patchwork" that should be eliminated by the imposition of uniform national standards.

The overall result was that the country cut in half the number of people on welfare at the same time as it saw a very significant drop in the number of people living in poverty and the number of people on low incomes.

The common objection to such reform, that it unleashes a "race to the bottom," whereby provinces compete with each other to abandon high quality services so as to cut taxes and spending, was not at all borne out in the evidence – and I can assure you that this is a matter that has been carefully researched.[180] It wasn't so much that spending on welfare declined overall as that we got much better value out of the money and it was focused on those who needed it most.

What I conclude from all this is that we make a mistake when we seek the kind of federal leadership that concentrates on eliminating the normal, constructive and informative "patchwork" in favour of imposing a one-size fits all solution to our health care sustainability problem that throws money at the problem and relieves those responsible of the need to think more carefully about reform.

What we need instead of the designers' failed prescriptions is to give the provinces the room and the authority to experiment, while simultaneously making it clear that they cannot pass along the costs to Ottawa, but rather must live within their means. Remember that welfare reform did not involve ending federal transfers. It cut and then capped transfers, so that provinces could see that *any improvements in their situation would come from their own actions,* not from lobbying for more federal money to bail them out of the difficulties created by a dysfunctional but centrally imposed system. If it is true that behaviour is driven by incentives, then these incentives were healthy and constructive ones.

But let me underline again that it was not enough to cut and cap transfers. Ottawa also had to *get out of the business of telling provinces how to run their welfare policy.* What resulted was a system tailored to local conditions that provinces could afford. We don't need to agree on the details of reform. The idea that there is a single reform agenda that can and should be centrally directed is itself part of the designer's delusion. Real leadership means creating the conditions in which provinces can experiment, and in which successful experiments will be copied and spread.

If we are to apply the gardener's lessons to health care reform, Ottawa needs to do two things. First, it needs to stop increasing the amount of money it gives to the provinces for health care. As long as the provinces believe that the easiest response to rising costs is simply to pass the blame to Ottawa and lobby for more money, there will be no change. I am glad to say that successive federal governments have essentially adopted at least part of the gardener's program. Provinces have been told that federal transfers will grow in line with nominal GDP growth with a 3.5 percent floor (in 2017-18) and no more.[181]

While this is progress, equally important is the other half of the gardener's advice: Ottawa needs to give provinces more room to experiment with how they run health care. That means at the very least changes in the way Ottawa interprets the Canada Health Act, and particularly its five principles.

Some changes of this kind have occurred from time to time in the past[182] but, damagingly, they are not dependable. The provinces will never take responsibility for health care and have the courage to put in place the reforms we need if Ottawa retains the designer's power to punish those whose reforms offend their aesthetic sense of how health care ought to be delivered. Once Ottawa learns to focus on general rules, like that no one will be denied needed medical care on the basis of the ability to pay, rather than micro-managing provincial policy, we will have put enough gardener-inspired incentives in place to begin to nudge the system in a healthier direction.

It is already happening, but fitfully, and different political parties at the federal level pull in different directions. The general trend, however, is still in the right direction, even if we are only taking hesitant baby steps. Put that together with the individual empowerment of Canadians by the *Chaoulli* decision that individual rights trump government policy when it endangers the health and well-being of the individual, and we have now, largely unwittingly, created a new framework for experimentation and therefore the breaking up of the old central planning mentality.[183]

Thus it is that Janice MacKinnon, former finance minister of Saskatchewan under the NDP government of Roy Romanow, could publish a paper[184] a couple of years ago lauding her province's experiments using private sector clinics to provide publicly insured services. This kind of baby step toward the unbundling of the old designer edifice, the separation of the functions of purchaser and provider of health care services will, if the old "progressive" reflexes are not allowed to reassert themselves, result in a system that is more experimental, more open to innovation, more entrepreneurial and, crucially, more oriented toward better care for patients. In turn, those patients inevitably will become more powerful voices within the system, especially as the Boomers, who have been assertive about everything they have wanted in life, age and become the major users of the system.

Medicare's moral deficit

The final thing I wanted to talk about was the moral and economic sustainability of a health care system whose greatest strength in the public mind is its roots in the best of intentions. I outlined at the beginning how Canadians' faith in the health care system in the abstract is in fact a form of endorsement of its moral or ethical foundation: that no one should be deprived of needed medical care on the basis of ability to pay. Of course it does no such thing, but then as I noted earlier Canadians seem to regard the system's actual failings as irrelevant; all that matters is its good intentions.

Beyond that there is a further ethical problem the system now faces. Of all the major determinants of health, we know that the health care system itself is in fact a relatively minor one. Much more important are things like education, community viability, quality of family life, personal habits and behaviour and individual and collective prosperity. Almost all of these things depend, among many other things, on public spending on things like schools, training and genuine infrastructure that raise our standard of living.

As we all know, health care spending already consumes basically half of provincial spending, and that is the level of government that provides many of those vital programs and investments that underpin prosperity, itself far more important to our health than health care per se. To be more specific, government health spending is on trend to exceed half of total available revenues in virtually every province within a few short years, up from only a quarter of provincial revenue in the early 1970s.[185]

If health care spending continues to rise at its current rates, if in the real world you cannot raise taxes without real consequences to Canada's competitive standing and if excessive public borrowing eventually crowds out program spending – as we learned in the '90s but seem to be forgetting again – the only alternative to genuine system reform such as I've been describing is to cannibalize other public spending. If you project current spending trends into the future, we can easily foresee health care spending squeezing our universities, transport, schools and all the rest.

So what are the ethical considerations involved in devoting the solid majority of all provincial spending to a service consumed (and no, health care spending is not an "investment," no matter how tempting it is to torture the English language to make it so) in the majority by those over age sixty-five,[186] at the cost of spending on real investments in people that pay large social dividends, such as education, infrastructure, environmental protection, etc.? And since the genuine investments we will be forgoing would pay the greatest benefits to the young (since they will live as long as the useful life of the investments themselves), this will be the cause of major intergenerational conflict. We cannot impoverish the rising generation to pay for the health care of the old.

I am not suggesting this will be the outcome, because clearly the inevitable adjustments will occur that will allow us to avoid this outcome, albeit narrowly. But the adjustments are made more difficult and painful by the politicized nature of our system. It may be inevitable that real reform will happen, but I am always amazed by how much effort it takes to make the inevitable happen.

To make health care reform happen will require a slow, incremental, ginger adjustment in the rate at which health care spending rises that can only be achieved by innovation, competition, and looking to the better-off to cover a little more of the costs of their own care. If we do that we will not only move our system toward sustainability, but quite likely we will be able to adjust the public health care coverage to ensure access to dentistry, drugs and other services for those on low incomes, adding another patch to the patchwork the designers decry but gardeners think is the secret of our success.

What will reform look like? The details will have to be worked out, but I think I see the principles fairly clearly.

First, public money will be concentrated on health services that confer the greatest public benefits and where individuals are least likely to be able to obtain appropriate and cost-effective insurance on an equitable basis.

Since health care spending will soon consume 50 percent of all program spending by the provinces, and that spending is crowding out other, vital, forms of public spending, ensuring we get value for money for that spending is critically important. In that context, consider that some very significant share of public health care spending produces absolutely no measurable benefit whatsoever.

Professor David Zitner, former director of medical informatics at Dalhousie University, says that something like 30 percent of all medical procedures performed today in Canada produce either no benefit, or are actively harmful. According to a study published by Drs. Baker and Norton in the *Canadian Medical Association Journal*,[187] for every 200 people admitted to a Canadian hospital as many as three die from preventable health system error – a higher rate, by the way, than in the United States. Many more are maimed and hurt because of preventable error.

David Cutler of Harvard Medical School says, "If you ask 'For what share of all the things that are done in the medical system is there good hard evidence that in that patient it is an effective therapy?' nobody knows the answer, but it is probably 20%."[188] In other words, the range of useless or even harmful procedures is somewhere between 30 percent and 80 percent of all those performed.[189] And with all those pushy Boomer consumers, with their access to the Internet and their determination to have access to all the latest diagnostic equipment and techniques regardless of what the system wishes them to have, I doubt that this is going to change any time soon as long as people using the health care system have no direct financial stake in the decisions they make about the health care services they consume.

Over and above that, we will have to get much more serious about distinguishing those services that provide real value to patients, and under what circumstances, and restrict public payment to those services. This will require us eventually to decide in advance what proportion of public expenditure we are prepared to devote to health care, and to rank all services in order of importance, looking to people to cover the cost of inexpensive services so that we can really focus on medicare's true justification: to ensure that no one is denied vital medical services because of an inability to pay. I will never forget the conversation I had with Tommy Douglas, the father of medicare, when I worked at the House of Commons and he was still the MP for Nanaimo-Cowichan-the-Islands. In private conversation Tommy expressed to me his frustration at how the debate around medicare had become all about whether the government should pay for every hangnail and runny nose. He told me that was never what he had in mind. What he wanted was to ensure that no one would find their lives destroyed by falling ill and finding the cost of the care they needed was beyond their means.

What this means becomes easy to understand if you look at specific examples, and not abstractions. I discovered a few years ago when researching health care in Nova Scotia that it costs the same to insure all Nova Scotians against the risk of upper respiratory infections (colds and flu) as it does to insure them all against the risk of needing coronary bypass surgery. Yet there are no effective treatments against upper respiratory infections which almost all of us get (as the old joke goes, untreated colds and flu last a week, whereas properly treated they last only seven days), whereas coronary bypass surgery is the sort of thing that even the wealthy cannot afford to pay for by themselves, and nobody asks for one just because it is free. If we want to share the risk of falling sick by spreading that risk across all taxpayers, which is the objective of medicare, and if there isn't enough money to pay for everything, it makes most sense to focus on sharing the risk of things individuals can never hope to pay for alone.

At the moment, we do the reverse. We welcome people with open arms in their GP's office to offer them totally free medical services, often of little or no value – services that they could usually pay for themselves out of pocket. If an analogy helps, consider if car insurance paid for ordinary maintenance, like oil and filter changes and putting on your winter tires, and if house insurance paid for a weekly cleaning service, having the lawn mowed, and maybe having the house painted every five years, insurance would be very expensive and inefficient, with people trying to get other premium payers to absorb the cost of minor things that each person should expect to pay for themselves. If, on top of that, insurance paid for the tire changes and the house cleaning fairly promptly, but made you wait ("queue") for years to get reimbursed if your house was destroyed in a tornado or burned down, well, that's medicare as we currently practise it.

In the cases of low-income people who cannot pay out of pocket, we can exempt them from the fee, which is the system in place in most of our peer countries that outperform us on health care results, including access. We give people unrestricted access to these services free of charge at the same time as we make them queue up for long periods to get treatment

for life-threatening diseases and excruciatingly painful conditions that no
one can afford to pay for out of pocket. This is the exact reverse of the
risk-sharing system you would choose for yourself – if you were allowed to
choose. Which of course you aren't.

I should also acknowledge that we don't welcome people with open arms
even in the GP's office. If you're lucky enough to have a GP, you can usually
get in to see him or her within a day (if it is a fee–for–service practice) or
a week or so if it is a rostered capitation practice. But there are thousands
of Canadians who are on no GP's patient list and cannot get even those
services unless they want to go to the local emergency room or wander
nomadically from clinic to anonymous clinic.

You may even have asked yourself why it is that while you can get immediate access to every kind of health professional *not* covered by medicare
(dentists, pharmacists, physiotherapists and so forth) just finding a doctor
is a struggle. This, too, is the fruit of designerism. Some bright spark in the
health care system noticed that wherever there were doctors, there were lots
of medicare billings.[190] The designer response was to strangle the supply of
new physicians, just as their response to the high costs of surgery was to create
a shortage of operating rooms, thereby controlling costs by creating queues.

Alas (and pretty obviously), the number of physicians was not the *cause*
of the medicare billings; the cause of the billing was the illnesses suffered
by their patients. So by squeezing the supply of physicians, designers simultaneously damaged access to health care while increasing the bargaining
power of physicians, who are in short supply. The usual designer outcome
was achieved: costs rose and service declined. Gardeners know there is no
bureaucratically determined right answer to how many doctors we need.
Only supply and demand, including the income that potential future
physicians can see coming from the health care system, can successfully
determine the right number needed at any one time.

The second principle of gardener-inspired health care reform is that
patients, not physicians, will become the primary agents of their own care.

In earlier times, people deferred to their doctors, who controlled access
to medical services. People took their doctor's advice. Now the old doctor-
patient relationship is dying, if not already dead.

Let me tell you about a conversation I had with a former head of the Canadian Medical Association. We'd been on a panel together and afterwards we were chatting and I said to him, "If you had to pick one thing, what would you say has been the single greatest change in the way medicine is practised in the past few decades?" Without hesitation he said that it was the number of patients showing up with print-outs from the Internet about their medical conditions and appropriate treatments. Many people are seeing alternative medical practitioners as their primary caregivers.

As Richard Bohmer, a physician and professor at the Harvard Business School says, "The development of programs and tools for patients to take more control of their health is based on 'a very important new assumption about how competent patients are' . . . The increase in knowledge specificity is 'the engine moving decision-making capability and therefore decision rights to the patient.'"[191]

According to a survey of health care consumers by the Change Foundation in Ontario:

> One out of every two people appears to be a "responsibility-taker," taking control of their health and actively searching out options. They believe that most of the responsibility lies with them. About half of respondents believe that, in general they have as much medical knowledge as physicians. About half (53%) agree that they are the prime decision makers on their own health and about half (48%) regard healthcare as offering a wide range of choices. These results point to a very empowered consumer who feels very able to make health care choices.[192]

Gardeners know you can't keep an empowered citizen down. Patient-consumers within our health care system are every day making themselves powerful agents of their own care. We need to recognize and celebrate this by giving them more choice and more control over and accountability for the health care spending they trigger, and by giving them more scope and incentives to take preventive measures to improve their long-term health while allowing them to act on their own knowledge of their health conditions.

I can hear the progressive designers huffing and puffing already. Their cry will be that physicians have so much more medical knowledge than patients have that physicians can recommend services that are medically unnecessary and whose sole purpose is to increase the physician's income. Poorly informed patients will not be in a position to question these recommendations. Such services are sometimes termed "remunerectomies," and the general idea seems not inconsistent with the observation that auto mechanics, who have the same type of informational advantage over many of their customers, are often believed to recommend unnecessary auto repairs.

The designer view is that wise and benevolent government control of health care budgets is needed to ensure that more of it goes on needed medical services rather than on what they call "supplier induced demand" (SID).

My view is rather different. The evidence of such physician-driven demand is weak.[193] It is often argued that physicians will abuse the asymmetry of knowledge between their patient and themselves. The patient has no way of knowing whether the physician is recommending services for no good medical reason.

This is a plausible argument, and a number of researchers have tested it, using data on service use by groups of patients distinguished by their degree of medical knowledge. The research has used a number of different measures of knowledge including, in some studies, looking at how physicians and their families use the health care system. The idea is that more knowledgeable patients should be resistant to inducement and that they should, therefore, make less use of medical care, controlling for other factors such as health status, age, sex, income and (in American studies) insurance status. In fact, these studies have consistently found that *not only do knowledgeable patients not use less care, but they frequently use more.* Whenever the asymmetric information version of the SID hypothesis has actually been tested, it has been rejected.[194]

Moreover, the barriers against physicians enriching themselves this way in Canada's current system are very weak: where physicians are on fee-for-service (as most are) there are almost no barriers to doctors and other suppliers of health services making their patients return for more billable visits than are medically necessary. If it is true that people are much more likely to spend their own money more carefully than someone else's, patients under a gardener's approach, where they decide where and when to spend their "share" of the health care budget, are more likely to question the need for proposed services than under a system where the service appears to be "free" when you actually get it (in the sense that no one hands you a bill when you go out the door – the bill comes later when you file your taxes).

It is just the case that people, aided by the Internet and many other information resources, are becoming increasingly sophisticated and demanding consumers of health care. Is there room for increased efforts at education of the users of the health care system about the options available to them? Of course. But this is no more true than in many other professional services available to consumers, including the choice of schools, lawyers, accountants and many other professionals who enjoy "knowledge inequalities" vis à vis their clients.

The paternalistic designer model that assumes people are incapable of choosing a reliable professional from whom to seek medical advice will be increasingly unacceptable to many people and both the empirical evidence and my own experience of the high professional standards of health professionals in Canada lead me to think that the physician-driven-demand objection to greater individual involvement in health care decisions is vastly over-rated.

Third in the gardener's reform agenda I note that technology will increasingly enable us to escape the designer-inspired health care system while changing even more fundamentally the way we relate to medical practitioners.

Virtually any kind of pharmaceutical product can now be purchased over the Internet from providers who are not in Canada and not subject to our government's controls. It is possible to have many kinds of diagnostic and other procedures carried out remotely, again by people who need not be in Canada. Your x-rays or MRIs can be read just as easily by a radiologist in Boston or Mumbai as by one in Toronto or Quebec City.

Several years ago Dalhousie University's Brain Repair Centre performed surgery on a patient from Saint John, NB. Nothing too remarkable there, until you realize that the patient stayed in Saint John and the surgeons never left Halifax. Increasingly surgery can be carried out in surgical booths equipped with video cameras and robotic arms, so that the surgery can actually be performed by surgeons physically separated from their patients.

Also, as the phenomenon of medical tourism demonstrates, well-off patients are quite capable of seeking out high quality treatments in corners of the world where they can escape both queues and government-imposed controls on access to medical services they wish to get. In Canada there are increasing reports of consumers travelling abroad for hip replacements, plastic surgery and laser eye treatment – and not just to the US, but to India and South Africa and France. At least one credible source reports 217,500 people left Canada in 2017 to get medical care.[195] In Europe the European Court has ruled that EU nationals may not be prevented by their national government from getting the treatment they want from other EU national health services. If ever the courts made a similar ruling in Canada, people would be able to escape local queues by choosing to get treated where the capacity existed right now, not when bureaucrats decided they had waited long enough.

In a world in which you can go to a surgical booth in Canada and be operated on by the best surgeon in the world, who may be at her office in London or Houston or Minneapolis, or where you can deal with a bonded medical services broker who can get you in to see some of the most reputable surgeons in the world in exotic locations, health care predicated on the notion of a closed national system in which people must take what public authorities decide they should have simply will not and cannot survive.

Fourth, contracting out and privatization will be used to introduce autonomy and accountability where appropriate, as well as to stimulate private investment and reward innovation in all aspects of health care, including in treatments, administration, timeliness, and quality – by the way, this is not the American model – it is the Swedish model of health care reform.[196] Providers of health care must be given more autonomy and responsibility so that they can act on their own knowledge of opportunities to improve service while helping their patients. The counterpart of this increased freedom, however, is that they must in turn be held more accountable for results, meaning that there should be more competition between providers for the health care dollars triggered by their patients and more and better quality information gathered on the quality and results of the health care system.

For such an approach to succeed governments will have to adopt an attitude of ever-greater neutrality between public and private suppliers of health care within our single-payer system. Provincial governments will act as purchasers of health care on behalf of their citizens, and will buy wherever they can get the best quality and best access at the lowest price in an open and transparent process with explicit quality standards. *Neither public nor private providers will get preferential treatment, unlike the status quo* where genuine private providers are still excluded from providing officially insured services in the vast majority of cases.

The old public sector monopoly model conferred huge power on ever-bigger hospitals, professions and trade unions who, together, exercised a stranglehold on the production of medical services. Not having alternative suppliers of services to turn to, provincial governments had little leverage over these giant organizations. Poor service, lengthening queues, high prices, inadequate technology; what was the alternative?

This is one of the major reasons why Ottawa has largely given up on the idea of pouring new funding into health care, and is unlikely to change that stance significantly. The government was too used to seeing the money disappear into the health system through increased administration, salaries and wages, with no increase in either the quality or the quantity of medical services. Even the otherwise free-spending Trudeau government has basically accepted the Tories' limitations on health care transfer increases despite having criticized the allegedly tight-fisted Harper government from the opposition benches for having starved the provinces of money.

Policy-makers are increasingly realizing that without a vital element of competition between health care providers, they will not be able to break this monopolistic stranglehold and ensure that they get full value for every health care dollar. Choice and accountability are a powerful discipline.

Of course the friends of the old system claim that there is no evidence that privately provided health care services are any more accessible or cheaper or of higher quality than publicly provided ones. But as Brian Ferguson, one of Canada's top health care economists told me in a private conversation, to make this case they rely on research by non-economists published in medical journals. You wouldn't want to be operated on by somebody who had learned their medicine in the *Canadian Journal of Economics*, and you shouldn't get your economic analysis from the *New England Journal of Medicine*. In fact, *the economics literature*, as well as practical experience in places like Sweden, France, and the UK, to choose just a few examples, show that there are lots of areas where private-sector providers can add value and help keep costs down. And Janice MacKinnon's work on Saskatchewan's private clinics is just one more piece of evidence that the same is true in Canada.

The real point, however, is that if governments were truly neutral between public and private providers, they wouldn't buy from *any* provider who couldn't meet tough accessibility, quality, price and accountability standards. Governments would no longer be in a conflict of interest where they are measuring and reporting on their own performance in running health care, thus avoiding what is known as "producer capture." And if private providers couldn't meet the performance standards, they'd go out of business. Strict reporting requirements would give government and the public an independent yardstick by which to measure the performance of health care institutions. And a little bonus: those institutions would have to provide better service, or else see their clientele leak away to better quality competitors, and their valued employees decamp to better employers. That's why monopolists always hate competition, and why we should embrace it in health care.

Finally, governments must focus their efforts on ensuring that no one suffers economic hardship to obtain needed medical care, that access to care is universal, that maximum information is made available on the performance of the health care system and its various components and that the transition to a new system is carried out under the watchful eye of an arm's length regulator, separating the function of service provider and service evaluator. In the present system the province is both provider and evaluator, an inescapable conflict of interest. Such a regulator would help give people confidence that quality and access are fully maintained under the new arrangements.

Let ten thousand health care flowers bloom.

CHAPTER X

Conclusion

PEOPLE CRAVE CERTAINTY and they fear risk. But because of all the things I've talked about – the limits of the human brain, the dispersed nature of knowledge, the unpredictable and dynamic effects of accelerating but unforeseeable knowledge discovery and so forth – the most successful societies are the ones that accept that knowledge and control and the idea of an overarching social design are all characteristic illusions of the progressive designer. Certainty is a rarity and risk inescapable, but we can increase certainty and manage risk as much as humanly possible. We just have to accept the trade-offs that requires.

In a free society of responsible individuals in which people act on their own knowledge and are thus unavoidably responsible and accountable for their character, their identity and their choices, we can achieve social order by making use of all the knowledge possessed by all the people who participate in society. We just cannot predict how this open and dynamic process will affect any individual person or group. Nor can we come along after the fact and "correct" the resulting distribution of goods, incomes, status, prestige and other desirable things without frustrating the plans and efforts of individuals. "Correction" of social "patterns" by political authority cannot mean anything else. And if individuals have been treated justly (in the sense that their choices have not been improperly obstructed by any other individual or organization) then the resulting patterns of distribution are not evidence of unjust treatment of groups.

We advance both in absolute terms and relative to other societies by marshalling more of the knowledge that allows us to achieve the purposes and objectives we have chosen for ourselves. We do this by creating a protected sphere in which people are empowered and entitled to experiment with what they know as long as those experiments do not intrude improperly on the protected sphere others enjoy.

Allowing political authorities to substitute their judgment for that of individuals and voluntary groups on the ground necessarily means that we as a society act on less, and less certain, knowledge because people in authority know less, not more, about our individual circumstances than we do ourselves. In other words, there is no alternative to letting people experiment with their identity, their character, and their resources, with all the potential good and bad consequences that may follow. The alternative isn't certainty and safety, but ignorance, stagnation and decline.

Every challenge we face, whether it is environmental degradation or economic collapse or mass starvation or a pandemic or nuclear war we have met effectively by becoming richer and using more knowledge to direct that wealth to achieve our purposes, not by becoming poorer and using less knowledge and therefore becoming less effective in the world. The fact that we didn't and couldn't know in advance how we were going to solve each of those problems does not negate the fact that we did. As a result, Canada and the other countries that largely use the approach I've described are cleaner, healthier, richer, safer and better fed than any other nations in the history of the world. That's a pretty good argument for not giving into despair and abandoning what has worked in favour of what doesn't and can't.

Designers will caricature this argument as one of quiescence, do-nothingism, trickle down, or some other bogeyman. But careful readers will see that what is laid out here is an approach that is far from doing nothing. Just as is the case in a real garden, in the metaphorical one of society there is an immense amount of work for gardeners to do. Unlike designers, however, gardeners recognize that the garden is not a machine, created by design, and which designers may manipulate in any way they wish to achieve any outcome they desire.

Every plant in the garden has its own character, its own process of unfolding and its own will to live according to its lights. Gardeners therefore approach the garden, as I said in the first chapter, with an attitude of gratitude and humility, not one of the will to dominate and the arrogance of those who believe it is all about them, forgetting that the flowers know better than those in charge how to be a flower and what it means.

That still leaves a huge program for the gardeners of our society, some parts of which I have alluded to in the preceding chapters.

The overarching job is to make progress possible by removing obstacles to people working together. People can and do work together when an overseer shows up and tells each person what to do, but that can only work for groups and organisations *within* society, not as an organizing principle for society as a whole.

Within society, we belong to groups of every kind on a voluntary basis, and we can leave them as well as join them. When we do come together, we negotiate the terms of our association. Because we then choose to agree on some shared objectives, authority is given to those in charge to organize us effectively in pursuit of those objectives. On a construction site or in a university classroom or a software lab or any other form of organized activity, there are things that have to be done to make the enterprise successful and there will be people who get to decide what role we will play and whether our contribution is up to standard.

In society as a whole, there is no such negotiated entry or agreement on the goals to be pursued. (The only real exception is wartime, or the response to some short term exigency like the COVID-19 virus, which creates a unique set of circumstances that warrant a whole other discussion. The key thing to remember is that the social survival imperative on which such special circumstances repose cannot be carried over into normal times once the crisis has passed. People will always want to return, rightly, to their own preoccupations and desires. More on this in a moment.)

In the state, membership is not voluntary but compulsory, although you can leave and become a citizen of some other society. But as long as you are here, you must be under the authority of the state.

Designers think there is an analogy between organizations within society and society as a whole. If we can agree to co-operate under authority in the army, in Walmart, in daycare centres and in car plants, surely it must be the same in the state. Designers believe that when there are elections and people are given political power, it is so that they can use their intelligence, backed by expertise, to tell people how to behave in order to make "society" work better and be more successful. Elections are contests to decide whose vision will carry the day and who gets to dictate what values we will pursue as a society.

The difference, though, is that "society" isn't a separate organization; it is merely the aggregate of everything that people do within it. Society does not pursue substantive "objectives," its job is not to "fix" the outcomes of social co-operation embodied in the activities of all the individuals and groups that, taken together, make it up. Were society to work that way, it would require our rulers to second-guess all of us and our plans for ourselves, and in doing so cause great disruption and frustration. That's because, of course, the people at the top always know only a tiny fraction of all that needs to be known about people, who they are, what they need and what their goals are. People know themselves best and a society that prizes individualism, shares knowledge freely, and allows people to negotiate their place in society based on what they contribute to others is a society where people have the greatest chance of successfully living their own best lives according to their own values and priorities.

If people genuinely thought that the grown social processes they participate in were vicious, oppressive and unjust, and they also thought that politics was the way to put things right, if they thought that the way we live prevents us from becoming the kind of people we wish to be and that politics was the way we put a moral stamp on immoral or amoral grown institutions, politics would preoccupy every one of us every waking hour.

Instead, what polling tells us is that people know little about the political sphere and the people in it. What designers mistake for a thirst on the part of people to use politics to inject morality into society is in fact a desire to see a moral renewal of the way we practise politics. And where people do take an interest in politics, it is often of a defensive kind, voting to protect the special benefits that have been conferred on them or to prevent others from getting such benefits at their expense. Just as gardeners predict, when it becomes permissible to use politics to confer benefits on yourself at the expense of others, energy is diverted from our real priorities, away from constructive social co-operation and into the destructive pursuit of tax-financed benefits or special government-conferred status.

I don't want to leave you with the impression, however, that gardeners don't believe in politics. Seeing politics as the agency that works tirelessly to perfect the rules of co-operation, rather than as an imposer of objectives, gives a big agenda to pursue. The vision of political society here isn't one where elections are winner-take-all contests where the losers must bow to the authority of the winners. Rather, in the gardener's world, politics is about how to come up with rules that allow people to work together successfully and energetically *despite not agreeing on ultimate values*. It is not a philosophy of winners and losers but a philosophy of peaceful co-existence in a world of diverse and sometimes irreconcilable values.

The beauty of the gardener's view is that we do not need to agree on ultimate values in order to be able to work together. And working together is the *sine qua non* of progress, if progress is understood as an ever-increasing ability of people to pursue their own values successfully because they have access to an ever-increasing body of genuine knowledge about what works. That knowledge cannot by its nature be centralized nor can our rulers have a useful overview of it and so when rulers try to tell us what is good for us, they have no legitimate claim on our acquiescence. The expertise which they so loudly and proudly hold out before them is little more than a primitive fetish stick.

As Steven Pinker from Harvard University points out,

> Progress is not magic. Progress is not perfection. Progress is not a miracle. It doesn't mean that everyone is maximally happy. It doesn't mean that everything gets better for everyone everywhere all the time and always. And that *would* be a miracle. That's not progress. The question is, however bad things are now, were they worse in the past?[197]

Ironically, progressives are the anti-progress party because they are designers; they think in terms of ends, and therefore "progress" can only be progress toward their vision of society. For them, progress is measured against an end point, which is their idea of what is good for us.

Gardeners think that progress is increasing the power of individuals to realize their own good, their own vision, their own objective, their own self-understanding. That means maximizing the knowledge available on which to act, but not seeking to interfere with the patterns or outcomes that result from people making their own choices. Progressives are anti-progress because they want society to act on what *they* know, not what *everyone* knows.

Gardeners, by contrast, are always looking for ways to extend and enrich the rules of social co-operation which are, you may recall, analogous to the rules of the road. They don't tell us where we want to go, only how to co-operate with other drivers as we each head for the particular destination we have chosen for ourselves. We do not need to agree on our destination in order to be able to use the road together.

The designer's view is that we need to use politics as a way to settle on a set of values that everyone must adhere to, regardless of how crude the choosing mechanism is and regardless of how offensive the values may be to large segments of society; the gardener's view is that genuine diversity of values, not superficial diversity of groups and colours and sexual orientations, is actually the motor of social progress.

That is because what motivates people is their vision of the good life: what they want for themselves and their family and their friends and others they care about. The gardener doesn't regard these choices of values as an obstacle to the great society just waiting to spring forth from the designing mind if only people wouldn't be so obstinate in choosing things other than what designers think are good for them. Instead these choices by individuals of what is important to them is the primary motivator of their actions and behaviours; respecting those values and giving them room to live and breathe is what makes people want to work with others in a society where we work together but no one tells us what we should want.

So focusing on process, not on ends, is one half of the gardener formula. The other half is to let people reward each other based on their evaluation of the value of the knowledge they put at our disposal. This rewards new knowledge discovery and creation and "distributes" the things people want, not on the basis of how those in authority feel about you (or your group or class), but on an impersonal society-wide evaluation of the worth of what you know how to do.

So by gratitude out of humility is born the next gardener's principle of governing: equality of treatment, or even-handedness among values and ways of life, neither advantaging nor obstructing the choices people make within the framework of the grown rules of social co-operation.

When designers use political power to impose preferences among ways of life, they don't cause social co-operation to cease. Instead, they distract us from seeking to use our knowledge to satisfy the wants of our fellow citizens, and instead the encourage us to put our energy into trying to capture political power for ourselves, so that if it is going to be used to advantage *someone* that someone will be me. Our knowledge is then used to gain benefits at the expense of everyone else rather than by satisfying the needs and wants of others. It is not a question of selfishness; as Adam Smith observed, even in a gardener society, selfishness (or at least "self-interest") is a primary motivator:

> It is not from the benevolence of the butcher, the brewer, or the baker that we expect our dinner, but from their regard to their own self-interest. We address ourselves not to their humanity but to their self-love, and never talk to them of our own necessities, but of their advantages.[198]

In the gardener version of society, self-interest is channelled in a positive direction, in the direction of a ceaseless quest to find and deploy knowledge that others find useful. In the designer's version, self-interest is channelled in a destructive direction, in the effort to seize political power to use it to confer benefits on ourselves at the expense of others, not because others have recognized the value of what we can do for them. The deeper we are pulled into this quagmire the more positive social co-operation is endangered and the more we quarrel over who gets to use the power of the state to impose their vision of the good life on everyone, including those who do not share that vision.

To use a concrete example that may help readers to see what's at stake, my view is that the current bout of Western Canadian alienation is a classic example of this kind of conflict. Ottawa doesn't understand the extent to which the West sees the federal government's behaviour as choosing favourites between, say, jobs and industry in Alberta, and jobs and industry in central Canada. The oil patch has been hard hit by both a cyclical downturn and the kind of intentional damage inflicted by obdurate public policy that I have discussed elsewhere in this book. Hostility to climate change cannot explain all of this since jobs at Bombardier in Quebec or in the car industry in Ontario, whose planes and cars generate lots of GHGs, have huge attention and energy lavished on them.

Openly manifesting a visible discomfort with one whole industry while acting as an enthusiastic cheerleader for others (even to the point of endangering the rule of law to "stand up for Canadian jobs" – as long as they're not in the oil patch) is the exact mirror image of not marching in a pride parade. In both cases what offends people is the suggestion that their choice of how to live is being rejected or impugned by the very authorities whose first responsibility is to protect the integrity of all law-abiding choices by all Canadians. If you are going to stand up for Canadian jobs, you must do so for all jobs consistent with the law and do so with equal fervour and enthusiasm. Likewise, if you are going to defend minority religions from criticism (i.e., laws against Islamophobia), you must do so for all religions. If you are going to make funding available to organizations to hire summer students, you cannot require that the applicants hew to the current federal government's position on abortion.[199] These are all examples of the obstructions imposed by Ottawa on the activities of Canadians of which designers disapprove. Designers are perfectly entitled to have their own views and disapprove of the views of others, with one significant exception. *When they hold public office* they are under a unique obligation of equal respect for all the legal choices Canadians might wish to make.

There are still plenty of things on which people can have real political disagreements in a gardener society where values are treated even-handedly by those in authority. I have referred to a few throughout the book.

Gardeners and designers agree, for example, that there must be a social insurance system that helps protect all of us from the risk of failure. Failure can happen to any of us and it is perfectly sensible and defensible to use the state to pool that risk and provide a minimum standard of living below which people cannot be allowed to fall. Legitimate political controversy attends the design and operation of such programs. My own view is that a guaranteed annual income, for example, is not ruled out by the gardener's philosophy but comes dangerously close to forcing people to subsidize permanently other people's life choices and is a poorly conceived design principle, but some other gardeners and most designers disagree.[200]

It is perfectly in order to say that no one should have to go without needed medical care based on ability to pay. It is not in order to say that no one should be allowed to obtain medical care outside a poorly performing monopoly system that no other country wishes to emulate, provided, of course, that our shared commitment to making care available regardless of ability to pay remains intact. How to organize medical care within the limits of the access principle is a proper area of political controversy.

Similarly, there is always room to review the rules of social co-operation to see whether our socially acceptable minimums, such as wages, working conditions, environmental and health and safety standards, are up to date. Since these can easily be used as a vehicle to enforce values on everyone, as opposed to setting basic minimums and letting people get on with whatever they want to do as long as they respect the minimums, this is an area that gardeners have to watch assiduously.

The same is true of the regulatory state. As I have mentioned at several points, there are two basic approaches to regulation. The designer's seeks to use regulation to impose preferred ways of doing things, so regulators tell bankers how to run their bank, telephony providers how to organize mobile phone service and greenhouse gas emitters how to reduce their emissions. Gardeners, by contrast, ask themselves what outcomes they want. Maybe they want stable banking, cheap but universal mobile telephony and certain GHG targets hit by a certain time. They then require the organizations they regulate to show how the way they want to organize their activities is consistent with those principles and outcomes, leaving the knowledge holders lots of discretion to organize their activities on the basis of what they know, rather than what regulators know.

As I suggested earlier in the book, there will always be questions about how to extend the grown social institutions we enjoy to new activities or to take account of externalities. Examples of the former are spectrum auctions or extending copyright protection to downloadable music or videos on the Internet. Examples of the latter are cap and trade for ozone-depleting CFCs or the carbon tax for GHGs. Because we don't always know what will work, and because whether legitimate externalities exist (pornography, drug use and controversial speakers all create externalities, but that does not necessarily mean they should be banned; in fact, in some cases, like the speakers, definitely should not be) can be matters of great controversy, these are areas of art, not science.

Other things I have not touched on here include the criminal justice system. Equality before the law requires that we not have competing systems where similarly situated individuals get meted out radically different treatment under the law, so some people will always feel the system is too lenient and others that it is too harsh. Again, lots of room for political disagreement.

Abortion, too, falls in here. There are clearly radically different views about the acceptability of abortion but it is an inescapably binary choice. Either it is allowed or it is not, so some people with deeply held moral convictions on either side will feel aggrieved by whatever policy is put in place. You can try to resolve this on the basis of the gardener's protected sphere of individual autonomy, and make it a pure question of women's rights, but this is not a particularly satisfactory answer. That is because the opposing view is that the foetus is a human being and therefore also entitled to its own protected sphere. I am not taking sides on this disagreement here; only observing that abortion is one of the hard questions of life and I have not seen the principled answer that rules it out of court as a legitimate area of political controversy.

The final example I will offer is in matters of war and peace. Canada as a whole has relations with other societies, and how those relations are conducted is done in the name of all of us. You can protest the decisions that are made and hold up signs saying "Not in my name," but the fact is that when our governments make decisions about how to relate to China or Iran or Russia or North Korea or even the United States, the United Kingdom and Australia, it inescapably does so in all our names. I have views about how those relations should be conducted but they do not spring from the gardener's philosophy, which is based on a series of assumptions that do not exist in the international order, which does not enjoy the kind of grown social norms and institutions that we enjoy domestically.[201] That said, I know we cannot surrender our ability to organize ourselves along gardener lines domestically in order to satisfy others, even if they cloak themselves in the rhetorical prestige of "the international community" and call themselves the Paris Accord, the World Health Organization or the United Nations.

Free trade is certainly a gardener's approach, but it increasingly needs to be hedged with some caveats, largely because the evidence is increasingly eloquent that our own very openness is being used as a weapon against us by regimes that do not wish us well.

China, for example, has used free trade as a kind of Trojan horse, a way to reach deep into Western societies, steal our technologies, insinuate state-owned corporations into strategic positions and not offer reciprocal access to their own markets. A case can be made that China has come to dominate certain industries as part of a drive both to bolster that country's own economic strength and to weaken our domestic economies for purposes of geo-strategic advantage.

There is evidence that China is exporting large quantities of opioids to Canada, contributing to a public health crisis of major proportions and then laundering the money by buying real estate, particularly in the Lower Mainland, and pricing Canadians out of the housing market in their own country. Beijing has tried to bully us into submitting to their will and abandoning the rule of law on the Meng Wanzhou extradition case, including by kidnapping our citizens and using them as pawns.

Finally, there is evidence that China is weaponizing its diaspora community in Canada, bringing pressure to bear on people resident in Canada to act so as to promote the interests of the People's Republic whether people wish to do so or not. None of that even mentions the loathsome ways in which China treats its own citizens such as Uighurs, Tibetans, Falun Gong practitioners, and those fighting for democracy in Hong Kong, all of whom are people entitled to rights and respect.

There is nothing in the gardener philosophy that requires us to sit still for this and much that requires us to take vigorous action to protect our interests, our values, and our citizens. Similar things could be said about Russia's efforts to sow confusion and loss of confidence in our institutions as a way of weakening the Western alliance. Gardeners know that many societies in the world are organized on anti-gardener principles and they seek to project their power and influence into the West. We are entitled and are duty-bound to act together with like-minded countries to ensure our safety and protect our interests.

The gardener's number one role is to protect the garden from predators, of whom there are many. We cannot rely on international law to control their behaviour, either because it is ineffective or because a great many of the people who pose a threat to us are in positions of power within international organisations. Yet Canada has allowed its ability to respond effectively and robustly (unless you think finger-wagging squeaky-voiced protests are effective and robust), and therefore its ability to protect its interests in concert with its allies, to fall into disrepair and desuetude. For gardeners this isn't merely ill-advised but deeply irresponsible.

A COVID coda

I was writing this book just as the COVID-19 outbreak was gathering steam and the manuscript will pass out of my hands and into those of graphic artists and layout designers and blurb writers before the immediate crisis is behind us. Voices are already making themselves heard, however, to claim that the coronavirus proves that we must put ourselves in the hands of experts for our survival and that the social and political cohesion we have achieved in the face of a common threat shows how we should tackle other pressing problems, such as combatting inequality or poverty or climate change.[202] COVID-19 and its aftermath are thus taken by some to vindicate the designer's approach and consign the gardener's to the dustbin of history.

Not so fast! Let's look first of all at the idea that COVID-19 proves that the experimental and incremental approach of the gardener isn't up to the job of protecting the population from this scourge. On the contrary, as I have already said, no one is more aware than gardeners that protecting us from predators, human and microbial, is Job One for those responsible for the state. Furthermore, because how people behave during a pandemic has enormous spill-over effects (or externalities), policy-makers are fully justified in taking strong action to preserve public order and minimize the spread of the disease. There is nothing in the gardener's creed that says that strong and decisive action cannot be taken when warranted.

On the other hand, the gardener clings stubbornly to the notion that the knowledge we possess, including knowledge about how to respond to viral outbreaks, is always and unavoidably partial and imperfect. This is doubly true when you consider that each outbreak has unique characteristics and the virus itself may be fast-evolving, presenting policy-makers with a moving target. So the gardener's view is that there is no contradiction between recognizing that decisive action may be called for while at the same time knowing that mistakes are inevitable and we have to take tough decisions on the basis of imperfect knowledge.[203] This is the human condition.

Then there is the notion that "expertise" saved us during the coronavirus outbreak. Yes, there were lots of experts peddling their expertise around the world, but those of us who actually looked at what they were recommending soon found that equally credible experts were often offering diametrically opposed advice.[204] Some experts' advice was followed in some places and it worked out well, as in Taiwan.[205] In other places different experts' advice was followed with less impressive results.[206]

So yes, public health crises like this require energetic action, and yes, it makes sense to seek the advice of those who profess to have the latest and deepest knowledge in framing appropriate policy. But the policy that was followed did not come about because policy-makers had to acquiesce in some expert consensus. Mostly what happened was that policy-makers listened to people who sounded convincing and had the policy-makers' ears. In the event their advice was sometimes correct, sometimes not, and sometimes simply neither particularly helpful nor harmful.[207]

Only when the crisis has fully passed, when it is too late to be of much use, will we really be able to sort out what was most helpful. Then when the next pandemic strikes, the lessons from COVID-19 will be trotted out by the experts when the state of our knowledge will again be partial and imperfect and COVID-19 may be more or less relevant. There is a reason why generals always fight the last war: because that's where their expertise truly lies.

When the smoke has cleared and we have enough distance to draw lessons from this particular public health crisis a lot of thinking will go into what those lessons are. Many of them will be unexpected and have nothing to do with public health or medical expertise. My suspicion, for what it is worth, is that we will find that a healthy dose of China scepticism was a positive factor, as Taiwan, Singapore, South Korea and others demonstrated when they discounted Chinese blandishments and the WHO's early advice about the seriousness of the outbreak and what it portended.[208] That suspicion, however, may not be borne out in the final analysis and other factors we cannot yet know may turn out to have been influential or decisive. Whatever the answer(s), it is certain that they will be only moderately useful next time, because circumstances will be new and therefore everyone's expertise will be of limited value.

It is important to dwell for a moment on the extent to which the public policy response to COVID-19 relied to an enormous extent on gardener strategies. Public health experts and epidemiologists and microbiologists are not, in the ordinary course of things, themselves experts on the thousand other areas of expertise on which a robust response to a pandemic must rely. They know little about how to make testing kits and whose testing kits will prove the most useful. They know little about manufacturing vaccines, supplying masks and other personal protective equipment, telephone tracking apps, logistics or the thousand other things that are or may be needed.

Governments and private donors didn't give to some single government lab, no matter how many experts they employed, the job of isolating the virus, analysing it, discovering the best way to test for it, developing a vaccine, or testing all existing pharmaceutical products against the virus to see if any of them worked. Instead, resources intended to hasten the discovery of COVID-related knowledge were handed to many public and private labs around the world, who then produced a plethora of experimental solutions and relied on a steady stream of discoveries from other labs to support their own work.[209] Different researchers are in effect competing with each other to find the most effective therapeutic agents or to design, test and then produce an effective vaccine[210] or to produce the cheap and essentially instantaneous COVID-19 testing kits which will be an indispensable part of a strategy to return to normal life as quickly as possible.[211]

In mid-March the Montreal General Hospital Foundation together with the Research Institute of the McGill University Health Centre launched a "global innovation challenge" backed by a $200,000 prize. This gardener strategy seeks to harness knowledge wherever it may be found in the world, regardless of nationality or public or private status, to find a design for a simple, low-cost, easy-to-manufacture and easy-to-maintain ventilator which could be deployed anywhere needed to save lives.[212]

All of these things are necessary because of the partial state of our knowledge and because the much vaunted expertise of those advising (some) governments on their response to the crisis is impotent outside their extremely narrow area of knowledge. And because of the urgency of the effort to gather relevant knowledge about the virus and effective treatments against it we have waived some regulatory barriers (say to testing on human subjects) that otherwise slow down the knowledge discovery process.[213] That, by the way, is precisely why gardeners think a light regulatory hand is best in general, because every unnecessary regulation makes us stupider by preventing us from discovering new knowledge and then acting on it.

Lots of people discovered new unsuspected things about themselves as a result of the spread of COVID-19.[214] Hockey equipment manufacturers discovered they could make face shields for medical personnel.[215] Car parts manufacturers shifted production to make the medical ventilators needed to turn ordinary hospital beds into ICU facilities – and opened up export markets into the bargain.[216] A pillow manufacturer swiftly became a high quality medical face mask producer.[217] Irony of ironies, the government of Canada is eagerly making deals with companies[218] to supply the spare capacity the health care system lacks in this hour of dire need, a solution they treat as an unacceptable attack on Canadian values the rest of the time. If things get really dire, we may well eventually see private suppliers constructing makeshift hospitals and other facilities to tide us over the worst of the crisis. For the moment existing hospitals have to content themselves with leasing convention centres and hotels to create extra space[219] when in normal times private investors would have been happy to build clinics and other specialized spare capacity we now cannot call on.

As for the notion that we should generalize from the social solidarity of the COVID crisis and apply its methods to resolving a host of other issues that seemed insoluble before, this is a vain hope. It is vain not because the social solidarity wasn't real (although I think it was much exaggerated, at least judging by the poor behaviour of many of the people in my local grocery store).[220] It is vain because the solidarity itself was born of very limited and special circumstances that are not normally present.

We saw a similar phenomenon after the end of the Second World War. In Britain six years of rationing and bombing and shortages and helping each other out led the Labour Party to promise to carry that spirit and those methods into running peacetime society. Their very slogan in the 1945 general election (which they won in a landslide) was "And now win the peace."

What they failed to realize was that war and peace are not the same thing. In the war there was an overriding existential objective to which all else was voluntarily subordinated by the vast majority of Britons: to defeat Hitler. When peace arrived, however, people went back to those things they wanted and valued for themselves and didn't have to agree on with their neighbours. They got tired of overweening public officials telling them what to do and how to do it in the name of the "spirit of Dunkirk." The public chafed increasingly under the privation of peace-time rationing. Above all else they craved a return to normality, by which they meant a state of affairs where they made their own decisions about what mattered to them. Without the shared overriding goal of victory in war, "social solidarity" rapidly came to be seen for what it was: licence for bureaucrats to order people around in accordance with other people's ideas, mostly the "experts" who were going to fix society's problems.

If it only took a year or two for people to begin to find the spirit of Dunkirk an increasingly irksome rallying cry, my guess is that the COVID-19 outbreak and our response will prove even more evanescent. Many people love the idea that everyone else will drop their stubborn attachment to their selfish priorities and sacrifice their narrow vision for the common good. But what they usually have in mind is that the rest of us should give up what *we* want and pursue what *they* want instead.

The fact of the matter is that outside times of rare crisis like war or epidemic, we as a society do not have a common set of concrete objectives on which we agree. And yet it is a consensus on overriding objectives that is the indispensable condition of selfless social co-operation on a large scale. The responses to most crises cannot be replicated once the crisis is over, when gardener values begin to look very attractive again.

My prediction is that people will be astonished at how quickly Canadians will want to return to the *status quo ante* COVID, even if individual pieces of our behaviour remain changed because we discovered during the crisis that we actually like those changes better than what we were doing before. My fitness group may never go back to meeting in person again because we discovered that meeting on-line is more flexible and convenient. This we would never have learned had it not been for COVID. And human beings, as I have already remarked repeatedly throughout this book, are condemned to learn, including from pandemics. We just will not learn what the fans of designerism hope we will.

Sunny ways are gardeners' ways

Humility, gratitude, even-handedness. That is the gardener's program, and it is at once modest and revolutionary.

It is modest because it eschews the designer's vaulting ambition of "fixing" society in accordance with some academic's theoretical scribblings. Canadian society is not something to be fixed. It is the framework within which we all make a life for ourselves and it makes possible our freedom, our autonomy and our flowering. It is something to be enjoyed, and its logic extended to new and unforeseen circumstances. It has evolved from a thousand years and more of experience and embodies knowledge and incremental improvements that have withstood the test of generations.

Our entire endowment of grown social institutions is the key to Canada's position as a leading nation of the world.

The gardener's program is also revolutionary because our grown social institutions are under siege and designers are manning the siege engines. So successful have they been in capturing the way we talk about politics that every party now campaigns on designer themes: who should get special tax breaks or credits, what groups should get special recognition, who has the better plan for implementing the Paris Accord, who is the best friend of abstract groups like the "middle class," who can create the most complete monopoly for the provision of public services like health care. As a result, Canada's standard of living has been in decline relative to our peers, the rule of law is under great stress, and Canadian society is riven by conflict over who will control the machinery of the state and use it to reward those it favours at the expense of everyone else, all in the name of "progressive" values.

This is a relatively new phenomenon whose evolution I traced in an earlier book.[221] All I will say here is that gardener values used to be the bedrock on which both Liberals and Conservatives governed this country. Gardnerism's main features are most obvious today in some of the larger currents within the Conservative Party, but contrary to what many people who know little of our history seem to believe, the gardener approach has deep roots within the Liberal Party and many of its tenants are biding their time, waiting for the progressive tide to ebb within their great party.

Sir Wilfrid Laurier, for instance, whose "sunny ways" have proven so great an inspiration to Prime Minister Justin Trudeau, was a gardener of the first water:

> . . . [Laurier] thought it vital to preserve and protect the institutions brought to Canada by our forebears, the "British liberty" composed of the rule of law, free speech, freedom of conscience and religion, respect of minority rights, habeas corpus, parliamentary self-government, minimal state interference, low taxes, respect of property and of contract. That liberty and those institutions were, Laurier believed, the catalyst that released the energy and dynamism of those who lived under them, whatever their ethnic origin or religious convictions. When people were

free to follow their own star, to determine what was important to them, to build their own relationships with family, friends and colleagues, they built well and energetically – they had confidence in the future, they took risks and reaped the reward.[222]

Laurier thought that people would flock to Canada (as they did during his premiership in record numbers) because of our long tradition of freedom, that people could come to Canada precisely because here they would be free to be themselves, not pieces on a chessboard to be moved around at the will of those in political power. Laurier believed "when people were expected to take responsibility for themselves and their family, they made better provision for their needs and directed their productive efforts where they would do the country and themselves the greatest good. When this natural necessity to strive was diluted by an easy access to the public purse, the ever-present danger was of the enervation of the individual and the stagnation of the progress of society."

"If you remove the incentives of ambition and emulation from public enterprises [by which he meant the economic undertakings of individuals and businesses, not state enterprise]," Laurier said on the subject in 1907, "you suppress progress, you condemn the community to stagnation and immobility."[223]

I could multiply the examples of similar sentiments expressed by our political leaders, both Grit and Tory, over the course of the first hundred years of our post-Confederation history, but in the last fifty, allegiance to gardener principles has proven to be the exception rather than the rule among our ruling class, as progressive designer values have displaced them, not because they work better, but because those values became fashionable and gardener values unfashionable. Those who believed in gardener values ceased making the case for them, then largely forgot how to defend them. This book is a contribution to the effort to reclaim for Canada and its main political parties the gardener values on which it was founded, values buried in our institutions where they labour still on our behalf, unloved, mischaracterized and often under threat, not from malice but misunderstanding and misplaced ambition.

When politics takes a wrong turn, the most progressive person is the one who shows the way back to the right road, and does so with patience, respect for tradition and a cherishing of Canadians as they are, not as some might wish them to be. That makes gardeners the only progressives worthy of the name in Canada today.

Endnotes

1 Cassie Werber, 2016, "How non-English Speakers are Taught this Crazy English Grammar Rule You Know but have Never Heard of," *Quartz*, 7 September.

2 Sean Speer, 2019, *A Dose of Reality: The Need for a Targeted Approach to Pharmacare*, Macdonald-Laurier Institute (June).

3 Paola Loriggio, 2019, "Toronto Public Library under Fire for Refusing to Cancel Meghan Murphy Event," *National Post* (October 16).

4 Sir Wilfrid Laurier, 1905, "Wilfrid Laurier: Let Them Become Canadians, 1905," *The Canadian Encyclopedia*, September 1.

5 Candice Malcolm, 2016, "Trudeau Says Canada Has No 'Core Identity,'" *Toronto Sun* (September 14).

6 Angus Reid Institute and CBC, 2016, "What Makes Us Canadian? A Study of Values, Beliefs, Priorities and Identity," Angus Reid Institute (October 3).

7 Sir Wilfrid Laurier, 1891, "Wilfrid Laurier's Speech to the House of Commons June 8, 1891," *The Macdonald Project* (June 9).

8 Joseph Schumpeter, 1942, *Capitalism, Socialism, and Democracy*, Harper & Bros.

9 See Pierre Berton's wonderful 1990 essay on this topic: "Wheels: The Car as a Cultural Driving Force," *Canadian Geographic* (December 1989/January 1990).

10 Jane Hart, 2020, "The Rapidly Changing Workplace," *Modern Workplace Learning 2020* (May 5). Hart's article forms the basis of much of this discussion about knowledge doubling, but see also C.H. Waddington, 1977, *Tools for Thought*, Granada Publishing, pp. 32-37.

11 I owe this term to Marc Rosenberg, 2017, "Marc My Words: The Coming Knowledge Tsunami," *Learning Solutions* (October 10).

12 See Samuel Arbesman, 2013, *The Half-Life of Facts: Why Everything We Know Has an Expiration*, Penguin Group.

13 Shane Parrish, 2020, "Half Life: The Decay of Knowledge and What to Do about It," *Farnam Street Media Inc.* Quoted in Hart.

14 Psychology Wiki, 2020, "Human Channel Capacity," *Wikia.*

15 *Miller, George A., 1956, "The Magical Number Seven, Plus or Minus Two: Some Limits on Our Capacity for Processing Information," Psychological Review 63, 2: 81–97.*

16 Philip E. Tetlock, 2005, *Expert Political Judgement: How Good Is It? How Can We Know?* Princeton University Press.

17 Tetlock, 2005, *Expert Political Judgement:* Abstract.

18 Stav Atir, Emily Rosenzweig, and David Dunning, 2015, "When Knowledge Knows No Bounds: Self-Perceived Expertise Predicts Claims of Impossible Knowledge," *Psychological Science* 26, 8 (August): 1295-1303.

19 Terry Goodrich, 2016, "People with Higher 'Intellectual Arrogance' Get Better Grades, Baylor Study Finds," News release, Baylor University (October 6).

20 Dan Kopf, 2016, "Data Shows that Using Science in an Argument Just Makes People More Partisan," *Quartz* (December 23).

21 William Davies, 2017, "How Statistics Lost their Power – And Why We Should Fear What Comes Next," *The Guardian* (January 19).

22 Helen Dale, 2019, "For Liberalism to Survive, We Must Renounce Technocracy," *CapX* (November 20).

23 Brigit Katz, 2020, "Human Body Temperature Is Getting Cooler, Study Finds," *Smithsonian Magazine* (January 16).

24 Matt Ridley, 2010, *The Rational Optimist: How Prosperity Evolves,* HarperCollins.

25 George Gilder, 2012, *Wealth and Poverty: A New Edition for the Twenty-First Century,* Regnery Publishing, p. XXVI.

26 Sir Roger Scruton writes that property is "The fullest right that can exist over anything, which includes . . . the right to possess, use, lend, alienate, use up, consume and destroy. More simply, property can be described as a right of use, which can exist in varying degrees, and subject to various conditions" (1983, *A Dictionary of Political Thought,* Pan Books).

27 Hernando de Soto, 2000, *The Mystery of Capital: Why Capitalism Triumphs in the West and Fails Everywhere Else,* Basic Books.

28 David Hume, 1739, *A Treatise on Human Nature,* Book Three.

29 John Stuart Mill, 1848/1909, "Chapter 1: Of Property," Book II: Distribution, *The Principles of Political Economy with some of their Applications to Social Philosophy,* William James Ashley, ed. (Longmans, Green, and Co., 1909, 7th ed.).

30 Which is why Taco Bell restaurants in the United States are now reportedly paying salaries of US$100,000 for managers of their fast food restaurants. (See Leslie Patton, 2020, "Taco Bell Is So Desperate for Workers It's Offering $100,000 Salaries," *National Post* (January 9).)

31 Philip Cross, 2020, "Busting a Few Myths about the Gig Economy," *National Post* and Macdonald-Laurier Institute (January 2).

32 Nassim Nicholas Taleb, 2016, "Inequality and Skin in the Game," *Medium: Incerto* (December 27).

33 Just in case the phrase "beer and popcorn" has passed from the popular imagination, let me recall that during the 2006 federal election Liberal communications director Scott Reid said that giving people money to "blow on beer and popcorn" was no substitute for a universal daycare system ("Federal Liberals Deride 'Beer and Popcorn' Money," *CBC* [Digital Archives] (December 11)).

34 Brian Lee Crowley, 2013, *Fearful Symmetry: The Fall and Rise of Canada's Founding Values*, Macdonald-Laurier Institute.

35 Encyclopaedia Britannica, 2019, "Moore's Law: Computer Science" (December 26).

36 ". . . a quick look at Amazon's financial statements shows it does pay taxes. In 2017, Amazon paid close to $1 billion in income tax. In 2018, the amount jumped to $1.18 billion, accounting for local, state, and international taxes" (see Stephanie Denning, 2019, "Why Amazon Pays No Corporate Taxes," *Forbes* (February 22).).

37 Just one small example: Amazon's purchases of vehicles have been a boon to the entire auto industry. "Amazon has built up a fleet of 30,000 last-mile delivery trucks and vans since creating its own delivery network in 2018, and currently handles about half of its own deliveries. That's good news for manufacturers of increasingly ubiquitous gray vans with the blue swoosh, which include Daimler's Mercedes-Benz, Fiat Chrysler Automobiles and Ford Motor Co." (See Gabrielle Coppola, 2019, "Amazon's Van-buying Spree Delivers a Gift to the Auto Industry," *Automotive News* (December 19).).

38 Joseph Schumpeter, 1942, *Capitalism, Socialism, and Democracy*, Harper and Brothers.

39 Haydn Shaughnessy, 2011, "Welcome To The $2000 Car: What Difference Does It Make to You? *Forbes* (June 29).

40 Tyler Cowan, 2014, "How Technology Could Help Fight Income Inequality," *New York Times* (December 6).

41 Frederic Bastiat, 1848/1995, *Selected Essays on Political Economy*, Online Library of Liberty, p. 144.

42 Elections Canada, 2020, *The 2019 Federal Election by the Numbers* [Data table], Elections Canada.

43 Gerald L. Gall, 2014, "Charlottetown Accord," *The Canadian Encyclopedia*.

44 Christian Leuprecht and Sean Speer, 2015, "How to Build a Long-Term

Refugee Policy," *From A Mandate For Change To A Plan To Govern*, *National Post* and Macdonald Laurier Institute (December 14).

45 Chris Selley, 2019, "Chris Selley: Our 'Illegal Carpooling Problem' Is Actually a Huge Opportunity," *National Post* (December 18).

46 Ashley Csanady, 2015, "Supply Management Costs Poor Families Five Times More Relative to Household Income: Study," *National Post* (February 27). Csanady documents the cost per family and notes that "According to OECD calculations, Canada's 'market price support' was an astounding $52 billion for supply-managed products from 2000 to 2017, or an average of just over $2.9 billion each year. Almost 90 percent of this overcharge was paid for milk: $46 billion, or nearly $2.6 billion every year." See also Michael Osborne, 2018, "It Really Is Time to Kick Canada's $2.6 Billion Dairy Habit," *Financial Post* (July 6).

47 Sean Speer, 2019, *Forgotten People and Forgotten Places: Canada's Economic Performance in the Age of Populism*, Macdonald-Laurier Institute.

48 Brian Lee Crowley, 2016, *Turning Canada from Agricultural Laggard to World Food Superpower*, MLI Commentary, Macdonald-Laurier Institute (June 24). See also Brian Lee Crowley, 2016, "Canada's Trouble with the Farm," *Globe and Mail* and Macdonald-Laurier Institute (June 10).

49 Peter Thiel, 2014, "Is Google a Monopoly?" *Fox Business* (September 29).

50 Oberlo, 2020, "Search Engine Market Share in 2019," Oberlo.

51 Google, Undated, "From the Garage to the Googleplex," Google.

52 Digital TechBlog, Undated, "April 2012 Search Engine Market Share," Digital TechBlog.

53 See Sean Speer, 2019, *Forgotten People and Forgotten Places: Canada's Economic Performance in the Age of Populism*, Macdonald-Laurier Institute (August).

54 Louis Jacobson, 2012, "Barack Obama Ad Says Women are Paid '77 Cents on the Dollar for Doing the Same Work as Men'," *Politifact* (June 21).

55 Warren Farrell, 2005, *Why Men Earn More: The Startling Truth Behind the Pay Gap – and What Women Can Do About It*, AMACOM; Valentin Bolotnyy and Natalia Emanuel, 2019, *Why Do Women Earn Less Than Men? Evidence from Bus and Train Operators*, Working Paper, Harvard University (July 5); Federico Anzil, 2020, "Is the Difference in Work Hours the Real Reason for the Gender Wage Gap? [Interactive Infographic]," *Visme*; Claudia Goldin, 2014, "A Grand Gender Convergence: Its Last Chapter," *American Economic Review* 104, 4: 1–30; John Phelan, 2018, "Harvard Study: 'Gender Wage Gap' Explained Entirely by Work Choices of Men and Women," Foundation for Economic Education (December 10); June E. O'Neill and Dave M. O'Neill, 2005, *What Do Wage Differentials Tell Us about Labor Market Discrimination?* NBER Working Paper Series 11240 (March), National Bureau of Economic Research;

Jeremy Staff and Jeylan T. Mortimer, 2012, "Explaining the Motherhood Wage Penalty during the Early Occupational Career," *Demography* 49: 1–21; Tim Worstall, 2015, "The Entire Gender Pay Gap Explained In Just One Number: 5.7%," *Forbes* (November 22); and Howard J. Wall, 2000, "The Gender Wage Gap and Wage Discrimination: Illusion or Reality?" Federal Reserve Bank of St. Louis (October 1).

56 Cody Cook, Rebecca Diamond, Jonathan Hall, John A. List, and Paul Oyer, 2019, *The Gender Earnings Gap in the Gig Economy: Evidence from over a Million Rideshare Drivers*, Stanford University (March 8).

57 Which is not to say there are never any instances of documented discrimination. No one is denying that discrimination does still happen occasionally, but the incidents are isolated outliers and are generally resolved quickly once brought to the attention of the authorities.

58 All job seekers go through this sort of calculus of course. Since this discussion is in the context of whether aggregate outcomes for *groups* are evidence of discrimination, however, I am going to use the example of a female job seeker.

59 Statista, 2020, *Number of Students Enrolled in Postsecondary Institutions in Canada in 2017/18, by Gender and Field of Study* [Web table], Statista.

60 Virginia Harrison, 2019, "How a University Dropout Built a Toy Empire," *BBC News* (December 16).

61 *Canadian Charter of Rights and Freedoms*, s 15 (1), Part 1 of the *Constitution Act, 1982*, being Schedule B to the *Canada Act 1982* (UK), c 11.

62 Jordan Peterson, 2019, "Jordan Peterson: Why the Western Emphasis on Individuals is the Ultimate Intersectionality," *National Post* (November 22).

63 The maximin principle was proposed by the political philosopher John Rawls. According to this principle, to be just a society should be designed to maximize the position of those who will be worst off in it. (See John Rawls, 1971, *A Theory of Justice*, 1st edition, Harvard University Press.)

64 Kaveh Shahrooz and Brett Byers, 2019, "Candidate Nominations in Canada are a Mess – Let's Fix That," *Toronto Sun* and *Macdonald-Laurier Institute* (December 4).

65 The OECD defines middle class income as anything between 75 percent and 200 percent of the median income of CA$59,800 (Organisation for Economic Co-operation and Development [OECD], "Governments Must Act to Help Struggling Middle Class," News Release (April 10), OECD.

66 Mark Gollom, 2019, "What You Need to Know about the Vice-Admiral Mark Norman Case," *CBC News* (May 8).

67 CBC, 2015, "Charbonneau Commission Finds Corruption Widespread in Quebec's Construction Sector," *CBC News* (November 24).

68   "Thatcher's premiership was a wrong, contradictory note for feminism; we regarded her as a man dressed up in a skirt suit" author Linda Grant was quoted as saying in *The Women's Blog* (Linda Grant, 2012, "Margaret Thatcher: A Feminist Icon?" *The Guardian* (January 5)).

69   A terminological note: I try to avoid as much as possible ugly bureaucratic terms as they are repugnant and discouraging to most readers. That is why throughout this chapter I am going to use the term "cities." City is a plain language term that experts define in different ways. Among urban geographers, the city has two functional definitions. One is the "metropolitan area," which is the labour and housing market. These are the Census Metropolitan Areas (CMAs), defined by Statistics Canada. The CMA includes the population centre and the area outside the population centre within the CMA, because the area of the CMA may contain non-built-up areas as well as built-up ones. Many people mix up "municipalities" and "CMAs" but this is a mistake. Referring to "built-up areas" gets us to the other relevant dimension (or "functional definition") of city in this chapter: the "population centre" in Canada. (It is called a "built-up urban area" in the UK and an "urban area" in the US and many other countries). This is the area of continuous development and the only definition from which meaningful population density figures can be obtained. For example, Statscan defines the Toronto population centre as generally from Burlington to the western border of the Durham region and up to Newmarket (excluding rural areas within). Where I think it helps illuminate the argument I will specify which functional definition of city I am using.

70   Gary Marr, 2015, "Don't Pull the Plug on the Suburbs Yet as Peak Prices Drive Home Buyers out of the Core," *Financial Post* (October 7).

71   It is important to acknowledge that outside of the central cities, planning decisions are often in the hands of people to whom the gardener approach appeals. But they are not the ones who dominate the public discussion. Those who are very much part of the discussion include the former Toronto chief planner Jennifer Keesmaat who says that Canada's cities were designed for cars and not people, a completely meaningless distinction unless the driverless car has come early to Toronto, because as far as I know, there are people in every one of those cars and they chose those cars over transit for some very good reasons, as we will see. (See Jennifer Keesmaat, 2018, "We Designed Canada's Cities for Cars, not People – and the People Are Dying," *The Guardian* (June 14).)

72   City of Vancouver population for 2019: 685,885; Surrey population for 2019: 584,526. Excel data sheet available at Government of British Columbia, 2020, "Population Estimates."

73 Wendell Cox, 2012, "Special Report: Census 2011: Urban Dispersion in Canada," *New Geography* (February 14).

74 Professor David Gordon, director of the School of Urban and Regional Planning at Queen's University summarized his school's research as indicating that "Canada is a suburban nation." Gordon notes that there is a tendency to "overestimate the importance of the highly visible downtown cores and underestimate the vast growth happening in the suburban edges" (David L.A. Gordon, Lyra Hindrichs, and Chris Willms, 2018, Still Suburban? *Growth in Canadian Suburbs, 2006-2016*, Working Paper 2 (August), Council for Canadian Urbanism, Queens University).

75 Joannah Connolly, 2015, "Infographic: TD Survey Reveals Home Buyer Attitudes on Urban Vs. Suburban," *Real Estate Wire [REW]* (May 24).

76 Robert Bruegmann, 2005, *Sprawl: A Compact History,* University of Chicago Press.

77 Wendell Cox, 2019, *Moving Toward More Accessible and Productive Transportation in the Puget Sound,* Washington Policy Center (October); and Wendell Cox, 2018, *Employment Access in Metropolitan Areas (2017),* New Geography (November 23).

78 Scott Beyer, 2019, "How Houston Is Becoming America's Next Dense City," *Catalyst* (December 18); and Joel Kotkin, 2014, "Introduction," *Opportunity Urbanism: Creating Cities for Upward Mobility,* joelkotkin.com (October 13).

79 As of February 29, 2020, Uber's market capitalization was US$70.72 billion (Markets Insider, 2020, "UBER (UBER) STOCK NYSE," (February 29).

80 Alissa Walker, 2016, "Look How Much Nicer Our Streets Will Be When They're Used by Self-Driving Cars," *Gizmodo* (May 3).

81 Ross McKitrick, 2012, "Gasoline Tax Would Need to Rise by $2.30 per Litre to Cut Motor Vehicle GHG Emissions by 30 Percent," Media Release (February 22), Macdonald-Laurier.

82 Airbnb, 2020, "Book Unique Places to Stay and Things to Do," [Home page], Airbnb Inc.

83 JustPark, 2020, "Find Parking in Seconds," [Home page], JustPark.

84 Nick Vivion, 2013, "Nosh Nations: The Monetization of the Sharing Economy Spreads to Food," *PhocusWire* (May 23).

85 Share Your Office [SYO], 2020, "Rental Offices, Meeting Rooms, and Coworking Spaces" [Home page], SYO.

86 Brian Flemming, 2015, *The Political Economy of Canada's Transportation Policies in 2015: The "What" is Easy; The "How" is Hard,* Van Horne Institute (May 20). Brian Flemming's remarks were then cited in another Canada Transportation Act Review chaired by David Emerson that reported in 2015 (Canada,

Transport Canada, 2015, *Pathways: Connecting Canada's Transportation System to the World*, vol. 1, p. 83).

87   Edward L. Glaeser, Joseph Gyourko, and Raven Saks, 2005, "Why Have Housing Prices Gone Up?" *American Economic Review*, 95 (May 2): 329-333.

88   Edward L. Glaeser and Joseph Gyourko, 2003, "The Impact of Building Restrictions on Housing Affordability," *Economic Policy Review* 9, (June 2): 21-39.

89   John M. Quigley and Steven Raphael, 2005, "Regulation and the High Cost of Housing in California," *AEA Papers and Proceedings: Regulation and the High Cost of Housing* 95, 2 (May): 323-328.

90   Real Estate Wire [REW], 2015, "Vancouver and North Vancouver Mired in the Most Development Red Tape: Study," *REW* (July 17).

91   The Economist, 2016, "The Grip Tightens: Faulty Land-Use Regulation is Throttling the Capital," Living in London, *The Economist* (April 30).

92   Wendell Cox, 2016, "LSE/Netherlands Research Documents Price Effects of Tight Housing Regulation," *New Geography* (April 12).

93   Randall Holcombe and Sam Staley, 2001, *Smarter Growth: Market Based Strategies for Land-Use Planning in the 21st Century*, Greenwood Press, p. 7.

94   Harry Kitchen, 2006, *A State of Disrepair: How to Fix the Financing of Municipal Infrastructure in Canada*, CD Howe Institute (December).

95   The original idea for such a list came from the author Michael Crichton in a speech he gave to the National Press Club in Washington DC on January 25th, 2005. I have updated it with more recent examples. (Michael Crichton, 2009, "Three Speeches by Michael Crichton," *Science and Public Policy Institute* (December 9).)

96   Wendell Cox and Hugh Pavletich, 2019, *15th Annual Demographia International Housing Affordability Survey: 2019 – Rating Middle-Income Housing Affordability*, Demographia.

97   Thomas Robert Malthus, 1798, *An Essay on the Principle of Population*, 1st ed., J. Johnson.

98   Gerald 0. Barney, 1998, *Global 2000: Report to the President*, Seven Locks Press.

99   "Rich countries use less aluminum, nickel, copper, steel, stone, cement, sand, wood, paper, fertilizer, water, crop acreage and fossil fuel every year, as Andrew McAfee documents in *More from Less*. Consumption of 66 out of 72 resources tracked by the US Geological Survey is now declining" (Johan Norberg, 2020, "Health, Wealth and the Environment are All Better than Ever: Norberg: The 2010s have been Amazing," *Human Progress* (January 15)).

100 And note that we in the West do not feed ourselves at the expense of people in the Third World. On the contrary, it is western innovation that has largely made it possible for the burgeoning populations of the world to be fed. And we are nowhere near the limit of what such innovation and inventiveness can accomplish. It has been estimated that if the very best technology were made available throughout the world, and property rights attached to agricultural land were sound everywhere, we could easily feed a billion more people than we do today.

101 The Conference Board of Canada, 2011, *World Income Inequality: Is the World Becoming More Unequal?* Conference Board of Canada; and Joe Hassel, 2018, "Is Income Inequality Rising around the World? *Our World in Data,* World Economic Forum (November 23).

102 In fact, according to the US NOAA, the quantity of volatile organic compounds (VOCs) found in LA's air has declined by 98 percent since the 1960s. VOCs are chiefly the result of car emissions and according to the NOAA, they are "a key ingredient in the formation of ground-level ozone, which, at high levels, can harm people's lungs and damage crops and other plants" (National Oceanic and Atmospheric Administration, 2013, "Los Angeles Air Pollution Declining, Losing Its Sting," *NOAA Research News* (June 4)).

103 Where hunger continues to be a problem, for example, it is due almost exclusively to two factors. One is politics and poor quality institutions that prevent investment in land, and the second is standards of living too low to allow access to the very latest in modern technology.

104 David Suzuki, 2017, "David Suzuki: Demanding Economic Growth on a Finite Planet Robs Future Generations," *ECOWatch* (August 9); and Mike Moffatt, 2018, "David Suzuki Needs an Economics Refresher Course," *The Globe and Mail* (May 9).

105 Katherine Martinko, 2016, "How Drip Irrigation Can Save the World," *TreeHugger* (December 13).

106 Food and Agriculture Organization of the United Nations, 2018, *The Future of Food and Agriculture: Alternative Pathways to 2050*, United Nations.

107 Asseng, S., F. Ewert, P. Martre, et al., 2015, "Rising Temperatures Reduce Global Wheat Production," *Nature Climate Change* 5, 2: 143-147.

108 Food and Agriculture Organization of the United Nations, 2018, *The Future of Food and Agriculture.*

109 Hannah Ritchie and Max Roser, 2019, *Natural Disasters*, Our World in Data (November 2019).

110 Michael Shellenberger, 2019, "Why Apocalyptic Claims about Climate Change Are Wrong," *Forbes* (November 25).

111 A good summary can be found here: http://www.lse.ac.uk/website-archive/ GeographyAndEnvironment/neumayer/pdf/EKC.pdf. See also James Van Alstine and Eric Neumayer, 2010, "The Environmental Kuznets Curve," in Kevin Gallagher (ed.), *Handbook on Trade and the Environment* (Edward Elgar): 49-59.

112 The US Environmental Protection Agency [EPA], 2017, "Air Quality Improves as America Grows," *Our Nation's Air: Status and Trends through 2016*, EPA.

113 Chelsea Follett, 2018, "How Human Ingenuity Can Protect the Environment," *Human Progress* (August 17).

114 Éric Grenier, 2019, "Canadians are Worried about Climate Change, but Many Don't Want to Pay Taxes to Fight It: Poll," *CBC News* (June 18).

115 Steven Pinker, 2018, *Enlightenment Now: The Case for Reason, Science, Humanism, and Progress,* Penguin Random House.

116 Shellenberger, 2019, "Why Apocalyptic Claims about Climate Change Are Wrong," (November 25).

117 Paul Read, 2019, "Arson, Mischief and Recklessness: 87 per cent of Fires are Man-Made," *The Sydney Morning Herald* (November 18).

118 John McAneney, 2013, "Climate Change and Bushfires – You're Missing the Point!" *The Conversation* (October 31).

119 Adam Voiland, 2019, *Building a Long-Term Record of Fire*, Earth Observatory.

120 Jean-François Bastin, et al., 2017, "The Extent of Forest in Dryland Biomes," *Science* 356, 6338 (May 12): 635-638.

121 Chi Chen, Taejin Park, Xuhui Wang, et al., 2019, "China and India Lead in Greening of the World through Land-Use Management," *Nature Sustainability* 2 (February 12): 122–129.

122 Shellenberger, 2019, "Why Apocalyptic Claims about Climate Change Are Wrong," (November 25).

123 Naomi Klein, 2014, *This Changes Everything: Capitalism vs the Climate*, Simon & Schuster.

124 In India, for example, "a developing country that is home to the world's second-largest population, the total fertility rate has shown a steady decline from 3.6 per woman in 1991 to 2.4 per woman by 2011. Over that 20-year period per capita incomes rose from 1,221 dollars to 3,755 dollars, going by the United Nations Development Programme (UNDP) figures" (Ranjit Devraj, 2018, "Declining Birth Rates Not Exclusive to Wealthy Nations," *Inter Press Service* (July 2)). Whether rising incomes is the direct cause of falling fertility or is what makes it possible to pay for better education (especially for girls) is neither here nor there. The point is that the increased wealth is a

necessary condition for the birth rate to decline. Again, remember that wealth gives societies problem-solving capacity.

125 Suzuki, 2017, "Demanding Economic Growth."

126 Amanda Connolly, 2019, "Tories Seize on Question of Carbon Tax Increase after McKenna Leaves Door Open," *Global News* (August 26).

127 Tom Adams, 2017, "Opinion: Ontario's Renewable Energy 'Disaster' Is What Drives up the Cost of Your Hydro," *Toronto.com* (March 9).

128 Massachusetts Institute of Technology, 2019, "Engineers Develop a New Way to Remove Carbon Dioxide from Air," *ScienceDaily* (October 25).

129 According to the BBC, scientists from round the world are seeking to improve ways of making money from carbon dioxide. They want to transform some of the CO2 that's overheating the planet into products to benefit humanity. Carbon dioxide is already being used in novel ways to create fuels, polymers, fertilizers, proteins, foams and building blocks (Roger Harrabin, 2019, "Turning Carbon Dioxide into Cash," *BBC News* (June 24).

130 Ross McKitrick, 2020, "Ross McKitrick: 'Believing the Science' on Climate Change Doesn't Mean Any Policy Goes," *Financial Post* (March 4).

131 Nicholas Stern, 2007, *The Economics of Climate Change: The Stern Review*, Cambridge University Press.

132 Rod Randolph Richardson, 2016, "Earth Day Shocker! Capitalism Saves the Planet! (Part I)." *The American Spectator* (April 21).

133 Note that according to one expert assessment it takes 12 years to turn over the existing vehicle fleet, so even with the very small carbon tax incentive change will happen at a rather glacial pace (Philip Cross, 2019, *The Case For a Carbon Tax: What Went Wrong?* Macdonald-Laurier Institute (July)).

134 Ross McKitrick, 2012, *The High Price of Low Emissions: Benefits and Costs of GHG Abatement in the Transportation Sector*, Macdonald-Laurier Institute (March).

135 Cross, 2019, *The Case for a Carbon Tax*.

136 Awkwardly for the Paris Accord enthusiasts, the US, which has withdrawn from the accord, led the world in absolute reduction in CO2 emissions at the same time as the economy experienced significant growth. Indeed the entire industrial world cut its CO2 emissions in 2018-19, in large part as a result of shifting from coal to natural gas for electricity generation (Michael Thomsen, 2020, "The US Cut Its CO2 Emissions More than Any Other Country in the World in 2019, Helping to Keep Total Global Emissions from Growing Past 2018's Record-Breaking High," *Daily Mail* (February 11)). The UK is a good example: "the UK's CO2 emissions from fossil fuels fell by 2.6% in 2017, driven by a 19% decline in coal use. This follows on the heels of a larger 5.8% drop in CO2 in 2016, which saw a record 52% drop in coal use. The

UK's total CO2 emissions are currently 38% below 1990 levels and are now as low as emissions were back in 1890 – the year the Forth Bridge opened in Scotland and Oscar Wilde's *The Picture of Dorian Gray* was published" (Zeke Hausfather, 2018, "Analysis: UK Carbon Emissions in 2017 Fell to Levels Last Seen in 1890," *CarbonBrief* (March 7)).

137 Recycling Council of Ontario [RCO], 2019, "Canada Recycles Just 9 Per Cent of Its Plastics," RCO (April 22); and Carolyn Jarvis and Megan Robinson, 2019, "Is Canada's Recycling Industry Broken?" *Global News* (May 28).

138 Karla Lant, 2017, "Stanford Scientists Are Making Wireless Electricity Transmission a Reality," *Futurism* (June 16); and Jayshree Sonawane and Sonal Benare, 2017, "Wireless Power Transmission Using Microwaves," *International Journal of Innovation Research in Computer and Communication Engineering* 5, 3 (March): 5143-5148.

139 Richard Walker, 2020, "Banning All but Electric Vehicles Could Backfire on the Environment," *CapX* (March 5).

140 And no, hydropower is not emissions-free by the way: "Many countries consider hydroelectricity a clean source of power because it doesn't involve burning dirty fossil fuels. But that's far from true. Hydropower is a significant source of greenhouse gas emissions: a new study shows that the world's hydroelectric dams are responsible for as much methane emissions as Canada" (Matt Weiser, 2016, "The Hydropower Paradox: Is This Energy as Clean as It Seems?" *The Guardian* (November 6)). There is little reason, therefore, to single out the oil and gas industry in Canada for emissions caps and so forth while leaving the hydroelectric industry untouched. This is just more designer prejudice at work. They like hydropower, even though they don't understand it, so it gets favourable treatment. They dislike fossil fuels, so that industry gets taxed even though they don't understand it either.

141 Stuart Thomson, 2019, "'If an Economist Says You Have To Use a Carbon Tax, They're Not Telling You the Truth,'" *National Post* (November 20).

142 Austan Goolsbee, 1998, "Investment Tax Incentives, Prices, and the Supply of Capital Goods," *Quarterly Journal of Economics* 113, 1: 121-148.

143 Quoted in Michael Asch, 2014, *On Being Here to Stay: Treaties and Aboriginals in Canada*, University of Toronto Press: 3.

144 J.R. Miller, 1996, *Shingwauk's Vision: A History of Native Residential Schools*, University of Toronto Press.

145 Documentation for this account can be found in these works: H. Brody, 1983, *Maps and Dreams: A Journey into the Lives and Lands of the Beaver Indians of Northwest Canada*, Penguin; Kenneth Coates, 1991, *Best Left as Indians: Native-White Relations in the Yukon Territory, 1840-1973*, Vol. 11,

McGill-Queen's Press-MQUP; Q. Duffy, 1988, *Road to Nunavut: The Progress of the Eastern Arctic Inuit since the Second World War*, McGill-Queen's Press-MQUP; J.D. Hamilton, 1994, *Arctic Revolution: Social Change in the Northwest Territories, 1935-1994*, Dundurn; and C. McClellan and L. Birckel, 1987, *Part of the Land, Part of the Water: A History of the Yukon Indians*, Douglas and McIntyre.

146 June Helm and William C. Sturtevant, eds., 1981, "6: Subarctic." *Handbook of North American Indians*, Smithsonian Institution; June Helm, 2000, *The People of Denendeh: Ethnohistory of the Indians of Canada's Northwest Territories*, vol. 24, McGill-Queen's Press-MQUP; June Helm, 1972, "The Dogrib Indians," *Hunters and Gatherers Today*, Holt, Rinehart and Winston; and T. Morantz, 2002,*White Man's Gonna Getcha: The Colonial Challenge to the Crees in Quebec*, vol. 30, McGill-Queen's Press-MQUP.

147 Gurston Dacks and Ken Coates, eds., 1998, *Northern Communities: The Prospects for Empowerment*, Boreal Institute for Northern Studies, especially the chapter by Lynda Lange, "The Changing Situation of Dene Elders, and of Marriage, in the Context of Colonialism: The Experience of Fort Franklin 1945-1985," pp. 23-32.

148 The idea that spending on Indigenous Canadians is much higher than what governments spend on other Canadians is widespread but is easily shown to be incorrect. Readers interested in learning more might consult the report of the Canadian Human Rights Tribunal on the case brought by Cindy Blackstone on child and family services (APTN News, 2019, "Federal Government Challenging Tribunal Order to Compensate First Nations Children in Care" (October 4); First Nations Child and Family Caring Society of Canada, 2016, "Victory for First Nations Children: Canadian Human Rights Tribunal Finds Discrimination against First Nations Children Living On-Reserve" (January 26); and Canadian Child Welfare Research Portal, 2020, "Blackstock, Cindy"). There is similar evidence regarding education funding (Indigenous Services Canada, 2019, "Government of Canada and Assembly of First Nations Announce New Policy and Funding Approach for First Nations K-12 Education on Reserve," *Cision* (January 21); and Assembly of First Nations, Undated, *Fact Sheet: First Nations Education Funding*).

149 There is strong resistance in many Indigenous communities to the creation of full individual property rights on reserves. My suspicion is that increased prosperity in the future will fuel demands from Indigenous people themselves for property rights. For the moment, however, wresting control over community property from Ottawa and putting it in the hands of the communities themselves is an important step in the right direction.

150 Missinipi Broadcasting Corporation, 2018, "Muskeg Lake Cree Nation, Saskatoon Celebrate 30th Anniversary of First Commercial Urban Reserve in Canada," (September 27).

151 Secwepemc First Nations, Indigenous Law and Research Unit, and the Shuswap Nation Tribal Council, 2016, *Secwepemc: Lands and Resources Law Analysis Project Summary*, Aboriginal Rights and Title Department (June 21).

152 Norah Kielland, 2015, *Supporting Aboriginal Participation in Resource Development: The Role of Impact and Benefit Agreements*, Library of Parliament, Canada.

153 This claim about strong traditions of accountability and openness arose in a private conversation I had with Professor Ken Coates, Canada Research Chair at the Johnson-Shoyama School of Public Policy at the University of Saskatchewan. It represents his assessment after a long career spent studying Indigenous communities and governments in Canada.

154 Stephen Buffalo, 2018, "We Are First Nations That Support Pipelines, When Pipelines Support First Nations," *Financial Post* (September 13).

155 Stewart Fast, 2017, *Who Decides? Balancing and Bridging Local, Indigenous and Broader Societal Interests in Canadian Energy Decision-Making. System under Stress – Interim Report #1*, University of Ottawa: 29.

156 Blaine Favel, 2019, *Commentary: Charting a Path to Economic Reconciliation with Indigenous Peoples*, Macdonald-Laurier Institute (April).

157 See, for example, Claudia Cattaneo, 2018, "'Eco-Colonialism': Rift Grows between Indigenous Leaders and Green Activists," *Financial Post* (January 4).

158 Jesse Snyder, 2020, "First Nations Chief Blasts 'Condescending' UN Anti-racism Directive That Called for Pipeline to be Shut Down," *National Post* (January 17).

159 Sergio A Rivera, 2014, "The Social License. Why It's So Hard to Obtain?" *MINING.com* (May 28).

160 Geoffrey Morgan, 2017, "B.C. to Proceed with Controversial Site C Dam, Cost Soars to $10.7 Billion," *Financial Post* (December 11).

161 David Ferry, 2017, "The Logging Company That Wants to Take Down Greenpeace," *Outside* (May 16).

162 Giuseppe Valiante, 2016, "NEB Cancels Energy East Hearings in Montreal after Protests," *CTV News* (August 29).

163 Philip Cross, 2018, "Philip Cross: Statscan's Latest Report Shows How Badly Our Governments Demolished Business Investment," *Financial Post* (March 1).

164 Kyle Bakx, 2016, "Pipeline Industry Concerned about Tampering and Vandalism," *CBC News* (March 9).

165 Richard Zussman, 2020, "Premier John Horgan Says Coastal GasLink Project Will Proceed Even with Wet'suwet'en Opposition," *Global News* (January 13).

166 Dwight Newman and Brian Lee Crowley, 2015, "MLI Commentaries by Newman and Crowley: Exploiting Social Licence Undermines Democracy," Macdonald-Laurier Institute (November 20).

167 Marieke Walsh, 2020, "More Details Needed Before Ottawa Makes Contentious Decision on Proposed Frontier Oil Sands Mine in Alberta," *Globe and Mail* (February 4).

168 Maarten Vinkhuyzen, 2019, "The EV Future – Volkswagen vs. Toyota in One Picture," *CleanTechnica* (August 16); Johnna Crider, 2020, "Oppenheimer: Tesla is an "Existential Threat" to Automakers," *CleanTechnica* (January 14); Dan Marcq Jr., 2019, "Innovative Technology to Combat Climate Change: Our 7 Favorite Solutions," *Bresslergroup* (November 14); and Matt Davis, 2019, "7 Climate Change Projects That Are Changing the Game," *Big Think* (March 27).

169 Sergei Klebnikov, 2019, "Saudi Aramco Reaches $2 Trillion Market Value in Record IPO's Second Day of Trading," *Forbes* (December 11).

170 Institute for Government, 2017, *The International Civil Service Effectiveness (InCiSE) Index 2017*, Institute for Government (July).

171 Eric C. Schneider, Dana O. Sarnak, David Squires, et al., 2017, *Mirror, Mirror 2017: International Comparison Reflects Flaws and Opportunities for Better U.S. Health Care*, The Commonwealth Fund; Aaron E. Carroll and Austin Frakt, 2017, "The Best Health Care System in the World: Which One Would You Pick?" *The New York Times* (September 18); and World Health Organization [WHO], 2019, *World Health Statistics 2019: Monitoring Health for the SDGs, Sustainable Development Goals*, WHO.

172 World Health Organization [WHO], 2015, "Population Data by Country (Recent Years)" Global Health Observatory Data Repository (June 15), WHO.

173 Janice MacKinnon, 2013, "Time to Overhaul the Delivery and Funding of Health Care, MacKinnon Says," Macdonald-Laurier Institute (January 31).

174 Niall McCarthy, 2017, "Canada Seen as the Most Positive Influence Globally," *Statista* (July 5).

175 Audrey Laporte and Brian S. Ferguson, 2015, *Changing the Way We Think about Drug Prices: Insights from Economics*, White Paper Series, No: 15W001 (October), Canadian Centre for Health.

176 As Nobel Laureate Milton Friedman observed, regulatory bureaucrats can make one of two mistakes: approve something new that is bad, in which case they lose their job; or block something that is good, in which case no patient ever knows about the benefit they might have gained. Of course, bureaucrats choose denial. (See Milton Friedman and Rose D. Friedman, 1980, *Free to Choose: A Personal Statement*, Harcourt.)

177 I owe this insight into the historical cost-control performance of Canadian medicare to my friend Brian Ferguson, health care economist at the University of Guelph.

178 To her great credit, Jane Philpott, then federal Minister of Health, said this was a myth (in a rare bit of honesty in a politician). (See Jane Philpott, 2016, "Remarks from the Honourable Jane Philpott, Minister of Health, to the Canadian Medical Association Annual General Meeting," Government of Canada (August 23).)

179 Co-authors Jason Clemens, Niels Velhuis and I told this story in some detail in Brian Lee Crowley, Jason Clemens and Niels Veldhuis, 2010, "Chapter Five: Reforming Canada's Entitlements – Glass Two-Thirds Full," *The Canadian Century: Moving out of America's Shadow*, Macdonald-Laurier Institute.

180 Crowley, Clemens and Veldhuis, 2010, *The Canadian Century*, p. 272.

181 Livio Di Matteo, undated, "Federal Transfer Payments and How They Affect Healthcare Funding in Canada," EvidenceNetwork.ca.

182 Michael Watts, 2013, "MLI Report: Debunking the Myths of the Canada Health Act," Macdonald-Laurier Institute (September 20).

183 *Chaoulli v. Quebec* (Attorney General), 1 S.C.R. 791, 2005 SCC 35 (2005). I do recognize, however, that the impact of *Chaoulli* has been blunted by its application being limited to Quebec and the stubborn refusal of the other provinces to recognize any real impact on their health care policies. If court cases like that being carried on by the Cambie Surgery Centre succeed in other provinces the impact may be greater (Will Johnston, 2018, "The Cambie Clinic Case Could Bring Us a Better Health-care System," *National Post* (December 20)).

184 Janice MacKinnon, 2013, *Health Care Reform from the Cradle of Medicare*, Macdonald-Laurier Institute (January).

185 Canadian Institute for Health Information [CIHI], 2019, *National Health Expenditure Trends, 1975 to 2019*, CIHI (October 31). It is not necessary to go as far as economist Don Drummond, who predicts that health care spending will consume 80 percent of provincial budgets by 2030, to know that the trends are unsustainable. (See Don Drummond and Derek Burleton, 2010, *Charting a Path to Sustainable Health Care in Ontario*, TD Economics Special Report (May 27).)

186 "For children aged 1 to 14, per-person average spending on health was $1,423, and for those aged 15 to 64 it was $2,663. The average for those 65 and older was $11,635. Predictably, the older the patient, the higher the average cost. CIHI reported that in 2014, per-person spending for seniors increased with age: $6,424 for those aged 65 to 69, $8,379 for ages 70 to 74,

$11,488 for ages 75 to 79, and $21,150 for those 80 and older. Provinces and territories spend almost 46 percent of all public-sector healthcare dollars on seniors" (Cynthia Levine-Rasky, 2018, "Don't Blame Seniors for Rising Healthcare Costs," Canadian Dimension (December 21). Fully one quarter of all health care spending goes on the final year of life according to Eric B. French, Jeremy McCauley, Maria Aragon, et al., 2017, "End-of-Life Medical Spending in Last Twelve Months of Life is Lower than Previously Reported," *Health Affairs* 36, 7 (July): 1211-1217.

187 G. Ross Baker, Peter G. Norton, Virginia Flintoft, et al., 2004, "The Canadian Adverse Events Study: The Incidence of Adverse Events among Hospital Patients in Canada," *CMAJ Group* (May 25).

188 Martha Lagace, 2004, "Does the Medical Industry Deliver Value?" *Working Knowledge* (November 22) Harvard Business School.

189 A qualification: There is a conversation to be had about whether medicine is a "production" or a "coping" organization (to use James Wilson's terms). Is it more like the post office, where we can see the work and see the outcome? Or is it more like policing, where we cannot see what "keeping the peace" looks like and we cannot measure how much peace has been kept? Former OMA President Shawn Whatley has some thoughtful remarks to make on this: Shawn Whatley, 2020, "How to Manage Doctors," Shawn Whatley MD (January 4). This is not the place to get into this discussion, but I will just observe that it is likely not an either/or matter.

190 Morris L. Baer and Greg L. Stoddart, 1991, "Barer-Stoddart Report: Toward Integrated Medical Resource Policies for Canada," *PubMed* 47, 11 (December): 6-8.

191 Martha Lagace, 2004, "The Changing Roles of Doctors and Patients," *Harvard Business School Working Knowledge* (November 22).

192 Julie Gilbert, Gale Murray, Ruth Corbin, 2001, "Consumerism and Healthcare in Ontario: Are Patients Becoming Consumers?" *The Change Foundation.*

193 The consensus now prevailing among health care economists is best summed up by Folland, Goodman and Stano, who conclude in a recent paper that ". . . it would be reckless to argue market failure, at least on the basis of SID, and to dismiss policy analysis based on standard models as ineffective" (Sherman Folland, Allen C. Goodman, and Miron Stano, 2017, *The Economics of Health and Health Care*, 8th edition, Routledge: 723).

194 J.P. Bunker and B.W. Brown, 1974, "The Physician Patient as an Informed Consumer of Surgical Services," *New England Journal of Medicine* 290: 1051-1055; J. Hay and M. Leahy, 1982, "Physician-Induced Demand: An Empirical Analysis of the Consumer Information Gap," *Journal of Health*

Economics 1: 231-244; and D. Kenkel, 1990, "Consumer Health Information and the Demand for Medical Care," *Review of Economics and Statistics* 52: 587-595.

195 SecondStreet.org, 2019, "Over 217,500 Canadians Left the Country for Health Care in 2017," SecondStreet.org (March 11).

196 It costs roughly $35 per physician visit in Sweden up to a maximum of roughly $350 per person per year. It is similar for prescriptions. Low-income people are exempted from the fee. Sweden's largest hospital, St. Goran's, has been privatized, and many paraprofessionals like nurses are not employees but contractors within the system. Sweden offers wait time guarantees – if a needed surgery or treatment isn't provided within 90 days, the public system will pay for the patient to get it elsewhere. For full information on the Swedish system, see Sweden Institute, 2019, *Healthcare in Sweden* (October 30).

197 Steven Pinker, 2018, *Enlightenment Now: The Case for Reason, Science, Humanism, and Progress*, Viking; Steven Pinker, 2018, "Steven Pinker: Can Numbers Show Us That Progress Is Inevitable?" *WYPR 88.1 FM*, TED Radio Hour, Episode: *The Story Behind the Numbers*, Part 1 (August 17).

198 Adam Smith, 1776, *An Inquiry into the Nature and Causes of the Wealth of Nations*, 2 vols., Strahan and Cadell.

199 Charles Lewis, 2018, "Restriction on Summer Jobs Funding Not the First Time Religious Rights in Canada Have Been Trampled on," *National Post* (March 16).

200 An overview of my thinking on a guaranteed annual income may be found at Brian Lee Crowley, 2015, "Guaranteed Annual Income the Wrong Solution to a Complex Problem," Macdonald-Laurier Institute (December 11).

201 As one author puts it, the international system ". . . is built on the illusion that there could be a higher force bringing order to the anarchy of international relations. In practice, the system is anarchic – there are just states. There is no world police that is independent from nations and governments. Instead, 'the strong do what they can, and the weak suffer what they must,' [according to] . . . Thucydides. The past 75 years have been the only time in the millennia of human history when a global supranational order in the form of the United Nations existed. When looking closely, however, it was merely a construct to amplify the power of the powerful. The most powerful countries agreed to grant themselves a veto power in the security council, that sits atop the rest of the member states. These so called Permanent 5 (Britain, China, France, Soviet Union/Russia, and the United States) still control most of the relevant committees and other powerful international organizations. Moreover [as David Kopolow indicates in his 2013 study, *Indisputable*

Violations: What Happens When the United States Unambiguously Breaches a Treaty, Georgetown University Law Centre], when domestic interests were at odds with the United Nations, the most powerful countries ignored or broke the rules. The Wilsonian belief in international law and order has been proven again and again to be unrealistic. While the United Nations definitely provides a platform for diplomatic exchange and has helped numerous people through its caritative organizations, it is at the grace of the great powers. International law is not a necessary outcome of international relations. It rests on the commitment of the powerful to respect and enforce the rules even when they would hurt themselves. This commitment never existed" (Dominik Wullers, 2020, "Germany, Wilsonianism, and the Return of Realpolitik," *War on the Rocks* (March 18)).

202 Sammy Roth, 2020, "Here's What a Coronavirus-Like Response to the Climate Crisis Would Look Like," *Los Angeles Times* (March 24).

203 Financial Times, 2020, "'Utterly Unreliable': The Mystery behind the True COVID-19 Death Rate," *National Post* (March 31).

204 For example, consider this piece by David L. Katz, a specialist in preventive medicine and public health, president of True Health Initiative and the founding director of Yale University's Yale-Griffin Prevention Research Center: David L. Katz, 2020, "Is Our Fight against Coronavirus Worse than the Disease?" *New York Times* (March 20). His advice contradicts that of some other equally well-qualified experts. Some governments followed advice that resembles Katz's; others rejected such advice as ill-informed or dangerous. Compare Sweden's "expert guided" COVID-19 response with that of many other countries. (See Maddy Savage, 2020, "Lockdown, What Lockdown? Sweden's Unusual Response to Coronavirus," *BBC News* (March 29). See also Terence Corcoran, 2020, "Terence Corcoran: Maybe Real Data on the Coronavirus Will End this Draconian Lockdown," *Financial Post* (April 1).)

205 J. Michael Cole, 2020, "How Taiwan is Leading by Example in the Global War on the Covid-19 Pandemic: New MLI Commentary," Macdonald-Laurier Institute (March 26).

206 Emerald Bensadoun and Kerri Breen, 2020, "Comparing Coronavirus Responses: What did Canada and the U.S. Do Differently?" *Global News* (April 1); and Shawn Whatley, 2020, "How We Got in a Covid-19 Fix and How We Start to Get Out: Shawn Whatley for Inside Policy," Macdonald-Laurier Institute (March 30).

207 Chris Selley, 2020, "Chris Selley: Official Nonsense on Masks, Travel Bans is Killing Ottawa's COVID-19 Credibility," *National Post* (April 2).

208 Cole, 2020, "How Taiwan is Leading by Example"; and Elisabeth Buchwald,

2020, "What We Can Learn from South Korea and Singapore's Efforts to Stop Coronavirus (Besides Wearing Face Masks)," *MarketWatch* (April 1).

209 See, for example, Robert Langreth and Susan Berfield, 2020, "Famed AIDS Researcher Is Racing to Find a Coronavirus Treatment," *Bloomberg* (March 20).

210 Gonzalo Schwarz, 2020, "Human Ingenuity Is Our Greatest Weapon against the Coronavirus," *The Hill* (March 25).

211 Michelle Fay Cortez, 2020, "Abbott Launches 5-Minute Virus Test for Use Almost Anywhere," *Bloomberg* (March 28).

212 Montreal General Hospital Foundation and Research Institute of the McGill University Health Centre, 2020, "Code Life Ventilator Challenge," Montreal General Hospital Foundation (March 19).

213 Eytan Halon, 2020, "Who Is Leading the Race to Develop the Coronavirus Vaccine?" *Jerusalem Post* (March 22).

214 Tom Cardoso, 2020, "Stuck in Self-Isolation, These Canadians are Using their Skills to Make Medical Supplies," *Globe and Mail* (March 31).

215 Joe O'Connor, 2020, "Game On: How COVID-19 Crisis Pivoted Bauer Hockey from Skate-Maker to Medical Face Shield Manufacturer," *National Post* (April 1).

216 Emily Jackson, 2020, "Canadian Auto Parts Makers Team up to Build Ventilators with Three Companies," *Financial Post* (March 27).

217 Rex Murphy, 2020, "Rex Murphy: It's the Ordinary Joes, Not the Liberal Elites, Who Are Allowing Society to Continue to Function During COVID-19," *National Post* (March 31).

218 Ryan Tumilty, 2020, "Government Looks to 'Made-in-Canada Solutions' to Mask, Ventilator Shortage as International Supplies Tighten," *National Post* (March 31).

219 Karen Howlett, 2020, "Ontario, B.C., Quebec Begin Building Makeshift Hospitals in Preparation for Rise in COVID-19 Patients," *Globe and Mail* (April 1).

220 And apparently I am not alone. (See Kayla Hounsell, 2020, "Grocery Store Staff Fed up with 'Social' Shoppers Who Flout Pandemic Rules," *CBC News* (April 3).)

221 Brian Lee Crowley, 2013, *Fearful Symmetry: The Fall and Rise of Canada's Founding Values,* Macdonald-Laurier Institute.

222 Crowley, Clemens, and Veldhuis, 2010, *Canadian Century.*

223 Doug Owram, 1986, *The Government Generation: Canadian Intellectuals and the State, 1900-1945,* University of Toronto Press, p. 35.

Bibliography

Adams, Tom. 2017. "Opinion: Ontario's Renewable Energy 'Disaster' Is What Drives up the Cost of Your Hydro." *Toronto.com* (March 9). Available at https://www.toronto.com/opinion-story/7144988-opinion-ontario-s-renewable-energy-disaster-is-what-drives-up-the-cost-of-your-hydro/.

Airbnb. 2020. "Book Unique Places to Stay and Things to Do" [Home page]. Airbnb Inc. Available at https://www.airbnb.ca/.

Angus Reid Institute and the Canadian Broadcasting Corporation. 2016. "What Makes Us Canadian? A Study of Values, Beliefs, Priorities and Identity." Angus Reid Institute (October 3). Available at http://angusreid.org/canada-values/.

Anzil, Federico. 2020. "Is the Difference in Work Hours the Real Reason for the Gender Wage Gap? [Interactive Infographic]." *Visme*. Available at https://visme.co/blog/wage-gap/.

APTN News. 2019. "Federal Government Challenging Tribunal Order to Compensate First Nations Children in Care." Aboriginal People's Television Network [APTN] (October 4). Available at https://aptnnews.ca/2019/10/04/federal-government-challenging-tribunal-order-to-compensate-first-nations-children-in-care/.

Arbesman, Samuel. 2013. *The Half-Life of Facts: Why Everything We Know Has an Expiration*. Penguin Group.

Asch, Michael. 2014. *On Being Here to Stay: Treaties and Aboriginals in Canada*. University of Toronto Press.

Assembly of First Nations [AFN]. Undated. *Fact Sheet: First Nations Education Funding*. AFN. Available at https://www.afn.ca/uploads/files/education/fact_sheet_-_fn_education_funding_final.pdf.

Asseng, S., F. Ewert, P. Martre, et al. 2015. "Rising Temperatures Reduce Global Wheat Production." *Nature Climate Change* 5, 2: 143-147. Available at http://eprints.whiterose.ac.uk/85540/1/Main_Asseng_2014-9-22.pdf.

Atir, Stav, Emily Rosenzweig, and David Dunning. 2015. "When Knowledge Knows No Bounds: Self-Perceived Expertise Predicts Claims of Impossible

Knowledge." *Psychological Science* 26, 8 (August): 1295–1303. DOI: 10.1177/0956797615588195.

Baer, Morris L., and Greg L. Stoddart. 1991. "Barer-Stoddart Report: Toward Integrated Medical Resource Policies for Canada." *PubMed* 47, 11 (December): 6-8. Available at https://www.ncbi.nlm.nih.gov/pubmed/1750305.

Baker, G. Ross, Peter G. Norton, Virginia Flintoft, et al. 2004. "The Canadian Adverse Events Study: The Incidence of Adverse Events among Hospital Patients in Canada." *CMAJ Group* (May 25). Available at http://www.cmaj.ca/cgi/content/full/170/11/1678.

Bakx, Kyle. 2016. "Pipeline Industry Concerned about Tampering and Vandalism." *CBC News* (March 9). Available at https://www.cbc.ca/news/business/cepa-chris-bloomer-pipelines-tampering-enbridge-vandalism-target-1.3480857.

Barney, Gerald 0. 1998. *Global 2000: Report to the Presiden.* Seven Locks Press. Available at https://www.cartercenter.org/resources/pdfs/pdf-archive/global2000reporttothepresident--enteringthe21stcentury-01011991.pdf.

Bastiat, Frederic. 1848/1995. *Selected Essays on Political Economy.* Online Library of Liberty. Available at https://oll.libertyfund.org/titles/bastiat-selected-essays-on-political-economy#Bastiat_0181_798.

Bastin, Jean-François, Nora Berrahmouni, Alan Grainger, et al. 2017. "The Extent of Forest in Dryland Biomes." *Science* 356, 6338 (May 12): 635-638. Available at http://science.sciencemag.org/content/356/6338/635.

Bensadoun, Emerald, and Kerri Breen. 2020. "Comparing Coronavirus Responses: What did Canada and the U.S. Do Differently?" *Global News* (April 1). Available at https://globalnews.ca/news/6737474/coronavirus-new-york-canada-responses/

Berton, Pierre. 1990. "Wheels: The Car as a Cultural Driving Force." *Canadian Geographic* (December 1989/January 1990). Available at https://www.canadiangeographic.ca/sites/cgcorp/files/images/web_articles/blog/berton.pdf.

Beyer, Scott. 2019. "How Houston Is Becoming America's Next Dense City." *Catalyst* (December 18). Available at https://catalyst.independent.org/2019/12/18/how-houston-is-becoming-americas-next-dense-city/.

Bolotnyy, Valentin, and Natalia Emanuel. 2019. "Why Do Women Earn Less Than Men? Evidence from Bus and Train Operators." Working Paper (July 5). Harvard University. Available at https://scholar.harvard.edu/files/bolotnyy/files/be_gender_gap.pdf.

British Columbia. 2020. *Population Estimates.* Government of British Columbia. Available at https://www2.gov.bc.ca/gov/content/data/statistics/people-population-community/population/population-estimates.

Brody, H. 1983. *Maps and Dreams: A Journey into the Lives and Lands of the Beaver Indians of Northwest Canada,* Penguin.

Bruegmann, Robert. 2005. *Sprawl: A Compact History.* University of Chicago Press.

Buchwald, Elisabeth. 2020. "What We Can Learn from South Korea and Singapore's Efforts to Stop Coronavirus (Besides Wearing Face Masks)." *MarketWatch* (April 1). Available at https://www.marketwatch.com/story/what-we-can-learn-from-south-korea-and-singapores-efforts-to-stop-coronavirus-in-addition-to-wearing-face-masks-2020-03-31.

Buffalo, Stephen. 2018. "We Are First Nations That Support Pipelines, When Pipelines Support First Nations." *Financial Post* (September 13). Available at https://business.financialpost.com/opinion/we-are-first-nations-that-support-pipelines-when-pipelines-support-first-nations.

Bunker, J.P., and B.W. Brown. 1974. "The Physician Patient as an Informed Consumer of Surgical Services." *New England Journal of Medicine* 290: 1051-1055.

Canada, Transport Canada. 2015. *Pathways: Connecting Canada's Transportation System to the World*, vol. 1. Government of Canada. Available at https://www.tc.gc.ca/eng/ctareview2014/CTAR_Vol1_EN.pdf.

Canadian Charter of Rights and Freedoms, s 15 (1), Part 1 of the *Constitution Act, 1982*, being Schedule B to the *Canada Act 1982* (UK), c 11.

Canadian Child Welfare Research Portal. 2020. "Blackstock, Cindy." Canadian Child Welfare Research Portal. Available at https://cwrp.ca/researcher/blackstock-cindy.

Canadian Institute for Health Information [CIHI]. 2018. *National Health Expenditure Trends, 1975 to 2018.* CIHI. Available at https://secure.cihi.ca/free_products/NHEX-trends-narrative-report-2018-en-web.pdf.

Cardoso, Tom. 2020. "Stuck in Self-Isolation, These Canadians are Using their Skills to Make Medical Supplies." *Globe and Mail* (March 31). Available at https://www.theglobeandmail.com/canada/article-canadians-use-crowdsourcing-to-produce-medical-supplies-for-health/.

Carroll, Aaron E., and Austin Frakt. 2017. "The Best Health Care System in the World: Which One Would You Pick?" *The New York Times* (September 18). Available at https://www.nytimes.com/interactive/2017/09/18/upshot/best-health-care-system-country-bracket.html.

Cattaneo, Claudia. 2018. "'Eco-Colonialism': Rift Grows between Indigenous Leaders and Green Activists." *Financial Post* (January 4). Available at https://business.financialpost.com/feature/eco-colonialism-rift-grows-between-indigenous-leaders-and-green-activists.

CBC News. 2015. "Charbonneau Commission Finds Corruption Widespread in Quebec's Construction Sector." *CBC News* (November 24). Available at https://www.cbc.ca/news/canada/montreal/charbonneau-corruption-inquiry-findings-released-1.3331577.

Chaoulli v. Quebec (Attorney General). 1 S.C.R. 791, 2005 SCC 35 (2005). Available at https://scc-csc.lexum.com/scc-csc/scc-csc/en/item/2237/index.do.

Chi Chen, Taejin Park, Xuhui Wang, et al. 2019. "China and India Lead in Greening of the World through Land-Use Management." *Nature Sustainability* 2 (February 12): 122–129. Available at https://www.nature.com/articles/s41893-019-0220-7.

Coates, Kenneth. 1991. *Best Left as Indians: Native-White Relations in the Yukon Territory, 1840-1973*, Vol. 11. McGill-Queen's Press-MQUP.

Cole, J. Michael. 2020. "How Taiwan is Leading by Example in the Global War on the Covid-19 Pandemic: New MLI Commentary." Macdonald-Laurier Institute (March 26). Available at https://www.macdonaldlaurier.ca/taiwan-leading-example-global-war-covid-19-pandemic-new-mli-commentary/.

The Conference Board of Canada. 2011. *World Income Inequality: Is the World Becoming More Unequal?* Conference Board of Canada. Available at http://www.conferenceboard.ca/hcp/hot-topics/worldinequality.aspx.

Connolly, Amanda. 2019. "Tories Seize on Question of Carbon Tax Increase after McKenna Leaves Door Open." *Global News* (August 26). Available at https://globalnews.ca/news/5814332/pierre-poilievre-carbon-tax-increase/.

Connolly, Joannah. 2015. "Infographic: TD Survey Reveals Home Buyer Attitudes on Urban vs. Suburban." *Real Estate Wire [REW]* (May 24). Available at http://www.rew.ca/news/infographic-td-survey-reveals-home-buyer-attitudes-on-urban-vs-suburban-1.1802963.

Cook, Cody, Rebecca Diamond, Jonathan Hall, et al. 2019. "The Gender Earnings Gap in the Gig Economy: Evidence from over a Million Rideshare Drivers." Stanford University (March 8). Available at https://web.stanford.edu/~diamondr/UberPayGap.pdf.

Coppola, Gabrielle. 2019. "Amazon's Van-buying Spree Delivers a Gift to the Auto Industry." *Automotive News* (December 19). Available at https://www.autonews.com/sales/amazons-van-buying-spree-delivers-gift-auto-industry.

Corcoran, Terence. 2020. "Terence Corcoran: Maybe Real Data on the Coronavirus Will End this Draconian Lockdown." *Financial Post* (April 1). Available at https://business.financialpost.com/opinion/terence-corcoran-maybe-real-data-on-the-coronavirus-will-end-this-draconian-lockdown.

Cortez, Michelle Fay. 2020. "Abbott Launches 5-Minute Virus Test for Use Almost Anywhere." *Bloomberg* (March 28). Available at https://www.bloomberg.

com/news/articles/2020-03-27/abbott-launches-5-minute-covid-19-test-for-use-almost-anywhere.

Cowan, Tyler. 2014. "How Technology Could Help Fight Income Inequality." *New York Times* (December 6). Available at https://www.nytimes.com/2014/12/07/upshot/how-technology-could-help-fight-income-inequality.html.

Cox, Wendell. 2012. "Special Report: Census 2011: Urban Dispersion in Canada." *New Geography* (February 14). Available at https://www.newgeography.com/content/002672-special-report-census-2011-urban-dispersion-canada.

Cox, Wendell. 2016. "LSE/Netherlands Research Documents Price Effects of Tight Housing Regulation." *New Geography* (April 12). Available at http://www.newgeography.com/content/005215-lsenetherlands-research-documents-price-effects-tight-housing-regulation.

Cox, Wendell. 2018. "Employment Access in Metropolitan Areas (2017)." *New Geography* (November 23). Available at https://www.newgeography.com/content/006149-employment-access-us-metropolitan-areas-2017.

Cox, Wendell. 2019. *Moving Toward More Accessible and Productive Transportation in the Puget Sound.* Washington Policy Center (October). Available at https://www.washingtonpolicy.org/library/doclib/Cox-Toward-More-Accessible-and-Productive-Transportation-in-the-Puget-Sound-REVISED.pdf.

Cox, Wendell, and Hugh Pavletich. 2019. *15th Annual Demographia International Housing Affordability Survey: 2019 – Rating Middle-Income Housing Affordability*, Demographia. Available at http://www.demographia.com/dhi2019.pdf.

Crichton, Michael. 2009. "Three Speeches by Michael Crichton." *Science and Public Policy Institute* (December 9). Available at http://scienceandpublicpolicy.org/images/stories/papers/commentaries/crichton_3.pdf.

Crider, Johnna. 2020. "Oppenheimer: Tesla is an 'Existential Threat' to Automakers." *CleanTechnica* (January 14). Available at https://cleantechnica.com/2020/01/14/oppenheimer-tesla-is-an-existential-threat-to-automakers/.

Cross, Philip. 2018. "Philip Cross: Statscan's Latest Report Shows How Badly Our Governments Demolished Business Investment." *Financial Post* (March 1). Available at https://business.financialpost.com/opinion/philip-cross-statscans-latest-report-shows-how-badly-the-governments-demolished-business-investment.

Cross, Philip. 2019. *The Case For a Carbon Tax: What Went Wrong?* Macdonald-Laurier Institute (July). Available at https://macdonaldlaurier.ca/files/pdf/20190621_MLI_COMMENTARY_Carbon_Tax_Cross_Fweb.pdf.

Cross, Philip. 2020. "Busting a Few Myths about the Gig Economy." *National Post* and Macdonald-Laurier Institute (January 2). Available at https://www.macdonaldlaurier.ca/busting-myths-gig-economy/.

Crowley, Brian Lee. 2015. "Guaranteed Annual Income the Wrong Solution to a Complex Problem." *Globe and Mail* and Macdonald-Laurier Institute (December 11). Available at https://www.macdonaldlaurier.ca/guaranteed-annual-income-the-wrong-solution-to-a-complex-problem-brian-lee-crowley-in-the-globe/.

Crowley, Brian Lee. 2016. "Canada's Trouble with the Farm." *Globe and Mail* and Macdonald-Laurier Institute (June 10). Available at https://www.macdonaldlaurier.ca/canadas-trouble-with-the-farm-brian-lee-crowley-in-the-globe-and-mail/.

Crowley, Brian Lee. 2016. *Turning Canada from Agricultural Laggard to World Food Superpower.* MLI Commentary. Macdonald-Laurier Institute (June 24). Available at https://www.macdonaldlaurier.ca/turning-canada-from-agricultural-laggard-to-world-food-superpower-mli-commentary-by-brian-lee-crowley/.

Crowley, Brian Lee. 2013. *Fearful Symmetry: The Fall and Rise of Canada's Founding Values.* Macdonald-Laurier Institute.

Crowley, Brian Lee, Jason Clemens, and Niels Veldhuis. 2010. *The Canadian Century: Moving out of America's Shadow.* Macdonald-Laurier Institute.

Csanady, Ashley. 2015. "Supply Management Costs Poor Families Five Times More Relative to Household Income: Study." *National Post* (February 27). Available at https://nationalpost.com/news/politics/supply-management-costs-poor-families-five-times-more-relative-to-household-income-study.

Dacks, Gurston, and Ken Coates, eds. 1998. *Northern Communities: The Prospects for Empowerment.* Boreal Institute for Northern Studies.

Dale, Helen. 2019. "For Liberalism to Survive, We Must Renounce Technocracy." *CapX* (November 20). Available at https://capx.co/for-liberalism-to-survive-we-must-renounce-technocracy/.

Davies, William. 2017. "How Statistics Lost their Power – And Why We Should Fear What Comes Next." *The Guardian* (January 19). Available at https://www.theguardian.com/politics/2017/jan/19/crisis-of-statistics-big-data-democracy.

Davis, Matt. 2019. "7 Climate Change Projects That Are Changing the Game." *Big Think* (March 27). Available at https://bigthink.com/technology-innovation/climate-change-projects.

Denning, Stephanie. 2019. "Why Amazon Pays No Corporate Taxes." *Forbes* (February 22). Available at https://www.forbes.com/sites/stephaniedenning/2019/02/22/why-amazon-pays-no-corporate-taxes/#76e67f7a54d5.

de Soto, Hernando. 2000. *The Mystery of Capital: Why Capitalism Triumphs in the West and Fails Everywhere Else.* Basic Books.

Devraj, Ranjit. 2018. "Declining Birth Rates Not Exclusive to Wealthy Nations."

Inter Press Service (July 2). Available at http://www.ipsnews.net/2018/07/declining-birth-rates-not-exclusive-wealthy-nations/.

Digital TechBlog. Undated. "April 2012 Search Engine Market Share." Digital TechBlog. Available at http://yogendratechblog.blogspot.com/2012/04/search-market-share.html?m=0.

Di Matteo, Livio. Undated. "Federal Transfer Payments and How They Affect Healthcare Funding in Canada." EvidenceNetwork.ca. Available at http://evidencenetwork.ca/federal-transfer-payments-and-how-they-affect-health-care-funding-in-canada/.

Duffy, Q. 1988. *Road to Nunavut: The Progress of the Eastern Arctic Inuit since the Second World War.* McGill-Queen's Press-MQUP.

The Economist. 2016. "The Grip Tightens: Faulty Land-Use Regulation is Throttling the Capital." Living in London. *The Economist* (April 30). Available at http://www.economist.com/news/britain/21697575-faulty-land-use-regulation-throttling-capital-grip-tightens.

Elections Canada. 2020. *The 2019 Federal Election by the Numbers* [Data table]. Elections Canada. Available at https://www.elections.ca/content.aspx?section=med&dir=bkg&document=num&lang=e.

Encyclopaedia Britannica. 2019. "Moore's Law: Computer Science" (December 26). Encyclopaedia Britannica. Available at https://www.britannica.com/technology/Moores-law.

Farrell, Warren. 2005. *Why Men Earn More: The Startling Truth Behind the Pay Gap – and What Women Can Do About It.* AMACOM.

Fast, Stewart. 2017. *Who Decides? Balancing and Bridging Local, Indigenous and Broader Societal Interests in Canadian Energy Decision-Making. System under Stress – Interim Report #1.* University of Ottawa. Available at https://www.uottawa.ca/positive-energy/sites/www.uottawa.ca.positive-energy/files/positive_energy-who_decides_dec_2017.pdf.

Favel, Blaine. 2019. *Commentary: Charting a Path to Economic Reconciliation with Indigenous Peoples.* Macdonald-Laurier Institute (April). Available at https://macdonaldlaurier.ca/files/pdf/20190405_Favel_COMMENTARY_FWeb.pdf.

Ferry, David. 2017. "The Logging Company That Wants to Take Down Greenpeace." *Outside* (May 16). Available at https://www.outsideonline.com/2185831/logging-company-sues-greenpeace.

Financial Times. 2020. "'Utterly Unreliable': The Mystery behind the True COVID-19 Death Rate." *National Post* (March 31). Available at https://nationalpost.com/news/world/utterly-unreliable-the-mystery-behind-the-true-covid-19-death-rate.

First Nations Child and Family Caring Society of Canada. 2016. *Victory for First Nations Children: Canadian Human Rights Tribunal Finds Discrimination against First Nations Children Living On-Reserve.* First Nations Child and Family Caring Society of Canada (January 26). Available at https://fncaringsociety.com/sites/default/files/Information%20Sheet%20re%20CHRT%20Decision.pdf.

Flemming, Brian. 2015. *The Political Economy of Canada's Transportation Policies in 2015: The "What" is Easy; The "How" is Hard.* Van Horne Institute (May 20). Available at http://www.mun.ca/harriscentre/aptf2015/Brian_Flemming_presentation.pdf.

Folland, Sherman, Allen C. Goodman, and Miron Stano. 2017. *The Economics of Health and Health Care*, 8th edition. Routledge.

Follett, Chelsea. 2018. "How Human Ingenuity Can Protect the Environment." *HumanProgress* (August 17). Available at https://humanprogress.org/article.php?p=1462.

Food and Agriculture Organization of the United Nations [UN FAO]. 2018. *The Future of Food and Agriculture: Alternative Pathways to 2050.* United Nations. Available at http://www.fao.org/3/I8429EN/i8429en.pdf.

French, Eric B., Jeremy McCauley, Maria Aragon, et al. 2017. "End-of-Life Medical Spending in Last Twelve Months of Life is Lower than Previously Reported." *Health Affairs* 36, 7 (July): 1211-1217. Available at https://www.healthaffairs.org/doi/full/10.1377/hlthaff.2017.0174.

Friedman, Milton, and Rose D. Friedman. 1980. *Free to Choose: A Personal Statement,* Harcourt.

Fuller, R. Buckminster. 1981. *Critical Path.* St. Martin's Press.

Gall, Gerald L. 2014. "Charlottetown Accord." *The Canadian Encyclopedia.* Available at https://www.thecanadianencyclopedia.ca/en/article/the-charlottetown-accord.

Gilbert, Julie, Gale Murray, Ruth Corbin. 2001. "Consumerism and Healthcare in Ontario: Are Patients Becoming Consumers?" *The Change Foundation.*

Gilder, George. 2012. *Wealth and Poverty: A New Edition for the Twenty-First Century.* Regnery Publishing.

Glaeser, Edward L., and Joseph Gyourko. 2003. "The Impact of Building Restrictions on Housing Affordability." *Economic Policy Review* 9 (June 2): 21-39. Available at http://www.nber.org/papers/w8835.

Glaeser, Edward L., Joseph Gyourko, and Raven Saks. 2005. "Why Have Housing Prices Gone Up?" *American Economic Review* 95 (May 2): 329-333. Available at http://www.nber.org/papers/w11129.

Goldin, Claudia. 2014. "A Grand Gender Convergence: Its Last Chapter." *American*

Economic Review 104, 4: 1-30. Available at http://econweb.umd.edu/~davis/eventpapers/GoldinConvergence.pdf.

Gollom, Mark. 2019. "What You Need to Know about the Vice-Admiral Mark Norman Case." *CBC News* (May 8). Available at https://www.cbc.ca/news/politics/mark-norman-case-explainer-1.5127752.

Goodrich, Terry. 2016. "People with Higher 'Intellectual Arrogance' Get Better Grades, Baylor Study Finds." News release. Baylor University (October 6). Available at https://www.eurekalert.org/pub_releases/2015-10/bu-pwh100515.php.

Google. Undated. "From the Garage to the Googleplex." Google (February 2). Available at https://about.google/our-story/.

Goolsbee, Austan. 1998. "Investment Tax Incentives, Prices, and the Supply of Capital Goods." *Quarterly Journal of Economics* 113, 1: 121-148.

Gordon, David L.A., Lyra Hindrichs, and Chris Willms. 2018. *Still Suburban? Growth in Canadian Suburbs, 2006-2016.*Working Paper 2 (August). Council for Canadian Urbanism, Queens University. Available at http://canadiansuburbs.ca/files/Still_Suburban_Monograph_2016.pdf.

Grenier, Éric. 2019. "Canadians are Worried about Climate Change, but Many Don't Want to Pay Taxes to Fight It: Poll." *CBC News* (June 18). Available at https://www.cbc.ca/news/politics/election-poll-climate-change-1.5178514.

Halon, Eytan. 2020. "Who Is Leading the Race to Develop the Coronavirus Vaccine?" *Jerusalem Post* (March 22). Available at https://www.jpost.com/International/US-researchers-begin-first-coronavirus-vaccine-trials-in-humans-621844.

Hamilton, J.D. 1994. *Arctic Revolution: Social Change in the Northwest Territories, 1935-1994.* Dundurn Press.

Harrabin, Roger. 2019. "Turning Carbon Dioxide into Cash." *BBC News* (June 24). Available at https://www.bbc.com/news/business-48723049.

Harrison, Virginia. 2019. "How a University Dropout Built a Toy Empire." *BBC News* (December 16). Available at https://www.bbc.com/news/business-50469922.

Hart, Jane. 2020. "The Rapidly Changing Workplace." *Modern Workplace Learning 2020* (May 5). Available at https://www.modernworkplacelearning.com/cild/mwl/about/.

Hassel, Joe. 2018. "Is Income Inequality Rising around the World?" *Our World in Data.* World Economic Forum (November 23). Available at https://www.weforum.org/agenda/2018/11/is-income-inequality-rising-around-the-world.

Hausfather, Zeke. 2018. "Analysis: UK Carbon Emissions in 2017 Fell to Levels Last Seen in 1890." *CarbonBrief* (March 7). Available at https://www.carbonbrief.org/analysis-uk-carbon-emissions-in-2017-fell-to-levels-last-seen-in-1890.

Hay, J. and M. Leahy. 1982. "Physician-Induced Demand: An Empirical Analysis of the Consumer Information Gap." *Journal of Health Economics* 1: 231-244.

Helm, June. 1972. "The Dogrib Indians." *Hunters and Gatherers Today.* Holt, Rinehart and Winston.

Helm, June. 2000. *The People of Denendeh: Ethnohistory of the Indians of Canada's Northwest Territories* (vol. 24). McGill-Queen's Press-MQUP.

Helm, June, and William C. Sturtevant, eds. 1981. *Handbook of North American Indians.* Smithsonian Institution.

Holcombe, Randall, and Sam Staley. 2001. *Smarter Growth: Market Based Strategies for Land-Use Planning in the 21st Century.* Greenwood Press.

Hounsell, Kayla. 2020. "Grocery Store Staff Fed up with 'Social' Shoppers Who Flout Pandemic Rules." *CBC News* (April 3). Available at https://www.cbc.ca/news/canada/nova-scotia/covid-19-pandemic-shoppers-grocery-stores-1.5518481.

Howlett, Karen. 2020. "Ontario, B.C., Quebec Begin Building Makeshift Hospitals in Preparation for Rise in COVID-19 Patients." *Globe and Mail* (April 1). Available at https://www.theglobeandmail.com/canada/article-ontario-bc-quebec-begin-building-makeshift-hospitals-in/.

Hume, David. 1739/1896. *A Treatise of Human Nature.* Book Three. Clarendon Press. Available at https://oll.libertyfund.org/titles/hume-a-treatise-of-human-nature.

Indigenous Services Canada. 2019. "Government of Canada and Assembly of First Nations Announce New Policy and Funding Approach for First Nations K-12 Education on Reserve." *Cision* (January 21). Available at https://www.newswire.ca/news-releases/government-of-canada-and-assembly-of-first-nations-announce-new-policy-and-funding-approach-for-first-nations-k-12-education-on-reserve-840380181.html.

Institute for Government. 2017. *The International Civil Service Effectiveness (InCiSE) Index 2017.* Institute for Government (July). Available at https://www.instituteforgovernment.org.uk/publications/international-civil-service-effectiveness-incise-index-2017.

Jackson, Emily. 2020. "Canadian Auto Parts Makers Team up to Build Ventilators with Three Companies." *Financial Post* (March 27). Available at https://business.financialpost.com/transportation/autos/canadian-auto-parts-makers-team-up-to-build-ventilators-with-three-companies.

Jacobson, Louis. 2012. "Barack Obama Ad Says Women are Paid '77 Cents on the Dollar for Doing the Same Work as Men.'" *Politifact* (21 June 2012). Available at https://www.politifact.com/factchecks/2012/jun/21/barack-obama/barack-obama-ad-says-women-are-paid-77-cents-dolla/.

Jarvis, Carolyn, and Megan Robinson. 2019. "Is Canada's Recycling Industry Broken?"

Global News (May 28). Available at https://globalnews.ca/news/5199883/canada-recycling-programs/.

Johnston, Will. 2018. "The Cambie Clinic Case Could Bring Us a Better Health-Care System." *National Post* (December 20). Available at https://nationalpost.com/opinion/the-cambie-clinic-case-could-bring-us-a-better-health-care-system.

JustPark. 2020. "Find Parking in Seconds." JustPark. https://www.justpark.com/.

Katz, Brigit. 2020. "Human Body Temperature Is Getting Cooler, Study Finds." *Smithsonian Magazine* (January 16). Available at https://www.smithsonianmag.com/smart-news/human-body-temperature-getting-cooler-study-finds-180974006/.

Katz, David L. 2020. "Is Our Fight against Coronavirus Worse than the Disease?" *New York Times* (March 20). Available at https://www.nytimes.com/2020/03/20/opinion/coronavirus-pandemic-social-distancing.html.

Keesmaat, Jennifer. 2018. "We Designed Canada's Cities for Cars, Not People – and the People Are Dying." *The Guardian* (June 14). Available at https://www.theguardian.com/commentisfree/2018/jun/14/canada-toronto-cycling-pedestrian-deaths-cars.

Kenkel, D. 1990. "Consumer Health Information and the Demand for Medical Care." *Review of Economics and Statistics* 52: 587-595.

Kielland, Norah. 2015. *Supporting Aboriginal Participation in Resource Development: The Role of Impact and Benefit Agreements*. Library of Parliament, Canada. Available at https://lop.parl.ca/sites/PublicWebsite/default/en_CA/ResearchPublications/201529E.

Kitchen, Harry. 2006. *A State of Disrepair: How to Fix the Financing of Municipal Infrastructure in Canada*. CD Howe Institute (December). Available at https://www.cdhowe.org/public-policy-research/state-disrepair-how-fix-financing-municipal-infrastructure-canada.

Klebnikov, Sergei. 2019. "Saudi Aramco Reaches $2 Trillion Market Value in Record IPO's Second Day of Trading." *Forbes* (December 11). Available at https://www.forbes.com/sites/sergeiklebnikov/2019/12/11/saudi-aramco-shares-jump-10-in-record-ipos-first-day-of-trading/#48e35d7855f0.

Klein, Naomi. 2014. *This Changes Everything: Capitalism vs the Climate*. Simon and Schuster.

Kopf, Dan. 2016. "Data Shows that Using Science in an Argument Just Makes People More Partisan." *Quartz* (December 23). Available at https://qz.com/869587/using-science-in-an-argument-just-makes-people-more-partisan/.

Kopolow, David. 2013. *Indisputable Violations: What Happens When the United States Unambiguously Breaches a Treaty*. Georgetown University Law Centre.

Available at https://scholarship.law.georgetown.edu/cgi/viewcontent.cgi?artic le=2902&context=facpub.

Kotkin, Joel. 2014. *Opportunity Urbanism: Creating Cities for Upward Mobility.* joelkotkin.com (October 13). Available at https://joelkotkin.com/00984-opportunity-urbanism-creating-cities-upward-mobility/.

Lagace, Martha. 2004. "Does the Medical Industry Deliver Value?" *Working Knowledge* (November 22). Harvard Business School. Available at http://hbswk.hbs.edu/pubitem.jhtml?id=4504&t=special_reports.

Lagace, Martha. 2004. "The Changing Roles of Doctors and Patients." *Working Knowledge* (November 22). Harvard Business School. Available at http://hbswk.hbs.edu/pubitem.jhtml?id=4502&t=special_reports.

Lange, Lynda. 1998. "The Changing Situation of Dene Elders, and of Marriage, in the Context of Colonialism: The Experience of Fort Franklin 1945-1985." In Gurston Dacks and Ken Coates (eds.), *Northern Communities: The Prospects for Empowerment* (Boreal Institute for Northern Studies): 23-32.

Langreth, Robert, and Susan Berfield. 2020. "Famed AIDS Researcher Is Racing to Find a Coronavirus Treatment." *Bloomberg* (March 20). Available at https://www.bloomberg.com/news/features/2020-03-19/this-famous-aids-researcher-wants-to-find-a-coronavirus-cure.

Lant, Karla. 2017. "Stanford Scientists Are Making Wireless Electricity Transmission a Reality." *Futurism* (June 16). Available at https://futurism.com/stanford-scientists-are-making-wireless-electricity-transmission-a-reality.

Laporte, Audrey, and Brian S. Ferguson. 2015. *Changing the Way We Think about Drug Prices: Insights from Economics.* White Paper Series, No: 15W001 (October). Canadian Centre for Health. Available at https://www.canadiancentreforhealtheconomics.ca/papers/changing-the-way-we-think-about-drug-prices-insights-from-economics/.

Laurier, Sir Wilfrid. 1891. "Wilfrid Laurier's Speech to the House of Commons June 8, 1891." *The Macdonald Project* (June 9). Available at http://macdonaldproject.com/education/wilfrid-lauriers-speech-to-the-house-of-commons-june-8-1891/.

Laurier, Sir Wilfrid. 1905. "Wilfrid Laurier: Let Them Become Canadians, 1905." *The Canadian Encyclopedia* (September 1). Available at https://thecanadianencyclopedia.ca/en/article/wilfrid-laurier-let-them-become-canadians-1905.

Leuprecht, Christian, and Sean Speer. 2015. "How to Build a Long-Term Refugee Policy." *From a Mandate for Change to a Plan to Govern. National Post* and Macdonald Laurier Institute (December 14). Available at https://www.macdonaldlaurier.ca/how-to-build-a-long-term-refugee-policy-speer-and-leuprecht-in-the-post/.

Levine-Rasky, Cynthia. 2018. "Don't Blame Seniors for Rising Healthcare Costs."

Canadian Dimension (December 21). Available at https://canadiandimension. com/articles/view/dont-blame-seniors-for-rising-healthcare-costs.

Lewis, Charles. 2018. "Restriction on Summer Jobs Funding Not the First Time Religious Rights in Canada Have Been Trampled on." *National Post* (March 16). Available at https://nationalpost.com/news/religion/ federal-restriction-on-summer-jobs-funding-is-not-the-first-time-religious-rights-in-canada-have-been-trampled-on.

Loriggio, Paola. 2019. "Toronto Public Library under Fire for Refusing to Cancel Meghan Murphy Event." *National Post* (October 16). Available at https:// nationalpost.com/news/canada/toronto-public-library-under-fire-over-event-by-controversial-speaker.

Malcolm, Candice. 2016. "Trudeau Says Canada Has No 'Core Identity." *Toronto Sun* (September 14). Available at https://torontosun.com/2016/09/14/ trudeau-says-canada-has-no-core-identity/wcm/60461a6d-7cb4-42a9-b242-05be9aaea46c.

Malthus, Thomas Robert. 1798. *An Essay on the Principle of Population*, 1st ed. J. Johnson. Available at https://oll.libertyfund.org/titles/malthus-an-essay-on-the-principle-of-population-1798-1st-ed.

MacKinnon, Janice. 2013. *Health Care Reform from the Cradle of Medicare*. Macdonald-Laurier Institute (January). Available at https://www. macdonaldlaurier.ca/files/pdf/Health-Care-Reform-From-the-Cradle-of-Medicare-January-2013.pdf.

MacKinnon, Janice. 2013. "Time to Overhaul the Delivery and Funding of Health Care, MacKinnon Says." Macdonald-Laurier Institute (January 31). Available at http://www.macdonaldlaurier.ca/time-to-overhaul-the-delivery-and-funding-of-health-care-mackinnon-says/.

Marcq, Dan Jr. 2019. "Innovative Technology to Combat Climate Change: Our 7 Favorite Solutions." *Bresslergroup* (November 14). Available at https://www. bresslergroup.com/blog/innovative-technology-for-climate-change-7-solutions/.

Markets Insider. 2020. "UBER (UBER) STOCK NYSE." *Markets Insider* (February 29). Available at https://markets.businessinsider.com/stocks/uber-stock).

Marr, Gary. 2015. "Don't Pull the Plug on the Suburbs Yet as Peak Prices Drive Home Buyers out of the Core." *Financial Post* (October 7). Available at https://business.financialpost.com/real-estate/property-post/ dont-pull-the-plug-on-the-suburbs-just-yet.

Martinko, Katherine. 2016. "How Drip Irrigation Can Save the World." *TreeHugger* (December 13). Available at https://www.treehugger.com/sustainable-agriculture/how-drip-irrigation-can-save-world.html.

Massachusetts Institute of Technology. 2019. "Engineers Develop a New Way to

Remove Carbon Dioxide from Air." *ScienceDaily* (October 25). Available at https://www.sciencedaily.com/releases/2019/10/191025170815.htm.

McAneney, John. 2013. "Climate Change and Bushfires – You're Missing the Point!" *The Conversation* (October 31). Available at https://theconversation.com/climate-change-and-bushfires-youre-missing-the-point-19649.

McCarthy, Niall. 2017. "Canada Seen as the Most Positive Influence Globally." *Statista* (July 5). Available at https://www.statista.com/chart/10157/canada-seen-as-the-most-positive-influence-globally/.

McClellan, C., and L. Birckel. 1987. *Part of the Land, Part of the Water: A History of the Yukon Indians.* Douglas and McIntyre.

McKitrick, Ross. 2012. "Gasoline Tax Would Need to Rise by $2.30 per Litre to Cut Motor Vehicle GHG Emissions by 30 Percent." Media Release (February 22). Macdonald-Laurier Institute. Available at http://www.macdonaldlaurier.ca/mli-paper-gasoline-tax-would-need-to-rise-by-2-30-per-litre-to-cut-motor-vehicle-ghg-emissions-by-30-percent/.

McKitrick, Ross. 2012. *The High Price of Low Emissions: Benefits and Costs of GHG Abatement in the Transportation Sector.* Macdonald-Laurier Institute (March). Available at https://www.macdonaldlaurier.ca/files/pdf/The-high-price-of-low-emissions-benefits-and-costs-of-GHG-abatement-in-the-transportation-sector-February-2012.pdf.

McKitrick, Ross. 2020. "Ross McKitrick: 'Believing the Science' on Climate Change Doesn't Mean Any Policy Goes." *Financial Post* (March 4). Available at http://business.financialpost.com/opinion/ross-mckitrick-believing-the-science-on-climate-change-doesnt-mean-any-policy-goes.

Mill, John Stuart. 1848/1909. "Chapter 1: Of Property." Book II: Distribution. *The Principles of Political Economy with some of their Applications to Social Philosophy.* William James Ashley, ed. (Longmans, Green, and Co., 1909, 7th ed.). Available at https://oll.libertyfund.org/titles/mill-principles-of-political-economy-ashley-ed.

Miller, George A. 1956. "The Magical Number Seven, Plus or Minus Two: Some Limits on Our Capacity for Processing Information." *Psychological Review* 63, 2: 81-97.

Miller, J.R. 1996. *Shingwauk's Vision: A History of Native Residential Schools.* University of Toronto Press.

Missinipi Broadcasting Corporation. 2018. "Muskeg Lake Cree Nation, Saskatoon Celebrate 30th Anniversary of First Commercial Urban Reserve in Canada." Missinipi Broadcasting Corporation (September 27). Available at https://www.mbcradio.com/2018/09/muskeg-lake-cree-nation-saskatoon-celebrate-30th-anniversary-of-first-commercial-urban-reserve-in-canada.

Moffatt, Mike. 2018. "David Suzuki Needs an Economics Refresher Course." *The Globe and Mail* (May 9). Available at https://www.theglobeandmail. com/report-on-business/economy/economy-lab/david-suzuki-needs-an-economics-refresher-course/article4602350/.

Montreal General Hospital Foundation and Research Institute of the McGill University Health Centre. 2020. "Code Life Ventilator Challenge." Montreal General Hospital Foundation (March 19). Available at https://www. mghfoundation.com/en/news/code-life-ventilator-challenge/.

Morantz, T. 2002. *White Man's Gonna Getcha: The Colonial Challenge to the Crees in Quebec* (vol. 30). McGill-Queen's Press-MQUP.

Morgan, Geoffrey. 2017. "B.C. to Proceed with Controversial Site C Dam, Cost Soars to $10.7 Billion." *Financial Post* (December 11). Available at https:// business.financialpost.com/commodities/energy/b-c-to-proceed-with-controversial-site-c-dam-cost-soars-to-10-7-billion.

Murphy, Rex. 2020. "Rex Murphy: It's the Ordinary Joes, Not the Liberal Elites, Who Are Allowing Society to Continue to Function During COVID-19." *National Post* (March 31). Available at http://nationalpost.com/opinion/ rex-murphy-its-the-ordinary-joes-not-the-liberal-elites-that-are-allowing-society-to-continue-to-function-during-covid-19.

National Oceanic and Atmospheric Administration. 2013. "Los Angeles Air Pollution Declining, Losing Its Sting." *NOAA Research News* (June 4). Available at https://research.noaa.gov/article/ArtMID/587/ArticleID/1473/ Los-Angeles-air-pollution-declining-losing-its-sting.

Newman, Dwight, and Brian Lee Crowley. 2015. "MLI Commentaries by Newman and Crowley: Exploiting Social Licence Undermines Democracy." Macdonald-Laurier Institute (November 20). Available at https://www.macdonaldlaurier. ca/mli-commentaries-newman-crowley-exploiting-social-licence-undermines-democracy/.

Norberg, Johan. 2020. "Health, Wealth and the Environment are All Better than Ever: Norberg: The 2010s have been Amazing." *Human Progress* (January 15). Available at https://humanprogress.org/article.php?p=2294).

Oberlo. 2020. "Search Engine Market Share in 2019," Oberlo. Available at https:// www.oberlo.ca/statistics/search-engine-market-share.

O'Connor, Joe. 2020. "Game On: How COVID-19 Crisis Pivoted Bauer Hockey from Skate-Maker to Medical Face Shield Manufacturer." *National Post* (April 1). Available at http://nationalpost.com/news/canada/game-on-how-covid-19-crisis-pivoted-bauer-hockey-from-skate-maker-to-medical-face-shield-manufacturer.

O'Neill, June E., and Dave M. O'Neill. 2005. *What Do Wage Differentials Tell*

Us about Labor Market Discrimination? NBER Working Paper Series 11240 (March). National Bureau of Economic Research. Available at https://www. nber.org/papers/w11240.

Organisation for Economic Co-operation and Development [OECD]. 2019. "Governments Must Act to Help Struggling Middle Class." News Release. OECD (April 10). Available at https://www.oecd.org/newsroom/governments-must-act-to-help-struggling-middle-class.htm.

Osborne, Michael. 2018. "It Really Is Time to Kick Canada's $2.6 Billion Dairy Habit." *Financial Post* (July 6). Available at https://business.financialpost.com/opinion/its-really-time-to-kick-canadas-2-6-billion-dairy-cartel-er-habit.

Outlook. 2019. "India, China Leading In Greening On Land Worldwide: NASA Study." *Outlook* (February 12). Available at https://www.outlookindia.com/website/story/world-news-india-china-leading-in-greening-on-land-worldwide-nasa-study/325307.

Owram, Doug. 1986. *The Government Generation: Canadian Intellectuals and the State, 1900-1945.* University of Toronto Press.

Parrish, Shane. 2020. "Half Life: The Decay of Knowledge and What to Do About It." *Farnam Street Media Inc.* Available at https://fs.blog/2018/03/half-life/.

Patton, Leslie. 2020. "Taco Bell Is So Desperate for Workers It's Offering $100,000 Salaries." *National Post* (January 9). Available at http://nationalpost.com/news/retail-marketing/taco-bell-is-so-desperate-for-workers-its-offering-100000-salaries/wcm/9c01a778-8df8-4c7d-9455-ead84be7a6dd.

Peterson, Jordan. 2019. "Jordan Peterson: Why the Western Emphasis on Individuals is the Ultimate Intersectionality." *National Post* (November 22). Available at http://nationalpost.com/opinion/jordan-peterson-why-the-western-emphasis-on-individuals-is-the-ultimate-in-intersectionality.

Phelan, John. 2018. "Harvard Study: 'Gender Wage Gap' Explained Entirely by Work Choices of Men and Women." Foundation for Economic Education (December 10). Available at https://fee.org/articles/harvard-study-gender-pay-gap-explained-entirely-by-work-choices-of-men-and-women/.

Philpott, Jane. 2016. "Remarks from the Honourable Jane Philpott, Minister of Health, to the Canadian Medical Association Annual General Meeting." Government of Canada (August 23). Available at https://www.canada.ca/en/health-canada/news/2016/08/remarks-from-the-honourable-jane-philpott-minister-of-health-to-the-canadian-medical-association-annual-general-meeting.html.

Pinker, Steven. 2018. *Enlightenment Now: The Case for Reason, Science, Humanism, and Progress.* Penguin Random House.

Pinker, Steven. 2018. "Steven Pinker: Can Numbers Show Us That Progress Is

Inevitable?" *WYPR 88.1 FM.* TED Radio Hour. Episode: *The Story Behind the Numbers*, Part 1 (August 17). Available at https://www.wypr.org/post/steven-pinker-can-numbers-show-us-progress-inevitable.

Psychology Wiki. 2020. "Human Channel Capacity." *Wikia.* Available at https://psychology.wikia.org/wiki/Human_channel_capacity.

Quigley, John M., and Steven Raphael. 2005. "Regulation and the High Cost of Housing in California," *AEA Papers and Proceedings: Regulation and the High Cost of Housing* 95, 2 (May): 323-328. Available at http://urbanpolicy.berkeley.edu/pdf/QR_RegAER0406.pdf.

Rawls, John. 1971. *A Theory of Justice*, 1st edition. Harvard University Press.

Read, Paul. 2019. "Arson, Mischief and Recklessness: 87 Per Cent of Fires are Man-Made." *The Sydney Morning Herald* (November 18). Available at https://www.smh.com.au/national/arson-mischief-and-recklessness-87-per-cent-of-fires-are-man-made-20191117-p53bcl.html.

Real Estate Wire [REW]. 2015. "Vancouver and North Vancouver Mired in the Most Development Red Tape: Study." *REW* (July 17). Available at https://www.rew.ca/news/vancouver-and-north-vancouver-mired-in-the-most-development-red-tape-study-1.2004750.

Recycling Council of Ontario [RCO]. 2019. "Canada Recycles Just 9 Per Cent of Its Plastics." RCO (April 22). Available at https://rco.on.ca/canada-recycles-just-9-per-cent-of-its-plastics/.

Reid, Scott. 2006. "Federal Liberals Deride 'Beer and Popcorn' Money." *CBC* [Digital Archives] (December 11). Available at https://www.cbc.ca/archives/entry/federal-liberals-deride-beer-and-popcorn-money).

Richardson, Rod Randolph. 2016. "Earth Day Shocker! Capitalism Saves the Planet! (Part I)." *The American Spectator* (April 21). Available at https://spectator.org/earth-day-shocker-capitalism-saves-the-planet-part-1/.

Ridley, Matt. 2010. *The Rational Optimist: How Prosperity Evolves.* HarperCollins Publishers.

Ritchie, Hannah, and Max Roser. 2019. *Natural Disasters.* Our World in Data (November 2019). Available at https://ourworldindata.org/natural-disasters.

Rivera, Sergio A. 2014. "The Social License. Why It's So Hard to Obtain?" *Mining.com* (May 28). Available at https://www.mining.com/web/the-social-license-why-its-so-hard-to-obtain/.

Rosenberg, Marc. 2017. "Marc My Words: The Coming Knowledge Tsunami." *Learning Solutions* (October 10). Available at https://learningsolutionsmag.com/articles/2468/marc-my-words-the-coming-knowledge-tsunami.

Roth, Sammy. 2020. "Here's What a Coronavirus-Like Response to the Climate Crisis Would Look Like." *Los Angeles Times* (March 24). Available at https://

www.latimes.com/environment/story/2020-03-24/what-coronavirus-like-response-to-climate-crisis-would-look-like.

Savage, Maddy. 2020. "Lockdown, What Lockdown? Sweden's Unusual Response to Coronavirus." *BBC News* (March 29). Available at https://www.bbc.com/news/world-europe-52076293.

Schneider, Eric C., Dana O. Sarnak, David Squires, et al. 2017. *Mirror, Mirror 2017: International Comparison Reflects Flaws and Opportunities for Better U.S. Health Care.* The Commonwealth Fund. Available at http://www.commonwealthfund.org/interactives/2017/july/mirror-mirror/.

Schumpeter, Joseph. 1942. *Capitalism, Socialism, and Democracy.* Harper and Brothers.

Schwarz, Gonzalo. 2020. "Human Ingenuity Is Our Greatest Weapon against the Coronavirus." *The Hill* (March 25). Available at https://thehill.com/opinion/technology/489422-human-ingenuity-is-our-greatest-weapon-against-the-coronavirus.

Scruton, Roger. 1983. *A Dictionary of Political Thought.* Pan Books.

SecondStreet.org. 2019. "Over 217,500 Canadians Left the Country for Health Care in 2017." SecondStreet.org (March 11). Available at https://www.secondstreet.org/2019/03/11/over-217500-canadians-left-the-country-for-health-care-in-2017/.

Secwepemc First Nations, Indigenous Law and Research Unit, and the Shuswap Nation Tribal Council. 2016. *Secwepemc: Lands and Resources Law Analysis Project Summary.* Aboriginal Rights and Title Department (June 21). Available at http://www.skeetchestn.ca/files/documents/Governance/secwepemc-lands-and-resources-law-analysis-summary.pdf.

Selley, Chris. 2019. "Chris Selley: Our 'Illegal Carpooling Problem' Is Actually a Huge Opportunity." *National Post* (December 18). Available at http://nationalpost.com/opinion/chris-selley-our-illegal-carpooling-problem-is-actually-a-huge-opportunity

Selley, Chris. 2020. "Chris Selley: Official Nonsense on Masks, Travel Bans is Killing Ottawa's COVID-19 Credibility." *National Post* (April 2). Available at https://nationalpost.com/opinion/chris-selley-official-nonsense-on-masks-and-travel-bans-is-killing-ottawas-coronavirus-credibility.

Shahrooz, Kaveh, and Brett Byers. 2019. "Candidate Nominations in Canada are a Mess – Let's Fix That." *Toronto Sun* and Macdonald-Laurier Institute (December 4). Available at https://www.macdonaldlaurier.ca/candidate-nominations-canada-mess-lets-fix-kaveh-shahrooz-brett-byers-toronto-sun/.

Share Your Office. 2020. "Rental Offices, Meeting Rooms, and Coworking Spaces." [Home page]. Share Your Office. Available at https://www.shareyouroffice.com/.

Shaughnessy, Haydn. 2011. "Welcome To The $2000 Car: What Difference Does It Make to You? *Forbes* (June 29). Available at https://www.forbes.com/sites/haydnshaughnessy/2011/06/29/welcome-to-the-2000-car-what-difference-does-it-make-to-you/#185280c76d7f.

Shellenberger, Michael. 2019. "Why Apocalyptic Claims About Climate Change Are Wrong," *Forbes* (November 25). Available at https://www.forbes.com/sites/michaelshellenberger/2019/11/25/why-everything-they-say-about-climate-change-is-wrong/#699b0c3212d6.

Smith, Adam. 1776. *An Inquiry into the Nature and Causes of the Wealth of Nations*. 2 vols. Strahan and Cadell.

Snyder, Jesse. 2020. "First Nations Chief Blasts 'Condescending' UN Anti-racism Directive That Called for Pipeline to be Shut Down." *National Post* (January 17). Available at https://nationalpost.com/news/first-nations-chief-blasts-condescending-un-anti-racism-directive-that-called-for-pipeline-to-be-shut-down.

Sonawane, Jayshree, and Sonal Benare. 2017. "Wireless Power Transmission Using Microwaves." *International Journal of Innovation Research in Computer and Communication Engineering* 5, 3 (March): 5143-5148. Available at http://www.ijircce.com/upload/2017/march/274_Wireless.pdf.

Speer, Sean. 2019. *A Dose of Reality: The Need for a Targeted Approach to Pharmacare*, The Macdonald-Laurier Institute (June). Available at https://macdonaldlaurier.ca/files/pdf/20190528_MLI_COMMENTARY_Pharmacare_Speer_Finalweb.pdf.

Speer, Sean. 2019. *Forgotten People and Forgotten Places: Canada's Economic Performance in the Age of Populism*. Macdonald-Laurier Institute (August). Available at https://macdonaldlaurier.ca/files/pdf/MLI_Speer_ScopingSeries1_FWeb.pdf.

Staff, Jeremy, and Jeylan T. Mortimer. 2012. "Explaining the Motherhood Wage Penalty during the Early Occupational Career." *Demography* 49, 1-21.

Statista. 2020. "Number of Students Enrolled in Postsecondary Institutions in Canada in 2017/18, by Gender and Field of Study." Statista. Available at https://www.statista.com/statistics/448911/enrollment-of-postsecondary-students-in-canada-by-gender-and-field-of-study/.

Stern, Nicholas. 2007. *The Economics of Climate Change: The Stern Review*. Cambridge University Press.

Suzuki, David. 2017. "David Suzuki: Demanding Economic Growth on a Finite Planet Robs Future Generations." *ECOWatch* (August 9). Available at https://www.ecowatch.com/earth-overshoot-day-2470973139.html.

Sweden Institute. 2019. *Healthcare in Sweden* (October 30). Available at https://sweden.se/society/health-care-in-sweden/.

Taleb, Nassim Nicholas. 2016. "Inequality and Skin in the Game." *Medium: Incerto* (December 27). Available at https://medium.com/incerto/inequality-and-skin-in-the-game-d8f00bc0cb46.

TD Bank Financial Group. 2010. *Charting a Path to Sustainable Health Care in Ontario: 10 Proposals to Restrain Cost Growth without Compromising Quality of Care.* TD Economics Special Report (May 27). Available at https://www.td.com/document/PDF/economics/special/td-economics-special-db0510-health-care.pdf.

Tetlock, Philip E. 2005. *Expert Political Judgement: How Good Is It? How Can We Know?* Princeton University Press.

Thiel, Peter. 2014. "Is Google a Monopoly?" *Fox Business* (September 29). Available at https://video.foxbusiness.com/v/3812081607001/#sp=show-clips.

Thomsen, Michael. 2020. "The US Cut Its CO2 Emissions More than Any Other Country in the World in 2019, Helping to Keep Total Global Emissions from Growing Past 2018's Record-Breaking High." *Daily Mail* (February 11). Available at https://www.dailymail.co.uk/sciencetech/article-7992751/2019-global-CO2-emissions-match-time-high-2018-cuts-emissions.html.

Thomson, Stuart. 2019. "If an Economist Says You Have to Use a Carbon Tax, They're Not Telling You the Truth." *National Post* (November 20). Available at https://nationalpost.com/news/politics/if-an-economist-says-you-have-to-use-a-carbon-tax-theyre-not-telling-you-the-truth.

Tumilty, Ryan. 2020. "Government Looks to 'Made-in-Canada Solutions' to Mask, Ventilator Shortage as International Supplies Tighten." *National Post* (March 31). Available at http://nationalpost.com/news/politics/government-looks-to-made-in-canada-solutions-to-mask-ventilator-shortage-as-international-supplies-tighten.

US Environmental Protection Agency [EPA]. 2017. *Our Nation's Air: Status and Trends through 2016.* EPA. Available at https://gispub.epa.gov/air/trendsreport/2017/#highlights.

Valiante, Giuseppe. 2016. "NEB Cancels Energy East Hearings in Montreal after Protests." *CTV News* (August 29). Available at https://www.ctvnews.ca/business/neb-cancels-energy-east-hearings-in-montreal-after-protests-1.3048563.

Van Alstine, James, and Eric Neumayer. 2010. "The Environmental Kuznets Curve." In Kevin Gallagher (ed.), *Handbook on Trade and the Environment* (Edward Elgar): 49-59.

Vinkhuyzen, Maarten. 2019. "The EV Future – Volkswagen vs. Toyota in One Picture." *CleanTechnica* (August 16). Available at https://cleantechnica.com/2019/08/16/the-ev-future-volkswagen-vs-toyota-in-one-picture/.

Vivion, Nick. 2013. "Nosh Nations: The Monetization of the Sharing Economy Spreads to Food." *PhocusWire* (May 23). Available at https://www.phocuswire.com/Nosh-nations-The-monetization-of-the-sharing-economy-spreads-to-food.

Voiland, Adam. 2019. *Building a Long-Term Record of Fire.* Earth Observatory. Available at https://earthobservatory.nasa.gov/images/145421/building-a-long-term-record-of-fire.

Waddington, C.H. 1977. *Tools for Thought.* Granada Publishing.

Wall, Howard J. 2000. "The Gender Wage Gap and Wage Discrimination: Illusion or Reality?" Federal Reserve Bank of St. Louis (October 1). Available at https://www.stlouisfed.org/publications/regional-economist/october-2000/the-gender-wage-gap-and-wage-discrimination-illusion-or-reality.

Walker, Alissa. 2016. "Look How Much Nicer Our Streets Will Be When They're Used By Self-Driving Cars." *Gizmodo* (May 3). Available at https://gizmodo.com/these-visions-of-a-self-driving-vehicle-future-are-incr-1774570917.

Walker, Richard. 2020. "Banning All but Electric Vehicles Could Backfire on the Environment." *CapX* (March 5). Available at https://capx.co/governments-move-to-ban-all-but-electric-vehicles-could-backfire/.

Walsh, Marieke. 2020. "More Details Needed Before Ottawa Makes Contentious Decision on Proposed Frontier Oil Sands Mine in Alberta." *Globe and Mail* (February 4). Available at https://www.theglobeandmail.com/politics/article-more-details-needed-on-teck-resources-emissions-plan-before-ottawa/.

Watts, Michael. 2013. "MLI Report: Debunking the Myths of the Canada Health Act." Macdonald-Laurier Institute (September 20). Available at https://www.macdonaldlaurier.ca/mli-report-debunking-the-myths-of-the-canada-health-act/.

Weiser, Matt. 2016. "The Hydropower Paradox: Is This Energy as Clean as It Seems?" *The Guardian* (November 6). Available at https://www.theguardian.com/sustainable-business/2016/nov/06/hydropower-hydroelectricity-methane-clean-climate-change-study.

Werber, Cassie. 2016. "How Non-English Speakers are Taught this Crazy English Grammar Rule You Know but Have Never Heard Of." *Quartz* (September 7). Available at https://qz.com/773738/how-non-english-speakers-are-taught-this-crazy-english-grammar-rule-you-know-but-youve-never-heard-of/amp/.

Whatley, Shawn. 2020. "How to Manage Doctors," Shawn Whatley MD (January 4). Available at https://shawnwhatley.com/manage/.

Whatley, Shawn. 2020. "How We Got in a Covid-19 Fix and How We Start to Get Out: Shawn Whatley for Inside Policy." Macdonald-Laurier Institute (March 30). Available at https://www.macdonaldlaurier.ca/got-covid-19-fix-start-get/.

World Health Organization [WHO]. 2015. "Population Data by Country (Recent Years)." *Global Health Observatory Data Repository* (June 15). WHO. Available at https://apps.who.int/gho/data/view.main.POP2040.

World Health Organization [WHO]. 2019. *World Health Statistics 2019: Monitoring Health for the SDGs, Sustainable Development Goals.* WHO. Available at https://apps.who.int/iris/handle/10665/324835.

The Women's Blog. 2012. "Margaret Thatcher: A Feminist Icon?" *The Guardian* (January 5). Available at https://www.theguardian.com/politics/the-womens-blog-with-jane-martinson/2012/jan/05/margaret-thatcher-feminist-icon.

Worstall, Tim. 2015. "The Entire Gender Pay Gap Explained In Just One Number: 5.7%." *Forbes* (November 22). Available at https://www.forbes.com/sites/timworstall/2015/11/22/the-entire-gender-pay-gap-explained-in-just-one-number-5-7/#66e24f61193a.

Wullers, Dominik. 2020. "Germany, Wilsonianism, and the Return of Realpolitik." *War on the Rocks* (March 18). Available at https://warontherocks.com/2020/03/germany-wilsonianism-and-the-return-of-realpolitik/.

Zussman, Richard. 2020. "Premier John Horgan Says Coastal GasLink Project Will Proceed Even with Wet'suwet'en Opposition." *Global News* (January 13). Available at https://globalnews.ca/news/6406240/premier-john-horgan-says-coastal-gaslink-project-will-proceed-even-with-wetsuweten-opposition/.

Index